DATE DUE

Traditional
Balinese Culture

Traditional Balinese Culture

Essays

Selected and Edited

by

JANE BELO

COLUMBIA UNIVERSITY PRESS

NEW YORK 1970 LONDON

The binding design by Hugh Dobbins,
derived from a Batik tapestry in
the Margaret Mead collection,
Museum of Natural History, New York

Copyright © 1970 Columbia University Press
Standard Book Number: 231-03084-3
Library of Congress Catalog Card Number: 68–54454
Printed in the United States of America

Foreword

JANE BELO TANNENBAUM died on April 3, 1968. This book is only one expression of a lifetime of generous and productive cooperation in anthropology and in the arts. She brought to her anthropological research not only precision and scholarship but also the sensitivity of a painter and a poet. In her monographs, *Bali: Temple Festival* and *Bali: Rangda and Barong*, and in her book, *Trance in Bali*, she has given us a unique record of Balinese ritual. Here in this book she has gathered together papers written by a group of us who had worked together in Bali in the 1930s. She had plans for other books, notably a study of Balinese painting and carving, which she had expected to call The Lively Arts in Bali.

She has been a lovely part of all of our lives for the thirty years we have studied Balinese culture together. She brought delight to all she touched.

MARGARET MEAD

The American Museum of Natural
   History, New York
August, 1969

Acknowledgments

GRATEFUL ACKNOWLEDGMENT is made to the following who have generously granted permission to use the material indicated.

Theodora M. Abel, for "Free Designs of a Limited Scope as a Personality Index."

Katharane Edson Mershon, for "Five Great Elementals, *Panchă Mahă Bută.*"

Gregory Bateson, for "An Old Temple and a New Myth," for "Bali: The Value System of a Steady State," and, as joint author, for "Form and Function of the Dance in Bali."

Claire Holt, for "Bandit Island," a Short Exploration Trip to Nusă Pĕnidă," the map of Nusă Pĕnidă, and the two photographs of the *baris jangkang* dancers, appearing in this volume as Plate XXIII; also, as joint author, for "Form and Function of the Dance in Bali."

Franziska Boas, for Holt and Bateson, "Form and Function of the Dance in Bali," which appeared in her *The Function of the Dance in Human Society*.

Faber & Faber, Ltd., for the excerpts from Beryl de Zoete and Walter Spies, *Dance and Drama in Bali* (London, 1938).

Shirley Hawkins, as executrix of Colin McPhee's will, for his "The Balinese *Wayang Kulit* and Its Music," for his "Children and Music in Bali," and for his "Dance in Bali."

Yale University Press, for eleven photographs from Colin McPhee's *Music in Bali* (Nos. 3, 8, 36, 61, 69, 104, 109, 113, 114, 116, 117), appearing in this volume as Plates XX, XXI, XXII, XXIV, XXV, XXX, XXXI, XXXVI.

Margaret Mead, for "The Arts in Bali," for "Children and Ritual in Bali," for "Community Drama, Bali and America," and for "The Strolling Players in the Mountains of Bali"; also, for the photographs from Colin McPhee's *Music in Bali* (enumerated above), for photographs from Margaret Mead and Martha Wolfenstein, eds., *Childhood in Contemporary Cultures* (Plates VI, VII, VIII, IX, X), appearing in this volume as Plates IX, XXXII, XXXIII, XXXIV, XXXV; for photographs from Gregory Bateson and Margaret Mead, *Balinese Character* (Plates 3:2,5,6; 4:1; 8:4,8; 11:1; 13:1; 15:5; 17:2; 23:3; 35:4; 75:5; 82:1; 84:1; 87:8; 94:1), appearing in this volume as Plates I, II, III, IV, V, VII, VIII, X, XI, XII, XIII, XIV, XVI, XVII, XIX, XXIX: also, for photographs from her collection, appearing in this volume as Plates VI, XV, XVIII, XXVIII (upper left).

The New York Academy of Sciences, for the photographs from Bateson and Mead, *Balinese Character*, listed above.

The University of Chicago Press, for the following material from Margaret Mead and Martha Wolfenstein, eds., *Childhood in Contemporary Cultures* (Chicago, 1955): Margaret Mead, "Children and Ritual in Bali"; Colin McPhee, "Children and Music in Bali"; Jane Belo, "Balinese Children's Drawing"; and also Plates VI (2,3), VII, VIII, IX, X, appearing in this volume as Plates IX, XXXII, XXXIII, XXXIV, XXXV.

Contents

Plates following page 330

Introduction

THE PEOPLE of Bali, during the years that I was privileged to live among them, were at peace with the outer world, and prosperous. Knowing their land to be an island, they referred to all outlying lands which stretched beyond their horizons as Djawă, or Java. This attributed peripheral homeland of European and American visitors to the island was thought to lie all around the island itself, which was the center of the known world. The peak of Bali, the volcanic Gunung Agung, was considered the highest mountain in the world and the abode of the gods. The head temple of Bali, on the upper slopes of the Gunung Agung, was the religious center where all important nation-wide ceremonials took place, and pilgrims from all parts of the island came there to do honor to the gods of Bali, making offerings, making an obeisance to the direction *kajă*,[1] and honoring the high priest who recited the liturgy of ancient Sanskrit prayers. And, in fact, in the 1930s, when they were told that the reason fewer tourists were coming to Bali than in previous years was that there was a world depression, the Balinese responded by celebrating an elaborate purification and propitiation ceremony at Běsakih, the head temple on the slopes of the Great Mountain, in order to bring the world depression to an end.

During these years the country, although it had a population estimated to be approximately one million, with an average density of six hundred to the square mile, was prosperous, and there was

NOTE: My data and the data on which the papers in this book by Abel, Bateson, Holt, McPhee, Mead, Mershon, and Spies and de Zoete are based date from the 1930s.

[1]Literally mountainward, in opposition to *kělod*, seaward. Thus, in South Bali, where I lived, *kajă* was translated as "north," whereas in North Bali the position was reversed. In North Bali, if you asked a man where *kajă* was he would point toward the south, and rightly so, for the central mountains lie to the south of the area known as North Bali. Thus Bali to the Balinese is really the center of all the earth.

plenty of rice grown in the wet rice paddies of the terraced central areas surrounding the mountain peaks and dry rice culture higher up on the mountain sides. Each house had its rice storage granary, and men, women, and children all helped with the harvest. Some rice was even exported to Singapore and beyond; fat Balinese pigs, raised in excess of the people's needs, were also sold to Singapore, for the Chinese population there relished good pork, although the Javanese next door did not offer the Balinese a market for their pigs, as the vast majority of them professed the Moslem faith. Other proteins in the diet of the Balinese were provided by small quantities of chicken or duck, occasionally eggs; on special feast days beef was provided from the meat of the sacrificial animals—cow, ox, bull, or water buffalo— offered in the ceremonials to the gods and demons of the Balinese pantheon, which, after the ceremony of offering it was completed, was shared out among the villagers belonging to the temple in question. Other feasts were conducted in the house-courts of ordinary villagers, the Malay *slamatan* to which neighbors and kinfolk were invited, or took place as celebrations in the "palaces" of princes attended by all their "followers," as in ancient times before the intro- duction of the Dutch colonial system. The occasions celebrated were many, beginning with the three-months-old "birthdays" of a new- born baby, through ceremonial tooth-filings, weddings, and especially the elaborate cremation rites.

The average Balinese man worked hard in the rice fields all day, and the women carried water from the spring, went to market, cooked, swept the house-court, and in their spare time created beautiful textiles on the hand loom or prepared on special pedestals the festive offerings of cakes and flowers and palm-leaf fringes for the gods. Both men and women looked after little children. When the men assembled at night, after the day's work, to practice in the continu- ally ongoing rehearsals of the *gamelan* orchestra, often they carried or held in their laps the babies born to them in the year or so past, and thus the little children received their first grounding in the complex rhythms characteristic of Balinese music. When the performance of a play, perhaps with hand-carved masks, was being prepared for the next celebration of a temple's calendrical festival, the small children sat in rows at the very front of the onlookers, and when a shadow play was given in the village the small children sitting in the front rows would doze and go off to sleep for a time, only to wake up, alert and bright-eyed, for the enactment of the most exciting scenes of the Hindu epics, the *Mahabharata* and the *Ramayana*, when gods appear, heroes and demons clash, or the more recent versions of old Javanese or old Balinese tales of the witch and her evil pupils wreaking havoc in the land.

Painting and sculpture both in stone and in wood were practiced by professionals and amateurs who could sell their products, always lively and curious, to the tourists. The temples were decorated with panels of carved stone in a design so well known by the villagers that two men could start the decorative motif at opposite ends of the strip of wall and meet in the middle, without any preliminary sketch and without breaking the continuity of the whole. Visitors from Djawă, or any land beyond the shores of Bali, were always impressed with the relentless creativity of the Balinese people.

Historically Bali had come under the influence of migrations from India and China, usually by way of Java, so that the old Indonesian pattern of village organization and that of the irrigation complexes (subak) of the rice fields were overlaid first with Buddhism, beginning around the ninth century, and later with Hinduism. Hinduism as a religion and the four-caste system of social organization has remained in Bali up to the present time. The Balinese call their religion Bali-Hindu, and this name is appropriate because of the importance made clear in the allocation of separate shrines in the temples, of ancestor gods, of gods of mountain, sea, and lakes, and of rites dedicated to the Indonesian rice goddess Dèwi Sri, alongside the worship of the Hindu Trimurti, Brahmă, Siwă, and Wishnu. According to the old caste system, the Brahmins (in Bali called Brahmană), or priestly caste, were the highest ranking; under them came the Ksatriyă, the ranking caste of princes and nobles, to which caste belonged the majority of the seven ruling kings (rajă) in power and in competitive relations and affiliations with each other at the time the Dutch took over the island, as late as 1906. Other rajă belonged to the Gusti or Vesya (in Bali Wěsyă) caste, in India traditionally the merchant caste, but in Bali merely a rank of the nobility less high than that of the Ksatriyă and Brahmană, none the less owning much agricultural land and possessing many "followers" or subjects who paid tribute to them as ruling princes and who sought their favor. Young girls would be taken into the "palaces" (open courtyards with thatched-roofed pavilions enclosed by walls and communicating with each other through a raised gateway like a stile, with steps going up one side and going down the other, said to be designed to keep the pigs and other livestock from wandering through the princely courts). These gateways were of ceremonial importance, often richly carved of paras stone and often with the figure of a temple guardian also carved in stone, on either side of the gate. At the sides of the gate were little shrines for the placing of offerings to the gods on appropriate days of the calendar. The young girls from among the villagers who were chosen to become part of the princely household served as some rustic "ladies-in-waiting" to the princesses and the consort of the ruling *rajă*. Young men from among the *agriculteurs* likewise joined the ranks of the prince's guard and were trained in battle lore, serving to attack and to defend the "country" of the prince from neighboring princes with whom relations had become strained. These fighting men were armed with iron-pointed spears and the knife-sharp Malay dagger of steel, cast in many curves and often with a carved and bejeweled handle and blessed by the priest. It was considered an especially significant and important part of a man's identity.

This system of the ancient Hindu caste rankings was reinforced in the fourteenth century when the great wave of Moslem religious conversion swept eastward through the whole Indonesian archipelago. Only the island of Bali and a portion of the neighboring island of Lombok to the east remained loyal to the Hindu faith, while the Moslem faith skipped around this staunch Hinduistic stronghold and passed on eastward to Timor, Flores, and the smaller islands of the three-thousand-mile chain. To this stronghold the ousted Hinduistic princes from Java came as refugees and as honored guests, bringing with them their palace retinue, dancers, musicians, artisans skilled in the arts of working in gold and silver and bronze, wood carvers, stone carvers, artists, and scribes who copied off the Hindu-Javanese manuscripts inscribed on *lontar* palm-leaf to preserve the literature in the collections of their Brahmană high priests and holy men. There are many legends pertaining to this period, from the time of the first intermarriage of a Balinese prince to a Javanese princess, the prince to inherit both the Balinese and Javanese thrones, to the time of the Javanese aristocracy taking refuge with their Balinese relations and receiving in Bali, because of the rich cultural heritage they brought with them, a royal welcome.

At the time of our field work in Bali, in the 1930s, the population of the total of the three high castes, Brahmană, Ksatriyă, and Wĕsyă, was estimated to amount to no more than 6 percent of the population. The remaining 94 percent of the population was of the Sudră caste, called in Bali, *jabă*, or "outsiders," referring to their living space, which was everywhere except within the courts of the priests and princes. Both high priests and princes received large grants of valu-

able land which was to be worked for their benefit by the indigenous
population, some hundreds or thousands of whom became the subjects, or "followers," of their high-caste leaders. For the rest, Bali
was organized in strong village communities (*désă*) divided into wards
(*banjar*), each with its village meeting-place, or clubhouse (*balé
banjar*); and each village maintained beside the small *sanggah*, or
household temple to the ancestors, several large and beautifully
decorated and designed temples containing the shrines of the Hindu
gods, those of the mountain- and lake-gods, and often those of the
ancestors of the ruling princes. At some as yet unfixed date a special
throne to the Sun God (Suryă) was set up diagonally across the northeast corner of the inner courtyard, bisecting the lines of the little god-
houses running the length of the northern wall and the length of the
eastern wall. Most villages maintained a *pură désă* (village temple), a
pură puseh (temple of origin), and a *pură dalěm* (temple of the dead).
Besides these, there were often temples built by the princes to com-
memorate their ancestors, to which the followers brought offerings
on the appointed festival days, and the *subak* temples common to
all the villages which drew from a common source the water for the
inundation of the rice fields surrounding the villages. According to the
old Indonesian pattern, this group was organized into village units
which had their own village limits bounded by the walls of the
contiguous courtyards of the villagers living at the edges of the
village complex and the outlying rice fields belonging to the villagers
of the community, all of which were known to be held and passed on
in the male line of descent within each individual family. Temples
also held lands for the support of the temple and of the simple
pěmangku, or temple priest, who worked the lands when he was not
officiating in the temple and called upon the faithful members of the
temple to help him when there was more work than he could do
alone, as at harvest time. Beside these there were the lands of the
princes, which might be bought, sold, or mortgaged—as the village
lands could not. White men, however, were not allowed by the Dutch
colonial government to buy land. We might rent land and put up
houses of bamboo and thatch, with wooden pillars as supports, to
shelter us while we conducted our studies. Simple foodstuffs could be
bought in the villages, and water was carried to us from the springs
by many willing carriers. For light there were only coconut-oil lamps,
and, little by little, kerosene lamps and the more glaring gasoline
pressure-lamps were being introduced. The climate was uniformly
warm except in the higher altitudes, where alone a blanket was

needed at night. To visit neighboring islands, outrigger dugout canoes, with or without a sail, were readily available. The life we led was one blessedly close to nature, and to the people who are the subject of these essays, the Balinese.

Bali, its natural beauty, its gracious people, and its richly rewarding culture had begun to be known to the outside world soon after 1906, when an expedition of the Dutch East Indian forces finally brought it under colonial rule. Dutch scholars, students of Sanskrit[2] and the classical old languages, archaeologists[3] interested in tracing relationships with Buddhist and Hinduistic sites in Java began to publish studies of Bali. When in a few years other Europeans and Americans happened to visit the island, they began to give it legendary fame. Men of outstanding discrimination praised it and without exception told with excitement how they had "discovered" the island, how they first happened to hear of it.

The painter Maurice Sterne went to Bali from Java in 1913. It was an accident. He had forgotten his father's watch in the hotel in Surabaya, went back to the port to fetch it just as he was to sail away, and missed his ship. With a number of days to wait for the next ship, he decided to make an excursion to Bali. There he was carried away by the beauty of the people, the men and women bare to the waist presenting perfect brown-skinned models for his brush, against a background of fantastically beautiful landscape. He exhibited his paintings on his return and continued to work from his many sketches, painting fantasy pictures of Balinese figures for all the remaining years of his life. In 1953, shortly before he died, I saw in his studio freshly done paintings of Balinese subjects as he remembered them. He was the Gauguin of Bali.

Shortly after Maurice Sterne's visit in 1913, the German photographer Gregor Krause published an album of outstandingly lovely photographs of Bali, the women carrying offerings on their heads, the temples, the terraced rice fields, the mountains, and the sea—an album which had wide circulation both in Europe and in America. The Mexican painter Miguel Covarrubias and his American wife Rose, herself a gifted photographer, state that they decided to go to Bali on an expedition (not till 1930) after seeing this album by Gregor Krause. Their book, *Island of Bali*,[4] with text by Miguel, many illustrations in his inimitable style, and an album of photographs by

[2]L. F. van der Tuuk, R. Goris.
[3]Dr. W. F. Stutterheim.
[4]New York, Knopf, 1936.

Rose testify that they were not disappointed. It is still selling as the outstanding book in the English language on the subject of Bali.

I suspect it must have been this same album of Gregor Krause's photographs that prompted the German novelist Vicki Baum to write in the introduction to her novel, *Tale of Bali*,[5] that she first saw photographs of Bali in 1916. "A strange relationship grew up between these photographs and me: as though I had known these people; as though I had often walked along these village streets and gone in at these temple gates." In her novel she attributes the photographs which influenced her to go to Bali to a fictitious character, a doctor resident in Bali, who is also responsible for the manuscript on which she bases her story. She did not go to Bali until 1935. "My first visit was the realization of a life-long wish without a hint of disillusionment."

And there was Walter Spies.[6]

Perhaps more than any one person in the period preceding World War II, he contributed to the knowledge and appreciation of Balinese culture in its many manifestations, by steeping himself in the lore of the people—their arts, their religion, their customs—and by taking up with great enthusiasm, combined with complete disregard for personal credit, the particular interest of foreign scholars or investigators who came to him for help.

His father was the German Consul General to Moscow in 1914, and Walter had passed his childhood there. At the outbreak of World War I he was detained in Russia and sent to the Urals where he lived in comparative comfort with the help of his family's funds. He grew up self-taught, learning to paint, to play the piano, to speak Russian, German, French, and English fluently. In the summer season he went out with the nomads into the mountains where the wild flowers grew as large as cabbages. With them he learned to herd sheep and to play the pipes of Pan. When the war was over he returned to his parents in Germany, but he did not like Europe. His paintings were exhibited with success, and he gave piano recitals. In 1923 he decided to ship as a sailor to Java, drawn by what he had heard in Holland of the fabulous beauty of the Indies. He skipped the ship in Weltefreden and managed, through his father's diplomatic connections, to get the necessary German citizenship papers issued to him by the German

[5]Garden City, N.Y., Doubleday, 1937.

[6]See Hans Rhodius, *Schönheit und Reichtum des Lebens Walter Spies; Maler und Musiker auf Bali, 1895–1942* (The Hague, L. J. C. Boucher, 1964). Walter Spies died in January, 1942.

consul in Batavia (now Jakarta). He found employment with the
Sultan of Djokjakarta, leading and teaching his European orchestra,
meanwhile studying the Javanese *gamelan* music. He learned Dutch,
Malay, and Javanese. Then he discovered Bali. Like Maurice Sterne
and Gregor Krause, he was completely carried away by the beauty of
the people and of the land. He sensed the varied complexities of a
culture which fostered the arts in an unending series of ceremonial
events, as yet untouched by foreign influences. In 1927 he moved
permanently to Bali and, with the proceeds from the sale of his
paintings, built himself in Ubud a spacious house in Balinese style
along the edge of a ravine "where two rivers meet." He loved the
Balinese people for their gentleness, gaiety, and creativity, and they
loved him for his charm, joyous sense of life, and his daily increasing
connoisseurship in their arts.

In 1936 Miguel Covarrubias, acknowledging his debt to Walter Spies
in the preparation of his book on Bali, wrote: "In his charming devil-
may-care way, Spies is familiar with every phase of Balinese life and
has been the constant source of disinterested information to every
archeologist, anthropologist, musician, or artist who has come to
Bali. . . . Much of his enthusiasm and energy has gone to help the
work of others, but he has achievements of his own, he was the first
to appreciate and record Balinese music, he has collected every pattern
of Balinese art, has contributed to Dutch scientific journals, has
created the Bali Museum, of which he is the curator, and has now
built a splendid aquarium. An authentic friend of the Balinese and
loved by them."[7]

Colin McPhee, my former husband, and I first came to be attracted
by and to love the Indies when we saw the Javanese shadow-play
figures, cut from buffalo hide, long-nosed, wide-shouldered, stylized
in the extreme. We wanted to visit the land which could produce such
absolute beauty. Then, in 1929, I think it was, we were given in New
York City the opportunity to hear the first recordings of Balinese
music, which had been made by Odeon under the direction of Walter
Spies. The records we heard were brought to us by Claire Holt and
Gela Archipenko (wife of the sculptor), who had just returned from
a visit to Java and Bali. We were enraptured by this music, such
tantalizing excerpts as could be recorded in those days. We decided
to go the following winter to spend six months in the Dutch East
Indies, as Indonesia was then called. That was in 1930–31. We were

[7]Covarrubias, *Island of Bali*, p. xxii.

going, of course, by ship, a trip which took three weeks from an Italian port or four weeks if one boarded the Dutch liner in Holland. We wanted to pass through Paris, where, at the International Exposition, a group of Balinese musicians and dancers had been playing. By great good luck we ran into Rose and Miguel Covarrubias on the Rue de la Paix—and they had just returned from their first six-months' stay in Bali and were bursting with enthusiasm. We sat down immediately at a sidewalk café, where Rose and Miguel gave us with their proverbial exuberance pointers on what we would find in Bali. They gave us letters to Walter Spies, the painter and musician, and Bobby Bruyns, the genial Dutch travel agent who would meet our ship. They also gave us the names and whereabouts of their Balinese hosts and chief informants while they lived on the island. There was not time for more.

The introduction to Walter Spies opened up vistas for us, and his first enthusiastic welcome to us was to be the beginning of a fast friendship between the three of us, that lasted all the years of our remaining life, and his, in Indonesia. We are both more deeply indebted to him than to any one single individual who had entered our lives during that period.

In Java we found Claire Holt again. A student of the dance and of sculpture, she had come into the orbit of the outstanding archaeologist of Java, Dr. W. F. Stutterheim,[8] of whose pioneering work in Bali I have already spoken. From him Claire Holt learned of all the wonders of Hindu and Buddhist archaeological sites in Java, and the reflections of these influences in the bas reliefs and dance postures to be found in the contemporary Bali. After World War II she was able to return to Bali to study the changes that had occurred and write her great work on *Art in Indonesia: Continuities and Change*.[9]

After we built our house in Bali, Claire would come over to visit and to undertake a course of training in the dance by a teacher, perhaps a recently retired *légong* dancer, who had just reached puberty. It was on one of these visits that she happened to join in on the expedition which Walter Spies and I had planned to make to Nusǎ Pěnidǎ (Bandit Island),[10] where the inhabitants had never seen a white woman and no official had visited for more than three years. It was lucky that she came along, though it meant short rations for the

---

[8]W. F. Stutterheim, *Oudheden van Bali, in het oude Rijk van Pedjeng* (Singaradji, Bali, K. L. van der Tuuk, 1929–30). 2 vols.

[9]Ithaca, N.Y., Cornell University Press, 1967.

[10]See Claire Holt, "Bandit Island," in this volume, p. 67.

rest of us, for without her we would not have the record of the trip to Nusă Pĕnidă.

During the time that Colin McPhee and I were living at Walter's house and building our own a few miles away in the village of Sayan, Katharane Mershon, a professional dancer, with her husband and dancing partner, Jack Mershon, came to Bali from California to build a house too, of native materials, but theirs was close to the sea at Sanur and not, like ours and Walter's, up in the hills, facing the rivers and the mountains. Katharane had been the director of the Pasadena Community Playhouse for the production of Eugene O'Neill's "Lazarus Laughed." Jack Mershon was also a brilliant photographer, to whom I am indebted for the most dramatic photographs included in my *Trance in Bali*.[11] He was also an expert gardener and made, by watering the sandy soil near the beach, California-wise, a beautiful garden in which even the elusive night-blooming cereus would bloom. We did not meet them, although they lived only a scant twenty-five miles away, until after they had built their lovely house and Katharane had established her famous "clinic" in which she dispensed most generously medicine to all the ailing Balinese of the district. This role, and that of learning the intricate rituals and prayers from the Brahmană high priests nearby, gave her an unqualified status as an important figure in the area. She was always cordial to others who came seeking information and awareness and would act as liaison with her numerous contacts among the high-caste Balinese. Over the years she has contributed massively to our knowledge of Balinese ways, and I shall always be grateful to her for her contributions of notes on which several chapters of *Trance in Bali* are based.

I fell into the way of going back to Bali, not via Europe and Singapore, but through California, across the Pacific to Honolulu, Samoa, Fiji, New Zealand, and Australia. Alternatively, one could go to Tahiti, the New Hebrides, New Caledonia, New Zealand, and Australia, which I did a couple of years later. Colin and I had made several trips to other islands of the Indonesian archipelago, to Sumatra, a thousand-mile trip merely to cross the island obliquely, from Padang to Medan; to Makasar in Celebes, and to Lombok, the island to the east of Bali, and the only island in the archipelago which showed Balinese influence. We had also several times made the trip north by way of Manila in the Philippines, to Hong Kong, thence up the river to Canton or up the coast to Shanghai. We used to joke that, after living for a year or two in the tropics, one had to run up to China to get a hot

[11]New York, Columbia University Press, 1960.

bath. But we never found anything as lovely as our beautiful Bali, and, as we returned, we always stood on the deck at sunrise, just as the ship which bore us was coming in to port, and saw the mountains looming in the early mist behind the stretches of beach and waving palms.

It was during these years that the Viennese ethnologist and explorer Hugo Bernatzik visited Bali on his way home from a field trip to the Solomon Islands and New Guinea. He was chiefly interested in the dramatic presentations of trance dancing and the high-pitched excitement aroused in the people at cock fights and cricket fights. We helped him by arranging performances in the daytime which he could photograph. He was an outstandingly brilliant photographer, as the illustrations in his book *Südsee: Travels in the South Seas*[12] show. Colin and I had recently taken up photography in earnest; we had invested in our first movie camera and, using a Rolleiflex and a Leica, were learning to capture the moment in the sequences of behavior. We profited by Hugo Bernatzik's experience in this work as he had profited by our experience in Balinese culture. About us and Walter Spies he wrote the following passages, just after his description of a cremation:

To me the cremation brought luck. During the ceremonies I met two European families, who had settled permanently in Bali far from the cultural centers of red gold. They were, strictly speaking, neither European nor families but a young American married couple and a German who had grown up in Russia. Among all the whites whom I met on my travels, they were the only ones who, amid the beautiful tropical scenery, did not live in barracks and had not, though their means would have allowed it, built themselves houses in the loud colonial style. They had real, artistic natures whose whole endeavour was to encourage and maintain the good characteristics and disposition which the Bali people so richly possess. In these circumstances it was no wonder that I soon made friends with them and gladly accepted the invitation to stay at one of the two houses. I had always in the Tropics avoided falling in with the invitations of planters and other white men. I had good reason to stick to this principle. But principles exist to be broken, and in this case, at all events, I had no cause to repent. My new friends knew the land well and most kindly put their knowledge at my service. Thus, in a few weeks I got to know the country in a first-rate fashion and my planned eight-days' stay expanded into many delightful weeks . . . .

Can my photos give a picture of that world in which I had all but lost myself? Everything "out there" all at once became void and immaterial for me, and who knows whether I should have returned so soon to Europe if wife and child had not been waiting for me there? It was almost pain to tear myself away. . . .

[12]Hugo Adolf Bernatzik, *Südsee: Travels in the South Seas* (London, Constable, 1935).

In every situation of life there is a climax, and after which a decline must inevitably follow. On this expedition I had survived much that was difficult, and even dangerous. Now I had been given the best that can be given to man in life as in death: to stop at the climax.[13]

During these years many celebrities visited Bali for short stays, and many of them carried off a recently completed oil painting by Walter Spies, thus affording him the wherewithal to continue living the good life in Bali for another five or six months. Among these visitors were Stokowski and his wife, Charlie Chaplin, Barbara Hutton, the Duke and Duchess of Sutherland, and Baron and Baroness von Plessen. To all of them Walter was gracious and helpful in orienting them to see what interested them most in the lovely island, whether the natural beauties of the landscape, the wild life of the jungle areas, the wonders of the coral reefs, or the ways of the people themselves. Of these visitors the most enthusiastic memories kept by the people themselves were of Charlie Chaplin's take-off of the little girls' *légong* dance which he made in impromptu fashion to a large audience—perhaps 1500 people—after witnessing a single performance by the highly trained little dancers. The crowd rocked with laughter at what was immediately understood by them as true comedy and the spirit of fun.

When Vicki Baum came to Bali, she was fortunate enough to encounter Katharane Mershon and Walter Spies, both of whom helped her enormously in gathering the material for her novel. She chose the dramatic incident of 1906 when the battle took place between the Balinese Rajă of Badung and the invading Dutch colonial forces. The story was laid in the territory of South Bali, where Katharane had her roots firmly established by the time that Vicki Baum met her, and much of the main theme and the particular detail of her book is derived from Katharane's intimate knowledge of the people. To Walter Spies she is indebted for the understanding she showed of the spirit of the Balinese people, their ultimate reliance on religion and the arts as an outlet for the expression of their emotional life when disaster overcame them, and the underlying theme of basic contentment in the agricultural of life, when it is plentiful. To both Katharane and Walter she acknowledges her debt (though not in so many words as I have here used), in the introduction to *Tale of Bali*.

During this time Colin McPhee was busy writing out the scores of the various musical compositions to be heard in Bali, in the more populous central villages where the artistic groups were in sharp competition with each other, for the reputation to be gained from

[13] *Ibid.*, pp. 149, 157–58.

possessing the best dancers and the best-trained *gamelan* ensembles, and in the remote areas where some of the classical old forms were still observable and could easily be brought back to a lively enthusiasm by the infusion of a little money and the interest of the foreign *tuan*.

Meanwhile I was devoting my time almost exclusively to tracing out the relationship of religious belief and customs to the practice of banning twins in Bali in the lower caste, and of celebrating their birth among the Balinese of high caste. When the work which forms the first essay in this book was done and the paper in press in Java, I returned to New York for a short visit to see about finances, for these were the years of deep depression in the economy of the world, and I was not sure we could all continue to work effectively in Bali where our interests were but where there was no way to make a living. For a year or two Walter had been assembling patterns of old Indonesian design to be seen on the *lamak*, the decorative panels made of cut-out green palm leaf pinned on to a panel of yellowish young palm leaf, which was hung from the religious shrines at New Year's and at every festival time. These patterns were abstract, all-over designs, or of a stylized tree—the tree of life—or of a spirit figure called a *chili*, with a wide semicircular headdress, a head, a triangular body, long arms with unusually elaborated hands and fingers, thought to represent the Goddess of Rice Culture. Walter's practice was to make a copy of each outstanding design he encountered, and they differed not only in every village but from one household to the next. He had by that time collected more than five hundred of them. Their chief interest, beside their infinite variety, was that they seemed to belong to Old Indonesian culture antedating Hindu influence. I took these designs to New York with me when I went, hoping to find a publisher for them as they made a very valuable collection.

In New York I went from publisher to publisher, without success, except that of finding an interested art editor, Mr. Perkins of Scribner's, who offered to publish the collection of designs if we could give the company a subsidy of $500. This miserable $500 has been plaguing me ever since, for we could not find any donor willing to put up the money—nobody seemed to have any $500 to spare—with the result that the collection was never published. To my great regret, I took the collection of designs back to Bali with me when I went, whence it was taken to Germany by some comparative strangers in an effort to find a publisher for it; the war came, and the collection was lost.

But my struggles in New York were rewarded in an unexpected way. I saw my first husband, the painter George Biddle, who suggested that I go to see Margaret Mead at the American Museum of Natural History. She had achieved a brilliant success in anthropology by her first books on Oceania, *Coming of Age in Samoa*, and *Growing Up in New Guinea*. I had known Margaret in a sociology course at Columbia when I was an undergraduate at Barnard in 1923–24. She, as a graduate student, was serving as assistant to Professor William G. Ogburn for his course on Cultural Factors in Social Change in which the first inklings of Freud's work and the developing science of psychoanalysis were presented to students. I, a sophomore, knew Margaret only slightly but remembered her as an outstanding personality. I was glad to have the chance to renew the acquaintance with her.

Margaret was at the time laid up at home with a broken ankle and unable to come to her office. But we arranged an interview. She still tells the story today of how I came in, lugging two enormous suitcases containing the collection of Balinese *lamak* designs; how we talked for three hours about Bali and our work there.

The next year we returned to New York, and I had an opportunity to show her some of our films, which influenced her in her choice of Bali for her next field trip. She notes that she had already thought of Bali because of a film on child trance dancing which she had seen several years before. She gave me good advice as to the journals to which I should submit my papers, "The Balinese Temper" and "The Balinese Family."[14] I had read her books and had been much influenced by her approach to what is now called behavioral science. There was at the time no accepted name for this type of study. Malinowski was also very much in the vogue at this time, and we discussed his approach and the teaching of Franz Boas, at whose feet we had both sat while we were students at Barnard, almost ten years earlier.

In 1934 Colin McPhee[15] and I made a return trip to America, where he worked on *Tabuh-Tabuhan*, a composition based on Balinese melody and rhythms, later played by the Mexican Symphony Orchestra conducted by our good friend Carlos Chavez. During that winter in New York, Margaret Mead invited us to a tête-à-tête dinner with Gregory Bateson, to whom she was not yet married, and we talked of Bali. Then he told us of his work in New Guinea with the Iatmul, a primitive tribe far up the Sepik River, that he had been studying

[14]Reprinted in this volume, pp. 85 and 350, respectively.
[15]Colin McPhee died in 1964.

since 1928 and among whom he had hatched his famous theory of schismogenesis to describe the continuingly split relations between the male and female sexes. He also told us some of his pidgin English folk tales, and the evening ended in merriment and good spirits. It was partly on account of what transpired at this dinner that Margaret and Gregory were able to complete their plans to make an expedition to Bali for a two-years' stay, beginning the following year, which later included a return trip to New Guinea for comparative purposes. We did not see him again until 1936.

He and Margaret had been working in Bali almost a year when I was able to join them in 1936, and they set out to train me in their newly devised method of doing field work in a literate culture. They introduced the method of using photographic stills of behavior sequences and a corroborating ciné film record of movement, together with notes compiled by a Western observer and notes in Balinese for the corresponding sequences taken down by a Balinese secretary, the whole record made coherent by the system of synchronizing our watches as we began our observations. Conversations and the trance talk of the oracles were taken down by the Balinese secretaries, who were also trained to note down kinship relationships between the prominent figures in any village setting. I found a charming young man, twenty years old, who knew Dutch and Malay as well as Balinese, and who had begun to typewrite, to act as my secretary. The Batesons' secretary Madé Kalèr instructed my Gusti Madé Sumung in the duties expected of him. A few months later, Katharane Mershon was also enlisted to make notes of village events and ceremonies in her district, and her fourteen-year-old Balinese adopted child proved an apt pupil in the role of secretary to her. At times the whole team would get together to cover an important festival, such as the Great Maligya, or post-cremation ceremony, which took place in the kingdom of Karang Asem in the year 1937.

While we were carrying on our research, Beryl de Zoete, an English woman and a good friend of the Orientalist Arthur Waley, came to Bali to do with Walter Spies a book about the dance and drama.[16] Their work took them all over the island, seeking out varieties of these artistic forms.

Margaret Mead and Gregory Bateson concentrated their studies for the first year in the mountain village of Bayung Gedé, but they also established dwellings in two other villages and developed ties with

[16]Published as *Dance and Drama in Bali* (London, Faber and Faber, 1938). Beryl de Zoete died in March, 1962.

these communities in which they worked. One of these villages, Batuan, was inhabited chiefly by people of the Brahmană caste, and the proportion of artists in this village was extremely high. In the other village their house was within the walls of the palace of the ruling Prince of Bangli, a man of Ksatriyă caste. This was a precaution they took against the possible charge that might be made in future years against their work, that Bayung Gedé was not a typical village such as those where the rest of us were working. Margaret Mead wrote many years later: "Although we find extreme and detailed differences between one part of Bali and another, or between the formal behavior of different castes, or between different priestly sects, the character structure seems to be extremely homogeneous, with little difference between the villages whose inhabitants never go into trance and those where almost everybody goes into trance."[17]

Gregory Bateson gave his version of the Balinese attitude toward the past in one of the essays reprinted in this volume.[18] He said further: "Sociologically we may see the incidents which have been narrated in this paper as the establishment of ceremonial links between the various communities concerned." Arthur Waley took up this point in the Preface he wrote to *Dance and Drama in Bali* by Beryl de Zoete and Walter Spies.[19]

In Bali, better than anywhere else, can be seen the processes by which dance and drama are linked together. . . .

Despite the interest which dagger dances and "possession" have aroused, and the prominence given to them in books and articles on Bali, I do not think that enough attention has been paid to "possession" as a training ground for and source of dramatic dialogue. In a recent article ["An Old Temple and a New Myth"], Gregory Bateson has transcribed the dialogue of a *balian* (medium) and a priest, both in a state of "possession." The *balian* (in this case, a woman) is possessed by the goddess of the village of Bayung, the priest by the god of the village of Katung. Through the mouths of these two mediums, the two deities converse and arrange the joint affairs of their respective villages. . . .

Why has Balinese culture, more than any other of which we at present have knowledge (it may turn out that parts of Africa run Bali fairly hard) tilted (away from playwriting) in the direction of dancing? What has made Bali a "special case," just as England is a "special case" as regards horse-racing, ball-games, and small religious sects? Perhaps Gregory Bateson and Margaret Mead, who have been studying Balinese society as it exists today [the 1930s] may be able to give an answer to this question in terms of the present.

[17]Margaret Mead, *Continuities in Cultural Evolution* (New Haven, Conn., Yale University Press, 1962), p. 352.

[18]Gregory Bateson, "An Old Temple and a New Myth," in this volume, p. 111.

[19]Pp. xvii, xviii, and xix.

Of the authors represented in this book, one may say: Each in his own way pursued the interests which attracted him throughout all the varieties and complexities of Balinese culture at that time. We were not exactly a team, yet we communicated and were aware of the ongoing studies being made by each of us. There was cross-stimulation, and cooperation when it was needed. Together we amassed quite a formidable amount of material which has been preserved, in large part, in the recesses and annexes of the little office which Margaret Mead has occupied for the past forty years at the American Museum of Natural History in New York. To her and to her colleague Rhoda Métraux we owe a debt of gratitude for helping to ferret out the different essays included in this book, many of which were out of print.

Margaret Mead published, shortly after her return from Bali to the United States in 1939, a paper in the *Transactions of the New York Academy of Sciences*[20] in which she states most felicitously her position on the study of Bali: "Bali is an extremely rich culture, rich in symbolic forms which may be studied in relation to the type of personality which they express on the one hand, and help to create on the other."

J.B.

[20]Ser. II, Vol. II, No. 1 (1939), p. 1.

Traditional
Balinese Culture

A Study of Customs
Pertaining to Twins in Bali

JANE BELO

Introductory Note

INTO A PEACEFUL AND ORDERLY SYSTEM of organization, a veritable bombshell of concern and agitation was dropped when twins were born. And especially serious was the case of boy and girl twins, for it was universally believed that the twins had had contact amounting to marital intimacy before birth, in the womb of the mother. For some this intimacy was a good and very portentous thing, and the high caste princes and priests claimed that the boy was born like a god, that he brought his wife with him out of the mother's womb. The young couple should be brought up with the idea that when they matured they would marry each other. This custom of very high-ranking nobility marrying the sister, finding no one else of suitably high caste, the Balinese shared with the ancient Pharoahs of Egypt and with the Inca of Peru. On the other hand, when boy and girl twins were born to the people of *jabă* caste—the other 94 percent of the population—it was considered a great evil and misfortune, an incestuous event, and so evil was it that the house of the parents had to be burned down, their possessions all destroyed or cast into the river "which carries its filth down to the sea," and the parents and the twins exiled from the village for a period of forty-two days, after which time they would have to provide a purification ceremony (*měcharu*) for the entire village at, to them, ruinous expense, containing meat offerings of a whole water buffalo, a pig, chickens, ducks, rice, fruit, cakes, and flowers, the services of a priest or *balian* (priestly

Originally published, except for Introductory Note, in *Tijdschrift voor Indische Taal-, Land-, en Volkenkunde*, LXXV, No. 4 (1935), 483–549.

doctor) to dedicate the offerings to the gods and their demon followers, providing a feast for the entire village. Here again the people believed the boy and girl twins were as if married in the womb, but the union, considered incestuous and evil, was punishable by the same ritual which was prescribed for other incestuous unions, as of a boy with his classificatory grandmother.[1] After the ritual of purification, the parents with the twins, if they survived, were allowed to return within the village limits where friends and neighbors would help them to rebuild their house on the old site.

For the low caste people the tragedy of the occurrence of any multiple births was met and atoned for with elaborate purification rites, for there was a deep-lying feeling that to bear more than one child at a time was to have children as animals do, in litters. The priests, who had been consulted over the centuries for advice as to how to turn off this evil, found in their sacrosanct books special prescriptions for twins of like sex, for triplets all of one sex, or of a boy with two girls, or a girl with two boys (especially bad). There is no case on record of a Balinese mother bearing quintuplets, but it is certain that, if one had, the babies would not have received the reception which America afforded the Dionne quintuplets.

It was my custom during the months when I was gathering material for the *Twins in Bali* study, to visit every village where twins were reported to have been born, to attend the ceremonies and interview the parents and the priestly authorities who directed them, to trace out records of twin births in the past and to look up any survivors of the ancient custom of marrying boy and girl twins to each other. The material I collected is presented in the following paper which was originally published in Java in 1935.

Let me just add a note to the effect that the Balinese booklore does not seem to distinguish identical (monozygotic) twins from fraternal (dizygotic) twins, though they are concerned as to whether there is one placenta or two. No elaborations have been developed of the close psychic and emotional ties between twins, especially monozygotic twins, such as have been explored in recent psychoanalytic and psychiatric studies of twins and their relationship to each other in Western culture. There is also to be found in the psychoanalytic literature evidence of strong sexually based attraction between boy and girl twins which comes to light in analysis, as of the adolescent boy-twin who would only find satisfaction by masturbating before a

[1] See Margaret Mead's article on "Incest," in *The International Encyclopedia of the Social Sciences* (New York, Macmillan, 1968), VII, 115–22.

three-way mirror, looking at his own anus and thinking of his sister.[2] Likewise to studies of homosexuality to be found in both of a pair of monozygotic twins.[3] I have nothing to add. The Balinese consider homosexual relations to be a form of play activity (*main-main*) not to be taken seriously—only heterosexual union is significant, and to be fittingly celebrated in the marriage ceremony of a young pair who are to carry on the family line by bringing forth children—often the ceremony is not celebrated until the girl has shown by her pregnancy that she is not barren but fully able to bear children. Women who have no children are believed to go to hell, and lurid paintings and drawings abound which depict the barren women in hell with enormous hairy caterpillars sucking at their dry breasts. No such fate awaits the homosexual, either male or female. Extramarital affairs and plural marriages are frequent occurrences, and not thought to "dirty the country" as does an incestuous union, however remote the kinship of the tie traced out, or the occasionally found attempt by boy herders to have intercourse with an animal. Nowhere is the real or fantasied relation between two partners as emotionally charged as in the Balinese reception of the fact of a boy and a girl having been born together at the same time and from the same mother.

Part I: Description of the Ritual at Sukawană, District of Kintamani, Bali

On the night of September 18, 1933, twins were born to a woman of Sukawană. When the family saw that the twins were a boy and a girl, they knew that this was a great wrong, that disaster had come upon their house and upon their village.

A brother of the father ran to the open place before the *balé agung*, the village temple. There he beat upon the *kul-kul*, the hollow wooden alarm, so that all the men of the village would come together to hear the direful news. And the sleeping villagers awoke in their tiny houses, still warm with the dying coals of the evening fire, and came forth wrapped in their blankets, for at night it is bitter cold on the slopes of the Gunung Pĕnulisan.

One by one they approached and took their places in the *balé sĕkăhă*, the meeting place of the men. The ancient men, two *kĕbayan*

[2]Jules Glenn, "Opposite-Sex Twins," *American Psychoanalytic Association Journal*, XIV, No. 4 (October, 1966), 736–59; originally presented at the Long Island Psychoanalytic Society, June, 1964.

[3]F. J. A. Kallman, "A Comparative Twin Study on the Genetic Aspects of Male Homosexuals (85 Homosexual Male Twin Index Cases)," *Journal of Nervous and Mental Disease*, CXV (1952), 283–98.

and four *bau*, priests and rulers of the village, sat cross-legged on the southeast side of the platform, for this is *kajă* and *luanang* in Suka-wană, the direction of the mountains, the abode of the gods, and the highest place. When it was known that Ni Jungir had given birth to twins, of which one was a boy and one a girl, the ancient men said, "That is *manak salah* [That is to have children in a wrong way]." And it was decided that at dawn of the next day the men should not go to their work in the coffee gardens but gather at the house of I Lèwèr and Ni Jungir. There they should tear down the cursed house, every post and board and rafter of it, and carry it away out of the sacred limits of the village to the unholy (*těngět*) land on the edge of the graveyard (*watěs sěmă*). And the father and the mother and the new-born twins should be banished (*kětundung*) from the village, to camp on the unholy ground for one month and seven days (*asasih pitung dină*). So did the village law decree. And during the time of banishment neither the father nor the mother of the twins might approach the village for any reason whatsoever. Their relatives would bring them rice, and the people of the village help to guard them at night from the dangers of the unholy place where they must sleep.

Furthermore, all the 175 men who belonged to the *balé agung*, although they came from the four distinct divisions of the village, Tanah Dăhă, Dajan Balé Agung, Kauh, and Kangin—these men and their families would be for forty-two days[4] unclean (*sěběl*). The doors of the temples must be closed, no one might venture even into the outer court, nor might he step into the little square of holy land on which is built his *sanggah*, the household shrine.

At the end of this period there must be a great ceremony for the purification (*měrěyaschită*) of the village, for the turning off of the curse (*malik sumpah*) on the unfortunate (*lachur*) parents, with many offerings both to the gods (*batară*) and to the demons and bad spirits (*kală bută*). When these ceremonies have been accomplished, the people of the village will again be allowed to enter the temples to worship the gods. But the great feast, the *usabă*, which was to have fallen on the next full moon but one, six and a half weeks after the birth of the twins, had to be postponed for two more moons. Instead a simpler *odalan* would be celebrated in the *balé agung*, and afterward the gods carried in procession to a temple one day's walk away, accompanied by four hundred of the villagers, to be fully cleansed

[4]The *sasih* is a month of thirty-five days. This month, plus seven days, makes forty-two days.

with holy water of the evil which had befallen them (*mĕlis, ngĕlun-gayang*). This is the way of old. The people must obey the laws of the *kramă dĕsă*, for, should they neglect the ritual in any form, famine would be upon the land, pestilence in the village, the crops fail, the beasts die. The birth of *anak kĕmbar bunching*, a boy and a girl, is the sign of disaster—only by strict adherence to the laws may the disasters be averted.

On the morning following the birth of the twins the men of the village tore down the house where they were born. It did not take long, for the houses of Sukawană are but a single chamber fitted with a raised sleeping platform on either side of a low hearth—three stones on a mud floor. The walls are of solid two-inch boards, the roof a shingle of split bamboo, turned inner side upward to make gutters for the rain. When the house was in pieces, the men loaded it on their shoulders and carried it off down the steep trail to the edge of the graveyard. Behind them came the women bearing mats, baskets, clay pots, a coconut spoon, all the furnishings and contents of the house. When they had finished, the place where the house had stood lay bare and empty, a break in the trim line of the compound, like the gap caused by a fallen tooth.

If the new house which was to be built up out of the materials of the old had been to accommodate only the family of the twins, the building would have been easy, for the wood is joined, the pillars fit into the beams, and the roof bamboos hang on their supports by slits cut in the lower side of each shingle. But the new *kubu* was to accommodate some fifty men. These were the watchmen, the *gĕbagan*, relatives and villagers who would take turns sleeping there beside the graveyard. Why must they watch? What must they watch for? Are they the keepers of the unlucky parents? No, the people say they come out of compassion, to help the banished ones, for it is lonely beside the graveyard and evil creatures (*léyak*) roam there at night, and one would not dare to be there alone, no, not even ten strong men would dare to sleep there, but if there are fifty it is noisy and no one is afraid.

So the villagers brought bamboo poles and rough mats of woven coconut fronds and sheaves of the long grass which grows upon the hillsides. With the posts of the old house and a few green trees as supports, they patched together a shelter some forty feet long by twelve feet wide. (The original house measured perhaps fifteen feet by nine.) At the northwest end (*tĕbènan*) of the building a private room was walled off for the parents with the twins and provided with a hearth for their use. The watchmen have two long rows of boards laid on stones for their sleeping place, and a kitchen outside to the southeast. The mother and the father of the twins may not cook their food in the same kitchen with the watchmen, for they are too unclean.

By evening the *kubu* was ready, a draughty and uncomfortable place, for the reception of the unlucky family. The mother of the twins, still weak from a difficult birth, was carried down the hillside and installed in this prison which she might not leave for a month and seven days. The grandmother of the twins carried in a coconut shell their joined placenta, wrapped in cloth, together with as much of the blood, amniotic fluid, and sack as could be collected. The *ari-ari* (placenta with umbilical cord) of any new born child is called his brother (*nyamă*) and must be buried in or before the house. A shrine is made for this ugly and terrifying brother, and offerings given to it daily so that it may watch over the living child. The *ari-ari* of the twins was taken to the *kubu* and buried under the hearth in the private room of the parents.

I have heard in Bali that twins such as these are "wrong" because the boy and the girl are as if married in the womb. I have heard also that, if a boy-child brings his wife with him out of the womb, it is a birth such as only gods and kings may have. For the common *sudră* it is an affront to the *rajă* (*mĕmadă rajă dalĕm*) to have children in this way.

But Sukawană is a Bali-agă village, where the Hindu religion has never quite penetrated, where no high caste people have ever lived, and every man is born the equal of his fellow. I Lèwèr, the father of the Sukawană twins, said he was pleased when they born, as a father always is to get a child. But his pleasure was offset and counterbalanced by the great trouble of their being boy and girl, for that meant a big expense to him. At the *mĕcharu* for the purification of the village he must provide a *kĕbo* (water buffalo), a calf, and a pig to be sacrificed. The many offerings which must be made, the quantities of rice and coconuts and fowls would be at his expense, except for the contributions of his fellow-members in the *balé agung*. The village law decrees that each man must help the poor (*lachur*) father with gifts according to his means, but all that is not given falls to the share of the father, and he alone is responsible for the complete array of the offerings. I Lèwèr also loses his house, already torn down, for at the end of the forty-two days the *kubu* constructed from its materials must be burned to the ground. And all his possessions, his mats, his clothes, and those of his wife, must be burned also, or cast away into the river, so that nothing may remain which has been connected with the uncleanness of the birth of the twins.

But I Lèwèr was not ashamed. He said: "I am troubled (*sěbět*), but I am not ashamed (*lěk*)." He knew only that the big ceremony must take place to avert disaster from the village. He opened his eyes wide with surprise when we asked if he had heard that this was the *rajǎ's* way to have children. "No," he answered, "I have never heard it."

We asked if people say that the twins are already married in the womb of the mother. I Lèwèr answered: "I do not know." And the old men sitting by said: "How can they, they are so small!"

But it was known in the village that if both children survived, they might, if they so wished when they grew up, marry each other.

As for the mother, Ni Jungir, she had nothing to say, except that she had much trouble at the birth of the twins, for it was hard, and she lost much blood.

Three days after their birth the knotted ends of the umbilical cord attached to the navels of the children had dried up and fallen off (*kěpus pungsěd*). Now could take place the ceremony called *mělěpas aon*—literally translated the "loosing of the ashes," a purification which for the ordinary child takes place in the house, and after the observance of which the father and mother are allowed to go out from the house-court into the village, and the baby may be taken for the first time out of the inner room where he was born. In the case of these twins the ceremony took place in the *kubu* on the edge of the graveyard. The offerings, which include *nasi sěgaan*, dedicated to bad spirits, tongs of bamboo and a blade of bamboo such as is used to cut the umbilical cord, and thorny branches of three kinds (traditional in many countries to drive off the evil spirits which attack newborn children)—these offerings for the twins were not double but followed the customary allotment for a single child. (The name of the ceremony is perhaps connected with an offering of cooked rice mixed with ashes, which must be included. But the meaning remains obscure and could not be explained by the people, except that it marks the freeing of the father, mother, and child from the uncleanness[5] of the birth, when the last "dirty" piece of cord has dropped from the navel.)

[5] The word used by the Balinese is *sěbět*. There is a tendency among European observers to give to the word a meaning connected with magic as well as its literal meaning of "unclean, impure." V. E. Korn, in *De Dorpsrepubliek Tnganan Pagringsingan* (Santpoort, Mees, 1933), says: "Bij de geboorte van het kind . . . zijn moeder en kind magisch zwak, men noemt dit sbel welk woord in de regel met 'onrein' wordt vertaald. Menschen die sbel zijn wegens de geboorte van een kind mogen geen bezoek van vreemden ontvangen. Dezen zouden de magisch zwakke kraamvrouw in gevaar kunnen brengen door hun eigen magisch vermogen" (p. 163).

On the ninth day the boy-twin died. He was buried in the graveyard. The graveyard of Sukawană has five divisions, running from
kajă, nearest the mountains, to *kĕlod*, nearest the sea. The highest
place, near the mountains, is reserved for young children who died
before losing their first tooth (*tondèn mĕkĕtus*). The lowest place is for
those who have died an unnatural or wrong death, who have died in
an accident or taken their own lives (*salah pati*). The boy-twin was
buried in the highest place. Alone amongst all the bodies those of the
little children *tondèn mĕkĕtus* do not have to be later dug up and
cremated. For cremation is a purification, and the little children have
not yet any sins. This twin child, then, was not wrong nor sinful in
himself.

On the twelfth day after the birth of the twins the ceremony
nyambutin was celebrated in the *kubu*. After *nyambutin* in Sukawană
the usual child and his parents are sufficiently purified to be allowed
to enter the temples. Although for the family of I Lèwèr there still
remained thirty days of exile, during which they might not even
enter the village, much less the temples, still these small offerings had
to be made according to custom.

But it seems to me confusing to impute such a meaning to the word *sĕbĕl*. The
Balinese language has no general term for magic, although there are special words
for charms, *sĕrană*, *gună*, and for "supernaturally powerful through holiness,"
sakti (*çakti*), and the word *tĕngĕt* is applied to things and places fearful in appearance
or charged with evil power, such as the witch *rangdă*, or the placenta of a newborn
child, or graveyards, certain temples, trees, and bridges where supernatural manifestations are frequent. The Balinese have no abstract conception of magic, and they
do not suspect that many of their customs and religious practices are considered by
Europeans as forms of magic. Therefore it seems incorrect in trying to render the
Balinese thought to bring in a concept which, though familiar to the observer, is
foreign to Balinese thought. A woman *pĕmangku* told me that she might never
enter a house, even of her nearest relatives, during the three days after the birth
of a child, for she who was in charge of the temple, where the gods are *sakti*, might
not come in contact with that which is *sĕbĕl*. Relatives are *sĕbĕl* after a death in the
family, and a woman at the time of menstruation. The high caste woman is for
three days banished from the *puri* of the princes, and literally imprisoned in a
special court. The Sudră woman at this time may not sleep upon the same *balé* as
her husband, although she bathes in the river and cooks his food. She may not enter
the temples or the *sanggah* (household shrine). In the village of Sayan, it is said that
the goddess Durgă must leave the temple once a month, when she is *sĕbĕl*, and take
up her place in the graveyard, where she may be given offerings at what is known
as the throne of Prajāpati. (A mystic explained that Prajāpati is really a woman in
the form of a man.) From these examples it will be seen that the word *sĕbĕl* means
unclean in the sense of "dirty" and in the religious and mystical sense of "impure,"
but in the Balinese mind there is no direct and conscious connection of the *sĕbĕl* state
with magical weakness.

During the last days the men of the village were busy at the *kubu* cutting trees into blocks for the chopping of the meat offerings, weaving rough trays of split bamboo, preparing skewers, and sharpening knives for the feast. It is a part of the custom that the villagers must not only contribute to the offerings but lend their indispensable aid in the making of them, for it is an array such as no single family could prepare alone. In return they are treated to a feast at the expense of the father of the twins. In the houses of I Lèwèr's erstwhile neighbors the materials were collected. Each man sent his share, according to his means. If a rich man should send a poor contribution, he would be too ashamed! The women cooked the rice and formed it into little cones, and into cakes of varied shapes and colors, and of sugar and rice flour they made still other dainties for the gods and for the demons. They wove plates of palm leaf, and decorative fan-shaped, circular, and trailing *sampéan* as top-pieces for the offerings, all of the young yellow leaf, cut with a knife in strong simple design. The part of the men is the killing and preparation of the animal offerings. On the day before the ceremony they killed the water buffalo, skinned it, and cut and cooked the meat in various ways. The next morning the calf, pig, goat, goose, ducks, chickens, and the three-colored dog ("red," black, and white) were killed and made ready. At eleven o'clock in the morning I Lèwèr's neighbors were still busy finishing the last dozens of palm-leaf decorations necessary for the offerings. When all was done the splendid array was laid out upon the bare ground where I Lèwèr's house had stood, and they were enough to cover the space completely. According to color and to kind the offerings were placed in specified positions, to the five directions, north, south, east, west, and center. At the *kajă* corner stood the *sanggar tawang*, a bamboo "throne" set up in honor of Suryă, the Sun.

The ceremonies were to be celebrated by a *sĕngguhu* priest, a non-Brahmană, called from a village some ten miles distant, assisted by the *balian* of the village (witch doctor and medicine man). *Sĕngguhu* priests belong to the older social order of Bali that existed before the Hindu castes were introduced, when the people were divided into guild-castes. What their role was before Hinduism is unknown, but today they are especially in charge of *mĕcharu*, formal offerings to the demons. At many big ceremonies, such as those at Bĕsakih, and in certain districts the yearly purification the day before *nyĕpi*, where the Brahmană *pĕdandă* officiate, the *sĕngguhu* is present to take charge of the *charu*. In such cases the *sĕngguhu* "follows" or obeys the Hindu high priest. But he may also officiate independently and alone, as was the case in Sukawană. The *balian's* position in Sukawană is anomalous. He has no place in the village council, the *saing-23*. At the formal sittings on the *balé agung* he has no special seat but is grouped with the ordinary villagers. In other words, he is not only not a priest for the gods of Sukawană but he has no official position in the *kramă désă*.

Toward noon on the forty-second day after the birth of twins, the *balian*, accompanied by thirty or forty villagers, went down the hillside to the place on the edge of the graveyard, for the *kubu* must first be burned. A preliminary ceremony took place in the private room of the parents. The offerings were small, and consisted of (*a*) *tĕbasan*, composed of rice and thread and *kèpèng* (cash), arranged on *dulang*, the offering trays, and (*b*) *karangon manchă limă*, five little banana-leaf plates of skewered pig meat and five little banana-leaf plates of rice. These are arranged according to the five directions. The *balian* repeated prayers in the old language and sprinkled the offerings with holy water. Before him knelt I Lèwèr and Ni Jungir. In the mother's arms was the girl-twin, swathed in white cloth. The father held a pseudo-twin swathed also in white cloth. This pseudo-twin was simply the dark red flower of the banana plant, with the primitive drawing of a person impressed in the surface of the bud—a head, two arms, and two legs roughly indicated, without attempt to denote the sex. The banana flower or bud is called *pusuh*[6] and resembles a large heart in shape, while the name for heart in Balinese is *pĕpusuhan*, as if derived from the flower. The people of Sukawană had no other name for this substitute twin than *pusuh*, but they made it clear that it was intended to take the place of the dead boy-twin in the ceremonies.

Both mother and father held in one hand a knife on the end of which an onion was impaled. This "weapon" is powerful against evil spirits and has to be carried on all occasions when a newborn child is

---

[6] In many districts of Bali such a "*pusuh*" is used at the ceremony called *mĕcholong* for newborn children, which takes place twelve days, forty-two days, or three months after the birth. It is one of a set of three *cholong*. The other two are a live chicken, and a *papah*, the stalk base of a coconut frond, on which a cross or a rough drawing of a person is made in chalk. The chicken may be stolen for use in this ceremony (*cholong* means steal). However the ceremony *mĕcholong* is for a live child and seems to carry the meaning of providing substitutes for the living child so that the evil spirits which molest young children will be satisfied and leave the child alone. *Mĕcholong* and this use of the *pusuh* are unknown in Sukawană. The *pusuh* in this case, the people definitely stated, was intended not for the living girl-twin but to take the place of the dead boy-twin.

taken out of its own house-court.[7] I Lèwèr and Ni Jungir never let these knives out of their hands throughout the day of the ceremony.

A fire was burning on the hearth in the parents' room. At the *balian's* direction the mother took a handful of dried corn from an offering plate and cast it into a new clay pot which rested over the flames. She stirred the corn about until it was brown. Then father and mother had to reach three times into the pot and eat a grain of corn. After the third time the father raised the pot and smashed it on the stones of the hearth.

Someone handed the father a torch of dry grass which he lit at the fire. He came out, bearing his false twin, his knife, and his torch, to set fire to his house. The mother followed with her child. The *balian* repeated a short prayer and then performed a final rite. In one of the offerings stood two cones of rice tied together at the top with a bit of thread, a *kèpèng* strung on to each. The top of each cone he pinched off, then he broke the joining thread. He rose, came out of the house, shut and bolted the door on the outside. None of the evil which was in that house must escape.

The villagers bearing torches lit from the father's fire set the house burning. In ten minutes the flames were leaping high, threatening the nearby forest. The *balian*, the mother, and the father, with a group of villagers and friends, stood on the hillside watching until the house crumbled to ashes.

Before the parents with the twins might reenter the precincts of the village, their house must be burned three times. So they told us. We

---

[7] This rite is mentioned in a popular verse sung to little children in Bali:

"Bibi anu, lamun payu luas manjus, atèngé tètèkang, yatnain ngăbă mĕsui, tyuk puntul, bawang anggon pĕsikĕpan.

"Anak lyu, bĕntjană dimargă agung, bajang alu bukal, mĕngisĕp nyonyo ngulanting, mĕngĕtĕkul mĕkrană tan pĕsu ĕmpĕhan.

"Sangkan hitung, tuyuhé mĕpală lampus, ngulah bĕtĕk basang, rarine juwă ngĕmasin, dadi lachur, nyén anaké sĕsĕlang.

"Sangkan lachur, numadi jĕlĕmă ĕluh, i mémé nyayangang, i bapă mĕpĕdang mati, yaning hidup, mĕméné anggon jalaran."

It may be translated:

Mother, whoever you are, when you go to bathe, bind tightly your breasts, take care to bring with you *mĕsui* bark [cortex sp.], and a dull knife with an onion as charm.

Many wicked people threaten on the highway, evil spirits in the form of flying foxes, which suck at hanging breasts, taking their place at the breasts, so that no milk comes out.

Take into account that trouble brings death, even though the belly is filled, the baby is the cause of the trouble, and if bereaved, who will there be to envy?

The trouble is that the child was born as a girl, her mother loves her, her father would wish her dead, but while she lives, her mother will take care of her.

followed the group of villagers up a steep trail, not the direct route to the village, to a place where it joined the trail leading to the grave-yard. A man carried a torch freshly lit with the same fire which had burned the big *kubu*. They had kept this fire alive by lighting a new torch whenever one burned down. In the center of the trail stood a small *kubu*, four posts set up and covered by a roof of grass-thatch not more than a meter square. Under this roof was an improvised *paon* (hearth) and a clay pot such as was used before. The fire was lit in this *paon* from the torch bearing the old fire.

The *balian* sat beside the little *kubu* and again set out the offerings *karangan manchă limă* in the five directions. The father and the mother knelt beside their hearth. The *balian* again dedicated the offerings, and the ceremony *nyah-nyah jagung* (to fry corn) was repeated exactly as described above. When the pot was broken, the father lit a torch at the fire on the hearth and ignited the roof of dry grass. It flared up like a match and was gone.

The people rose and made their way toward the village. Someone carried the torch which the father had used. When they came to the place just outside the wall of the outermost house-court, another small *kubu* stood waiting. With another set of the same offerings, again the mother and father cooked their corn and ate three times from the pot. When this *kubu* was burned, the torches could be cast into the flames. Three times I Lèwèr had taken fire from his kitchen and burned down his unclean house.

The *balian* explained: Three times the parents of the twins have just come to a new house, they have cooked and eaten there, and then set fire to it—this is to show that they are miserably poor, they have nothing (no house, no possessions), so that the people of the village will take pity on them. Someone in the village will have to give them shelter in his house, since they have no longer any house of their own. [8]

[8] The *balian* did not give the obvious explanation that the parents had to burn their house three times lest they might bring a curse upon the house in which they would live. If there were any chance of disaster accompanying them, no villager would receive them into his house. A *lontar* from Tonjă states that, if anything is lacking in the ceremony, twins may be born three times in succession. I did not find anywhere else in Bali the custom of burning two small *kubu* after the real one. But in general the case does not come up that the parents must be given hospitality in another house, for the village plan of Sukawană differs from the usual village made up of individual family courtyards. The usual Balinese house consists of several separate buildings, and only the *balé pěgat* or the *mětèn* where the children are born must be torn down and burned—sometimes not even that. So that the parents on their return still have other buildings to inhabit in their own house-court and are not obliged to seek hospitality elsewhere.

I Lèwèr and Ni Jungir, after forty-two days of exile, were now free to enter the village. They walked slowly and with dignity down the street where their old house had stood, each carrying a "twin" and each firmly grasping a knife with an onion impaled. There was no greeting from the villagers, nor any sign of joy or sadness on the faces of the parents. Before they reached the site of their house, twenty yards away down the street, mats were spread for them. There they must sit and wait in the street for perhaps three hours, while the ceremony *malik sumpah* would take place—the ceremony of turning off the curse that was upon them, but in which for the time they had no part.

Immediately opposite the entrance to the house-court the feast for the villagers was going on. Many men sat cross-legged on the *balé*, enjoying their portion of rice and succulent morsels of meat. In the roadway pits had been dug for roasting, and ducks, chickens, pigs, and sausages were being given a final turn on the spit. The villagers who had witnessed the ceremonies outside the village now had their share of the feast.

The *sěngguhu* priest took his place on a mat spread among the offerings on the site of the old house. Before him were arranged his holy instruments—the figure of a man seated on a lion in ancient Chinese pottery, containing holy water, a bronze lamp containing glowing coals of sandalwood, a bronze bell, a bronze "astrological beaker" with the signs of gods and zodiac in raised relief, and bearing the date 1248 (Çaka = 1326 A.D.). This beaker was filled with holy water and the chopped petals of flowers. During the ceremony the *sěngguhu* priest several times after ringing his bell immersed it in this beaker of holy water.

The two most honored ancient men, the two *kěbayan* of the village, came and sat behind the priest. The *balian* also sat near and assisted in the ritual. The *sěngguhu* began with prayers and offerings *bědu'ur*, "above," made facing the *sanggar tawang*, to the gods. He then returned to his place among the offerings arranged in the five directions. These included the water buffalo, calf, pig, goat, goose, chickens, duck, and dog, and the thousand minute offerings of rice and palm which must be provided according to rule and no one of which may be omitted. The dedication seemed to follow the order of Bali-Hindu ceremonies, with *mantră* (prayers in the old language) repeated by the priest, the ritual of fire and holy water, the ringing of the bell, and the sprinkling of the offerings using two broomlike bunches of young coconut leaves, called the *lis* and the *těgtěg*, or *tugtug*. To the *lis*, which they said was male, was attached a small woven "basket" of leaf called *kĕtipat pusuh*, and to the *tĕgtĕg*, female, one called *kĕtipat tulud*.

Toward the end of the ceremony the *sĕngguhu* took out from a basket the great conch shell which is traditional in the ritual of his priesthood. While he rang his bell and repeated prayers the *balian* blew great blasts upon the conch, calling the *kală* and the *bută* from afar to come and receive the meat and rice and palm wine spread there for them.

The final rite was again the breaking apart of the two cones of rice tied together with a bit of thread, just as was done in the *kubu*. The priest said the offering was called *pĕras*. But the meaning of the rite he could not explain.

Now the priest rose, and the *balian*, and the men and women of the village who had assembled to watch the proceedings. They turned to the entrance of the house-court, where, at the bottom of the stone runway leading down to the lower level of the street, stood the parents with the twins. Now at last they were to have a part in the ceremony.

I Lèwèr and Ni Jungir had on all new clothes. (This was another expense of the day for them.) There in the street they had discarded the filthy clothes worn night and day during the forty-two days of their exile, and donned fresh bright batiks and crisp shirts. Ni Jungir carried her child in a new *slèndang*, and both twins were wrapped in clean white cloth. The parents knelt in the roadway. At the *balian's* direction a woman relative sprinkled the four unclean ones with holy water, three times with the *lis*, three times with the *tĕgtĕg*. They were more doused than sprinkled, so thoroughly did she wet them with the purifying *toyă*. Then the clay pot which held the water was dropped and smashed behind the parents, scattering its remaining contents upon them.[9]

But not yet were the unfortunate ones sufficiently pure to enter the house-court where they had lived. They turned away, following the priest and the *balian* toward the village temple, the *balé agung*. There they squatted at the foot of the steps which lead up to the temple gate—not allowed to go further until several other ceremonies had been performed.

---

[9] This is called *ngĕlukat* in most villages in Bali and is usual in the purification ceremonies for twins. But in Sukawană the word *ngĕlukat* was unknown, and the priest said this was part of the *mĕrĕyaschită*.

The priest entered the first court of the temple, where stand the two long buildings called *balé agung*, one used for the formal sittings of the village council at dark moon, the other at full moon. On the ground of the court, before the temple gate, the offerings were set out to the north, south, east, west, and center. But this time only fowls were used in the ceremony, the bigger offerings of pig and goat and calf and buffalo were not necessary. Some of the villagers came in to watch the priest at his prayers, but no one was yet allowed to enter the higher court of the temple where the shrines of the gods stand and where the sacred *pĕrtasti* are kept. Later on in the evening, after the full order of the purification had been completed, they would be allowed to enter the courts of the gods.

The priest dedicated the offerings as before. This, he said, was the *mĕrĕyaschita* of the temple.

It was now time for the *mĕsakapan*[10] of the parents and the twins. This took place at the foot of the temple steps where they sat waiting. The instruments of the ceremony were the following live animals: a white duck; a chicken "with feathers going the wrong way"; a red, white, and black chicken; a chicken with feathers like casuarina-tree needles; and a small pig, uncastrated.[11] These beasts are required to "eat out" the uncleanness of the parents and the twins. Each beast was to act on a separate part of the body, divided thus; the head, the two shoulders, the two hands, the body, and the two feet. The *balian*, performing the rite, took each one in turn and made as if the beast ate at the skin of the person. The words used for this filth-eating were *ngĕkĕh* for the three chickens and *ngolsol* for the duck and the pig, because they have different ways of eating. The chicken scratches with its feet and pecks; the duck and pig snuffle it up!

These animals were not sacrificed but set free before the temple, to live out their lives. No one would take them, the people said.

It was nearing sunset. A procession started for the Meeting of Rivers, the *champuh*, a holy place some half hour's walk distant from the village. About fifty relatives and friends of the twins' family accompanied I Lèwèr and Ni Jungir. Women carried on their heads baskets containing the old clothes of the unclean ones, and all the

---

[10] *Mĕsakapan* as generally known in Bali is a wedding ceremony and does not resemble this ceremony, which is usually called *nyĕkĕhan*.

[11] The beasts' names and the divisions of the body on which they act were as follows: *bĕbĕk putih*, on the head; *ayam sidamală (sudă mală)*, on the hands; *ayam grungsang*, on the shoulders; *ayam bulu chĕmară*, on the body, up and down; *kuchit butukan*, on the feet.

utensils and receptacles for food which had been in their possession
before the disaster and had not been consumed in the *kubu* fire.
Arrived at the *champuh* all these things were cast away into the
water (*anyudang*) which leads down to the sea. There were prayers
and a few offerings, and then these people rushed into the icy water
to cleanse themselves thoroughly of the *sěbĕl* state. The *pusuh*, the
pseudo-twin, was also cast away into the stream. On their return Ni
Jungir, carrying her child, walked still armed with the knife and the
onion, but I Lèwèr, having cast away his twin, no longer had any
need for his weapon.

I Lèwèr and Ni Jungir and the remaining twin were at last
purified. They were taken into the house of his brother, where they
warmed themselves at the evening fire, and were glad that they might
once again sleep in security within the walls of their village. There,
with two families crowded into one tiny house, they would have to
remain for some months. I Lèwèr means to rebuild his house on the
former site, which stands waiting and bare. But for the time he has no
resources to buy the necessary materials—all that he had in cash and
in worldly goods has gone in turning off the curse of the birth of the
twins. From the labor of his hands and from the fruit of his land he
will in time reestablish his homestead.

That night there was no more village activity. Each family retired
to its house, where the fires were burning, the women crouching
beside them frying meat left over from the offerings. The men sat
upon the raised *balé* on either side of the hearth, and the children
squatted on the floor, or sat quietly in the laps of their grandfathers,
listening to the talk of their elders. We were guests in the house of
the *perbĕkĕl*, the headman of the village by order of the official Dutch
government. This man has himself no place in the village council.
But his father, who is now an old man to whom no one pays much
attention, was once *kĕbayan*, holding the highest position in his half
of the village.[12] According to the village laws a *kĕbayan* is super-
annuated when his youngest child is married. He becomes *sayă*, a
place of honor without power, and the position of *kĕbayan* is filled by
the next highest member of his half of the village council. To the
house of the *perbĕkĕl* came that evening several of the elders from the
council—there were things to discuss in the order of the ceremonies
to come. In three days' time would begin the *odalan* in the temple,
replacing the big *usabă* ceremony which was due on that day, at full

[12] The villagers are divided into two groups, *tĕngĕn* (right) and *kiwă* (left), into
which they are born and remain throughout their life. Each group has its *kĕbayan*.

moon. The *odalan*[13] would last two days, and afterwards the gods must go away. They must be carried in procession to the sea or to a holy bathing place, where they would receive their "bath of purification" (*ngĕlungayang* or *mĕlis*). For in the case of the birth of boy and girl twins even the gods are dirtied. So far it had not been decided to which place the procession would go, nor on what day. The *perbĕkĕl* would have to inform the *punggawă*, head of the district, who would report to the Dutch Controleur what was being done in Sukawană. But that night nothing was decided. When the fire began to burn low, the visiting elders went away, and the people of the house rolled themselves in their blankets to sleep.

On the morning following the big *mĕrĕyaschită*, we were surprised to find offerings for *mĕcharu* again laid out in the court of the *balé agung*. The *sĕngguhu* was present to officiate. The ceremony he called *manchă satah* this time, and the offerings included five chickens and a duck. He could not explain why a second *mĕcharu*, or formal offerings to the bad spirits, had to be made in the temple, so closely resembling the ceremony performed the previous evening. After the return of the people from the Meeting of Rivers anyone who wished was allowed to enter the upper court of the temple. Perhaps this second *mĕcharu* in the temple was to drive away any evil spirits which might have rushed in at the opening of the gates which had been closed for forty-two days. But neither the priest nor the people gave any explanation of it—only, "that is the way it is done."

When it was over the *sĕngguhu* returned to his village. His part in the ceremonies was finished. The next day nothing happened. There was visiting in the houses of the elders. Many cups of coffee were drunk in the give-and-take of hospitality. At the end of the day, without any formal meeting of the council, it had been decided that the gods should go, on the third day after the *odalan*, not to the sea but southward over the mountains to the temple of Pausan, some thirty miles away. They would be carried in procession, riding in their pagoda houses, accompanied by more than four hundred men, women, and children. It would take a day to walk there. Two days they would remain there, making offerings and sprinkling the gods

[13] The *odalan* is not described because it was a ceremony belonging to the ordinary calendar of festivals in the *pură balé agung* and had nothing to do with the ceremonies occasioned by the birth of the twins. It is curious, however, to note that the *odalan* took place between the twin ceremonies, that is, after the *mĕrĕyaschită* and before the *mĕlis*. In other villages where *mĕlis* was required for the birth of twins, it was arranged to take place before the *odalan*, and the people believed that only after *mĕlis* could an *odalan* be celebrated.

with the holy water of the place. Then they would return to their village, up over the mountains, to reinstate their purified gods in the temple. That is the end of the ceremonies required for the birth of twins who are a boy and a girl.

Part II: Variations of the Ritual and Taboos in Different Districts of Bali

As with all other customs in Bali, marked variations are found from village to village. I have visited a dozen different villages where twins have been born in the past few years. These villages lie in the districts of Dèn Pasar, Tabanan, Mèngwi, Gianyar, Klungkung, Bangli, Kintamani, and Bulèlèng. I have read *lontar* prescribing the ritual and special taboos applying to each of these districts except Kintamani. The contents of those *lontar* which it was possible to transcribe are given in Part IV. Of course the villages of a certain district will not necessarily follow the dictates of a *lontar* found in that district but are more apt to go by their own individual rulings, referring to the authority of the texts in the possession of the priests only in case of difficulty or uncertainty. On account of the autonomic system of village law, the differences are innumerable, but there are some points on which most of the villages agree. The order followed in Sukawană, described above, is as typical as any, if it be remembered that in such an old and isolated village the ceremonies are fuller, the offerings greater, and prescriptions more strictly adhered to than they are in villages more subject to influence from the outside.

Among the major differences in the custom of the various villages is that of the duration of expulsion of the twins with their parents. This is generally forty-two days, but in Trunyan (at the Batur lake) it lasts three months of thirty-five days, as it is also in the rules of the *sĕngguhu nabé* (teacher) of Pĕjatĕn, near Tabanan. In an old *lontar* from Bulèlèng the time is stated as three *tilĕm*, or dark moons. There is also the question whether the three Galungan (yearly festivals) following the birth may or may not be celebrated. We shall see later that the *lontar* do not agree on this point. In certain villages, as in Kĕtèwèl (district Ubud, near the south shore), the sacred vessels for holy water kept in the temples must be overturned (*choblong mĕlingĕb*), and the temple gates closed up with thorny branches, so that the gods will not enter there and become contaminated during the time that the village is *sĕbĕl*. According to a *pĕdandă* from Sanur, and to a *lontar* from Tabanan, signs (*sawèn*) of the thorny pandanus must be put up before each household entrance gate.

It is not always customary to tear down the house or building where the twins were born. In Klungkung it is not done; neither did it happen in Tĕgĕs Kawan (Pĕliatan) nor in Kutri (Singapadu) in cases I investigated. When the house is not torn down, a hut is built for the exiles out of bamboo and woven coconut fronds. The place of the _kubu_, where the twins and their parents must live for the period of their banishment, can be on the edge of the graveyard, as in Sukawană, or in the graveyard itself, as in Tĕgĕs Kawan; at the cross-roads (_pĕmpatan_) as many of the _lontar_ state and as we found in a case of twins on the island Nusă Pĕnidă, in the village of Julingan; at the place where three roads meet (_talung tambi_) as at Taro; outside the village on the road to the graveyard, as in Nyĕstanan (Sayan) and Kutri (Singapadu); outside the village to the south as in Bu'ungan[14] (Susut); or on the seashore, the old custom of Klungkung and of Sanur. All of these spots are of course relatively unholy ground, all graveyards and crossroads being favorite haunts of the bad spirits, whereas the seashore, as the "lowest" place, farthest away from the mountains and the abode of the gods, is fit for the reception of unclean people banished from the village limits. The number of watchmen (_gĕbagan_) considered necessary is a curious point of variation, for whereas in Sukawană the number reached fifty men who slept in the hut with the parents and the twins, in Taro there must be only ten or fifteen; in Klungkung, in Kĕtĕwèl, in Kutri (Singapadu) five or ten villagers suffice, whereas in Tĕgĕs Kawan the _dĕsă_ does not provide any watchmen, but four or five of the relatives of the banished family join them to keep them company. In contrast, when twins were born in Nyĕstanan the entire _banjar_, or village group of sixty men, watched every night during the period of exile.

The names applied to the purification ceremonies are various. Undoubtedly the same ceremony is called by different names in different villages, and probably a single name is often differently understood and applied to unlike rituals.

These I have found in use:

mĕrĕyaschită or _pĕrayaschită_	in Sukawană, Klungkung, Bangli, Gianyar, Pĕliatan
ngĕlungah	in Taro, Bu'ungan, Kĕtĕwèl, Tonjă,

---

[14] References to the customs of Bu'ungan and of Lumbuan are taken from the report of Idă Bagus Adiptă, "Menjelidiki adat-adat koena didésa-désa dalam bilangan negara Bangli," published in the _Bhāwanāgara_, II, Nos. 7, 8–9 (1932–33), and III, Nos. 2–3, 4–5 (1933).

	Tĕnganan,[15] Bangli, Gianyar, Pĕliatan, Tabanan
mĕsakapan	in Sukawană, Tabanan, Julingan (Nusă Pĕnidă), Bu'ungan
mĕtĕlah-tĕlah dĕsă or *mĕsadi*	in Taro, Lumbuan,[16] Bu'ungan
mĕpĕrisadi or *mapri saddhi*	in Ubud, Gianyar, Bangli, Pĕliatan
mĕcharu by these names:	
malik sumpah	in Sukawană, Taro, Klungkung, Nyĕstanan, Sanur
panchă walikramă	in Sanur, Tonjă
panchă sanak	in Sanur
panchă kĕlud	in Pĕjatèn, Tonjă
labuh gĕntuh	in Sanur, Pĕjatèn
wrĕspati kalpă	in Sanur, Tonjă
yamărĕsi gană saptă	in Tonjă
mĕdudus	in Ubud, Gianyar, Bangli, Pĕliatan
ngĕlukat or *mĕlukat*	in Klungkung, Julingan (Nusă Pĕnidă), Gianyar, Bangli, Pĕliatan, Ubud, Bu'ungan, Taro
mĕkiis or *mĕlis*	in Taro, Bangli, Gianyar, Pĕliatan, Bu'ungan, Kutri, Tabanan, Sanur, Tonjă
ngĕlungayang (same as *mĕlis*)	in Sukawană
ngĕlungahang (not to the river but only to the boundaries of the village)	in Lumbuan

These last two are to be distinguished from the *ngĕlungah* above, which, in Taro for example, is the initial ceremony to be celebrated, first in the house where the birth took place, and then in the *balé agung* temple. In Sukawană, it will be remembered, at the *ngĕlungayang* a great number of the villagers went in procession with the gods to a temple far away. At the *ngĕlungah* in the temple at Taro the villagers are not even allowed to be present, for they are still too unclean to enter the temple, and the ceremony is performed by the *pĕdandă*, who has been called from afar, and the maker of the offerings, a man also from another village, since the inhabitants of Taro itself are considered too unclean to prepare the offerings. After

[15] References to the customs of Tĕnganan are taken from V. E. Korn, *De Dorpsrepubliek Tnganan Pagringsingan.*

[16] See footnote 14.

the *ngĕlungah* in the house and in the temple, in Taro, comes the *mĕkiis* not to the sea but to a river, then the *mĕtĕlah-tĕlah désă*, and finally the *mĕcharu* called *malik sumpah* at which a *sĕngguhu* officiates. It will be noted that not only the names but the order of the ceremonies can vary, for it is certainly usual to have the *mĕcharu* first and later the *mĕkiis* or *mĕlis*.

The celebration of the ceremonies may be entrusted to a *sĕngguhu*, as in Sukawană; to a *pĕdandă* alone, either Siwă or Bodă, as in Klungkung, Tĕgĕs Kawan, Kutri, and Trunyan; to a *pĕdandă* functioning with a *sĕngguhu*, as in Bongkasă, in Taro, and as many of the *lontar* dictate. Or the ceremonies may be carried out by the local priests, using holy water prepared and blessed by a *pĕdandă*. This is done is Julingan on Nusă Pĕnidă, and also in Tĕnganan.[17] In Lumbuan, the *pĕmangku*, the temple-guardian priest, officiates, and in Bu'ungan the *balian konèng*, a sort of witch doctor, but both villages use holy water prepared by a *bujanggă*, probably a *sĕngguhu*. In Kĕtèwèl, where the purification differs for two sorts of twins, the more serious is celebrated by a *sĕngguhu* and a *pĕdandă*, the less serious by the *pĕmangku* and a *pĕdandă*. It would seem that a *sĕngguhu* should rightly be in charge of the *mĕcharu*, for offerings to the bad spirits are his special field, and a *pĕdandă* should dedicate the offerings to the gods. But the services of a *sĕngguhu* are difficult to obtain, for these priests are rare and, although in caste they rank much lower than the Brahmană *pĕdandă*, they may charge a higher fee. For this reason the *sĕngguhu* is often dispensed with. The *pĕdandă* has power to make offerings to the bad spirits, just as in Sukawană the *sĕngguhu* also made offerings to the gods.

In the matter of offerings the variation of the ritual is hard to tabulate, because the extent of the array depends not only on the custom of the village where the twins are born, but upon the rank and relative wealth of the individual family. Only in the older, more strictly organized villages such as Sukawană, Trunyan, Taro, Lumbuan, and Bu'ungan does the *adat* dictate an elaborate set of offerings which cannot be diminished even if the family of the twins is destitute. In such villages the array must be guaranteed by the members of the village group, and that which the family is not able to provide is supplied for it, creating a debt to the village and putting the family lands in pawn until the debt can be repaid. But in the more usual, less strict villages where the feeling for the unity and common

[17] See footnote 15.

interest of the group is less intense, the extent of the offerings is allowed to depend upon the resources of the affected family, and a small *mĕcharu* for poor people is considered equivalent in effectiveness to a great *mĕcharu* offered by people able to afford it. The rule is that the ceremony is low, middle, or high, according to the "birth" of the people, whether low, middle, or high (*nistă, madyă, utamă*). The reference to birth seems to cover their worldly wealth as well as their caste. The *mĕcharu* given for twins born in Tĕgĕs Kawan and in Kutri included, as animal offerings, only five chickens, a duck, a pig, and a dog, and the other offerings were correspondingly less than those used in Sukawană, for instance, where a buffalo, a calf, a goat, and a goose had to be offered as well as the less expensive beasts. But to say that in Tĕgĕs Kawan and in Kutri the *mĕcharu* for *manak salah* comprises only offerings of five chickens, a duck, a pig, and a dog would be incorrect, for twins might conceivably be born to a family there which considered itself sufficiently "high" to give one of the more elaborate *charu*.

In connection with this it may be noted that whereas in the old villages the members of the *balé agung* are generally required to contribute to the ceremonies, upon each man falling the burden of his share, it is more customary for the father of the twins to go begging from door to door, receiving contributions which may not amount to more than a cent per household. In many districts he begs not only in his own *balé agung* but in three, seven, ten, or eleven nearby *balé agung*, until he has collected the necessary funds. It is said that he may not be refused, no matter how small the contribution. This custom probably originated in former times when the entire *nĕgară*, the kingdom ruled by a certain *rajă*, was rendered *sĕbĕl* by the birth of boy and girl twins in one of its villages (so I was told by Chokordă Anom of the ruling house of Klungkung). The *lontar* say such twins *ngĕlĕtĕhin jagat*, or *bumi*, or *nĕgară*. This can be translated "to make unclean the country," and originally must have meant the whole kingdom, although now it is interpreted to mean a single *balé agung*. But the custom remains of asking contributions in a number of surrounding *balé agung*, as a leftover of their participation in the *sĕbĕl* state in former times. Today not more than a single *balé agung* is considered *sĕbĕl*, and sometimes only the *banjar* (one of the village groups which make up the *balé agung*) in which the birth of the twins occurred.

In nearly all the villages studied the birth of twins of like sex, two boys or two girls, is not *manak salah*, does not require banishment of the family nor special ceremonies of any kind. Exceptions are the old villages of Lumbuan, Bu'ungan, and Taro, where certain ceremonies are prescribed, and Trunyan and Kětèwèl,[18] where the twins and their parents are also banished from the village. Such twins are called *anak kěmbar*, whether or not they are considered a bad sign.

Although according to some *lontar* only members of the ruling Ksatriyǎ or Wésyǎ family, and the families of Brahmanǎ priests escape being branded *manak salah* if they bring forth boy and girl twins, and, although a Bulèlèng *lontar* states it to be a bad sign for people of all the four castes, in nearly all the villages of South Bali it is only considered a bad sign if *jabǎ*[19] (ordinary people, Sudrǎ) have twins who are a boy and a girl, and a good sign if Triwangsǎ (people of Brahmanǎ, Ksatriyǎ, or Wésyǎ caste) have such twins. They are called *anak kěmbar bunching*,[20] which means "twins bride and bridegroom." Among ordinary people it is known that such twins may marry. Everywhere I was told this, by all sorts of people. But a Brahmanǎ scholar and holy man, Idǎ Putu Maron of Ubud, stated that *jabǎ* twins may not marry each other, because they are *salah*.[21] On the other hand, it is a very good sign if high-caste twins marry each other.

In the present generation of the princely *chokordǎ* family of Ubud there are such twins who did not marry each other, because, the boy said, if he had married his sister, he would not have been allowed to take any other wives, and, although he was pleased with her, he did not care to commit himself to having only one spouse throughout his life.

In Batuan twins of a "small Ksatriyǎ" family, whose titles are Déwǎ Gědé and Déwǎ Ayu, married each other and were happy for two years. Then a powerful man of higher rank (Ksatriyǎ caste, *chokordǎ*) stole away Déwǎ Ayu from her twin-husband. Both the young twin-husband and the father of the twins seemed distressed at this arbitrary breaking of the intended order.

These twins were brought up in the same house. But people often say that it is better if the children can be separated when they are small, so that they will be pleased to wed when they meet again at

---

[18] In Kětèwèl a special reason exists. See pp. 39–41.

[19] According to estimate the *jabǎ* are 94 percent, the Triwangsǎ 6 percent, of the population of Bali. The population is supposed to be approximately a million.

[20] Van der Tuuk's dictionary has *bunching* = bride and bridegroom. Note also that current high Balinese for "to marry" is *měkaryǎ pěbunchingan*.

[21] Although the Balinese are supposed to follow the dictates of the Hindu priests, it often happens that the common people go their own way without consulting the priest. When they are at variance with the Hindu custom as strictly held by the Triwangsǎ, the priest excuses them, saying paternally, "They do not know."

the marriageable age. A member of the *sěngguhu* caste (classed as *jabǎ* but on account of their priestly functions often considering themselves as good as Brahmanǎ) told me that the twins should be placed as far apart as possible, for instance, one in Bulèlèng and one in Badung (Dèn Pasar). He said: "When twins are a boy and a girl, it is called *manak salah*, and people say that the boy brings his wife with him out of the womb, and therefore is like a god. The village in which it occurs becomes unclean, the subsequent Galungan may not be celebrated in the village. Afterward the largest *měcharu* must be held to purify the village before it can take part in the Galungan festivals. The people of the village are very angry when such twins are born.

"But the mother and the father are very pleased. The legend (*chěritǎ*) is that this boy must become king, since he has brought his wife out of the womb, like the kings of old.

"After the time of banishment and the purification, the boy and the girl are separated while they are still very small, and placed in houses as far apart as possible, as in Bulèlèng and in Badung. When they have reached the marriageable age, they are brought together and married to one another. It is hoped if the legend comes true and the boy becomes king the wife will bring him power over the faraway land where she was reared, and all the land between.

"But it is a very rare occurrence that such twins live. Usually either the boy or the girl, or both, die at an early age, and often even the parents die."

Unfortunately this charming version of the separation is not true all over Bali. Not one of the parents of *jabǎ* twins whom we questioned had heard that this was "to have children like the kings of old." They knew only that it was a bad sign, and a costly one to them. Since it is impossible for a *jabǎ* to become king, and has always been so, the explanation is one which would only occur to the imagination of a proud *sěngguhu*. Later it will be shown to what extent *sěngguhu* consider themselves exempt from the taboos imposed on all *jabǎ* twins.

In Nyèstanan, a village near Ubud, *jabǎ* twins born twelve years ago were separated by the adoption of the boy into a household in the same village. A year afterward the woman who had taken the boy died suddenly. This was a bad sign. The boy was returned to his parents, for no one else would take him. Now the boy and girl, who are near puberty, state most vigorously that they do not wish to marry each other, since they were brought up as brother and sister.

J. de Vroom, writing more than sixty years ago, mentions as an old custom of forgotten times that *kěmbar bunching* had to marry each other.[22] I did not find one person, *pĕdandă*, prince, or ordinary man, who stated that such marriage was compulsory.

De Vroom reports also that people say *kĕmbar salah* mostly die. It is curious that in seven cases I investigated one or both twins died before the period of banishment was over. In Taro boy and girl twins have been born three times in the past two years, to unrelated families. In each case the girl has died.

In connection with the frequently reported death of twins one is reminded of the custom of putting to death one or both twin children, found in the great area extending from British India to New Guinea and Australia. Frazer, in *Totemism and Exogamy*, quotes from the Rev. B. Danks's article on the New Britain Group (Northern Melanesia) that in the Duke of York Island "if twins are born, and they are boy and girl, they are put to death because being of the same class (of two exogamous classes) and being of opposite sex, they were supposed to have had in the womb a closeness of connection which amounted to a violation of their marital class law."[23] Again, Frazer tells of the tribes near King George's Sound, in southwest Australia, that "when twins were born, one of them was killed; if the children were of different sexes, they killed the boy and preserved the girl. The reasons which they gave for destroying a twin were 'that a woman has not sufficient milk for two children, and cannot carry them and seek her food'."[24] Edgar Thurston states that "in Madras . . . twins are sometimes objects of superstition, especially if they are of different sexes, and the male is born first. The occurrence of such an event is regarded as foreboding misfortune, which can only be warded off by marrying the twins to one another and leaving them to their fate in the jungle. Cases of this kind," he continues, "have however, it is said, not been heard of within recent times."[25] W. H. R. Rivers has written of the Todas (southern India) that "twins are called 'omumokh,' and it is the custom to kill one of them, even when both are boys. If they should be girls, it is probable that both would be killed, or at any rate would have been killed in the past."[26]

[22] J. de Vroom, "Aanteekening uit eene Balische Adversaria," *Tijdschrift voor Indische Taal-, Land-, en Volkenkunde*, XVIII.

[23] B. Danks, "Marriage Customs of the New Britain Group," *Journal of the Anthropological Institute*, XVIII (1889), quoted by Sir J. G. Frazer, *Totemism and Exogamy* (London, Macmillan, 1910), II, 122.

[24] Frazer, J. G., *Totemism and Exogamy*, I, 549, on authority of Scott Nind, *Journal of the Royal Geographical Society*, I (1832), 39.

[25] Edgar Thurston, *Omens and Superstitions of Southern India* (London, Unwin, 1912), p. 54.

[26] W. H. R. Rivers, *The Todas* (London, Macmillan, 1906), p. 480.

Certainly the feeling that twins are an evil omen is widespread throughout this extensive area. But I found no evidence to show that the Balinese ever went so far as to kill the children, except in the case of triplets which were two boys and one girl. A *pĕdandă* from Sanur and a *lontar* from Kabă-Kabă (Tabanan) stated that these were to be thrown in the sea or abandoned on the shore; but my informants added that "other people," that is, not the parents, might take them up and care for them. Probably the high mortality of twins in Bali is sufficiently explained by the undesirable removal of them the day after birth, the sojourn in an inadequate shelter during the first weeks, and perhaps the physical and mental effects on the mother of the whole anxious period before the purification.

Another point must be mentioned in connection with the early death and the separation of the twins. I was told by Chokordă Anom, keeper of the genealogy (*babad*) of the ruling family of Klungkung, that in the time of the Balinese kings all twins and triplets were taken into the *puri* of the *rajă* to become his slaves (*parĕkan*). The *rajă* had the right to take these children, whether two boys, two girls, or whatever the assortment of the sexes. The *rajă's* power over them continued throughout their lifetime. It happened in Taro in the last generation that a boy-twin was separated from his sister when they reached puberty, by order of the Anak Agung (prince) of Tĕgallalang, whose *parĕkan* the boy became. Later the boy was released from servitude. He returned to Taro and married his twin. He is now dead, and his widow is an old woman. This is the only case I found where a twin or triplet was taken by a prince, although De Vroom speaks of finding in *lontar* that boy and girl twins may be dedicated to the prince, who will have them educated.[27] And this case also is too far in the past to make sure that it was on account of his being a twin that the boy was taken into servitude. Princes in Bali still can find ways of casting their subjects into temporary servitude, and this must have been more true before the influence of the Dutch government overspread the island. However, if it *was* the custom for twins to become slaves, that might explain both their reported high mortality and their custom of separation (regardless of whether or not they proposed to marry). For the old *rajă* of Bali ruled their kingdoms loosely, leaving each village its independent organization, themselves rarely venturing beyond their palace walls. From time to time they sent a *patih*, or emissary, to collect tribute, or to bring back some

[27] See footnote 22.

offender against the crown to have his head chopped off. (Such is the picture suggested by the literature, the popular legends and dramatic plays representing older times.) In cases where two or more children had been born at once, it would have been easy enough to cheat the *rajă* of his slaves by the adoption of the extra children into other houses and the reported death of any child whose liability to servitude threatened. However, the death of one or more of the children does not release the parents from the full obligation of banishment and the purification ceremonies prescribed by the village law. A crime against the community and a crime against the *rajă* were two distinct things. In Kutri (Singapadu) boy and girl twins were born in September, 1933. Both died the day of their birth, before the *kubu* on the road to the graveyard had been finished for their reception. But the parents were banished just the same, and the full order of ceremonies took place after forty-two days.

This brings us to the question of whether the "wrongness" of boy and girl twins in *jabă* families is a concept rooted in the ancient belief of the Balinese people antedating their conquest by Hindu-Javanese princes or a concept spread among them by those conquerors. As has been seen from the notes on various peoples quoted above, the concept is characteristic not only of Southern India, but widespread in great reaches of Oceania. It has been reported from the Philippines that the Nabaloi people, inhabiting Benguet, North Luzon, believe "if there are twins, one is the child of the *ampasit* (a malevolent spirit belonging to each locality, itself the child of an incestuous union of brother and sister). We do not know the child of the *ampasit*. A twin should marry a twin. If another person not a twin marries a twin, the *ampasit* will become angry and kill him." [28] Such a belief, although not directly related to that found in Bali, is interesting in the suggestion which it offers of a perhaps similarly primitive belief existing in the primitive Bali, which might have been later overlaid by the Hindu concepts. If this were true, all twins would originally have been objects of superstition. Yet most intelligent Balinese attribute the taboo directly to Hindu-Javanese influence. The *lontar* definitely state that "it is an affront to the king—*mamadă Rajă Delĕm*." But much evidence points to an earlier fear of twins. Why do we find in four old-style Bali-agă villages twins of like sex considered bad, and only in one Hinduized village, where the special reason of twin ancestor gods exists to explain the unusual taboo? (Kĕtèwèl, see pp. 39–41.) Why are

---

[28] C. R. Moss, "Nabaloi Law and Ritual," *University of California Publications in American Archeology and Ethnology*, XV, No. 3 (October 28, 1920), 273.

there bizarre elaborations of the rite in old villages?[29] Why are the offerings in the villages greater where Hindu influence is less? Why do the clever Hindu priests find in their *lontar* excuses for avoiding the taboos, based on hair-splitting differences in the birth—was the boy born first or the girl, were there two placentas or one, which child "brought the placenta," at how great an interval of time were the children born[30]—all differences unknown to the ordinary *jabă* and rarely relied upon to squeeze out of the trouble of *manak salah*? Does it not look as if the true Balinese concept is that such twins are a bad thing, and the newly arrived Hindu-Javanese rulers simply claimed their right to have such children honored in the royal and priestly families? Rather than attempt to destroy the established popular superstition about twins, they would have at first only denied any evil pertaining to their own twins, then propounded the belief that this was their own special way to have children (especially a boy and a girl together), finally strengthening their own position by stating that the commoners affronted the *rajă* when they dared to have children in his privileged way. Eventually the popular superstition about boy and girl twins would have been reinforced by the royal prescription, and the superstition about twins of like sex would tend to die out. Of course, even in the primitive belief boy and girl twins must have been the more terrifying sort, on account of the obvious incestuous connotation which could not but offend again the marriage laws, whatever they were. Therefore it would be easier for this taboo to survive than that on twin brothers or twin sisters. Meanwhile the royal and priestly families were taking wives from among the com-

---

[29] Such elaborations, for instance, as thrice burning the *kubu*, and the use of the *pusuh* as a substitute for the dead twin in Sukawană. Also, in a case of twins recently in Sělulung, the following rite, which was witnessed and related to me by Walter Spies: A *pusuh* was again used as substitute for one of the twins which had died, and, when the crowd of villagers went down to the river, not only the *pusuh* but the mother and the father and the remaining twin were cast into the stream (*anyudang*). This took place at a *champuh*, or meeting of rivers, and a dam had been constructed across the stream just below where the two rivers came together. The father, the mother holding the child, the *pusuh*, with various *cholong*, coconuts, and so forth, were cast in the water above the dam, and then the dam was broken up, so that with a rush of water all were carried some little way downstream. Below this were stationed some fifteen men armed with spears, who with much shouting and excitement tried to pierce the *cholong* and coconuts as they swept past.

Still another barbaric custom is that prescribed in Těnganan, when, after the parents of twins have been driven out of the village, their house is stoned by the villagers. See V. E. Korn's transcription of the *Awig-awig Désă* in his *De Dorpsrepubliek Tnganan Pagringsingan*, p. 245.

[30] See below excerpts from the Tabanan *lontar*, pp. 44–47.

moners, producing children of Ksatryă and Brahmană caste who yet
were not sufficiently well-born to escape being "wrong" if they or
their descendants happened to have boy and girl twins. These people,
we must suppose, the small nobility, appealed to the priests to clear
them of the wrong. For they, on account of their caste, were brought
up in the Hindu tradition. Probably it was for their benefit that the
priests evolved the complicated differences in the birth of twins,
whether there were two placentas or only one, whether the boy was
born first, and so forth, and posited that only in one special combination of conditions could the offending parents be said to "affront the
rajă." Even on these points the priestly authorities do not agree, so
that even more leeway is afforded by their varying doctrines.
Theoretically a man could go from authority to authority seeking one
whose version would absolve him from his wrong. In Pĕliatan the
question came up in the case of twins whether the village should
follow the dictates of the *pĕdandă Bodă*, who said that three Galungans
could not be celebrated after the birth, or the words of the *pĕdandă
Siwă*, who said that the Galungan immediately following the purification might be celebrated. In Sanur where there are twenty-one
pĕdandă, the scope of opinions is infinite. But the ordinary *jabă*,
unaccustomed as he remains to Hindu thought, rarely appeals to the
priest for an excuse to escape his dilemma.

Perhaps it should be explained that all investigations which touch
upon the religion of Bali are hampered and obscured by the confused
background of the people, about which very little is definitely known.
The only histories are genealogies kept by the various royal families,
which do not agree with each other, which "have holes in them and
do not join" as one Balinese put it, and whose very names for the kings
cannot be identified with the kings of the tales and legends kept alive
in the minds of the people. If one tries to sift out what part of a rite
or custom is of Hindu or Hindu-Javanese origin and what part Old
Indonesian, one gets into difficulties—for not only is every village
different from every other village in Bali, but no purely Hindu village
or household exists, and probably no Bali-agă village exists which has
not been at some time and in some way influenced by Hindu custom.
The great body of the religion of Bali seems to be ancestor worship,
combined with a certain amount of animism in the worship of
mountain-, lake-, and sea-gods—the whole overlaid with a coating
of Hinduism differing in profundity. Where Hindu influence has
been greater Hindu thought and terminology is more widespread,
even among the "ignorant outsiders," the *jabă*. In other places the

old style seems to have resisted the religious persuasion of the conquerors to such an extent that even today the inhabitants refuse to tell the name of their gods, to let them be seen by strangers, even in some temples Hindu *pĕdandă* are refused admittance. Yet the scholars and thinkers are chiefly Hindu priests and Hindu-caste princes, who are ready to explain every act of the people in a Hindu way—and these thinkers are the only ones of the Balinese able to give reasons. The simple man says, "That is the way it is done," or, "That is the way the old men tell," or, "That is the way my father taught me." The great mass of the Balinese behave according to tradition, without question and without need for explanatory thought. And if one listens to the Hindu-thinking Balinese, who has always a rational-sounding answer, one has little assurance that his answer actually reflects the cause of true content of the commoner's behavior. To give an example: The *sanggah kamulan*, perhaps the chief shrine of the household temple, is found all over Bali. It has a characteristic form, with three doors. Nine out of ten simple Balinese will tell you when asked the name of the god whose shrine it is, that they do not know any name for the god. If asked what *sanggah kamulan* means, they will answer that it means the "place of the forefather," the founder of the family. They cannot tell why it has three doors. Yet the tenth man, of Hindu caste, or trained or tinged with Hindu thought, will answer: "It is for Batară Guru," or, "for Siwă," or, "for Brahmă-Siwă-Wisnu, the Trimurti." If you insist and ask why others say the shrine is for their ancestor, this man will say: "Yes, that is true, for Siwă is the First Ancestor of all men, it was Siwă who made all men." And yet even a *pĕdandă* told, when a question came up of installing figures of the gods in the *sanggah kamulan*, that the figure of only one god with his wife, either Siwă or Wisnu, could be placed there. He said that to place Brahmă, Siwă, and Wisnu, with or without their wives, behind the three doors, was impossible. I never heard a satisfactory explanation of the three doors, which appear to be such an obviously Hindu form. Yet the *sanggah kamulan* is unquestionably the shrine of the ancestor in each individual household and has nothing to do with Siwă in the minds of the householders to whom each shrine belongs and who give offerings there.

Besides the difficulty of receiving Hindu-thought explanations for customs probably of non-Hindu origin, one has to remember that certain Hindu rites may have been taken over into the laws of the old Bali-agă villages as magic or medicine considered efficacious against misfortune. As in Sukawană, where the worship of the gods is in the hands of the villagers and their Council of Elders as priests, a *balian* exists who performs certain ceremonies outside the temples, and the *sĕngguhu* is called in from another village for *mĕcharu*. In Trunyan, known to be so strong in its old organization and strict in its religion, a *pĕdandă* from Bangli, we were told, must be called for the *mĕcharu* following the birth of *kĕmbar bunching* twins. And in Taro a *pĕdandă* must officiate with the *sĕngguhu*. In Tĕnganan, according to Dr. Korn, the ceremony must be carried out with holy water from the *pĕdandă* Siwă-Bodă. The presence of these Hindu practices in non-Hindu villages does not prove that the whole twin-purification ceremony is of Hindu origin, but it may be due to the magical power ascribed to Hindu ritual by the villagers, so that they believe the presence of the Hindu priest or the use of holy water prepared by him will reinforce their own ways of driving off the disasters. As will be seen, the custom of banishment, and certain more barbaric rites for multiple births than were performed in Sukawană, mentioned in some of the *lontar*, have much in common with the old incest ritual of some of these villages.

Part III: Divers Points of View, Together with Some Explanatory Legends

I have said that the Balinese authorities do not agree. I shall report some of the opinions and stories expressed to me in conversation with various Balinese—priests and educated men, and princes—on the subject of twins. This seems to me a good method for approaching the subject as it exists in their minds. The same people might modify or revise their beliefs after referring to the *lontar*—later we shall take up the information that these contain—but their original statements are more illuminating for grasping their actual living concepts.

Here is the mystical point of view, as presented by a Ksatryă, Chokordă Ngurah of Ubud:

The word *bunching* means the same as *ardă nari swari* (Skr.*ardhanareçvarī*), which, applied to the gods, means the male and the female, the god and his wife in one person. As Batară Siwă has only one wife, Giri Putri, but she has many names and forms, according to the different aspects in which she is worshiped (literally: "the different places where she is seated," *mĕlinggih*). She is called Durgă, Umă, and so forth. All the gods, Batară Wisnu, Batară Bramă, each has only one wife.

And so to be born with a wife is to be born as a god, and the twin boy if he marries his twin may have only that one wife, like a god.

Now it is written that Batară Siwă made all men. First he made Brahmă, and Brahmă made the world, and his children were the four castes, Brahmană, Ksatryă, Wésyă, and Sudră. So that all men are in a sense the children and descendants of Batară Siwă, and therefore it is possible for them to be born as gods, as *kěmbar bunching*. But it is only right for people of high caste (Triwangsă) to be born or to have children in that way, and people of Sudră caste are not allowed to have children in that way. If they do, and they can because they also are descendants of Batară Siwă, they are *salah* and must be purified, together with the village where the disaster occurred.

For Triwangsă people it is a sign of prosperity if boy and girl twins are born. The rice fields will yield great plenty, and the king and the country will prosper and grow rich.

For *jabă* it is a sign of disaster, pestilence, famine to the land.

It is a better sign for Triwangsă if the boy is born before the girl. It is a better sign if the children have only one placenta instead of two. For *jabă* it is a much more *salah* happening if the boy is born before the girl, and also if there is only one placenta.

(This matter of the placenta has nothing to do with physiological fact. The Balinese have no knowledge or concern over identical and nonidentical twins, and they make no difference between a single placenta and two which adhere, appearing as one. The result is that cases of "two placentas" are extremely rare, for they must appear absolutely separately to be considered as two, and most Balinese will say that they have never seen such a thing, many that they did not know of its possibility. However the more erudite Balinese distinguish between a birth with one or two *ari-ari*, although they differ as to which is to be considered the more serious offense.)

As a contrast to the high-flown reasoning of Chokordă Ngurah, let us see what a young Brahmană, a schoolteacher, nephew of the *pědandă gědé* of Bongkasă, has to say:

The story is that boy and girl twins have had sexual contact in the womb, and the people believe this. They are ignorant, and therefore they are afraid.

The *rajă* of old were jealous of their own royal rights and customs. For instance, a certain day, as *rědité manis*, is an excellent day for people of high caste (Triwangsă) to have a cremation. But the *jabă* were not allowed to use that day. And so the *jabă* do not dare to use it, they are afraid, they say, "It is not a favorable day for us." If the *rajă* wears red, he forbids the *jabă* to wear red. And in the same way, as male and female twins are a good sign for the *rajă*, they are a very bad sign for the *jabă*. It was forbidden by the *rajă*, but as the people were under the rule of different *rajă*, the customs differ.

If the girl is born before the boy, of twins born to a *rajă*, they may not marry, for she is older. Therefore it is not *salah* for the *jabă* if the girl is born before the boy.

Perhaps the custom arose because once a *rajă* had boy and girl twins which were lucky, and once a *jabă* had such twins which were unlucky. Superstition arises when people are afraid.

This young man, so superior to the superstition of the people, still admits that *jabă* are *salah* if they have male and female twins of which the boy is born first. On this point he is in agreement with Idă Putu Maron, a Brahmană scholar of Ubud, who said:

It is only called *bunching* if the boy is born first. If the girl is born first it is called simply *kěmbar*. In this case it is not a good sign for the Triwangsă, nor is it *salah* for the *jabă*. But the people do not know this. They proceed with the purification of the village just as if it were *salah*.

There was once in the ancient Pèjèng dynasty a *rajă* who was a twin. He is called Dalĕm Bunching. After this, the *rajă*, to enforce their power, ordered the *jabă* to be *salah* when they had twins in the way of the *rajă*. This was to make the people humble.

When we asked this informant about the twins' sexual connection in the womb, he said that he had never heard such a thing, but perhaps it was told the people by the *rajă* to make them ashamed, so that they would realize how *salah* they were.

Although Idă Putu Maron applies the name *bunching* only to twins of which the boy is born first, we have seen that it is generally applied to all male and female twins. But according to the *lontar* of Sanur and of Tabanan *bunching* is the name when the girl is born first, whereas if the boy is first it is called *silih asih*. The old men of Taro also said *bunching* if the girl is born first, and *salit* if the boy is first. The *pĕdandă gĕdé* of Bongkasă also calls it *silih asih* if the boy is born first, saying that it is a better sign for Triwangsă, but no worse for *jabă* than the reversed order. He says that twins with one placenta are worse for the *jabă*, because that is their way, and with two placentas are better for *rajă*, for that is their way. I was also told by the father of Kĕtut Wijanagară, the administrator of the Liefrinck van der Tuuk Library, that in the old days in Bulèlèng the case of one placenta was considered more *salah*, but if the girl was born first it was not *salah* at all.

I have encountered still more divergent meanings for the word *bunching*, as, for instance, when the *sĕngguhu* priest of Lukluk told me that he called boy and girl twins *bunching* if they had two placentas, and *silih asih* if they had only one, regardless of the order of their birth. He added that he had never heard of a case with two placentas. And recently in Bandă, a village near Blahbatu, where triplets were born, the *perbĕkĕl* (government headman) called triplets in which the sexes were mixed *bunching*, whereas if there were three boys or three girls they would be called *kĕmbar*. In this particular case there were two boys and a girl, which generally is considered a very bad sign, as the people say two men may not share a wife, and the family must be banished, the village purified. The custom in Bandă we cannot consider very orthodox, for, although they planned to have the *měcharu malik sumpah*, they did not banish the family for the reason that the triplets died within a day of their birth. The death of the offending children does not, in stricter villages, absolve the parents from banishment. We may consider this application of the name *bunching* a case of ignorance. The old name is *katijuru*, perhaps deriving from *juru katrini*, that is, "the three officials," a term occurring among the names of officials in older language. There are other fanciful names applied to triplets, as *tunjung apit tělagǎ*, "a waterlily on either side of the pond," given when there are two girls and a boy, for it is a good sign when the boy is born with two wives (Batuan). If there are two boys and a girl, they are called *butǎ*, demons, because they must fight over the girl. I have also heard two boys and a girl called *panchoran apit bulakan*, two girls and a boy *bulakan apit panchoran*. These are two sorts of springs, the *panchoran* water coming from above and flowering out of a spout, the *bulakan* water bubbling up from beneath in a hollow rock—obvious male and female symbols.

The people are vague about the significance of triplets, as these are, of course, rarer in occurrence than twins. In a case of one boy and two girls born about seven years ago in Bongkasǎ, the people did not know what to do. Although at that time the *perběkěl* of the village was the son of the *pědandǎ*, the *pědandǎ* apparently could not advise him, so he reported the case to the *punggawǎ*, the head of the district. The *punggawǎ* again reported to the Dutch Controleur, but, as the *perběkěl* told me: "They did not order anything to be done, so the village did nothing." This exemplifies how much the people still hold in their minds that unusual births are a crime against the *rajǎ*—although they know that the power of the *rajǎ* is long past, they suppose that the Dutch government will also consider it an affront if anyone has twins or triplets!

Another such case was when five or six years ago boy and girl twins were born in Kabǎ-Kabǎ (near Tabanan). The parents happened to be *sěngguhu* people, who, because of their priestly caste (although not of the three higher Hindu castes) considered that they had the right to have such twins and not be *salah*. The village, however, did not agree and insisted that the parents provide the ceremony for the purification of the "country." As the *sěngguhu* family insisted on their rights, the village brought a formal action against them. The decision was referred from one high official to another until finally it was brought to the Governor General. Meanwhile a year had passed. The villagers took the matter into their own hands and banished the family from the village for life. The exiled ones moved to Tabanan, where they had relatives who took them in, "for they had known of people with twins who had left out the ceremony."

In the effort to trace the historical or legendary figure of Dalĕm Bunching, the original king who was a twin and to whom the people attribute the origin of the twin customs, I was told the story of Mĕsulă-Mĕsuli. The story comes in part from the Usana Bali. It was long ago, in the time when the great mountain Gunung Agung had just been made. A fierce and terrible Détya, Mayă Danawă, was in power over the land. He was jealous of the gods and did not allow the people to give them offerings. The gods banded together to fight the demon Mayă Danawă, and a war ensued in which many people were killed. Finally Batară Indră was able to overpower Mayă Danawă, but in killing him his plan was to make him alive again, dividing him into a male and a female part, to become the first *rajă* of Bali. The spirit of the demon was placed in a coconut flower, and on the slopes of the Gunung Agung the gods came down and blessed it, and out of the coconut flower they made to come two children, a boy and a girl, who were called Mĕsulă-Mĕsuli. Mĕsulă-Mĕsuli became the first *rajă* of Pĕjèng, and all the people who had not been killed in the great war became their subjects.

Mĕsulă-Mĕsuli, the boy and the girl, had children, who were again a boy and a girl and were also called Mĕsulă-Mĕsuli. These twins married and again had twins, and so it went until there had been seven generations of Mĕsulă-Mĕsuli. Now each time the *rajă* married his sister, and he might not have any other women. But the seventh Mĕsula-Mĕsuli was a handsome young man, and his sister was black and ugly, and he did not care for her. He sat watching a *gambuh* play, and, when a beautiful young dancer appeared, he fell in love with her. So strong was his desire that, going against tradition, he married her instead of his sister. And after that there were no more Mĕsulă-Mĕsuli, no more twins were born to the royal family.[31] The child of

[31] Although I was told by various people of the repeated generations of Mĕsula-Mĕsuli, they are not always mentioned. C. C. Berg, in *De Middeljavaansche historische traditie* (Santpoort, 1927), gives the story simply: "There was a coconut tree near Batu Madĕg, two children came out of this tree, a male and a female. They were called Masula and Masuli, and married each other. He was made king of Bali by Mpu Kuturan." In the Kidung Pamañcangah (folio 1b–2a) the story is: "A man of great *sakti* (supernatural power), of demonic character, a *danawă*, was killed by Puruhuta (Indra) with his *bajră*. He had to stay a long time in the *ayatană* (space between heaven and hell) after which he was to be reincarnated. He was born in Tatakalapa (in Mĕdang) and taken as a child by a hermit of the To-Langkir (Gunung Agung). Afterwards he was appointed king of Bali and named Masula-Masuli. He married his younger sister."

the last Mĕsulă was a son, Bédahulu, who had the head of a pig (*bedă*, different, (*h*)*ulu*, head).

The story goes that this son was very strong in magic power. So strong was he that he was able to take a kris and cut off his own head, and then place it back upon his shoulders again. Often in the palace he would tell his servant to cut off his head, and then replace it. But one day he was playing beside the river, and, when he ordered the servant to cut off his head, the servant did so, and the head fell into the stream and was swiftly carried away by the current. The servant, in despair, saw a pig nearby, so he cut off its head and placed it upon the shoulders of the Prince. That is why he was called Bédahulu.

When he became *rajă* his palace was moved from Pèjènb to Bĕdulu (called after him). He used to sit on high in the *balé tĕgĕh*, and the people were not allowed to look up at him. When they ate the long limp ferns, they might not lift up their heads and drop them into their open mouths. If they disobeyed, they were instantly killed, by a weapon hurled down from on high by the *rajă*. But a little child looked up and went unnoticed, and so the news spread among the people that their *rajă* had the head of a pig.

According to tradition this Bédahulu was the king who was defeated by Gajă Madă, the emissary of the royal family in Java to which the present rulers of Klungkung trace their ancestry. I have quoted his story because it makes the only link between the legendary Mĕsulă-Mĕsuli and any line of Balinese *rajă* which extends to the present day. But how slender is the historical significance of this link may be judged from the legend of that ancestry, as related to me by Chokordă Anom, the keeper of the genealogies of the royal house of Klungkung. He said that in the beginning was a Brahmană *pandită*, who as a result of many penitences begat from a stone a son, called Sri Krĕsnă Kĕpakisan. This son married a *wijadari*, a heavenly nymph. Although he himself was a Brahmană, because he had not married a Brahmană his four children by the nymph were Ksatriyă. It was his *patih*, Gajă Madă, who defeated Bédahulu and so put an end to that dynasty. The four children became rulers in Pasuruan, Blangbangan, Sumbawa (the queen), and Bali, the youngest, Dalĕm Kĕtut, coming to Bali after its conquest to set up his palace in Samplangan. His son moved the palace to Gèlgèl, and after five generations the *rajă* moved to Klungkung, where the line has ruled up to the present time. The story of Sri Krĕsnă Kĕpakisan is supposed to refer to the conquest of Bali by the Majapahit forces.

Just how intimately the descendants from this miraculous past take their legendary tradition is shown by the affirmation of Chokordă Anom that all the Měsulă-Měsuli, the seven generations of them, were born with two placentas. Such a birth, then, is the way of the *rajă*. It is curious that the tradition of the twin king should have been kept alive by this Klungkung dynasty, which claims that its ancestors defeated and put an end to the Pějèng and Bědulu dynasty to which the legendary Měsulă-Měsuli belong. If it had been a king of the Klungkung or Gèlgèl dynasty who was a twin, one could better understand their insistence that for common people to have twins was an affront to the *rajă*. Chokordă Anom stated that there had never been a twin in those dynasties. But the *pědandă* of Intaran (Sanur) had a story to tell of twins in the Gèlgèl dynasty. There were three generations of boy and girl twins, he said, each of which grew up to marry each other. The twin of the third generation was the king Dalěm Sěganing. In those days the kings were so holy that they did not die, but when they grew old and their life was over, one day their bodies disappeared (*moksah* or *musnă*). They went straight to heaven. But Dalěm Sěganing was not satisfied with the one wife who was his sister, and he took many women. And so when his time came he died and his body remained. It was necessary to cremate him, and a *nagabandhă* (a great serpent which precedes the cremation tower of high nobles) was used for the first time to lead his soul to heaven. And *nagabandhă* have been used ever since.

Sěganing, or Sagěning, as a king of Gèlgèl, is another traditional character, many times mentioned in the Kidung Pamañcangah, but there is nothing about his being a twin. The story is a legend which has become attached to his name. It shows several points of similarity with the Měsulă-Měsuli story, the repeated generations of boy and girl twins, who were allowed only to marry each other, and the arresting of the divine cycle of twins if the king wed any other than his sister. Although I did not find this particular point in any other legend, stories of the supernatural birth of a boy and a girl who become the ancestors of a tribe or family are not rare in Bali. Here is one from Kětèwèl, as told by the *perběkěl* of his own ancestry.

When Kětèwèl was still a jungle, a *dukuh*, a very holy man, dwelt there. He built a *sanggah* (household shrine) of bamboo.

The Rajă Dalěm Gèlgèl came to the forest to hunt. He was accompanied by his priest and many of his subjects. But they saw neither birds nor beasts. They came to I Dukuh and asked why they saw no prey. I Dukuh answered: "If the *rajă* wishes to see birds and beasts in plenty, he must worship at my *sanggah*."

The *rajă* was very angry at this impertinence. He returned to his palace. But the following day he sent two hundred men with the order to put I Dukuh to death. They came in canoes along the shore. But as their canoes touched land at Kětèwèl, a heavy rain came down, and the two hundred men fell ill upon the beach and died.

When this news had reached the *rajă*, he believed I Dukuh to be indeed a very holy man. And the next day he sent his high priest with only six men, to ask for the soul (*jiwă*) of I Dukuh. The *rajă* wished to get this powerful soul for himself.

The high priest came to I Dukuh in the forest and told him the king's desire. I Dukuh agreed. He said: "First I must purify myself, and then you may do as you like with me." He bathed himself and washed his hair, and, when it was done, the followers of the priest killed him. The priest ordered his body to be buried, but, when the men wanted to bury him, they found the body had disappeared (*musnă*).

A child of I Dukuh heard voices speaking in the forest. He looked about, but there was no one there. Then he heard that the voices issued from a *kětèwèl* tree. He took an axe and cut open the tree, and out came two children, a boy and a girl. It was the spirit of I Dukuh which had been reborn (*numitis*) in these children.

The children were called Iri Suchi and Mas Suchi. They grew up and married each other, and their descendants are the family of the *perbĕkĕl*, which has lived there ever since, in the place called Kětèwèl after the tree from which the children were born.

There exist in Kětèwèl twin gods, Déwă Kěmbar, in the form of sacred bronze figures kept with a number of others in the Pură Jogan Agung. They are two males, called Mas Mětěkèl and Mas Murug. Such figures are believed by the archaeologists to represent dead kings whose memory was perpetuated by the making of their likeness to be worshiped as gods. I found no legend relating to these Déwă Kěmbar, but an unusual reversal of the customs regarding twins is due to them. In Kětèwèl, because of the twin gods which are two males, the birth of twins of like sex, either two boys or two girls, is considered more *salah* than the birth of a boy and a girl. Twins of like sex are banished for forty-two days to the graveyard, and ten people must watch them, whereas *bunching* twins are placed before the *pură désă*, and only four *gěbagans* are thought necessary. When the time comes for the ceremony of purification, a larger *měcharu* is given for *anak kěmbar*, with a dog, a pig, a duck, and five chickens as offerings, and a *sěngguhu* officiates with the *pědandă*. For *anak bunching* only five chickens are offered, and the *pĕmangku* assists the *pĕdandă*. In neither case do they have the *mĕlis*.

Likewise the caste distinctions are more strict in Kĕtĕwĕl, for only Brahmană and *rajă* Ksatriyă have the right to have twins, either *kĕmbar* or *bunching*, and all the smaller nobility together with the *jabă* are *salah*. The people know, of course, that their taboo on *anak kĕmbar* differs from the custom of the surrounding villages. They say it is because in Kĕtĕwĕl they have gods which are twins and the others have not. The idea that the figures are representations of ancient kings is unknown to them. But every village may have its own gods in its temples, which are worshiped by the people of that village, and the people of other villages have nothing to do with them.

Part IV: What the Lontar Say

One of the Balinese *lontar*, called Bhagawan Gargă, has in part to do with twins. A copy of this *lontar* was in the possession of a *pĕdandă* Siwă in Bangli, another in Gianyar, and a third belonged to the *pĕdandă* Bodă of Pĕliatan. All three priests referred to this *lontar* when questioned about *manak salah* or *kĕmbar bunching*. The story of the one from Bangli may be roughly summarized as follows:

This is the story of people with boy and girl twins.

The *rajă* of Bali goes to meet the holy man, Idă Bagawan Lindu Tawang, in Lĕmah Rékă (Lĕmah Tulis). The holy man receives him at his meditation place. The *rajă* takes a humble place on the lower level (*pemarĕkan*), but, when he has introduced himself as a pupil of Bagawan Sunyă Murti Bali, the holy man welcomes him and leads him inside the palace. Because the prince has followed the teachings of Bagawan Sunyă Murti Bali, the holy man gives him his daughter in marriage. Sang Mpu Pradah (the holy man) becomes teacher-priest in Maospait.

Now Idă Mpu Kuturan had a son, called Idă Sang Bujanggă Bali, who in turn has a son already three months old, in appearance like a perfect jewel, his body perfect, he has no flaws. Mpu Kuturan gives him the name of Idă Batară Guru. Because he is the son of Idă Sang Bujanggă Bali, he must become the teacher of the *rajă* of Bali. When Idă Mpu Sunyă Murti had explained how he became super-latively *tri murti*, pure, he died and went back to the home of the gods.

It is said Batară Bagawan Indră Chakru (the child above called Idă Batară Guru?) taught the prince of Bali. When the pupil had learned what the teachings were, Bagawan Chakru died. The *rajă* addressed his people thus: If there are people in the country of Bali who affront the *rajă* by having twins *bunching*, the country of the *rajă* becomes unclean; if twins *bunching* are born in the land of Bali, within the limits of the village, every house of man, every man is unclean in the unclean village. If it happens, they are banished by the people of the *dĕsă*, far from the village. They must be placed at the crossroads where it is lonely, they may not come near the village. Up to the time of the ceremony, the country of the *rajă* is threatened, the meditations of the *rajă* are disturbed, rice is dear, plantings do not prosper, water is scarce, there is famine in the country of the *rajă*. After forty-two days' time, these people must have the purification—*prayaschita, těbusan, amanchă panggungan, linukatan (ngělukat); ngělungah* at dark moon, *měkiis* at full moon, in the presence of *Bujanggă* and *Siwă* (interpreted *sěngguhu* and *pědandă* Siwă), each of these must officiate, so that the microcosmos and the macrocosmos may be purified. Moreover the Galungan festival may not take place for three times, if it is not three times stopped, calamity to the Two Worlds, many beasts fall dead, all the plantings fail, the meditations of the *rajă* are burned up. If the right way is strictly followed, the Two Worlds become prosperous, the beasts and plantings healthy. If a *rajă* or a Bujanggă or a Brahmană has twins *bunching*, the country prospers and there are no disasters.

After this, the king died. He who became king was one of boy and girl twins. He prayed and prayed, he studied and meditated to become holy, he prayed at the Gunung Agung, day and night he fasted and did not drink nor sleep, for he was in real *ascesis*. He concentrated in the *lumbung (sanggar)* on the Gunung Agung (Běsakih) on the day of full moon in the tenth month, together with the Bujanggă and Siwă (*pědandă* Bodă and Siwă), as witnesses. This was the behavior of the *rajă*, meditation on the *lumbung*, in order that the rule of the *rajă* of Bali should be strong and long-lasting.

It will be seen that this "story" is far from clear, and Balinese scholars themselves do not seem to understand it. The various names given to the characters cannot be definitely identified with those to whom they refer. And other obscurities of language are interpreted according to the prejudice of the reader. For instance, in the passage "if there are people in the country of Bali who affront the *rajă* by having twins *bunching*," the word *wong*, meaning simply people, is taken by the authority from Bangli to mean "people of Sudră or Wésyă caste." Another would interpret it to mean only Sudră, another all people except the *rajă* himself and his priests, as stated later on in the passage. But this again is not clear, for the phrase *Sang Bujanggă Brahmană* is extremely obscure and open to many interpretations. *Bujanggă* is a title claimed not only by Siwă and Bodă *pědandă* but by *sěngguhu* as well. *Sěngguhu* would here claim that the word Bujanggă refers to them, and the word Brahmană does not modify it, that is, giving immunity from *manak salah* to *sěngguhu and* to Brahmană. When referring to the celebration of the ceremonies, the phrase *bujanggă* Siwă was interpreted *sěngguhu* and *pědandă* Siwă; when referring to the meditations of the *rajă, sang bujanggă* Siwă was interpreted *pědandă* Bodă and *pědandă* Siwă. I merely call attention to these discrepancies so that the reader may take them into account. It will be noted that the name of the king who was a twin is not disclosed.

The *lontar* Bhagawan Gargă has a further passage on twins:

It is the way for people with wrong children (*manak salah*), male and female born, to be banished by the people of the village, to be sent out from the house, to be placed at the graveyard, for a month and seven days they remain at the grave-yard and may not return home to sleep. After the time is up they may come back to the village, and have the ceremonies *amalukat*, *maprisaddi*, *mĕdudus dĕning chatur kumbă* [= purifying (bathing)] with water from the four vessels, at the big crossroads [here the offerings are enumerated] . . . the ceremony *pĕdudusan* [bathing] to be accompanied with *mantră* [prayers] of the complete *prayaschită*, that is, *Sayam Brahmă*, *Ganastawă*, *Bhuwanéswari*, *Nadayă*, *Astupungku*.

They must make the *Sanggar Tawang* [bamboo shrine for the gods]. [The offerings are enumerated, both to be put up in this shrine for the uranic gods (*suchi*) and to be set out on the ground for the chthonic gods (*charu*).] Those who officiate are *Sang Siwă* (*pĕdandă* Siwă) and *Sogată* (*pĕdandă* Bodă), offerings *daksină* and *pras*. As soon as the people are purified (*adudus*), the house in the graveyard is burned, is sprinkled with holy water, using the necessary offerings *prayaschită* and *sĕsayut*. When this is done, the uncleanness of the people with twins is erased. Then they may go back to their house. This is required by divine law.

[More about the offerings] . . . and the possessions of the people with twins may not be taken and used for ceremonies nor for *charu* before they have been purified (*mĕlukat*). After they have been purified, the festivals may go on in all the temples. And the people of the village are forced to contribute according to their means (*nistă*, *madyă*, *utamă* [poor, middle, rich]). The people who have twins must beg for contributions in ten *balé agung* before the ceremony *malukat*, but they may not sleep in the villages.

Here we find in two different passages of a single *lontar* sets of rules which do not correspond. The first text which the *rajă* expounds to his people banishes the twin-family to the crossroads, the second text names the graveyard. In the second no mention is made of *ngĕlungah*, nor of *mĕkiis*. Although we found *mĕkiis* (carrying the gods to the sea or to the river) or *mĕlis* customary in most villages after the birth of twins, we were told in Klungkung and in Kĕtĕwĕl that it was not done there. It will be noted that in the Bhagawan Gargă *lontar*, the *rajă* tells his people that three Galungan may not be celebrated after the birth, although the later section does not speak of it. Another *lontar*, from Tabanan (Kabă-Kabă) specifically denies the restriction. And as I have told, the *pĕdandă* Bodă from Pĕliatan recommended this measure in a case of twins there, but his advice was not followed, and I have never happened to find a case where the stopping of three Galungan festivals did occur.

Rarely one finds the time of banishment for the family of twins extended to three months. In the old village of Trunyan, for instance, twins of unlike sex are placed at the *trugtug*, where the dead are not buried but only exposed, for three months (*sasih*), whereas twins of like sex are only banished to a hut in the fields outside the village limits, for forty-two days. J. de Vroom apparently was told that *manak salah* entails banishment to the graveyard for three months of thirty-five days.[32] And the *sĕngguhu* Rĕsi Nabé from Pĕjatèn (near Tabanan), who is a most famous priest and teacher of *sĕngguhu*, and whose pupils practice all over South, North, and West Bali, also said *bunching* twins were to be banished for three *sasih* months of thirty-five days. We found in the following fragment of a *lontar* from Bulèlèng, Sīma déça Bulèlèng, the time stated as three *tilĕm*, or dark moons, which is, of course, not the same thing as three *sasih*.

If a full member of the society of the *balé agung*, or a person living in the *désă* Bulèlèng, begets *anak salah* even though they are Brahmană, Wésyă, Ksatryă, or "people of the fields," it makes the country dirty, the entire village. They must be banished [temporarily] by the villagers and placed at the *talugtug* [junction of three roads] of the graveyard, and the house of the "wrong ones" must be brought there, for three dark moons. As soon as three dark moons have passed, the wrong ones must purify the village as above, *anapuhin prayangané tiga sakti* [purify the *pură balé agung*, *pură dalĕm*, *pură pusĕh*]; and they must *mĕkiis* and give a feast to the villagers, including a performance of the *gamelan* gong. Before the country, the entire village, has been purified, and the offerings made to the gods *kĕtiga sakti* [of the three temples], they may not worship the gods. The offerings are dedicated by the *sĕngguhu*. If this is done, all is well with the country; if it is not done, the gods may not be worshiped, the ceremony *angrasakin* [for the agricultural gods] is forbidden, making the rice-goddess Nini in the fields is forbidden, that is, called the country impure (*sampĕt*), all the ceremonies must not be. If this ruling is disobeyed, the fine is 22,500 [*kèpèng*].

It may be noted that the Bhagawan Gargă *lontar* specified *ngĕlungah* at dark moon. If this took place on the dark moon following the forty-two days of exile, it might very well fall on the third dark moon after the birth. The following *lontar* from Tabanan also places *ngĕlungah* at dark moon. It has much to say about the names and varieties of twin births:

If twins are born with one *ari-ari* [placenta], it is called *tunggal* [one, single]; if they are male and female, and the female has no *ari-ari*, the name is *tunggal* [male]. If the male has no *ari-ari*, the name is *tunggal* [female]. If there is only one *ari-ari*, it is not necessary to banish the people, for it does not make impure. But they should have a ceremony. . . . [Here the offerings are enumerated, specifying what the father of the twins must give, and that the villagers must help to contribute what the father cannot supply.] He should have the ceremony, because it is called *kĕnchĕlan ing déwă* [a dirtying of the gods]. This is the way of the ceremony.

---

[32] J. de Vroom, "Aanteekening uit eene Balische Adversaria." *Tijdschrift voor Indische Taal-, Land-, en Volkenkunde*, XVIII.

And if both have an *ari-ari*, but one is born *mahĕlatan* [later, separated by a space of time from the first child], it is also called *tunggal*, everything thereafter is *tunggal*, the offerings *tunggal*. . . . The people should bathe in *yèh suddhămală*, *yèh mangĕning* [water from sacred springs].

The rules for *manak salah* follow, giving the offerings required for. the purification (*sasakapan*) at (1) the *kubu*, the hut of the banished family, (2) the *kĕmulan*, the household shrine at their original house, (3) the *pĕmpatan*, the crossroads, (4) the *pĕkĕn*, the market place, (5) the *blulangan yèh*, an island or piece of land with water running on either side of it, (6) the *balé agung* temple, and (7) the *balé pĕgat*, the building where the birth of the children took place. The cere- monies are performed by a *pĕdandă* (*Brāhmană*) and a *sĕngguhu* (*yajamānă*), in order to rid the country of the evil (*pāpă*). If these rules are not obeyed, disasters and epidemics increase.

And if triplets (*katijuru*) are born, they must be banished to the seashore. If there are two boys, famine and illness to the country. Other people [not the parents] should take them up and have the ceremony for them. They should be taken up and a ceremony performed at the *balé agung*.

If there are two girls and one boy, it is not necessary to banish them, for it is said to make the country fertile.

This is the way of the *désă* Kabă-Kabă.

This is the law: If there are two children born in one day, and the girl is born first and the boy after, it is called born *bunching*. Because the *bunching* birth is an affront to the *rajă*, the country is dirtied, they must be banished and placed at the big crossroads for forty-two days. The people of the village must put up *sawèn* [signs of pandanus] before every courtyard gate. When the time is up, the people who have made the village unclean must have the ceremonies *masakapan amanchă panggung*, *ngĕlungah* at dark moon, and after *ngĕlungah* the people of the village must *mĕkiis* to the sea at full moon.

The people who have made the village unclean must surrender all their utensils for the ceremony to the head of the village, money 10,100, rice 200 measures, and the other offerings for the gods (*widhi-widhănă*), and firewood, *arèn* leaves, coconut leaves, bananas, laths.

There follow instructions about the offerings. The father is to go begging for three days, asking contributions. But it does not say to beg in a number of other *balé agung*, as I found customary in many other places—in Taro, eleven *balé agung*, in Tĕgĕs Kawan (Pĕliatan) the same number, in Sanur seven, in Kutri (Singapadu) three, in Bongkasă, Ubud, and, according to the Bhagawan Gargă, ten. Then come directions for *mĕkiis* to the sea, and the statement that, after the village is entirely purified, Galungan may be celebrated for three times. This seems to be a denial of the rule found elsewhere that the Galungan festival is to be three times held up.

Next we have another sort of twins:

And if two children are born in one day, and the boy is born first and the girl afterward, it is called *salilyasih* [*silih asih*, exchange of love]. This does not dirty the country, it "washes" the queen, it blesses the country below and above.

And if anyone has twins (*manak salah*) which dirty the country, they must be banished by the villagers, and placed at the big crossroads for forty-two days. All the people of the village must put signs of pandanus before all the courtyard doors. When the time is up, they must have *matatĕbasan* at dark moon, *amanchă panggung* called *manglungah*, offerings and full honor to the gods as before, let none be lacking.

Then are given the offerings for *pracharu* for *manak salah*, to be set out at the *balé agung*, the crossroads, the market place, the spring or bathing place, the *balé* where the birth took place, and the household shrine. Once more the instructions for *atatĕbasan* at the *pură désă*, then *mĕkiis* to the sea at full moon. It is specified that the village must make the *charu* according to custom, building the *sanggah tutuan*, and all the villagers must be purified with the *lis*, and give honor to all the gods.

An explanatory sentence, referring to a section above, says that a birth is called *hĕlatĕn* when one, two, or three *da'uh* (period of an hour and a half) intervene between the appearance of the two children, even though both come in the same night. This was called *hĕlatĕn* in olden times.

Lastly, the births called *bunching* and *silih asih* are of Triwangsă people (high caste, Brahmană, Ksatryă, or Wésyă), and according to the prince in the palace at Tabanan, all those who are not of high caste are *salah*.

That is the end of this unusually full *lontar* regarding twins. A case of twins born to Chinese people living in Bulèlèng occasioned discussion of the various customs in the Balinese magazine *Bhāwanāgara*.[33] One author recommends the *adat* from Kabă-Kabă, Tabanan, as a good one to be followed, and quotes from a *lontar* originating there. The quotations are in modern Balinese but must be taken either from the same *lontar* which I have summarized, or from a transcription of it, for it agrees on all points with the other text. Although not so full in directions for the ceremonies, the various differences in the births, with their special names, correspond—for one placenta, for a difference in time between the births, for the birth of the boy first, or the girl, for triplets of which two are boys, and triplets of which two are girls, and the same distinction between

---

[33] "Pertanja'an tentang adat," *Bhāwanāgara*, III, No. 8 (1934), 126, and "Indik Manak Salah," *ibid.*, p. 127.

ordinary people and those of high-caste birth. The *lontar* is very generous in the exemptions from *manak salah* which it allows. Firstly, all high-caste people seem to be exempt, not only the king and the high priests as we found before. Then any birth which can be called "single," either because there is only one placenta, or because the children are born with an intervening time period, does not seem to require banishment. And of boy and girl twins, if the boy is born first, it is a good sign—although the last paragraph suggests that this does not hold good for Sudră.

A Brahmană scholar of Sanur made the following report after consulting the *lontar* of his *pĕdandă*:

If, in Bali, Sudră people have twins *manak salah*, it is called *bunching* when the girl is first and the boy comes after. This is said to threaten the safety of the country, and so the children and the mother and father must be moved to a hut at the crossroads or on the seashore, until the children are forty-two days old, in Balinese called *nyĕpi* [this term is usually applied to the yearly purification of the village, after a *mĕcharu*, when the people retire to their houses and leave the streets "lonely," so that the bad spirits will depart]. And the villagers of a single *balé agung* put up signs of pandanus before the middle of the door of each courtyard, and it is called *sĕbĕl* [unclean] within that village.

Before the arrival of a favorable day (*déwasă*) for *nyĕpi* the father of he twins must beg alms of the people of seven different *balé agung*, asking contributions for the ceremony to purify the country, and the people of a single *balé agung* (his own) must help him. The father must provide money to the amount of 10,100 *kĕpĕng*, rice, coconuts, eggs, and so on.

As soon as the children are forty-two days old, the people of the single *balé agung* must make the offerings *charu* and *mĕkiis* to the sea. The names of the offerings and the *charu* depend upon the estimate of the *pĕdandă* and the desire of the villagers, for example, *manchă walikramă, malik sumpah, manchă sanak*. The *charu* is celebrated by a *pĕdandă* Siwă and a *pĕdandă* Bodă, assisted by a *sĕngguhu*.

As soon as the offerings are completed, the children are purified (*kĕjayă*) at the *balé agung*, at the temples, at the market place, the river, and the sea, and only after this may the children be taken home to their house.

Likewise if people have twins *manak salah*, but the birth happens differently, so that the boy is born first and the girl afterward, that is called *silih asih*. In this case, according to the explanation of the *lontar*, no uncleanness results, but an obscure statement suggests that it brings evils and misfortune just as *bunching* described above.

The explanation of the *lontar* further states that when people have a boy and a girl born at the same time, but with only one placenta, one of the children is "wrong," *salah*, and it is not called *bunching* nor *silih asih*. Thus:

1. If the girl brings the placenta and the boy does not, that is called *kĕmbar tunggal* [twins single], which means that it is as if both were girls.

2. If the boy brings the placenta and the girl does not, that also is called *kĕmbar tunggal*, as if both were boys.

Neither of these sorts of twins threatens the country. But the *lontar* says it is just as well to have the ceremony or the *charu*.

And if anyone has three children born at once, of which two are boys and one a girl, that is called *katiruju* [*kati-juru* in the Tabanan *lontar*] and is extremely dangerous to the country, and these children must be set down on the seashore. According to custom two of the children are cast away and then picked up by another person, not their mother. In this case there must be the ceremony *mědudus* at the *balé agung*.

And if anyone brings forth one boy and two girls, they do not become *sěběl* and their house is not moved, because in this case, it is said, the country begins to be prosperous and healthy, and diseases will not spread.

This set of rules makes apparent gradations in the wrongness of *manak salah*, so that the only really evil birth seems to be when to low-caste people a girl is born before a boy and there are two placentas —except of course in the case of the very rare unlucky triplets. And the matter of the placentas is not based on physiological fact, for if the two adhere they are considered as one. The obscurities in the texts allow room for interpretation in favor of those concerned. In a case of boy and girl twins born to Jabă people in Sanur last year, the family was not banished, no *měcharu* was held, and the villagers did not consider themselves *sěběl* but continued to go to the temples only because the boy had been born first. The *pědandă* of Intaran and the Brahmană *balian*, who normally should have officiated, did not approve of their omitting the ceremonies and said that at the latest the people must have a *měcharu* during the ninth month (four months after the birth).

A report has been made in the magazine *Bhāwanāgara* covering the ancient *adat* of two Bali-agă villages in the district of Bangli, Bu'ungan[34] and Lumbuan.[35] The ancestors of the inhabitants of these villages lived in the district of Karang Asěm, but in a time of war with Bulèlèng the people moved *en masse* to the present sites in the Bangli district, bringing with them their *lontar*, sacred objects, and the rules for their whole complex social organization. In Bu'ungan the rules for twins are reported as follows:

If anyone bears twins which are two males or two females (*anak kěmbar*), as soon as these children are aged one month and seven days and as soon as the ceremony *tutug kambuhan* has taken place, at once must be the ceremony *měsakap* (*matělah-tělah désă*) at the crossroads, performed by the *balian konèng* (trance-doctor). The offerings are the same as enumerated for marriage which wrongs the *adat*.

[34] Idă Bagus Adiptă, "Menjelidiki adat-adat koena didésa-desa dalem bilangan negara Bangli," *Bhāwanāgara*, III, No. 4–5 (1933).

[35] *Ibid., Bhāwanāgara*, II, No. 8–9 (1933).

After three days the *kramă dĕsă* [group of villagers] must *mĕlis*, and the twins with the mother and father receive holy water (*mĕlukat*) to be freed from their uncleanness (*sĕbĕl*).

The expenses of this and also of the *pĕmĕndak Batară* [the reception of the gods] on their return from *mĕlis* are all to the account of those who have the twins.

Before we consider the rules for *manak salah*, it will be well to note what is said about wrong marriages in Bu'ungan, where the *mĕsakap*, *mĕlis*, and *pĕmĕndak Batară* correspond with those for twins of like sex. It is in such connection that one wonders if the whole twin superstition does not rest, not on the idea of incest itself, but on the same basis as that for incest taboos—the concept of the way of animals in contradistinction to the way of men. For if it is the way of animals to mate with their near relatives, it is also their way to have more than one child at a time. Twins of like sex are already bad because they are born like beasts, and twins of unlike sex are worse because of the incestuous connotation, the improper intimacy of brother and sister in the womb. The Bu'ungan report definitely states the thought connection of animals with incest:

As regards all marriages which are thought to bring famine to the village and to make dirty the temples, according to the *adat* of Bu'ungan the behavior of the people who commit this wrong is thought to be just as the behavior of animals.

For example, when it happens that someone marries the mother of his cousin (*rĕramă di misan*), or the mother of his second cousin (*rĕramă di mindon*), on the male or on the female side, they must have the ceremony *mĕsakap* at the crossroads of the village with the following offerings:

a. *Panchă-limă*
   bèbèk bĕlang kalung [duck]
   in the center, *nasi wong-wongan tumpĕng 10*
   one small *sorohan*
   offered to the earth (*ibu pĕrtiwi*).
b. Pig, chopped
   sorohan agung [large]
   other offerings which go with it, making a high altar (*panggungan*) as a place
      for these offerings to the Sun god, *Suryă*

As soon as the *balian konèng* has dedicated (*ngantĕb*) these offerings facing east as he should, at this time the man and the woman who have committed the wrong together crawl on all fours, their necks hung with the bar of bamboo in the manner of animals [pigs], the man from the south and the woman from the north approaching a *palungan* [drinking trough] made from a dap-dap tree, which has been filled with the water in which rice was washed [pig food], the two, man and woman together drink the rice-water in the drinking trough.

The report states that before this incest rite the man and the woman must remain for a month and seven days outside the village, to the north (whereas for *manak salah* the time of banishment is the same, but the place to the south of the village). Three days after the *měsakap* the whole group *gěbog satak* of two hundred villagers must *mělis* to a meeting of rivers, carrying with them not only the gods but all the possessions of the temple including the *gamelan*. All are purified with holy water from a *bujanggǎ*.

On the return from *mělis*, the reception of the gods is celebrated with offerings of a pig and *sorohan agung* and performance of the *baris* dance. A feast is given to the *kramǎ désǎ* by the family of the incestuous pair. After this the two are banished from the village for a year, not allowed even to enter the precincts of the *gěbog satak*. The penalty if they disobey is the offering of a pig to the temple *purǎ balé agung* and of a goat to the temple *purǎ dalěm pingit*. When the year is up, they may return to the village and must go through the usual marriage ceremonies. In case the family concerned is not able to pay all these expenses the village takes them over, seizing or putting in pawn all their lands until the amount is repaid.

For most serious incest, as of a man with his brother's mother, his own mother, or his sister, the ceremony *měsakap* is the same, but there must also be the ceremonies *ngělungah* and *měsadi* as for *manak salah*. The people are banished from the village for life, and the lands of the family may be seized on the male or on the female side.

We now come to the rules for *manak salah*:

If anyone bears *anak bunching*, male-female, it is called *manak salah*. The people of the village quarter (*kramǎ banjar*) must move these people (the mother and the father and the two *anak salah*) to the outskirts of the village, on the south side, near the graveyard, with the entire house where the children were born, which must be taken apart and put up again outside the village. The people of the *banjar* take their turns helping, but in the matter of food the "wrong ones" must make their own provision. The "wrong ones" stay there one month and seven days.

When twelve days have elapsed after the birth of the children, the ceremony *ngělungah* [small *mětělah-tělah*] takes place inside the house-court where the children were born. Offerings *panchǎ limǎ*, celebrated by *balian konèng*, holy water from the *bujanggǎ*.

As soon as one month and seven days are up, the ceremony *měsadi* [big *mětělah-tělah*] takes place before the temple *purǎ pěnetaran* in the village of the people with the twins. The ceremony requires one small male pig and one female calf whose nose has not yet been punctured for the rope, skinned and spread out on the ground, together with offerings *sorohan agung* and *bayang-bayang*, all to be set out on the ground facing south, to be offered up to the gods of the sea and of the earth (*pěrtiwi*). And one white goose, skinned and spread out with offerings *sorohan agung* are placed in the *sanggar tawang* [bamboo altar] for Batarǎ Suryǎ [Sun god]. One female black goat, a duck *bělang kalung*, chickens of five colors (*manchǎ warnǎ*) are placed according to the five colors, white to the east, red to the south, yellow to the west, black to the north, and many-colored in the center, together with *sorohan panchă* to be offered to these gods: Iswară, Brahmă, Mahadéwă, Wisnu, and Siwă. After this to the *bută-bută* [the demons]. Then one full-grown black pig skinned and spread out with *sorohan agung*, *běbangkit*, *suchi*, and all the various offerings which must accompany it are placed in the *panggungan* to be offered to Batară [the god of the temple]. . . . During this time Batară Sakti Bujanggă is invited to descend, to be present before the temple where the holy water is asked for. The *balian konèng* performs the ceremony called *ngantěb* [to deliver the essence of] these offerings.

As soon as the *ngantěb* is over the people with twins receive holy water, and their house is also burned on the spot. Then they may return to the village, for their uncleanness (*sěběl*) is erased.

Three days after this, the *kramă désă* [group of villagers] must *mělis*, following all the gods to be purified. The entire *kramă gěbog satak* (200) go to *mělis*. The reception of the gods on their return and the putting them away is the same as was described above for marriages against the *adat*.

As regards the expenses of all the ceremonies, it is said that they are evenly divided, half to fall on the *kramă désă* and half on the people with twins.

So much for Bu'ungan. In Lumbuan, the other old village whose *adat* is covered in the *Bhāwanāgara* report, if *anak kěmbar*, twins of like sex, are born, the ceremony *mětělah-tělah* is the same as that required in cases of *salah pati*, when a man hangs himself. Although for the suicide the house must be taken down and burned at the graveyard, this does not seem to be necessary for the twins of like sex. The ceremony takes place before the house where the disaster occurred, one month and seven days after the event, and includes building the *panggungan* in which *sorohan agung* and a pig are offered, and before this on the ground the chickens of five colors, the duck *bělang kalung* (white collared), a dog *bělang bungkěm* (red and black with a white mouth) and a goat, set out in the five directions. Here it is called *měcharu*, for the *kală bută* (demons). The *pěmangku* officiates, prayers are made to the gods of the temple *pură pusěh balé agung*, and the *pěmangku* asks for holy water with which to purify the house-court of the disaster and the whole village.

When *anak bunching*, boy and girl twins, are born, it is called *manak salah* for people of *jabă* caste. The members of the *banjar* (village quarter) beat the *kul-kul*, assemble, and remove the parents with the twins and their house to the outskirts of the village, where they must remain a month and seven days. The members of the *banjar* take turns watching over them. But for their food the family with the twins must be themselves responsible.

After one month and seven days, the ceremony for the purification of the village is held, called *měsadi*, with offerings for *měcharu* including a goat, a goose, a duck, a calf, and a dog. They are set out as before, the *pĕmangku* officiates, but the holy water is got from the *bujanggă*. There are prayers to the gods of the temple *pură pusĕh balé agung*, and holy water is asked before the temple *pura pĕnataran*. Here also the people with the twins are purified (*mĕtĕlah-tĕlah*).

After twelve days all the gods of all the temples are carried out to be purified, as far as the boundary of the village to the north and the boundary of the village to the south. This is called *ngĕlungah*.

The expenses of the *mĕsadi* are taken over by the village if the parents of the twins are too poor, but later they must repay the village.

It will be noted that the offerings for *manak salah* in such an old village as Lumbuan are extensive, including, as regards the animal offerings, a goat, goose, duck, calf, dog, pig, and five chickens. Many of these are to be of special "colors" and are often difficult to find. Still stricter are the villages of Sukawană, Trunyan, and Taro, where a *kĕbo* (water buffalo) must also be used. But in most of the villages of South Bali the five chickens, duck, pig, and dog are considered sufficient for the *mĕcharu*. There is in existence, however, a *lontar* which surpasses all bounds in this respect, giving instructions for the use of a tiger and a rhinoceros in the consummate *mĕcharu*! This curious document is in the possession of a *sĕngguhu* in the village of Tonjă, near Dèn Pasar. Much of it seemed obscure to the owner himself. I shall try to quote from it.

The *lontar* called Indik Manak Salah, says: "If each has a placenta this affronts the [*rajă*] Idă Dalĕm, it is necessary to purify (*mĕrestistă*) the country. Such is the purification ceremony (*pĕngĕlungahan*) for *manak salah* born in the village, by order of the kings of Bali." At great length the offerings are enumerated, the various sorts of coconuts, the array of clothes, for both men and women, the offerings of elaborate composition containing rice, fruit, flowers, thread, money, spices, and palm-leaf decorations, each of which is known by its individual name, and the number of *kèpèng* which must appear among each set, and which the *bujanggă* takes for himself after the ceremony. Some of these are to be dedicated at the *balé agung*, some at the house, some at the *mĕlis* or *mĕkiis* to the sea. Among the offerings at the house are a plough and the instrument with which the earth of fields is smoothed over. In connection with this the *sĕngguhu* told me, although it is not written in the text, that the custom was in the case of *manak salah* for the inside of the courtyard where the unlucky birth took place to be ploughed up and then smoothed over, using a *yos brană* and an *anggrèk ulan*—a black water buffalo born from a white mother and a white one born from a black mother! He said that in case these animals were not to be found, the parents of the twins must themselves be hitched to the plough. The use of the two rare buffalo for the occasion of a big *mĕcharu* was verified by the *sĕngguhu nabé*, the teacher, of Pĕjatèn, but he had not heard of hitching up the parents, only saying their legs were to be tied up lightly with three-colored thread. The three-colored thread is mentioned in this *lontar*.

Other offerings at the *mĕlis* are a roast pig, a duck, and five chickens, a new fan such as is used in the kitchen, a new clay cooking pot. At the house must be also a roast pig, duck, five chickens, and four new pots, and at the *balé agung* a roast pig, two ducks, five chickens, the throne to the Sun god. It is repeated many times that the *bujanggă* gets 1700 *kèpèng* at the *ngĕlungah*, at the return to the house from the *mĕlis*, etc., but the order of the writing is so confused that it is hard to tell how often this fee is to be paid. He gets also many of the offerings, and after officiating at the *désă* temple, on return from *mĕlis*, he gets 3200 *kèpèng* and an entire set of clothes. At this time, among other things, fifteen ducks, twenty-five chickens, a pig, and five ducklings are offered. And the water used for purification is of eleven kinds, including that from the sea, from the lake, and from the various sorts of springs.

The *lontar* then states that the people with twins (*manak salah bunching kĕmbar*) must be banished by the villagers for forty-two days and must pay for the offerings *amanchă-sangă panggung*, one *panggung*, or altar-ful, to be placed on land surrounded by water, on the edge of the village, beside the bridge, at the crossroads, at the *balé* where the birth took place, at the *balé agung*, at a meeting of three roads, and at the house. When the gods are carried to the sea there are more offerings on the seashore and on the return to the *désă* temple.

Do not be short of the way of this writing [it says] lest twins be born again. According to the birth of the people, the way of the ceremony must be: high for the high, middle for the middle, low for the low.

If there is *mĕcharu* at the *balé agung* of the whole country, at each *banjar* must be a small *pĕngĕlungahan*, outside the house small offerings . . . at the household shrine . . . at the *balé agung* must be the great *mĕcharu ékadasă ludră* with buffalo, cow, tiger, rhinoceros, the contents of the forest, the contents of the sea, the contents of the rice fields, a complete set, with metal and gold and gilded cloth. . . . If the ceremony is *mĕpanchă walikramă*, five, if *mĕwrĕspati kalpă* three times the animals [are reduplicated], if *yamă rĕsigană saptă* five, if *mepanchă kĕlud* once, for each, the low, middle, and high, a dog of three colors. The descendant of the *bujanggă* officiates.

These are the names for the various forms or levels of the *mĕcharu*, *ĕkadasă ludră* the highest, *mepanchă kĕlud* the lowest. The sense of this passage seems to be that the highest born people should have the most elaborate *mĕcharu*, which includes the buffalo, cow, tiger, rhinoceros, etc. Lower people would be content with less, and their offerings would be acceptable because of their inability to provide more. One can interpret the *ĕkadasă ludră*, which carries the meaning of "ten times," even to reduplication of the tiger, buffalo, etc., ten times. But more probably the reduplication refers only to lower animals, such as chickens and ducks. There are many names for *mĕcharu*, and their requirements vary according to the "authority." For instance, the *sĕngguhu* priest called Juru Rĕsi in Lod-tunduh (district Ubud) has a *lontar* in which *ĕkadasă ludră* calls for twenty-six buffalo and is to be celebrated at Bĕsakih. Nothing is said about tigers and rhinoceroses. According to his text the *charu* are:

> *panchă sanak*, the lowest
> *panchă kĕlud*, with goat and goose
> *balik sumpah*, with cow and pig
> *taur gĕntuh*, with one buffalo
> *sapuh sapuh*, with three buffalo
> *panchă walikramă*, with five buffalo
> *ĕkadasă ludră*, with twenty-six buffalo
> *mĕnyĕgjĕg bumi*, with forty-six buffalo

this last only celebrated at the time the country was "made to stand." Both this *sĕngguhu* and the one from Tonjă admitted that their rules were obsolete, "for tigers are now too hard to find." The rhinoceros, they said, must have come from Java (which means to the Balinese any country outside of Bali), for it has never been known in Bali.

After the naming of the various sorts of *charu* the Tonjă *lontar* straightaway gives a *mantră* or prayer to the *kală bută*, the demons. This, with the *mantră* to Siwă which comes at the end, the *sĕngguhu* was unwilling to read out, whether from ignorance of the old language or from fear of the consequences should the magic words be sounded under inappropriate circumstances, I was unable to discover. The *lontar* is considered very sacred, and offerings had to be made before it could be "opened." After the prayer to the demons, the *lontar* continues:

This is the law for wrong birth, *bunching kĕmbar* female-male, they must be banished by the villagers to the big crossroads for forty-two days, they must pay for the set of offerings. The offerings are given at the *balé agung* to purify the country, offered to all the gods. The gods are placed on the *balé panjang* [the *balé agung*, here denoting the long platform, to distinguish it from the temple which is called after it *pură balé agung*]. All the *pĕmangku* are called. All the people must make offerings to all the gods in the temples *désă* [=*balé agung*], *dalĕm*, *pusĕh*, *pĕnataran*, *mĕlanting ring pasar* [the market]. When the gods come out, an uncastrated pig must be sacrificed before the big inner gate of the temple.

This is the story if anyone has twins born *bunching kĕmbar*, exactly as these letters have given it. If anyone does not follow it, he will have twins *bunching* again. Beware lest he have them three times.

A *mantră* to Siwă ends the *lontar*.

The Balinese, as a people in great part illiterate, have an exaggerated respect for the written word. They take the *lontar* most seriously, considering the prescriptions voiced in them to be as law—a law sometimes obsolete, obscure, unexplainable, but still holding in its content the right way. This in spite of the many disparities which, as we have found, exist between one text and another, and the illogical, confused order, even contradictions, appearing within a single text. It is to be said, however, that there is no reason why the texts originating in different districts should coincide, for these were in the old days under the rule of different princes. As the years went by each royal family developed its laws independently, and, as we have seen, the people considered the laws for *manak salah* to come from the king. And the custom within individual villages would tend to take on its own character, for there was and still is little connection between the doings of one village and the next. The position of the *sĕngguhu* is curious, for, as these priests are rare, they generally have to be called from a distant village to officiate in the village where they are needed. Then, although they may have their own rules to be followed, they merely play their role according to the custom of the village which has engaged them. In Taro, where twins were born three times within two years, because the disaster occurred in three different families, each of these chose to call in a different *sĕngguhu* priest. But the way of the ceremony remained the same, following the laws of Taro. So that in the case of the *lontar* of the *sĕngguhu* in Tonjă, it is possible that it would never be referred to except when *manak salah* happened in that very village.

It is clear, I think, from this review of the events and of the differing opinions of the priestly authorities consulted in cases of multiple births in Bali that such multiple births are charged with emotion in the Balinese scene. This is true whether they occur in families punishable according to village law or in families whose higher caste entitled them to view the event with favor.

It is a matter of concern not only to the individual parents but to the community as a whole.

Five Great Elementals
Panchă Mahă Bută

KATHARANE EDSON MERSHON

THE OUTLINE of the Five Great Elementals was given by a Brahmană priest (Sivaite), Idă Pĕdandă Madé Sidĕmĕn of Intaran, South Bali. He explained that one could not understand the complexity displayed in Balinese rituals without knowing how the gods descended into the world and what role the elementals played in their relationship to mankind.

There are delicate tokens of worship, *bantèn*, for the deities, *dèwă*, which are placed in shrines raised some considerable height above ground level, befitting emissaries from heaven. There is another set of offerings termed *charu*, which are used to honor and placate elementals, the *bută*. These are invariably placed upon the ground, hence spoken of as "ground offerings."

Charu offerings may range from a simple coconut shell filled with pungent incense placed at the entrance to a compound, *lĕbuh*, to elaborate assortments of various shapes and sizes in trays, containers, and *isinyă*, "fillings." In these fillings lies the significance of the offering. At the "Coming-of-Age" ceremony one sees the extra-ordinary adherence to these *bută*, for the first blood of the menstrual period issues in a manner similar to the blood discharge of birth. The blood *bută* is thus in control.

Technical books, *lontar*, give lengthy descriptions of the relation-ship of the gods to mankind, beginning with information concerning the Absolute, Sanghyang Sunyă Sĕpi. (Sanghyang is a deific title, while Sunyă is derived from the Sanskrit word *Shunya*, the Void, the Emptiness, the Absolute in Unmanifest State. *Sĕpi* is a duplicating

Manuscript published for the first time with permission of the author.

word in Balinese for Sunyă.) The "form," "color," and "seat" of each deity is described and the appropriate offering to be associated with him is explained in the *lontar*.

Wisnu (Skr. Vishnu) is described as having a circle form, being dark blue or black in color, and seated north. Each deity occupies a cardinal point: Brahmă, south; Iswară, east; and Mahadèwă, west. Brahmă resides in the kitchen, being Lord of Fire whose color is red. (Balinese kitchens are generally located to the south in a compound.) Iswară occupies the house shrine, and his color is white. Mahadèwă takes the rice barn for his abode as he represents the earth and its produce, rice. The barn is established to the west, and the color for this deity is yellow.

Bută follow a similar pattern, for they are described as coming down from heaven with mankind and as taking places of residence, both in temples and, more intimately, in the body of man. The *bută* are thus honored with elaborate and often intricate tokens of worship, *bantèn*, also given as *labanyă*. Just as the *dèwă* are providers and protectors of mankind, so the *bută* are equally at home in man's body and function as powerful protectors if man will only give them thoughtful concern and attention, evidenced by *charu* offerings.

Balinese have immense belief in becoming "magically endowed," *sakti pisan*, and it is to the *bută* that one must look and seek their favor. This is especially necessary because the *bută* have taken possession of certain parts and functions of man's body and therefore are in a position not only to shower their "brother" with magical energy but also to withhold aid.

Pĕdandă Madé Sidĕmĕn not only translated the *Panchă Mahă Bută lontar* but clarified passages which seemed obscure. When engaged in a culture so foreign to one's own, it is necessary to have an attentive guide. Such was Pĕdandă Madé.

Dr. C. Hooykaas concerned himself with clarification of Sanskrit words and their relationship to the Balinese text. He was kind enough to aid in the translation of some of the difficult passages of the concluding chant, *mantră*, at the end of the *Panchă Mahă Bută* outline. For his minute care and scrutiny of my text and his gracious suggestions to augment my knowledge I am particularly grateful.

Pĕdandă Madé Sidĕmĕn spoke as follows:

"Three gods and mankind came down from Heaven. These gods took as their dwelling-places three kinds of temples, *purǎ*.

"The first temple was a *purǎ dalĕm*, which they situated outside of a village in the fields. The god, *dèwă*, who took this temple as his abode was Sanghyang Sunyă Mertă [Sunyă, the Void, the Infinite, coupled with *mertă*, elixir of immortality (Skr. *amerta*)].

"These temples, *pură*, are also represented in the body of mankind. Sanghyang Sunyă Mertă took for his holy spots the mouth and the throat as well as the crown of the head—the 'door of Siwă'—Siwă *duară*.

"One must obtain help from these gods to be magically endowed, *sakti*, seated as they are in their respective shrines in the body. Sanghyang Sunyă Mertă is the ruler of the *pură dalĕm*; he changed his name when he manifested in human form to Aya Mas Rangdă, who is feminine in aspect. [Ayu, sex appelation; Mas, honorific title meaning "gold"; *rangdă*, a widow. This explains why the dance drama in which the *rangdă* appears is almost invariably held in the forecourt of a *pură dalĕm* or in the roadway in front of one.]

"The second temple chosen for habitation by one of the three deities was the village temple, *pură désă*. It is ruled by Sanghyang Yogi Suară [Yogi, one who meditates on union with the Divine; *suară*, sound].

"The center in the body corresponding to this temple, *pură désă*, is the forehead, the exact center between the eyebrows, *sĕlaning lĕlata*. The deity governing this center is Sanghyang Sĕmară Bawă, from whom one must obtain sanction to become *sakti*. Sĕmară Bawă chose his place in the body as the lower abdomen, ovaries in women, and glands of procreation in men, as there are only three deities to control all bodily functions. [This Sĕmară appears dramatically in the ritual for "Coming-of-Age."]

"The third temple is the *pură pusĕh*, navel temple or temple of origin. It is ruled by Sanghyang Nilă Sĕrayă. He rules the top of the head, a spot that will open with due meditation. It is called *usaran*."

[These three temples are honored throughout Bali. *Pură dalĕm*, situated in the fields near a graveyard, though not in one, is referred to as the "Home of Siwă," Creator of the Universe as well as Destroyer. Here the Absolute is personalized by Siwă, whereas in other references it is termed the Infinite Void, Sunyă Sĕpi. These three temples with their corresponding body centers control the magical energy, *sakti*, which flows through mankind.]

"The five great elementals, *panchă mahă bută*, have equal power over bodily functions and are represented by actual temples, just as the first three gods who came down with mankind took abode in *pură* and in man's body.

First Bută

"Yèh Nyom is white in color and called *bută putih*. Each *bută* has an 'essence,' *rasă*. The white *bută*-essence is termed *angga pati* (*sang séds rasă*).

"Yèh Nyom is the amniotic fluid of birth and as such is called one of the Four Brothers of Birth, Kandă'mpat. Yèh Nyom not only manifests as water of birth, but 'he leaves the body as perspiration, which is good, freeing it of filth.'

"The temple controlled by this *bută* is located at Jembaran and is known as Ratu Ngulun Swé, whose god is Ratu Ngurah Tankĕb Langit [Ratu, title of high-caste persons; Ngurah, name for first-born; *tangkĕb langit*, to catch the sky].

"This *bută putih*, water, rules every kind of shrine, or *sanggah*, small wayside niches to hold offerings, such as a *tugu* or *bĕdugal*.

"He has power to 'hear for men,' as he is sensation, for, besides being the amniotic fluid, he is represented by the skin of the body, the 'clothing for hearing,' as he knows everything through the skin. As the deity controlling the skin, his name is Sĕgară Tăn Pĕtĕpi [Sea without Limit]. He rules also the semen in men and the ovaries in women.

"He is known as *pĕluh*, perspiration, when leaving the body.

"Ratu Ngurah Tangkĕb Langit, 'to catch and hold the sky,' is also the god for all animals.

"His sound in a *mantră* (chant) is *sang*.

"The sign of his presence is when the sky is clear of all clouds, or, if at night one should see a drum tower, *kul-kul*, standing in the middle of the road, then he would be there."

Offerings for him, *labanyă*, are: (*a*) pickled eggs, *taluh kasĕm*; (*b*) one handful of rice, *channang păsuchian*; (*c*) meat-filling for an offering, *ikan*; (*d*) black rice, onion, ginger (*jai*), salt mixed with charcoal, *tasik arĕng*.

Second Bută

"The second great elemental is blood, *gĕtih*, called *bută abang*.

"His essence, *rasă*, is red in color and is termed *mĕrajă pati*.

"He is the second Brother of Birth, the blood.

"The temple holding his magical energy is at Kapal, the Pură Sédă.

"The god administering his power at Pură Sédă is Ratu Nyoman Tĕbă. [The gods bear names like the pattern of persons: first-born, Nguruh (sometimes Ngurah); second-born, Madé; third, Nyoman; and fourth, Kĕtut.]

"He is the god of mountains, forests, places of walking, *margă* [from Skr., path].

"He governs all journeying from place to place. He also guards the spot just outside the entrance to a home, *lĕbuh*.

"He is the flow of blood in the body, as well as an element in the semen, for 'there is a blood-making element in the seed else how could it germinate into a body of a child?' This blood element is called *kamĕn dalu*. This *gĕtih bută* is the strength in the blood, the red part. He guards through this red strength of his against sickness both at night and in daytime.

"His sound in the *mantră* is *bang*.

"The sign of his presence is generally fire, but he sometimes takes on the appearance of a mountain or forest, as they are symbols of his strength."

Offerings for him, *labanyă*, are: (*a*) rice cooked in little pillow-like baskets, *kĕtipat galĕng*; (*b*) eggs, *ulam taluh*; (*c*) one handful of rice (must be *red*), *channang păsuchian*; (*d*) one handful of red rice, onion, ginger; salt mixed with charcoal, *tasik arĕng*.

Third Bută

"*Banas pati* is the third *bută*, whose color is yellow. He is the covering, *bungkus*, for he is the flesh of the body as well as the natal cord of the child. He is the third of the Four Brothers of Birth, Kandă'mpat.

"His place is in any *pură pusĕh* (navel temple or temple of origin), owing to his being the natal cord.

"This guardian has two names for his powers or essences: I Ratu Mas Kuwindu and I Ratu Madé Jĕlawang.

"His manifestations include: 'inside a yard surrounded by walls' and 'inside a house surrounded by walls.' These walls refer to the bundling up, enclosing, *bungkus*.

"He is the *déwan karang*, house deity, in the sense of actual abode. He expresses himself also as *tĕgal abian*. [*Tĕgal* is ground that has *not* been planted, while *abian* refers to soil which has plants within it.] He represents thus 'the meat or flesh of the soil,' depicted by the plants. In man's body he is the flesh.

"His sound in the *mantră* is *tang*.

"His seat, *chakră*, is at the base of the spine, designated as *mĕrtă kundalini*. [*Kundalini* (Skr.) is depicted as a serpent coiled at the base of the spine, which rises level by level (*chakră*) until it reaches the crown of the head where it opens the "door of Siwă" and one becomes enlightened.]

"Hair on the body, such as hair in the nostrils, eyelashes, and pubic hair, belongs to him, as it guards the flesh.

"One sign of his presence is a strong wind; and, if one is walking and suddenly sees a wall across the road or a house standing in the middle of the road, these would be signs of his presence."

Offerings, *labanyă*, are: (*a*) little baskets woven in the form of a goose in which rice is steamed, producing a "goose form," *kĕtipat gangsă*; (*b*) different kinds of meat broiled on a skewer, *saté, saté gĕdé*; (*c*) one handful of yellow rice, *channang păsuchian*; (*d*) one handful of yellow rice, *sĕgă kĕpĕlan kuning*; (*e*) a handful of yellow rice, onion, ginger, and salt mixed with charcoal, and *iwak*.

Fourth Bută

"Banaspati Rajă is the name of the fourth *bută*. He is the real binding together of veins and arteries, for he is the placenta, *ari-ari*, 'younger brother or sister,' and as such is the strongest Brother of Birth.

"Banaspati Rajă is the black elemental, *bută irĕng*, for his color is black.

"His abode is in any *pură dalĕm*. His name, when in the temple, is I Ratu Nyoman Sakti Pĕngadĕgan.

"He is the lord of graveyards, streams (*tukad*), brooks (*pangkung*). He governs the little fairies of forest and stream, the *dété* and *tonyă*.

"He is the god of jinns, magicians, named Déwan Sămar."

[When anyone becomes entranced, as in a *barong* ceremony or at temple rituals when persons are "taken by the gods," it is he who has power over their bodies. His name Pĕngadĕgan is derived from the verb *adĕg*, to stand up. When trance subjects are "stood up by the gods," such a temple rite bears his name, *pĕngadĕgan*.

Through his name, he bears a triple relationship: Banaspati Rajă, lord of graveyards; Banaspati Rajă, the protector lion of the *barong*; and Banaspati Rajă, the placenta. These three aspects unite to guard one from birth, through life, and on into death where one is deposited in his care until the soul is freed by cremation.]

"As the deity governing males, Bătară Sĕmară, he has power over all entertainment, *unèn-unèn*. He enters [the *dalang*] spokesmen for shadow plays, and it is owing only to his power that they can be successful. He has control over every type of foretelling, *tĕnung*, and over persons who perform any of these arts, such as fingernail prophecy. [This type of reading is accomplished by placing a drop of magically potent oil upon the nail surface, where the observer endeavors to see "the answer in a mirror." A black frying pan may be used for a similar type of oil reading. Tossing coins, divination by holding objects, discovering the location of water (for wells), recovering lost objects, all of these fall under the jurisdiction of Banaspati Rajă.]

"His sound in a *mantră* is *ang*.

"He issues from the body in the form of urine.

"His power may be displayed by kindness and pity or through rage and violence.

"He makes all rain and power to stop it as well.

"He may create all manner of sickness, or he may cure every illness.

> "'Every sort of tree must sometime know the wind;
> Every sort of man must at some time know sickness;
> But, whether the sickness is great or little
> Depends upon the will of Banaspati Rajă.'

"He is able to make vendors sell their goods (*dagang laku*).

"He guards metal workers, whether they work in bronze, silver, or gold. He also guards the carvers who fashion statues.

"He has power to create all illusion, *mayă*, all apparitions, or spirit manifestations.

"He governs all appetites, whether for food, drink, clothes, intercourse with women, or just chewing *sirih* and tobacco.

"His presence is manifested by various signs: sometimes like a bird; or falling rain; even like a stream; or, in a graveyard, he may appear as a person. Sometimes he assumes the form of an old man wearing a black-and-white-checked *kain*; or he will manifest himself in the body of a flower."

Offerings for him, *labanyă*, are: (*a*) rice steamed in a small woven basket in the shape of a gong, *kětipat gong*; (*b*) fried egg, *taluh guling*; (*c*) a handful of black rice, *channang păsuchian*; (*d*) onion, ginger, salt mixed with charcoal, and *iwak*.

Fifth Bută

"This fifth *bută* is the smallest one of the five great elementals, Yèh Ninginging. He is the most delicate of fluids within the body (*yèh*). There are two aspects of his essence: *bută* of five colors, *bută panchă warnă*, and the *bută*-essence which rules all elementals, *bută kală děngěn*.

"He is also guardian of day and night.

"His abode is in any village temple, *pură désa*, where he exerts power. His name, when called within this temple, is I Ratu Kětut

Pĕtĕng. [I designating that he is male; Ratu, title for a high-caste person; Kĕtut, fourth-born; and *pĕtĕng*, night.]

"He is guardian for pregnant women and all small children.

"Within the body, he guards by the very fineness of his form, the delicacy of his element, which is practically like *prană*, the vital life of the body as displayed by the power to breathe.

"His seat in the body (*ragă*) is in the marrow of the bones, *jahjah di dalĕm tulang*.

"He is thus the fluid within the bones, *mertă pawitră*.

"His sound in the mantra is *ning* or *ying*.

"He manifests as 'feeling in the bones and sensations over all the body.'

"By his great refinement he is able to combat sickness and cure it, even though the sickness manifests as a great plague.

"Signs which indicate his presence are: the sight of a very large market; a group of small children (*anak raré*). He may also assume the form of a most beautiful woman.

"He is the deity for all insects."

Offerings for him, *labanyă*, are: (*a*) rice cooked in little baskets, *kĕtipat lĕpĕt*; (*b*) five little baskets of steamed rice, which grouped together form one offering (five different colors of rice must be used for he is the *bută* of five colors, *bută panchă warnă*), *kĕtipat nasi padă mekelan*; (*c*) eggs, *ulam taluh*; (*d*) five handfuls of rice of five different colors, *channang păsuchian sĕgă kĕpĕlan bĕrumbun*; (*e*) onion, ginger, salt mixed with charcoal, and *iwak*."

Mantră

What follows now is the chant, *mantră*, which one should employ if one desires help from these different deities.

"If you wish fervently to call him to you, speak in this manner: '*Iki pangarodană penghrahan ring dalĕm*' [to call the gods from their places of majesty and depths (*dalĕm*)]."

Here is the *mantră* [the following gives the names of the five deities to be called]: "Ih Ratu Tangkĕb Langit; Ratu Wayan Tĕbĕ; Ratu Madé Jĕlawang; Ratu Nyoman Sakti Pĕngadĕgan; Ratu Kĕtut Pĕtĕng."

Then comes the plea:

"Aji, siră laliasanak ring ingulun,
Apan ingulun tăn lali ring siră
Hon padă mĕtu siră maring Tunianing adnyané
Wĕhĕn tă anédă nugrahă, sakti sisip nguchap. Ong!"

[I express the hope that you, brothers, may assume a playful
   attitude toward me

For I am standing in a most playful attitude toward thee, in
   dead earnest,

All of you appear going toward the Voidness of Knowledge
   (Tunianing, from Sunyă)

Bestow, that I may be allowed to ask for favor, supernatural
   power (*sakti*) on me

——— (name), forgiveness, in case I make a mistake in
   speaking.]

The last lines that follow convey that the *mantră* should be spoken
with closed lips, secretly (*rahasiă*); that the name of the person on
whose behalf the *mantră* is recited should be mentioned silently, in
thought (*angan—Hanganset*)

   "Winuraiti rahasiă muke Hanganset sirě sarining Mertă
   Kěsumă, namă suakă, I ano [give the name of the person]."

Mertă Kěsumă we judge to mean holy water with flower petals in it.

This translation of the *mantră* is a free one and judges the intention
of the prayer as accurately as we are able.

Whatever is asked for in good faith may be granted, even if the
mantră is not known, provided the offerings listed are used in sufficient
quantity. If the *labanyă* tabulated are not available, and a *bantèn
pajegan* is substituted, it must be presented with manners showing
honor to a prince, *anak agung*. The wish will be granted. Offerings
listed here are those deemed most necessary if the *mantră* is not
pronounced. These *bantèn* are additions to the previously listed sets:
(*a*) pig meat, *ulam bawi*; (*b*) assorted purification offering, *suchi
assoroh*; (*c*) wearing apparel, in this case black-and-white checkered
cloth, *rantasan*; (*d*) all kinds of liquors: beer (*tuak*), alcohol (*arrack*),
wine (*běrěm*); *tětabuhan gěněp*.

   "If you wish to put into your body all of these five enchanted
relatives and seek holiness!

   "Măkaryă kramanyă yen mayun aděgan kasidian ragă:

[Calling the five great elementals and the three temples, *dalěm*,
pusěh, and *désă*. If one uses these methods he will be aware of these
five *bută* within his body (*ragă*).]

   "Ayot Idě: Sanghyang Panchă Mahă Bută muang ring dalěm,
pusěh, désă, sami sěrup a ring ragă."

There now follows a description as to what form of manifestation these *bută* will assume:

1. If the body has a sense of greatness and gives forth water profusely, it is Sanghyang Tangkĕb Langit who has taken possession. All sickness will vanish. This is the white *bută*, water.

2. If one has a sensation of intense heat, it means that *bută* Wayan Tĕbă has taken the body. Any sickness produced by evil beings, such as *gĕring*, will be lost. This is the red *bută*, blood.

3. If one has a feeling of goose flesh, with hair beginning to rise on the body, one is then in possession (*chirin*) of Ratu Madé Jĕlawang. This is the yellow *bută*, flesh.

4. If one has a sensation of trouble, it is Ratu Nyoman Sakti Pĕngadĕgan who gives this intuition. He cures all troubles, as well as sicknesses. He is the fourth *bută*, black in color, and is the placenta.

5. If during one's natural life one is just an ordinary sort of person, neither brilliant nor extremely dull, and if one on certain occasions suddenly talks brilliantly, fluently, entrancing one's listeners, then it is Ratu Kĕtut Pĕtĕng who has taken possession of one's body. If one has been extremely angry at someone but, when that person makes an appearance, one loses all sense of rage, that is also the influence of Ratu Kĕtut Pĕtĕng. He is the fifth *bută* who governs the life force in breath (*prană*).

"These are their works and paths—this do not forget!"

It can be seen by this outline of what great importance the *panchă mahă bută* play in their roles of Four Brothers. Offerings are made to them in every ritual dealing with Balinese life, from birth through death and on into that beyond where the deities then assume control.

As the colors and seats are given, one notices that pig meat is often used. Pig flesh, blood, entrails—all play an important role in ground offerings, *charu*. There must invariably be present in these offerings water, blood, flesh, combinations of these elements to represent the placenta, and strong liquor for the subtle body of breath (*prană*).

Lontar dealing only with lists of offerings for various rituals contain minute descriptions for these offerings, and animals may be involved from the tiniest chicken sacrificed during trance seances to enormous water buffalo (*kĕbo*) and, even for *rajă*, a rhinoceros. We are not elaborating upon these *bantèn*, merely presenting the ground work upon which offerings to *bută* depend. Even in the *mantră* quoted, the *bută* are addressed as Brothers and Relatives. Such is the intimate aspect which the elementals confer upon persons, behavior, and ritualistic procedure.

"Bandit Island"
A Short Exploration Trip
to Nusă Pěnidă

CLAIRE HOLT

FROM THE SOUTHEASTERN COAST of Bali one may sight on a clear day, almost within reach, the greenish-violet mass of another island. It has no sharp peaks of high mountains, no spectacular curves in its formation. Just an evenly rising mass with fairly steep slopes toward the sea. One is told that this is Nusă Pěnidă—and very little more.

It is natural that one should be curious about so close a neighbor of Bali. Looking up books, however, does not prove very helpful. Information about this island and its inhabitants seems very scanty indeed, and among the known facts one finds the following: that originally the island's name was simply "Nusă," which is to be translated as "the island"; that "Pěnidă," later attached to it, means *pamor*, the white meteorite metal worked into krisses; that on early Dutch maps it appeared under the name "Noesa Pandita" (*pandita* = wizard, recluse); and, finally, the English seafarers chose to designate it as "Bandit Island." This last name, aside from its phonetic relationship with *pandita*, had its justification in the evil reputation of the island, for it was the place of banishment for all criminals and undesirable subjects in the kingdom of Klungkung to which it belonged. Thus a small Siberia of Bali!

But what about the people inhabiting the island now? Are they the same as the Balinese? Do they toil on terraced flooded *sawah*? Do they worship their gods in temples similar to those of the Balinese?

Originally published in *Djawa*, XVI, Nos. 1, 2, and 3 (1936). Reprinted with permission of the author.

Do they enjoy the same riot of colors in their clothing and do they apply their artistic gifts in sculpture, painting, music, and dance in the same way as their neighbors in Bali do?

All these and similar questions, which could find no ready answer anywhere, prompted our small expedition. There were three of us[1] and our interests were divided: our "arts-and-crafts department" was mainly interested in the architecture and sculpture of the temples and also wanted to make special inquiries about the local weavings. Family customs were the chief interest of the other member of our party. And I myself was most anxious to see some dances of Nusă Pĕnidă as compared with those of Bali and Java.

So on a beautiful quiet morning, just before the rays of the sun burst into the drowsy skies, our two *jukung*, shaped like big, narrow, light blue fish with upraised tails, and resting on the outriggers as on wings, were pushed off the shore at Kusambă, a small Mohammedan settlement at the southeastern coast of Bali. On the shore stood, like little toys, rows of square grey houselets which are in some way connected with the production of salt. As our *jukung* were struggling away from shore, jerkily brought forward by the round paddles of their owners, the violet top of Gunung Agung appeared very high up above the clouds, as if benevolently surveying our departure. And below, on the shore, the rows of the tiny uniform grey houses seemed to be marching off in humble discipline. And then the sails were hoisted, and we turned to Nusă Pĕnidă, our boatmen silently praying for favorable winds, which would save them all the rowing.

With favorable winds one could sail across to Lĕmbongan, an oblong small island near the *nusă besar* (big island), in about four hours. Having to struggle with currents and adverse breezes however, we spent six hours in the *jukung* before we could set foot on the beach at the village Jungulbatu. There is another, still smaller, island, Chĕningan, between Lĕmbongan and Nusă Pĕnidă, and its legendary origin is an overturned *prahu* (boat).

There once was a man from Java who came to Bali in a *prahu*, the legend relates. On his way back the Gunung Agung obstructed his way. So he ran against the mountain of the gods wanting to split it, with the unexpectedly natural result that his *prahu* overturned and was thrown aside to the place where Chĕningan lies now, this name being derived from the name of the overbearing man from Java. The anchor of the ill-fated *prahu* is still seen in the big rock across the

[1] Jane Belo, Walter Spies, and the author.

strait near the coast of Bali. A scientific and philological explanation of Chĕningan would simply be "little island," and very little the island is indeed.

After all these digressions let me say that we wanted to walk through Lĕmbongan and Chĕningan first before entering Nusă Pĕnidă proper.

What a different atmosphere from Bali! One senses it the moment one sets foot on Lĕmbongan. In the first place the *désă* Jungulbatu itself has an original appearance all its own with everything speaking about the sea. Wherever possible jagged sea-stones are used for construction.

The enclosures of the houses and the main street are lined with low walls made of these porous and irregular grey stones. In some of the yards, filled with the heavy odor of drying fish, lie extraordinarily large sea shells. We were puzzled by quantities of oblong, flat snow-white bits of something hung in the yards on lines and obviously drying in the sun. They were slices of *katella* (sweet yams) later to be stamped into flour, which together with *jagung* (maize) constitutes the main food of the population, here as well as on Nusă.

At the southern end of the main street the way leading across the island starts upward in wide steps, almost in little terraces, hewn into the slope of the stony hill. The vegetation is that of a land poor in water—big cactuses, low trees, sudden patches of green, small flowers. On the whole somewhat as one would imagine Palestine to be or perhaps some rocky part of Spain. No abundance of little streams and *panchuran* (water spouting from a bamboo conduit) as in Bali. The villages, if fortunate, have deep wells, and, if very fortunate, of sweet water, and near the well is the bath, which has, as a water vessel, a large rectangular stone, hollowed out like a sarcophagus without cover and placed on the wall of the enclosure surrounding the bath. But for us these enclosures were by no means an assurance of privacy during our trip—they served as marvellous observation points for all children of the various *désă* (villages) where we stopped, as might easily be imagined.

Leaving Jungulbatu we came across a strange effigy put up near the entrance of the temple of the death-goddess, the *pură dalĕm*. It was a flat long figure cut out of the spine of a palm leaf, without arms or legs, and only with a round disk at the top on which human features were drawn in chalk. Little matted bags of withered palm leaf (*kĕtipat*) were suspended at each side of the effigy, and a multitude of offerings scattered nearby. This was something to be investigated and proved of special interest to our "family department." We were told that this effigy was a *chĕmplongan* which is customarily put up in front of the *purǎ dalĕm* when a newborn child reaches the age of one month and seven days. There is a similar custom in Bali, only there the shape of the effigy, its name, the placement, and its point of time are different. As far as I know it is put near a river or at crossroads, but this matter concerned our "family expert."

It does not take more than forty-five minutes, perhaps, to cross the whole island of Lĕmbongan. We lingered however on its highest ridge before descending to the south coast. Here, magnificently situated, lies the *purǎ pusĕh* (temple of ancestors) of the *désǎ* Lĕmbongan. Standing at its gate one can overlook the sea from both sides, Bali appearing at the north side and Nusǎ Pĕnidǎ to the south, preceded by little Chĕningan bathed in the brightest of blue-green edges by the snow-white of breakers.

This first gate of the *purǎ pusĕh* Lĕmbongan appeared of unexpectedly solid and beautiful architecture. Its crown-shaped top is flanked by four melon-shaped pieces which together are somehow reminiscent of the Prambanan temple in Java. In the niches of the gate, however, are several humorous-looking figures of birds, apes, and squatting men, the latter very similar to the figures on the gate of the former palace in Klungkung.

As we found later, Klungkung is in general the center of culture and fashion for Nusǎ Pĕnidǎ and its little brothers—a sort of Paris. Often would we hear a man say with pride: "This comes from Klungkung," or, "I have once been to Klungkung," or, "It was told to us by a man from Klungkung." Everything is relative indeed. What an important bright place Klungkung becomes when one is on Nusǎ Pĕnidǎ and what an immense country Bali!

Had the tide been low we could have walked over to the "little island." This not being the case, a small *jukung* brought us over to Chĕningan at Purǎ Bakung where a temple feast was in full swing. A cock fight was being held. There were offerings put up in the inner temple court not unlike those of Bali, but far poorer and smaller.

Our pitching the tents under the palms near the beach proved an additional great diversion for the people who gathered at the temple feast. Somebody remarked that it would have been still better had we brought along a *wayang kuda* (a circus)!

With the tide receding before sunset we wandered out to the coral reefs between the two small islands. In the transparent luminous pools left by the sea glimmered fantastic miniature landscapes of lightly agitated plants nestling in the multicolored coral rocks, more exquisite than the miniature Japanese rock gardens and animated by small and large inhabitants of the southern seas of the most varied shaped and colors. Here were crabs, and jelly-like heavy-breathing creatures, and parasites like gay moss, and flower-like half-animals half-plants instantly vanishing into the sand at the slightest touch. Each pool a little world of wonders. And all over on the rocks and in the water were scattered the originally decorated starfish—each a model in design and color combination for a jeweler or fashion designer. There were mauve-colored stars with salmon-red protruding round points set like semiprecious stones; or beautifully shaded grey ones studded with lazuli-blue buttons; softly glowing stars of burnt sienna shades with a black pattern, and some again as if covered by a lizard skin, or of an even cobalt blue. Within a few minutes we could build a one-meter-high pagoda out of the stars putting them one on top of the other.

As the evening fell we returned to our camp. The people gathered around our lamps, and we sat there quietly chatting and transacting the necessary business. Throughout our voyage we could always find somebody speaking Malay, otherwise the Nusă language differs but slightly from that of Bali. While purchasing food we found that silver money was a source of great confusion and inconvenience, and here our "*kèpèng* period" began—from now on we carried along the heavy strings of *kèpèng*, the Chinese pierced coins with a value of about one seventh of a cent on Nusă, and we transacted business in hundreds and thousands.

From the people we learned that there was no Triwangsă on either of these islands, thus no castes of Brahmană, Ksatriyă, and Wěsyă, but that, nevertheless, just as in Bali, they burn their dead; that for important occasions a *pědandă* has to come over from Bali, there not being a single such priest either in Nusă Pěnidă nor on any of the two smaller islands.

It was only the second morning of our voyage, and already it seemed a long, long time since we left Bali. Now we were to start for Nusă Pěnidă proper.

Embarkation on an ocean liner is child's play in comparison with a voyage in a *jangolan*—a large *prahu* with a steeply sloping roof over its bunk, which is the regular passenger ship between the islands. The *jangolan* was booked to capacity. Men, women, and children filled the bunk and crouched on the roof. We were also assigned "seats" on the roof, where, after much sliding and battling with the ever-menacing sail boom, we found it at last most comfortable to sit astride on the ridge. This was real seafaring! What excitement every time the wind became capricious, and the sail had to be turned. How we shot across the waves only to stop again after a while with listlessly hanging sail, the rowers swearing under their breath. And when we finally arrived—Toyă Pakĕh was the name of the "port"—all our numerous belongings, tents, cameras, provision baskets, and empty gasoline tins (for water—we were warned!) and even ourselves had to be carried ashore held up high amid the breaking waves. It was a jolly, sporting affair with such splashing and laughter till everything was assembled on the beach under the scorching sun. And there we were parked.

It is easier to climb the Merbabu, I suppose, than to persuade a Nusă-Pĕnidian to oblige you and to become temporarily a carrier even for fair pay. In Toyă Pakĕh it took us about four hours to hire five men willing to carry our luggage to Pură Pèd, which lies in about one-and-a-half hours' walking distance and is one of the most important temples on the coast.

Most of the inhabitants of Toyă Pakĕh are Mohammedans, but in this respect the *désă* seemed to be an exception. Wherever we passed later we found no traces of Islam. The stately *pĕrbĕkĕl* (*désă* head) in Arab turban was obliging enough to forward our message with a request for horses to Sampalan, the next large settlement on the coast whereto we were heading.

A smooth, intimately pleasant avenue along the beach, lined intermittently by low roundish trees like the small oaks of California, cactuses, and wild bushes, such was the way leading to Pură Pèd. "What I would like to see," said one of us, "is a tree full of white cockatoos!" And this was truly like magic. We were approaching the high-branching masses of ancient trees usually found at holy sites, and there suddenly a swarm of white cockatoos started up from a magnificent old waringin, and we could hear their shrill calls and chatterings till sunset when we had already set up our tents near the temple.

The cockatoo question is most puzzling. Why should multitudes of them swarm about Nusă Pĕnidă and not one live in Bali, which is so near? A local man tried to explain this by relating that once upon a time the cockatoos misbehaved most terribly in Bali, stealing and plundering, and therefore they were—banished to Nusă Pĕnidă! Bandit Island—of course! We got the flavor of it too when the next morning a man with a pock-marked face presented himself as a carrier and cheerfully announced that he had been in jail in Tabanan for the murder of a woman. Why did he kill her? Oh, he believed she was a *léyak*, a witch.

As for Purǎ Pèd itself, aside from being a very beautiful complex in layout, it has an interesting addition very rarely found in Bali. It is the so-called *taman* (garden) which is a quadrangular pond in the midst of which a small shrine is installed as on a miniature island. A narrow bamboo bridge connects it with the grounds. With the exception of Batu Kauh we have never seen such a *taman* as part of a temple complex in Bali, though a shrine or even a larger structure, like a *balé kambang*, a structure in a garden surrounded by a quadrangular water basin, is not uncommon there and may be found, among other places, in Klungkung, in Ubud, and in the *puri* (palaces) of Kěsiman and Gianyar. Later we saw on Nusǎ another, even larger, *taman* also as part of a temple, namely that of Batu Mědau near Swana.

The *klian* (village official) of the nearest *désǎ* was very kind and helpful and promised us carriers for the next morning. He would also send us a man who could sell us some eggs. Just about midnight, when

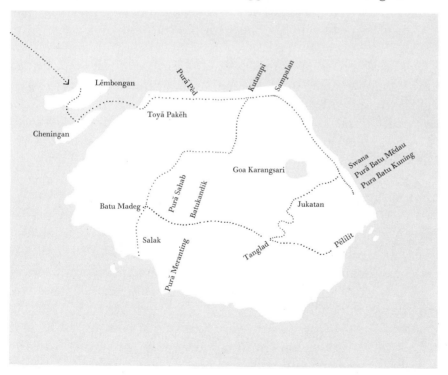

The island of Nusǎ Pěnidǎ, showing the journey of Claire Holt, Jane Belo, and Walter Spies

we were deep in slumber after a strenuous day, we were aroused by voices. The eggs had arrived!

It was a great joy and surprise to find that horses had actually come from Sampalan the next morning. So, again along the same pleasant avenue, off we went, the carriers trotting much faster than our little horses.

Sampalan is the big capital of Nusă Pěnidă. One may even find there such a luxurious institution as a Chinese *toko* (shop)—the second and last one we saw on the island. Again a trial of patience and diplomacy. If two horse owners agree to rent out their horses for fifty cents a day for the rest of our trip, why should the third insist on three guilders a day? We needed his horse. But three guilders a day! We sat on the porch of the school arguing with the man for hours. Our arguments were most ingenious, the question was approached, illuminated, and discussed from every conceivable angle. The afternoon advanced. We had a long trip ahead. The man kept playing with a knife belonging to our camping outfit. When we were ready to give up, exhausted by his incomprehensible obstinacy, he suddenly said: "All right, you may have my horse for the rest of your trip free of charge, if you give me this knife." He wanted it for cock spurs. The bargain was quickly closed. And with the setting sun we rode off to Swana.

I do not know what the road from Sampalan to Swana looks like during the day time. It was incredibly beautiful in twilight and at night with only the stars illuminating the sky. Gradually rising, the way wound itself in deep curves higher and higher above the beach. There were fantastic silhouettes of trees against the void above the sea. Every time we came out of the darkness at the inner curve of the road, where the horses could just feel their way, there was the magnificent expanse of the sea viewed from high above. As the evening advanced, bright moving flames, sometimes blinding the horses, flared up below in the water near the beach. These were torches of fishermen catching octopuses, which are a delicacy much sought for. In the distance the flames of the torches gathered in rows and looked like lights of a big city. Very soon they all vanished, and there was only the sky with blinking stars.

Late in the evening we arrived in Swana, and now, by the light of the moon, we could distinguish a tremendous old waringin in the central square of the village, a kind of *alun-alun* (plaza), and around the base of its huge stem a square stone terrace for the people to sit on, like the one we had already noticed in the *désă* Lěmbongan. On the side toward the sea was a well and the baths with two "sarco-phaguses," *panchuran*; on the opposite side the *balé banjar* (communal pavilion); to the right the *désă* school and to the left houses. We spent the third and fourth nights of our trip under the hospitable shade of the giant tree in the middle of Swana, for during the whole day between them there were many interesting things to be seen.

About one kilometer north of Swana there lies a tremendous cave, the Goa Karangsari. Walter Spies descended into it through a small traplike opening and found himself in complete darkness. Walking downward through a narrow passage, he suddenly came into a larger cave and from there into still another one, till, finally, there were large vaulted halls with stalactites hanging down and all the hollow uncanniness of deep caves. This seemed to be a whole hollow moun-tain. After a fair amount of wandering about the man accompanying Spies told him to stop. He was to go no further. Before them lay a small pool of brilliantly transparent water. "This is the bath of the *dĕdari* (heavenly nymphs)," declared the guide. (His name, by the way, was Kichig, and a preciously helpful soul Kichig proved after-ward!) So beyond the bath of the heavenly nymphs no one should pass.

It must be a peculiarly fascinating spectacle—the celebration held by the people of Swana at their Galungan feast in the Goa Karangsari. They enter there with torches, and at the light of their flames offerings are brought and dances performed under the trembling shadows of the stalactites.

Our precious guide Kichig brought us to two temples a short distance south of Swana. In the first Pură Batu Mĕdau, containing two stately high *mèru* (pagoda-like temple structure), we found a confirmation that the plain rectangular stone terrace, which we had already seen previously in *pură*, is not an accident but a typical con-struction in the temples of Nusă Pĕnidă. It is obviously an altar approximately ranging from three to five meters in length and two to four in width and with an elevation of about one meter from the ground. It looks like a simple base for a *balé* or a foundation of some other structure, has no roof, and offers a plain large surface for offer-ings. Another characteristic feature was the crown of the gate shaped like a flattened *pĕdandă* hat with an open small niche going through its middle. In Pură Batu Mĕdau we also found two stone ancestor figures with rather long faces and of much finer work than the two withered small stone images we had previously seen in Lĕmbongan. This long-faced stone couple was rather reminiscent of the Hinduistic figures on Gunung Pănulisan in Bali. There was also a large *taman* surrounded by glorious *camboja* trees, whose miraculous branches, some fallen to the ground and just lying there as if doomed to waste away, continue to bring forth fresh flowers—the smooth ivory-colored *kĕmbang jepung* with dazzling sweet smell. These solid simple blossoms play such an important role in all rites of the people—one always finds these trees on cemeteries and in temples, and their blossoms tremble in the crowns of the dancers, arise heavenward in the flower ornaments crowning the offerings, and oftentimes they are dipped into holy water by officiating priests and then thrown through space by their nimble fingers plying themselves into the mysterious *mudras*.

Everybody knows, or can easily imagine, what a torturing thing thirst can be and this on a tropical midday near a sun-scorched beach. The only well of Swana furnished water richly salted. Therefore our morning coffee had been salted far beyond the limits prescribed by coffee connoisseurs. No wonder then that, while resting in the shade of a *balé* at Purā Batu Kuning, the next temple along the beach, and while delighting in the sight of the bright sea playing beneath its walls, we were also dreaming of ice-cooled drinks or at least of young sweet coconuts. There wasn't a soul in sight, however, who could have possibly provided even the more reasonable of the two blessings, the *kĕlapă*. But then Kichig burst into cries of joy—a man was coming along the beach with two long bamboo containers suspended from his shoulders—there was drink, drink, drink—even though it was *tuak* (palm-wine)!

Kichig was very communicative and so full of initiative and explosive outbursts of temperament that it was tremendously refreshing after our contact with so many phlegmatic Nusă-Pĕnidians. So we had to learn that for his wife he had paid 30,000 *kèpèng*, which was a little more than the average price for a nice girl; that in matters of wooing difficulties *gună-gună* methods are usually applied, with love potions and quick-forget-medicines furnished by the *balian* (medicine men), who, by the way, are all men on Nusă. We also had to discuss the "twin problem." This lay within the special scope of interests of our family expert who already in Bali had investigated many of the customs following the birth of twins in a village.[2] It is a big calamity indeed when twins of different sexes are born. In fact, before we left Bali, messengers had come to Ubud from the *désă* Trunyan in the

[2] See Jane Belo, "A Study of Customs Pertaining to Twins in Bali," in this volume, p. 3.

Batur mountains with a warning that the next big feast, for which preparations were already being made and which we had intended to witness, would not take place because a woman of Trunyan had the ill luck to give birth to twins of both sexes. Poor mother of such twins! We visited such a mother in the heart of Nusă Pĕnidă—but this is another story.

It is the fifth day of our trip, and we feel that only now we shall at last go to the real Nusă Pĕnidă, to the villages in the mountains.

Kichig, having attached himself to our retinue, and another horse with the indispensable "horse-man" hired as a valuable addition, and a double set of carriers—this time eight of them turned up instead of four, none of whom we could dismiss without injury to our reputation —our small caravan bids goodby to the sea and turns inland. Yet, the further we advance, steadily rising, all the broader and more magnificent becomes the outlook on the sea, and for hours and hours yet we can contemplate it from the plateau above and even get a view of Lombok in the distance.

The way is stony and hard on the feet of the walking men. Everywhere, up to the highest places, which are only about five or six hundred meters above sea level, one finds the coral rocks and the rugged stones eaten out by the water. Sometimes one even finds sea shells in the hills, which makes us wonder how short or long a time ago this island arose from the waters.

And now the country. No *sawah* (wet rice fields) to be sighted anywhere. Only dry fields with young sprouts of maize in curving terraces along the slopes of the round hills. There are few coconut palms and only here and there a small grove of slender pinangs arises in a corner of a valley. Along the road we are greeted by bright dark blue small and butterfly-shaped flowers nestling near the ground, flaming bushes of small velvet red and orange blossoms, the gay plant said to have been introduced to the Indies by Marquis de Serrière; also tall bluish-white stiff flowers that look like giant hyacinths made of porcelain and from which, I am told, belladonna is obtained. Before we know it, we have reached the first mountain village, Jukutan.

As we enter one of the grey compounds with low stone walls, which seem to run around and between the courtyards like a labyrinth puzzle, what a joy for our companion seeking information about the craft of weaving, to find two women at work at their looms. In fact, we found that nearly every house had a loom or two, for the women of Nusă Pĕnidă all weave their own *tapih*—gay multicolored striped cloths which they wear under the dark-blue or black upper *kain*,[3] so that only a small piece of the striped *tapih* shows near the feet. Black and blue were also the short *kain* worn by the men. There was none of the suspicious reserve which one encounters in Madura for instance. Long explanations, interrupted by many interjections from the gathered crowd and by violent disputes between the spokesman and some older female expert of weaving, poured forth. It took a long time before the technical details of the looms, the enumeration of materials used, and the colors were noted down, with the necessary sketches. Yes, leaves of the *taum* for black and blue, roots of the *sunti* for all shades of red, fruit of the *kunyit* for the yellows. How beautifully deep are these colors gained by primitive methods, how hard and empty our aniline dyes look beside them !

We were permitted to visit their temple, Purǎ Gunung Anyar, situated, like all *purǎ* inland, on a hill. Only the horses had to be left behind. Here, apart from several guardians in crudely executed Balinese style, but with childishly thin flat and unexpansive limbs, we found in the inner court installed on an altar what was termed by my companion "a natural stone of unnatural shape." It was a fairly large porous sea-stone, absolutely untouched by a carver's hand, yet by the whim of elements rendering the shape similar to the head of a horse or of some other long-jawed quadruped. What the people of Jukutan saw in it we could not ascertain. But we remembered now that in almost all the other temples we had visited heretofore such "natural stones with unnatural shapes" were installed, either on three corners of the large plain stone altar mentioned before, or on a pile of stones under an old tree, or on a base of a shrine. They would recall the shape of a bird or an animal or evoke in the imagination the forms of some fantastic being.

After Jukutan the road became much steeper, and we had to entrust ourselves completely to the horses, who displayed an astounding energy when it came to climbing, the wisest discrimination at dangerous descents, but who were exasperatingly disinterested and slow on an even smooth path. The landscape now displayed enormous amphitheaters composed of evenly curving semicircular terraces of maize fields descending into valleys. And some of the round hills with their terraces running around the slopes looked like formidable spiral sea shells.

Just before sunset we arrived in Tanglad, and there we discovered that the finest place to camp in a native village is the *balé banjar*.

[3] A rectangular cloth wrapped around the hips and reaching to the ankles.

There are no pigs bumping against your tent at night—the pigs of Nusă are enormous beasts—no lamenting babies carried out at night to forget their tears at the sight of strange visitors hidden behind the *kĕlambu* (mosquito nets) of their funny little houses. And there is the enormous advantage of the spacious *balé's* floor covered with fresh mats, where all the *barang-barang* (luggage) can be conveniently unpacked and where meals can be held at ease with endless conversations. What a lovely and sociable institution, and what a blessing is a *balé* [4] per se in a country where there are no hotels, no rest-houses, and not even *warung* (roadside shop).

One of our reasons for coming to Tanglad, which is a large village, with solid stone houses and steep roofs, picturesquely sprawling on the different levels of the hills, was the prospect of seeing the *baris jangkang*. We had heard about this peculiarly interesting dance performed by the men of the *désă* Pĕlilit which lies near the coast southeast of Tanglad.

So in anticipation of the next morning, which promised to be exceptionally strenuous, the way to Pĕlilit being so steep that the use of horses was out of the question, we indulged in a *babi guling* (roast pig) feast, which cost us 750 *kèpèng* and the preparations for which called for a multitude of "assistants." It was a grand feast for ourselves and the boys and their assistants, a roasted pig probably seldom enjoying such appreciation. Following this we descended to a lower situated part of the *désă*, *banjar* Julingan, and there, late in the evening, *gandrung* (special boy dancers) were showing us their art.

In the dark court of the *balé banjar* with only one oil lamp illuminating with reddish light a circle in the middle, two boys in tightly fitting white shirts, bright silk cloth around their hips, and with green "hair" made of some fine grass streaming out of their headdresses similar to the Balinese dance crowns, danced side by side subtly moving their undulating bodies. Later they were gliding past each other, meeting and separating, and coming together again, all the while manipulating in one hand a flat object substituting for a fan. Their formations were not unlike those of Western folk dances, while their stately fine steps and inclination of the body were vaguely reminiscent of the Russian dance of the "boyaryshny," the young court ladies entertaining their princesses in the gay wooden palaces of ancient Russia.

So very strange are the affinities of gestures! One could discover the same spirit in the old Chinese dances performed by the inimitable

[4] An open, elevated, pillared wooden structure with a roof.

Mei Lan-fang—yet little direct similarity is there between the dance movements of the great Chinese artist and the *gandrung* of *banjar* Julingan of the *désă* Tanglad in Nusă Pĕnidă.

The road to Pĕlilit certainly exceeded our expectations. When, having started out early the next morning, we finally arrived, after descending what might be called the wall of the hill closing off this little world, my knees and ankles shook as after the first skating party following several seasons' rest. But this and the breath-robbing ascent back again was worth while indeed.

In about one hour's time the *jangkang* dancers were assembled. Most of them were old men, some of them of that marvellous dignity one finds among the elders of "primitive" tribes. Two or three out of the nine dancers were young. They started dressing, putting on first close-fitting long pants with red and black stripes and triangles not unlike those of the American Indians. Over the pants they wrapped a multicolored or white *kain* not quite reaching the knees and hanging down in long ends in front. Then a large wooden kris was stuck into the belt. Covering the kris again, and therefore protruding to the side, a bright piece of silk was put and tied over the breast. On the head they each tied a headkerchief in most individual fashion, but always so that the glistening black hair was showing. Then they all took up long poles, and, accompanied by the music (which was rather a rhythmical clatter of differently manipulated small gongs called there *dèng-dèng*, *kĕmpul* and *pĕtuk*, two small drums (*kĕndang*) played on by sticks, and three cymbals (*chèng-chèng*), which gave strongly syncopated accents), the dancers came on to the open place in front of the *balé*, spreading themselves evenly into three rows of three.

They were to show us three different *baris jangkang* dances: the *gaok* (crow), the *chĕlatik* (rice-bird), and the *èlo*—a word whose meaning they could not explain but which seems to be the same as the Javanese *ngigel* (prancing, as a peacock). And was there a story to these dances?

—Oh, yes, there was a small story.

—All right, so what about the crow?—The crows were stealing offerings.

—And then?—Well, that's all.

—And how about the *chĕlatik*?—The *chĕlatik*, oh, they are making "*plĕsir-plĕsir sajă*" (just enjoying themselves).

The *èlo* remained as mysterious as in the beginning.

During the dance the performers stayed in the places they had

occupied in their original formation, keeping their symmetrical rows
of three. (See Plate XXIII.) But, having completed a certain dance
period, they sometimes made a quarter turn and danced facing in the
new direction. It seemed to me that I could distinguish in their movements, especially when they all crouched down with one arm outstretched, winglike, and their heads moving obliquely from side to
side, birdlike, a stylized imitation of a bird's movement. Yet there
entered so much of manly grace combined with a peculiar softness,
when they gradually lowered themselves, balancing in one hand the
horizontally lying pole. Then again some attitudes would appear for
a passing instant which made one think of the flat Pharoahs holding
their inclined staff in an outstretched arm on the reliefs of ancient
Egypt. And when they jumped over their poles in light, springy,
tapping steps with their elastic bodies bent forward, American Indian
dances flashed to mind again. It is futile to make comparisons. But
how can one otherwise convey impressions about so elusive a thing
as a dance which cannot be fixed in words?

There was a slight variation in the second, *chĕlatik*, dance, and the
mysterious *èlo* was in essence almost the same. Yet we rejoiced,
because all the better the beauty of these movements could be fixed
in our memories and, above all, by the moving-picture camera.

Back to Tanglad we visited a mother of twins. The boy had
"fortunately" died on the fourth day after his birth while in the
pură dalĕm. It is the custom, when such twins are born, that the
parents with the babies stay for a month in the temple of the death-
goddess, and there they are taken care of in turn by some old women
of the *désă*. It seems to be a purification procedure. And we were also
told that in way of a test (but most likely for another forgotten reason
connected with ancient beliefs) the parents have to sit down for a
moment on the lap of their children! In Bali, if the twins survive,
they may not stay together in the parents' house, and one of them
is sent away as far as possible and is brought up away from his
twin brother or sister. But when they grow up, the two may marry.
Since the old people, who seemed to know everything that the present
generation knows no longer, are all dead ("*orang tua samua mati*" is
the usual reply to a question to which no explanation can be given),
it is difficult to get at the root of this old superstition, traces of which
are still alive in Java, too.

As for the parents of the twins—the mother feels most ashamed and
depressed to have given forth such ill luck bringing omens to the *désă*.

This one, a bewildered, poor-looking woman with scabies-eaten skin showed us her remaining little daughter with the expression of a tigress shielding her cubs. Otherwise she was speechless and obviously disturbed by the additional publicity of her unfortunate case. There seem to be many tragedies of a kind entirely unknown to us—among them that of a mother of twins in a society haunted by ancient superstitions.

Now, the seventh morning of our trip, we are crossing Nusă Pěnidă from east to west, riding all the while along the plateaus of its central hills. After about two hours' ride we reach the *désă* Batukandik, and it is here that we make what we consider the most interesting discovery of our trip in the sphere of temples.

As usual we went to the most important temple of the *désă*, and in this one, named Purǎ Meranting, we found a *sanggar* (a highly elevated throne for the Sun-god Suryǎ, found also in every temple of Bali) of most striking form and of a style quite different from anything in Bali. Due to the pyramidical form of its stone mass, it was slightly reminiscent in style of Chandi Sukuh on the western slope of the Lawu in Java.

Instead of the usual architectural base supporting the seat of the sun god, this one was resting on the head and the uplifted hands of a huge stone woman, standing on widely spread legs half hidden in the pyramidical mass of steps descending as if pouring out of her lap. Her face had a peculiar grin due to the small fangs protruding at each corner of her mouth. And behind her head, fixed to the back wall of the *sanggar* and quite invisible from the front, there was a wonderfully carved head of a cow or bull, with similar fangs and also as if grinning.

There were many interesting details on and around this unique figure too numerous to be described here, but the knowledge of which might prove of value to students of Indonesian antiquities.[5]

Our tin gasoline can had developed a leak, and no water could be carried along in it. So from Batukandik we had to take along a youngster, who just happened to come along with two big calabashes filled with water brought from a long distance away. The youngster was willing to sell us his water, but for no money would he part with

---

[5] Published since by W. F. Stutterheim as "Eeen interessante Sūrya-Zetel van Noesa Penida," in *Bijdragen tot de Taal-, Land-, en Volkenkunde van Nederlandsch-Indië*, XCII (1935), 206–10.

his calabash-vessels and would rather trot along with us till the water was used.

After a while we came to the only piece of jungle left on Nusă. It was so refreshing to enter its humid shade, to see the large plants, big ferns, and the heavy trunks of trees overgrown by creepers after the comparatively bare expanse of the hills. This was the holy forest of Sahab hiding an important temple. The squat, heavy figure of the luck-bringing elephant god Ganesa is kept there, which is used for "making rain," the image being dipped into water when supernatural help is sought for the coming of rain.

Perhaps Sahab is the place whereto runs the legendary tunnel connecting Bali with Nusă Pěnidă and which is said to start from a hole in *pură pusěh ring* Jagat of Pèjèng? There is by the way a resemblance between the numerous Hinduistic figures, about thirty in all, arrayed on the shelves of different *balé* in Pură Sahab, and the antiquities of Pèjèng. I don't know anyone who has actually seen the remarkable hole, the entrance to the said tunnel in Pèjèng. But since its existence and significance is insistently perpetuated in the folklore, why dispute its reality?

Thus Sahab remained in our memory as the place where the close connection with old Bali seemed to have left its deepest traces, the many images representing departed kings or nobles, almost all holding up in each hand a fruit (or perhaps it is a closed flower?), *linggas* held in the grip of *nagă*, the beautiful *chaturmukă* (four-faced image) whose four heads have still preserved the fine features—all of them being of the same kind as the images that once were worshiped in the temples of the old kingdom of Pèjèng.

With the evening we reached the *désă* Batu Mаděg and, according to already established custom, invaded the *balé banjar*. In no time all the *balé* and the space on the ground was occupied by an eager public contemplating the unique spectacle we offered. Our clothing was at this stage of the voyage in deplorable condition. For a minimum of luggage naturally also demands a minimum of dresses and suits. My tattered riding breeches had to be substituted by wide green pajama trousers. So if the people of Nusă Pěnidă should henceforth have some quaint notions about the clothing of white women—they saw these peculiar beings for the first time in their life, they asserted—we are responsible for it.

Having eaten our chicken and rice—rice is a rare luxury in the hills of Nusă and we were wise enough to have brought some along—we had for after-dinner music a short *prèrèd* concert. This *prèrèd* is a kind of trumpet, blown almost without gasping pauses by skillful manipulation of the outgoing and indrawn breath. And its sounds are remarkably well rendered in the phonetics of its name—a *prèrèd* "praeraeae-ae'ds" in broad, lamenting, cackling, brassy tones. The concert did not last too long.

It is our last day on Nusă Pěnidă, and we are going down to the south coast via the *désă* Salak, where our horses can at last still their thirst, drinking water being so scarce in Batu Mǎděg. It is still early in morning hours when we reach the coast. We rush to the edge of the high shore, a vertical wall of yellowish rock, and more than two hundred meters below, the bright turquoise of the gently agitated sea. For a long time we lie on our bellies looking down into the dazzling turquoise-green. In some places the water is quite transparent. Of what tremendous size must be this almost triangular fish with slowly flapping fins, which appears to us the size of a dog. Now we can also discern turtles that look no larger than coconuts. And there is a strange rock in the water with a large opening in the middle and looking just like a gate. We look at the marvellous shades ranging from almost white to deep blue-green and think that the same waters continuing the vast distance southward also carry the swaying icebergs at the South Pole.

The same day we managed to cross the whole island from Salak to Kutampi, a village near Sampalan. And the next morning we boarded a *jukung* which was again a large fish with upraised tail and resting on the outriggers on wings. The wind god was benevolent to us that day. Gunung Agung was beckoning from a distance, and in four hours we reached the south coast of Bali at Sanur.

Not far from the place where we had landed, a massive stone pillar with a mysterious inscription had been discovered the preceding year (ca. 1952). When the engraved weather-eaten script was deciphered, it appeared that the pillar was erected by a South Balinese king in the first half of the tenth century. Repeated in two languages—Kawi (Old Javanese) and Sanskrit—the text commemorates a glorious expedition undertaken by the king's fleet from Sanur to Nusă Pěnidă.

The Balinese Temper

JANE BELO

IN EXAMINING the psychological character of a people such as the Balinese, who number more than a million, we have no choice but to take up one by one the simple habits of the individual which are common to the people as a whole, noting the patterns occurring in the adult, and how the child by his early conditioning is molded into a personality essentially Balinese. If, in an effort to cast light upon problems of personality, one wished to set forth special traits, special individual developments to be found among the Balinese, one would find it difficult to make one's self understood unless some picture had previously been drawn of the people's psychological nature, as evidenced in the general character of their ways of behaving. For what are among them universal traits might be mistaken for individual deviations. Therefore it seems advisable to describe the general trend of personality development against a background suggesting the tenor of the life, the modes of feeling and of activity, which may range from a subdued stillness to states of exalted animation without being excluded from the habitual and universal trends.

By the Balinese temper I mean the nature and ways of the people as a whole. In my presentation individual examples will serve as illustrations of the general trends and in certain cases indicate deviations from them. I believe that the Balinese exemplify by their behavior

This study is based on four years' acquaintance with the people, during which I resided with my husband, Colin McPhee, in a wholly Balinese village, making studies of the arts, music, legends, and rituals in their intimate correlation with Balinese life.

Originally published in *Character and Personality*, IV, No. 2 (December, 1935), 120–46; reprinted, with permission, in Douglas G. Haring, ed., *Personal Character and Cultural Milieu*, 3d rev. ed. (Syracuse, Syracuse University Press, 1956), 157–79.

how closely the individual may be required to conform to patterns laid down by the social group, with what rhythmic and unstrained ease he may, under such laws, accomplish the tasks exacted of him, and in what apparent contentment he may exist, when no problem is without an answer in his scheme of things. A description of the making of such adjustments, and the formation of the personality through them, may be of interest because of the foreignness of the setting, of the society in which they are made. My method will consist in an enumeration of a series of patterns of behavior, beginning with the simplest, which give to the outsider his initial impression. The simplest passages of behavior differ from our own no less than do the highly complex thought mechanisms, so closely interlocked with them. Ordinary behavior, the way of walking, of sitting, of greeting acquaintances, of taking nourishment, speech habits, gesture, and facial expression, all these differ from our own, and all are founded not only on the way of life but on the people's conception of it and of the place of the individual in relation to it. And conversely, the higher concepts are built up out of component units, the simpler habits of ordinary behavior. In a discussion of the Balinese temper we shall have to consider both phases, and we shall find them often interdependent and inseparable.

Bearing and Pace

To a Westerner, the most striking characteristic in the ordinary behavior of a Balinese is the absolute poise and balance of his bearing, noticeable in his posture, his walk, his slightest gesture. All mature men and women have this poise, and even the small children develop it with remarkable rapidity. Almost never does one see a stooped or curving back even among the old people, and clumsiness and lack of coordination are rare. The impression is that of a nation favored with an unusually fine physique, with natural dignity and ease in every motion. But together with the impression of ease, one remarks a sort of *carefulness* in the bearing, as if each foot were placed in its appointed place, each turn of the head or flick of the wrist calculated not to disturb an equilibrium delicately set up, and hanging somewhere unseen within the individual. One learns that the Balinese is never unconscious of his position in space, in relation to *kajǎ*,[1] north,

---

[1] The mountains which form the central part of the island are conceived as the abode of the gods, and the highest and most holy place. The sea is by contrast the lowest place, and although there is also a god of the sea, the sea and the seashore are conceived as unholy, and all that is filthy must be cast there, or into the rivers which

which is the direction of the mountains, and *kĕlod*, south, the direction of the sea; and in relation to his position above the ground, which should not be higher than that of his social superior. It would seem that a great deal of the "carefulness" in the manner of the Balinese springs from his habit of adjusting his position according to the laws of his cosmology and his social group. The other great factor is the habitual avoidance of any impulsive movement which could shock or otherwise momentarily disturb the feeling of well-being in the body.

The individual Balinese moves slowly, with deliberation. Westerners, seeing for the first time films representing the Balinese at their daily tasks, are immediately struck by the slow tempo of their actions. If a man seated in one pavilion of his house-court suddenly wishes to show something which is in another pavilion, he will rise to his feet and saunter across the intervening space, quite as if he were going for a casual stroll. He will never hurry, as we would, eager to grasp the object which has come to mind. There is plenty of time, and to hurry would be unusual, unnecessary, and stupid—a waste of energy. Walking along the roads, each individual progresses with an even, measured step. The custom is to walk in single file, probably because the trails are narrow, and even today when the gravel-covered motor roads are used for long distance walking, there is only a narrow track at the side which is comfortable to bare feet. Rarely does one individual walking in the single file pass another, for all go at the same rhythmic pace. This pace seems to be kept over long distances as well as short and is hardly influenced when the walker carries a medium load (about forty pounds). Women carry such a load with facility, balanced on their heads. Men usually carry much heavier weights, divided in two parcels, one of which is slung at either end of a bamboo pole balanced on the shoulder. Invariably, when the load is heavy (a hundred pounds or so), the man with the shoulder bar proceeds at a short run, almost a trot, and he keeps up this pace without ever slowing down to a walk. The idea is not to get there more quickly; but the motion of the trot vibrates the pliant shoulder bar, so that the weights at either end swing up and down, thus relieving the pressure on the shoulder. This pace, however, has become customary to people heavily laden, and a woman bearing on her head one of the large

---

carry their own filth down to the sea. As the present observations were made in South Bali, for the sake of convenience *kajă* is translated north and *kĕlod* south. On the other side of the mountains, in North Bali, *kajă* means south, and *kĕlod* north, since the relative position of the inhabitants to the mountains is reversed. *Kangin*, east, and *kauh*, west, remain the same in both localities.

offerings of rice, fruit, and cakes (often a cone four or five feet high) will proceed with the same accelerated steps that the men use under their heavy shoulder bars.

A test of the evenness of the habitual pace, kept up over long distances, came on the occasion of an annual ceremony at a temple on the southernmost shore. A Balinese whose house stood next to mine visited the temple on that day, accompanied by his two wives and two children, approximately eight and ten years old. All carried offerings and supplies of food and betel for the journey, but no member of the little group could be said to be heavily laden. They started "in the hour before dawn," which would be about five o'clock in the morning. When I arrived at the temple by motor, they were seated outside taking their meal, having already made their prayers and presented their offerings. Shortly afterward they must have started homeward, for I passed them on my return, proceeding at an even steady pace along the road. At half past three in the afternoon they reached home, apparently not the least exhausted by their walk of over fifty miles, as registered on the speedometer of my car. Even if one assumes that they spent only half an hour at the temple, they covered the fifty miles in ten hours, averaging certainly no less than five miles an hour. The road led up and down over several steep hills, and at least half of the way through arid fields, with no tree to give shade. This family, whose expedition I was able to time, was only one of hundreds visiting the temple on that day, and their excursion was in no sense unusual.

Physical Exertion and Well-being

A great part of the land lying between the high mountain district and the shore is formed in longitudinal ridges which run parallel to each other and no great distance apart. Between these ridges are the steep-walled ravines, where the rivers flow and where are found most of the drinking and bathing springs. Villages are apt to be placed on the high ground, so that in inter-village traffic, walkers going north and south follow an easy up or down grade along the top of the ridge. But a person travelling east and west finds many a steep climb and precipitous descent along his path. Every member of the family is accustomed to go down at least once a day to the river or the bathing place for his bath, and many must climb up and down several times in a day—the women and girls carrying water for household needs, the men going to and fro in their work in the steeply terraced rice fields, the small boys escorting their special charges, the ducks and the water buffalo, down from the dry ground for their daily immersion. Mothers carry babies on their hips, at the same time balancing a forty-pound jar of water on their heads, yet never do they waver in their erect posture nor vary their slow even pace on the steep and often slippery incline. Little girls of five or six already carry a coconut shell full of water on their heads. Gradually the weight of water is increased, until, on reaching maturity, the slender girl can manage as heavy a load as her mother and aunts. Neither do the aged women shirk the task. Kintil, whom I judged to be no less than sixty and who lacked only a few months of being a great-grandmother, made the daily descent of more than two hundred feet along an almost vertical trail and, in wet weather or dry, never failed to carry up her jar of water. She would, I believe, hate to give up carrying water, for that would constitute an admission of her failing strength.

There is an undercurrent of superstition in the Balinese mind that to "give up" will cause weakness and increased vulnerability to the dangers of illness. For illness is conceived as imposed from the outside by malevolent forces, which lurk everywhere, ready to rush into the body of anyone whose strength and purity (both physical and spiritual) are for the time below the normal, outbalanced by the share of weakness and impurity which form a part of every human being. That is why people who have undergone a trying ordeal are not spared and pampered but urged to get up and go on as if nothing had happened to them. Women who have just given birth to a child go down to the river for their bath as soon as the three days of sequestration within the house are passed; and this sequestration (during the period of "uncleanness" following the birth) is as much to protect the village from contamination by the mother and child as to protect the latter from the attacks of evil spirits, to which they are especially vulnerable at this time. Rantun went down to her bath as soon as she could walk following an exhausting bout of fever, and she attempted to carry up her jar of water, although the household was well supplied. Probably this unnecessary exertion brought on the relapse—she fell down on the trail, then clambered up with her empty jar and went to bed for several more days. But the desire for the daily bath is so strong in the Balinese who dwell in the hot regions that they will take any risks rather than forgo it. The bath at the end of a long day in the heat is considered essential to the feeling of well-being within the body. "If I have my bath, I shall feel well," argues the Balinese, even in illness. And Rantun undoubtedly believed she would regain her strength more quickly if she carried up the jar of water.

The same refusal to admit weakness and to spare the sick person was shown in two cases which I witnessed. A boy fainted and remained unconscious for an hour and twenty minutes. His relatives showed great concern and exerted themselves tirelessly to bring him to, blowing in his ears and eyes, rubbing his feet and hands, going to fetch arrack and hot peppers, which they put down his nostrils. But when at last he had regained consciousness they insisted that he should walk home, a distance of half a mile or more, and refused either to allow him to be carried or to remain in a strange house. The best thing was for him to walk home as if nothing had happened. On another occasion a woman was found unconscious in a field, knocked in the head with an axe. When she had been brought to and her wound attended, she was forced to attempt to walk the hundred yards to her house, although she was a tiny thing and her husband or any one of the men present could have carried her with ease. They did support her under the arms and, on arrival at the house, lift her onto her bamboo couch. But no matter how weak, she was not to be carried home like a corpse.

Orientation in Space

The question of position is so significant to the Balinese because of their acute consciousness of their position in relation to the surrounding space of their world. There are three ways for a man to be: erect (standing or "going"); seated (sitting or squatting); and recumbent (the words for sleeping and lying down are the same). Even children never stand on their heads nor turn somersaults. There is felt to be something wrong about the inverted position, with the head where the feet ought to be; and one of the best-known demons, who is pictured on the astrological calendar standing on his hands, is called Kală Sungsang, to be translated Demon Upsidedown. Babies are never seen to crawl—they are held or carried until old enough to stand on their two feet. Only animals walk on all fours. I have spoken elsewhere of an incest punishment in which the offending pair are forced to crawl on all fours to a pigs' drinking trough.[2] To fall down is considered an unlucky sign, a presage that worse things may happen, occasioned by the evil forces which are only "trying their strength" in causing the harmless fall. When one of the members of my household fell and broke her arm, the entire group seemed more concerned over the fact that she had fallen than over the actual

[2]See Belo, "A Study of Customs Pertaining to Twins in Bali," in this volume, p. 49.

injury. They said that several of them had fallen, that now things were getting worse, and that the place should by all means be purified by a great *mĕcharu* ceremony, to drive away the demons and bad spirits who were growing bolder. Falling is a shock which upsets the nice balance of well-being, just as the feeling of a rush of blood to the head in an inverted position is uncomfortable, and must therefore be wrong.[3] Fathers and grandfathers who hold their young children in their laps for hours at a time never swing them about nor cast them in the air as ours are apt to do. Men and women will always endeavor to keep their erect posture, their even pace, their absolute balance, regardless of obstacles in the way, and to cultivate this tendency in the child. White men who scamper down a hillside, in an excess of good spirits and momentum or who leap over a stream will always evoke laughter in the Balinese, who walks sedately on, stepping into the water as if it did not exist, so long as the even measure of his gait is not interrupted. Because his feet are bare and the water warm, there would seem to be no reason to exert himself to jump over the stream. If it were not that the Balinese never jump, one would say that their habits are only better adjusted than ours to a climate uniformly hot, where it is better to conserve one's energy for those exertions required in the daily work. But the systematic avoidance of all shocks and pains and disturbances of the circulation of the blood characteristic of all adult Balinese would indicate that a more specialized consciousness of the body is involved. And this theory is supported by the fact that the average Balinese, although he has plentiful supplies of distilled arrack and palm wine, does not like to get drunk. The feeling of confusion, the lack of his usual surefootedness and sense of equilibrium are so unpleasant to him that he does not often risk the experience. And the whirling of the universe which precedes nausea is positively terrifying. Then he is indeed *lost*.

Malay people have a term for the sensation of being lost, *kĕliru*. In the Balinese language the word is *paling*. To be *paling*, they say, is "not to know where north is"; in other words, he is *paling* who has lost his sense of direction, or who has lost the sense of his own position in relation to the geography of his world. One man whom I knew was taken for a trip in a motor car. He fell asleep during the ride. When

---

[3] The Balinese do not express in words the idea that to upset balance is wrong, but they do express it in their affective response. A look of pain, of fear, or of anxiety appears on the face of an adult who tumbles, or of a child who is held upside down, which far surpasses in feeling the response we should expect and is comparable only to the responses called out by other "wrongs" against the social and religious laws.

the car stopped, he awoke and, leaping out, looked about him desperately, crying, "Where's north, where's north? I'm *paling*."

So accustomed are the Balinese to know where they are in relation to the points of the compass that all instructions of direction are given in these terms, rather than in "right" and "left," or such designations as "toward me," "away from the wall," and so forth. The Balinese says, "When you come to the crossroads, take the turn to the west"; "Pull the table southward"; "He passed me going north"—not "going toward the market"; even among musicians, "Hit the key to the east of the one you are hitting." When for any reason this sense of direction is temporarily lost, when, as we phrase it, a man feels "turned around," he is not only uncomfortable but he is quite unable to function. We once sent a small boy of eight to a distant village where he was to learn to dance, living in the house of his teacher. Riding in the car, the child lost his sense of direction. When we visited him three days later, he had not begun his lessons, for he was still *paling*. "How can I tell him to turn to the east, to advance toward the north, when he is *paling*?" said the teacher. The boy was returned to his village, where, once on familiar ground, he found himself. After several days he went back to the house of the teacher, intently watching every curve of the winding road. But it was no good—he was again *paling*. He grew anxious and was unable to eat and sleep. Then someone thought of taking him out into the fields, where he could see the high cone of the Gunung Agung, the highest mountain, rising to the north. He was cured of his trouble on the spot and had no recurrence of it during the six weeks of his stay in the village. He seemed happy there and made great progress with his dancing.[4]

As a rule the small children are not bothered with the responsibility of direction, for they play within the circumscribed limits of the particular *banjar* (division of the village) which is theirs, or in the outlying rice fields. On this ground they are at home. When they visit other villages, they go in the company of their parents or near relatives, an older brother or cousin, who knows the way. But their consciousness of position in space develops naturally together with the

---

[4] It is probable that an important factor in what we know as homesickness is the dislocation of the sense of direction in unfamiliar surroundings. In the life of the civilized being, who continually moves about and changes the habitual interior from which he orients himself, this sense must be seriously disturbed. Wild animals seem to be perfectly oriented. And domesticated animals manifest uneasiness and make definite attempts to orient themselves, or to return to familiar surroundings, when they are removed from one place to another.

use of language, and the words *kajă*, *kĕlod*, *kauh*, and *kangin* are frequently heard in the chatter of the four- and five-year-olds. When such a group was making drawings at my house, they arranged between them which was to have the south wall, which the east, and so on.

Every Balinese sleeps with his head either to the north (in North Bali, south; see footnote 1) or to the east. He may not even lie down for a moment in the opposite direction, for the feet are dirty and may not be put in the place of the head. To lie in the reversed position is said to be "lying like a dead man," although the Balinese in South Bali are not buried with their heads to the south. The implication is that only a dead man, who could not help himself, would lie in this dangerously wrong way.

Sense of Social Orientation

By imitation of their elders the children soon learn also on which "level" they should sit at formal gatherings. Within the courtyard of the Balinese house are a number of pavilions, each on a foundation of sandstone varying in height from two to four feet. On the platforms so formed are couches of bamboo, constructed between the pillars which support the roof. It is customary to sit either upon the clay floor of the foundation platform or on the couches, which also may vary in height. Thus are provided a hierarchy of sitting-places, whose relative height may be easily ascertained, as the pavilions are without walls.

In family groups no particular attention is paid to the arrangement of levels, and a little girl does not have to stop to think whether or not she is sitting higher than grandfather. But on the advent of a visitor, especially if he be of higher caste than the family of the host, politeness requires that he be given the highest place. At a wedding which I attended of a young man of noble birth, a nephew of the *rajă*, or regent of the district, the most formal rules were observed in the seating of the guests. On the floor of the highest pavilion sat the high priests. On a nearby lower pavilion sat the men of rank, and across the court on a still lower pavilion, the women of the family, also of noble birth. Some chairs were provided for the male guests of the "advanced" type, but these were avoided by the more humble members of the group. Even those seated on chairs were on a level inferior to that where the high priests sat, cross-legged on the floor. Servants and retainers, people of low caste, came and went through the court. Other pavilions for their use were provided in a rear court, where they would eventually receive a share of the feast; but, if any man wished to be seated in the court of honor, he might, after making a reverence with joined hands, squat down on the ground anywhere without fear of offending his social superiors. When all were assembled, the *rajă* appeared. He marched across the courtyard, mounted the steps of the pavilion where the high priests sat, and seated himself cross-legged on the bamboo couch which formed the highest level within the court.

The Place of the Children

On occasions such as this when the strictest etiquette must be observed, the children are not much in evidence, so quiet are they, so intent on watching their elders and imitating their behavior. Small babies may be present, but they are not heard to cry, for at the first whimper they are given the breast of the mother. This applies to children up to two and three years old, provided no younger brother or sister has taken their place. Aunts, cousins, and elder sisters (from the age of eight or nine) habitually carry or hold children of this age. But it is not customary for a woman other than the mother to suckle the child. A youngster may scuttle across the intervening space which divides the women from the men, scramble into its father's lap, and sit there quiet and solemn-eyed. This is not in the least embarrassing to the fathers, who are extremely affectionate and proud to show off their young. It is not unusual to see a player in the *gamelan* orchestra holding on his knees for two or three hours his small child, while he reaches around it, beating the keys of his resounding instrument.

As the children grow older, the boys tend to clan together in groups of their own age, whereas the girls stay more closely beside their mothers. One often sees a gang of small boys playing in the village street, flying kites made of a leaf or a captive dragonfly, or playing "jacks" or gambling games with pebbles. In contrast to their elders, they do run, skip, and tumble, but rarely does the play take a rough turn. Quarrels consist of brusque words and threatening gestures on the part of the stronger child, while the weaker immediately assumes an attitude of submission, or, if he is struck, utters the plaintive "*adoh!*" equivalent to our "ouch!" The utterance of this pain word seems to satisfy the oppressor, who desists. I never witnessed nor heard of a case where one small boy "beat up" another. Certainly the hierarchy of ages recognized in any family group tends to discourage fighting, for every child knows that he is allowed to "speak down to," scold, and order about his younger brothers and cousins, just as he himself is spoken down to and ordered about by brothers and all relatives older than he. The system works smoothly, for, if one is humiliated by an elder, one may take out one's venom on a younger member of the familiar group. The accumulation of ill-humor does not fall too heavily upon the youngest child, for he can always take refuge behind the protective skirts of the mother, who is older and therefore in authority, over his oppressor. So are the scales balanced.

Very small girls are sometimes seen in the company of the boys who play in the streets. But by the time the girls reach the age of responsibility—seven or eight—they are more apt to remain in the house-court with the mother, taking a part in her work. Or if they are seen along the road, they carry on their hip a younger child entrusted to their care.[5] These diminutive nursemaids saunter up and down, or stand watching the play of the boys, prevented from joining in the activity by the responsibility and the actual weight of their charges. Girls do not play games, for gambling is a man's occupation. Neither can they share in one of the boys' favorite diversions, that of drumming away for hours on the instruments of the village orchestra, which are generally left in an open pavilion accessible to the children. This is another occupation which belongs to the men. The girls stand by watching and do not think of trying their hand at it, although they are not actually forbidden to do so. I have known one or two girls, dancers, who had developed quite a proficiency as musicians, but their cases were exceptional. In the same way girls are not expected to paint and draw. When I sent out a call to a number of villages for the drawings of children from four to ten years, and distributed materials sufficient for all, not a single girl sent in a drawing, nor would the little girls of my own village attempt any drawings even under repeated encouragement. Yet these same girls are learning from their mothers the complicated arts of making offerings, cutting designs from palm leaf, and weaving.

Behavior at the Plays

Whenever there is a performance of dancing, drama, or the shadow show, the entire village attends. The audience is packed closely around the four sides of the "stage"—an oblong of level ground marked off with bamboos. The first arrivals squat as near as possible, folded up into the least possible space and pressed against each other,

---

[5] Boys also carry babies, without shame, in imitation of their fathers who habitually dandle the small children.

the late comers stand in rows eight or ten deep at the back, the rear-most able to catch only an occasional glimpse of a performer's head-dress. In this tight formation the audience remains from the beginning, which for a play may be anywhere between the hours of nine and midnight to the end which comes about dawn. The whole temper of the audience is, from the actor's standpoint, ideal—watching, concentrated as one man, happy and pleasantly disposed in the warm contact of a large group of their kind, in festive mood, ready to enjoy themselves to the utmost. On the appearance of a hero, particularly graceful and gorgeous in his attire, a whispered "*bèh!*" of admiration issues from a hundred mouths; and when the clowns cavort or a rough joke is made, the entire audience rocks with mirth, the high shrieks of the women's laughter rising above the guffaws of the men. The smallest children, from two or three years upward, constitute the first rows of the audience surrounding the stage. They arrive long before the performers have any thought of beginning and sit, in quiet expectancy, sometimes for several hours before the play begins. If for any reason a child arrives late, he will with confidence squeeze his way through the crowd, pushing past people of higher rank and superior in age, to a good place in the very front. During the performance, the children watch every detail of the action with intentness.[6] Generally even the tiniest ones stay through the night, although they fall asleep for hours at a time and only manage to wake up for the most exciting parts, battles, or the enacting of bewitchment.

Older boys and girls, especially those who have passed adolescence, come to the performance in groups of two or three friends, the girls with their arms entwined about each other, the boys often holding hands. Such a group of boys will arrange to sit down in a place imme-diately behind a group of girls, so that, as the press in the audience increases, they will be huddled more and more together. It would be unseemly to stroke or to caress a member of the opposite sex in public. But if a girl is so placed that she must lean against one's knee, or her

---

[6] In connection with the close integration of the Balinese children with the life of their elders, one sees a parallel with the gentle and maternal Arapesh people, as described by Margaret Mead. She says of their children: "Games are played very seldom. More often the times when children are together in large enough groups to make a game worth while are the occasions of a feast, there is dancing and adult ceremonial, and they find the role of spectatorship far more engrossing." And again: "Early experience accustoms them to be part of the whole picture, to prefer to any active child-life of their own a passive part that is integrated with the life of the community." Margaret Mead, *Sex and Temperament* (New York, Morrow, 1935), pp. 57–58.

shoulder touch one's shoulder and her sleepy head droop, who can find fault? In the dim light—for the stage is illumined by only one or two flickering oil lamps, and the audience is in almost complete obscurity —flirtation is favored. Occasionally a girl rises and leaves the audience, to be followed after a short interval by the youth who has been seated near her. One supposes that a rendezvous has been arranged for a few moments of stolen love in the surrounding darkness.

Development of Decorum

By the time boys and girls have fully matured, they must behave with the decorous composure proper for adults. A boy of fifteen who belonged to my household was sometimes guilty of acts of clumsiness or thoughtless irresponsibility. He broke a plate in the washing of it, or he quietly made away with half a jar of the master's jam. These misdemeanors I was apt to excuse on the grounds of his youth. But the mature men were more stern with him. "Among us," they said, "a boy of that age is considered already big. He may not behave like a small child." Very marked was the change which came in Champlun, a talented little dancing girl, as she passed adolescence. When I first knew her she was a wiry child of eleven or twelve, the points of her breasts barely beginning to show. At that age she was a little devil, nervous and full of life, wriggling about, always up to some prank or mischief. A gifted mimic, she would make fun of anyone or anything and go off into hilarious laughter at her own jests, bending her slim body back and forth, slapping her thighs or the shoulder of any person who happened to be near her. Two years later she had grown tall, and her breasts had rounded out. She was no longer eligible to dance in the group of three little *légong* dancers of her village, although it was to a large extent her own talent which had made these dancers famous, so that they were in demand to play at festivals in the sur- rounding district. Champlun trained a new set of six-year-old dancers for her village. Then she was engaged by various other villages within a radius of ten or fifteen miles to train their dancers. The fact of her growing up was forcibly impressed upon her by the change in her social function. She began to behave with dignity: to carry herself decorously, to sit down carefully with both legs to one side, not sprawling anywhere, to speak when she was spoken to, to keep upon her face an habitual expression of composure. As she learned manners, she lost a great deal of the vivid, spontaneous charm of her personality. But in restraining her wild ways, she acquired a new charm, that of a demure and gracious feminine creature. When still another year had passed (which would make her about fourteen or fifteen), I saw her dance again, demonstrating before a new pupil. By this time the restraint in her bearing had become natural to her, and the change was strangely reflected in her dancing. She went through the dance in which she had so excelled as a child, without the slightest deviation from the traditional motions, postures, and step figures which she had always used—and yet the whole flavor of the dance was different. Instead of the wiry, electric little body whose sticklike arms bent in sharp angles, accenting the beat of the music, whose fingers quivered in the classical hand positions, whose little head sat stiffly on a rigid neck, whose feet stamped out with tense exactitude the vibrant music —instead of this stylized, puppetlike figure was a woman, with rounded arms, and hands of classical perfection, on her face a blank composure almost beautiful, who moved forward sedately, or glided sideways with easy grace, her curves softening the intended angles of the postures. This smooth performance of an accomplished dancer, now grown to maturity, had a beauty of its own. But it was not *légong* dancing as it should be. Seeing it, one could not help agreeing with the Balinese, who say that only children can dance *légong*. For the very grace and womanliness of a bigger girl infuse a disturbing element into the dance, which is in its essence sexless, impersonal, acute, and pure in its stylization.

Champlun still laughs and makes jokes, and her eyes snap with merriment. But her role has changed from that of a talented child to that of an unwed maiden, whose behavior shows modesty and restraint —for those are the qualities which will attract a desirable husband.

Etiquette in Speech, Posture, and Manners

I have tried to give a suggestion of the strict order in the behavior of the Balinese people, and how this order is dictated by their way of life, their social and religious concepts, which hold them to a rigid pattern of what is fitting. In the use of language, as in other matters, definite and complex rules must be followed. The Balinese language, rich in terms with minutely differentiated meanings, is also stratified into words of all levels, which may be roughly subdivided into High and Low Balinese. Low Balinese is the familiar and current language, used between members of a family and to all friends and intimates, except when there is a disparity of caste between the speakers. A man of low caste must address his social superior in High Balinese, and he will be answered in Low. The matter is further complicated when a man of intermediate caste is being discussed, for the commoner must

choose a word in referring to him neither so low as to be insulting to
the ears of the noble he is addressing, nor so high as to be discourteous,
for the very highest words should be reserved for reference to the
noble himself.[7] Special words are to be used only in reference to
animals, and to apply one of these lowest words to a man constitutes
an unforgivable insult. Strangers who meet address each other in
High Balinese, asking "Whence do you come? Where are you
going?" and follow this immediately with a leading question designed
to discover the rank of the interlocutor, so that the language appropriate to him may be at once adopted. There is no "farewell" in the
language. Visitors must ask their host's permission to depart, and the
answer to this request may be either the common "yes," a dismissal,
or a choice of a polite word for "go," carrying a courteous inflection
because of the relative highness of the word used.

Less complex, but equally rigid, rules prescribe the actual way of
sitting. Both men and women habitually squat on their heels, and
this is the position most readily assumed when anyone stops for a
moment what he is doing, either for conversation or for a short rest
from hard labor (and it may be noted in passing that the Balinese
seem to take, automatically, a rest of five or ten minutes out of every
hour of hard work; look at any ten men at work in the sun, and two
will be sitting under a tree; half an hour later, two others will be
resting). The squatting position may also be held over long periods,
in the fulfillment of any task conveniently done on or near the
ground, such as the playing of certain musical instruments, or the
chopping and hashing of foodstuffs on a wooden block, in preparation
for a feast. In taking the position the Balinese, be he a man of eighty
or a child of eight, lowers himself with the back held straight, at the
same time pulling the loincloth with his two hands tight over the
thighs, so that the folds will not hang and expose him indecently.
Women are, of course, equally modest, and the little girls learn this
trick earlier than the boys, for they are generally given a strip of
cloth to wrap around them at the age of four or five, whereas the boys
run naked several years longer.

Women sit with their legs bent back from the knees, both legs to
one side. They may not take the cross-legged position which is proper
for the men. A high priest, who has a right to the place of honor, will
on entering a European house choose not the most softly cushioned,

---

[7] It is as if we were to choose between the expressions "he has eaten," "he has
dined," and "he has partaken of his repast."

but the highest chair, and he will cross his legs upon the seat of it. Certain ascetics of noble caste, who have bound themselves to strict rules of behavior, may not sit down to eat facing in any direction except north or east. In the palaces of the nobility men of humble rank may sit or squat, but they are not allowed to stand or walk while a prince is seated. When they have to move about, fulfilling orders, they advance in a half-crouching position. So strongly felt is the matter of relative height that a man may ask one's permission before venturing to climb up a coconut tree to bring one refreshment.

The Balinese prefer to eat alone, and it is forbidden to speak to anyone who is eating. To speak to him would anger the god that is in him.[8] In some villages there used to be a fine imposed on any man who entered another's house and disturbed him while he was eating. Of this fine, part was paid directly to the affronted person, part to the community, in compensation for disturbing the peace. Within the household there is no sitting down to a family meal. Each member takes his leaf plate of rice at his own pleasure, carrying it off into a corner, often turning his back on his friends and relatives.[9] It is only proper to take food in the right hand while eating, although of course both hands are used in the preparation of it. Along the roads, at the markets, and at all performances are little stalls where refreshments are sold. But I have known several Balinese who said it was improper to eat in the street, and that they were "too ashamed" to do it.

The feeling of modesty—no other word seems to apply—attached to eating does not apply to drinking, and anyone will drink anywhere, without making a fuss about it. Similarly no shame is felt for urinating, which is done by both men and women along the public roads, in the open fields, anywhere except within the house-court or on holy ground. But for defecating the people retire to relative privacy, "where the pigs are," out of sight. The many pigs and dogs act as scavengers and may be relied upon to do away with all the filth.

Where there are gushing springs, bathing places are constructed, with walls dividing off the place of the women from that of the men. When the rivers are used for bathing, the sexes divide into groups, the men taking the upstream position, the women the downstream. But within each group modesty is shown, and the genitals may not be

[8] Here again, indigestion as a disturbance of bodily well-being is to be feared and avoided.

[9] In my own house I often surprised a boy or girl crouching alone in a dark cupboard absorbing the allotted plateful of rice, while a merry group who were not at the moment eating sat chatting without.

exposed even to a member of the same sex. The men cover themselves
with one hand, the women lift their skirts gradually, and suddenly
plunge waist deep in the water. Dressing and undressing may be done
in public by both men and women, for their clothes are of such a
nature than they can be changed without immodesty.[10]

Manifestations of the Emotional Life

The Balinese are universally afraid in the dark, and the fear of *léyak*,
living male and female sorcerers in supernatural form, is intensified
between the hours of midnight and dawn, when these creatures are
supposed to roam. Even grown boys and men will not visit at night
unholy places such as the graveyard, the crossroads, certain trees and
bridges where supernatural manifestations are frequent. They are
afraid to walk along the dark village streets at night, unless accompanied, but if a man must go alone he sings in a loud voice to frighten
away the *léyak*, or to keep his spirits up. His house-court is his haven.
The encircling clay walls, the high ceremonial entrance gate, and the
magic strip of wall immediately within this gate (to block the path of
evil spirits) give him a feeling of security, sleeping upon the open
pavilions. But he prefers not to sleep alone. If he has passed the age
when he wishes to sleep next to his wife, he will take one or two of his
little sons to bed with him. Small children sleep with their parents or
grandparents, or huddle in a group together. When a group of men
who are strangers are passing through a village, they may take shelter
for the night in the men's communal pavilion which stands by the
roadside—an unprotected place. They curl up as close as possible to
each other, like young puppies, the body of one curving around that
of his neighbor, with often an arm or a leg thrown over him. A group
may be so compact that if one turns over the whole group must turn.
The language contains terms for light and heavy sleepers, but as a
rule they sleep soundly and are hard to rouse. They are afraid to
awaken each other, lest the soul of the sleeper be wandering. But the
taboo seems to imply more danger to the one doing the awakening
than the one awakened, for a boy who says "I do not dare to wake
him" will show no objection if a foreigner takes upon himself the
responsibility of awakening one of his fellows.

As has been mentioned, a man may not touch a woman, even his

[10] For the breasts, of course, the women show no modesty at all. It is only the
region from the knees to the waist which must never be exposed. The Balinese feel
about exposure of the thighs of women as Westerners feel about their breasts, and a
woman in a Western bathing suit is extremely shocking to them for that reason.

wife, before others. He may not touch a woman's clothes, nor should his clothes touch hers, as, for instance, in a trunk. If it is necessary to pack them together, the man's clothes must be on top. But in the privacy supplied by darkness the taboos are lifted. Lovers and married people may caress each other freely. Favorite caresses are the *chium*, the affectionate or passionate "sniff" which replaces our kiss, and the *saling ngaras*, "exchange of strokings," a term applied to the rubbing of cheek on cheek, both slowly turning their heads from side to side, so that the lips do come into play as they brush past each other. Love scenes depicted in the paintings and described in the literature suggest that many of the refinements of the art of love which belong to Hindu tradition have been taken over by the Balinese. But for reasons of their own, which have already been made sufficiently clear, the Balinese do not use the reversed posture, nor may the woman be above. In sexual play only the left hand may be used, since the right is used for eating.

A woman is popularly supposed to have within her a *manik*. The term *manik* is applied to jewels and to a sprite which sits in coconut trees and is pursued by Kilap Krèbèk Gĕrudug, Thunder-and-Lightning, who, when he catches the *manik*, causes the coconut tree to be burnt up. But the *manik* in a woman is of a different sort. In sexual intercourse her *manik* is repeatedly "hit," and this contact causes it to become larger and larger until it becomes a child. After the birth of the child, she gets a new *manik*. It is possible, though by no means sure, that the Balinese conceive orgasm of both man and woman to be caused when the male organ finally achieves contact with the *manik*.[11]

Although a free display of the affection between the sexes, except in private, is forbidden, the Balinese have a strong tendency to hold on to and caress each other in all relations where no sexual connotation is implied. Fathers and mothers, grandfathers and grandmothers, love to fondle the young children, to press their faces into them and

---

[11] The reproductive function of semen is not unknown to them, as is illustrated in the popular legend of the creation of Kală, to whom Sivă gave birth alone, by producing a single drop of semen. The parallel with the *manik* idea is, however, interestingly carried out in the legend, for it is only on being repeatedly struck by the arrows of the gods that the drop of semen becomes alive, gets arms and legs, a head, genitals, etc., and finally stands up and shouts, a fully formed Kală. It is difficult to tell whether the theme of the repeated striking refers to the rhythmic motion of copulation, or to an idea that a single sexual act is not sufficient to cause the development of the embryo, and that the man must continue to "strike" during gestation, so that the child will grow.

"sniff" them, just as in the relation between a man and a woman. Two girls, two boys, or two bearded ancients will stroll along a road holding hands or with their arms about each other. Such gestures should not be misconstrued as evidences of homosexuality, for they are no more than the habitual expressions of a demonstratively affectionate people.

Manifestations of anger are remarked much less frequently than those of love, fear, and affection in the everyday life. An equable temper is certainly the characteristic one among the Balinese. If a man is easily angered, he is said to have *kepala angin*, a Malay expression meaning "a windy head." Although one often hears voices raised in explosive and admonitory speech, they can hardly be said to be expressing anger, for among the adults, as among the children, superiors have always the right to call down their inferiors, an elder brother to speak harshly to a younger, a man to "order" (never simply to ask) his wife to do something for him. Each Balinese is habituated to thinking of himself as relatively more or less powerful than all the other members of his familiar group. And if he is less powerful, he obeys naturally and usually without remonstrance. By contrast, in larger groups, such as communal organizations, whose members are on a less intimate footing with each other, great care is taken to preserve the equality between the members. Each man is reluctant to appear to be giving an order or dictating in any way to his social equal. For this reason, in any group of workers the man whom we would call the "foreman" seems always inefficient and lacking in administrative powers; and the resulting accomplishment has a lively, if haphazard, character, brought about by the enthusiasm of the various individuals working together virtually without a leader. One has the impression that it is fear of angering his fellows which prevents the Balinese from assuming a dominant attitude toward persons outside of his familiar group.

When anger does appear, it usually follows the pattern of the Malay "running amok," also recognized in Bali. The literature is filled with episodes in which a man, even a prince or *rajă*, who is overcome with grief or thwarted in his desires, "becomes confused in his mind, and retires to his sleeping apartment, where he lies for many days and many nights, refusing both food and drink." This brooding state is the first stage in the pattern, when the man remains alone, nursing his grievances, until he has worked himself into a trancelike state, and he will have the strength to rush out and commit deeds of violence. Tales of warriors describe the stirring-up of anger before going into combat; and all war dances have brooding passages interspersed between the gestures and expressions of fierce and terrifying advance. Bravery in itself is not highly valued. It is considered more natural for a man to be under the sway of fear than of anger. A man shows no embarrassment over his fear—he says quite simply, "I do not dare," whether the project in question is a midnight visit to the graveyard, or climbing a coconut tree on a day of the astrological calendar when it is forbidden. The things which a man will not dare to do are those which the experience of his forbears have shown to be unwise, and to behave with intrepidity without good reason would be to court disaster, not only for himself but perhaps for the whole community.

Deviants

We have seen that in such a social scheme each individual has his place, and he has only to do what is expected of him to fit with nicety into the life of the group. But there are occasions when an individual finds it impossible to conform, and at these times disturbance and maladjustment appear. Certain temperaments, for instance, are not amenable to the national habit of submissive obedience. Women with fiery dispositions may run away from their husbands, taking shelter with their own families and refusing to return, or departing with a lover.[12] A small boy of eight told the following story of his rebellion against his father's authority, the events described having occurred when he was no more than six or seven:

My father beat my mother too hard, and I became too angry. Then my father beat me very hard. I followed him when he went out to work in the rice fields. I took money from the pocket of his jacket which he had laid down on the edge of the fields. I ran away. For a month I did not go home.

With the money I bought rice in the market, and I stayed out all day in the rice fields, and I never saw my father and my mother. At night I would go into the house of one of my other fathers [uncles] and sleep with the children. My father and mother did not know where I was. Then one day my mother saw me. She wept, and begged me to come home. I went home.

My father was only silent.

In this encounter, since the father did not beat him on his return, the child seems to have triumphed over the man.

Another deviant is Madé, who rebelled not so much against paternal authority as against the prescribed rules of tradition. He is a young man of impulsive temperament, with ways unusually quick and

[12]For cases of runaway wives see Belo's "A Study of a Balinese Family," in this volume, pp. 367–68.

nervous in a Balinese, quick to laugh and quick to be angered, extremely efficient when engaged in tasks which interest him, lazy and unreliable at all other tasks. Born in a small hamlet far from the town, and at several miles' distance from the motor road, he decided when still a boy to become a chauffeur. He left his farmer parents and went to live with relatives in the town. There he attended school, learned to speak Malay, and began to pick up from older boys the knowledge of his chosen trade. He served his apprenticeship with them, receiving their teaching in return for the performance of menial duties. When he had sufficient knowledge, he in turn got a job as chauffeur and was able to marry, buying with the money he earned the rice which he had not been able to raise on his family land. (So strong is the farming background in Balinese life that any man who has had employment and loses it, automatically goes back to tilling the land until he can find new work.) Although Madé is skillful as a driver and mechanic, he is not very successful. The very qualities which made him turn from the environment and occupation to which he was born, and to which his forbears had for generations conformed, impede his progress as a chauffeur. He refuses to carry out orders unless it pleases him. He is impatient with any part of his work which is not mechanical. He will drive tirelessly for several hundred miles and cheerfully apply himself to any necessary repairs in a breakdown. But if after a short journey he is asked to lift out a parcel from the car, he calls another to do it for him—a very unusual thing in Balinese who are not of high caste, as they are universally reluctant to ask their equals to serve them. Another unusual quality is his lack of the sense of relaxation common to most Balinese. Generally they will sit for hours without impatience, waiting for something to happen, and they seem to find pleasant the state of doing nothing. Often they drop off to sleep. But Madé could not be left alone for ten minutes in a car; he would be off on some errand of his own, to bargain for coconuts or to flirt with some pretty girl at a market stall. He took rebukes from his masters with ill grace, flaring up in insolence or sulking and glowering to himself. To cover up his impetuosity and his shirking of explicit orders, he developed habits of dishonesty. All these things caused him to make an unsatisfactory chauffeur, and he repeatedly lost his position, whether he worked for Europeans or for Chinese or Arab car owners. He is an impulsive spender, vain about his costume and the prestige afforded him by his possessions. The money that he earns is soon gone, and he will probably never save enough, as many of the young men do, to buy a secondhand car of his own. This is the case of an unusually ill-adapted Balinese. It is curious to note that such a type cannot adjust itself to the new order any more than to the old. He makes many friends and many enemies among the Balinese. Men and women respond to his spontaneous charm, his vivacity and gaiety as a companion. But in his friendly relations he is always getting into trouble, for he will not stick to the rules of the game.

The Force of Tradition

It is in contemplating the character of such a man that one realizes, in contrast, how closely the majority of the Balinese do conform to the scheme laid down by tradition, and how well-mannered, balanced, and relaxed they appear. The babies do not cry, the small boys do not fight, the young girls bear themselves with decorum, the old men dictate with dignity. Every one carries out his appointed task, with respect for his equals and superiors, and gentleness and consideration for his dependents. The people adhere, apparently with ease, to the laws governing the actions, big and small, of their lives. Since the material conditions of their existence have remained for many hundreds of years static, it has been possible for these laws to grow up, to be sifted and tested over a long period, until they have reached a code eminently suitable to the people whom they govern. For this reason it becomes easy for the child to take over the ways of his elders —the more forcibly impressed upon him because of the weight of tradition behind them, and the fear of transgressing the laws which have been shown by experience to be acceptable to the ever-present gods and demons. Actually the child is afforded no choice at all under the sanction of the community. He has only to obey the prescriptions of tradition to become an adult happily adjusted to the life which is his. And if the child is a girl, she begins very early to feel how her role is differentiated from that of a boy. The women accept without rancor the role of an inferior. It is simply that they have their being on a different plane from the men. In a society with so many stratifications, that of age within the family, of rank and of relative wealth as between families, the place of woman as an inferior is not seen as a hardship. The system of stratification works smoothly as a rule, and all those individuals who conform to it seem happy. It is a part of the very order which gives to the life of the Balinese its stability.

When the Rules May Be Broken

The Balinese way of life even provides an organized release from the rigid code, times when individuals who feel the need of it may break

almost all the rules of decorum. These are the occasions of intense and
fevered group activity. There is no space here to describe these manifestations in detail, and a few examples of what I mean must suffice.
In the prolonged and enthusiastic rehearsals of musicians, actors, and
dancers, when all work together in a group, no attention is paid to
relative rank, and a performer of noble birth takes his place in
equality with the group—he sits on a level with his social inferiors
and bows to their will in matters of artistic production, if their talent
be superior to his. At communal feasts men who are accustomed to
eating in private gather in groups to partake of the unusual viands
and delicacies which they have prepared. Here the taboos do not quite
break down, for although they regale themselves with relish, no conversation is allowed between the members feasting together. At the
celebration of cremations, several hundred men together cast off their
habitual carefully poised bearing, and, taking up the body of their
friend, or the tower which is to convey him to the cremation place,
they shout, they leap, they lift their arms in threatening gestures,
they whirl around and around in a mass of vigorously stamping,
kicking, and entangled limbs, falling down, trampling upon their
fellows, hurling themselves into a pool of mud and besplattering each
other with howls of glee. Again, a group of villagers wishing to divine
the will of the gods goes into trance—tears stream down the face of a
young girl, a woman sobs hysterically, an old man trembles as in an
ague, a youth with rolling eyes and thrashing limbs tries to force
burning coals into his mouth. Or in a ceremony for the propitiation
of the King of Demons, in the form of a grotesque figure of a lion, a
group of men and boys clusters about, shouting, prancing, pressing
with all the strength of both arms the point of a kris into their own
naked chests. One holds the handle of the weapon on the ground, with
the point upward, and hurls his body upon it, throwing both feet in
the air so that he will strike with all his weight. The term *ribut*, a
Malay word meaning "storm," is applied to a group in such an
excited state. Acting under the powerful stimulus of mass emotion,
each man forgets to be cautious, to be dignified, to be afraid. The
minor fears of pain and bodily disturbance are for the time forgotten.
When the frenzy is carried to the pitch of trance, the Balinese is to a
great extent in a state of anesthesia, able to dance upon hot coals or to
wound himself with a dagger (although they themselves say that if
the trance is sufficiently deep the flesh will resist the dagger and no
wound will be sustained). But even without trance, every individual
who participates in the excitement is free to break the rules without

experiencing fear or shame for his unusual behavior. He is secure in the consciousness that he is one of many, that the crowd moves as he does.

It has seemed necessary to mention, however briefly, these forms of activity which are in sharp contrast to the slow deliberate tempo, the quiet dignity and balanced equilibrium of the habitual movements. For the Balinese at their daily tasks lead a life of reserved, steady—almost plodding—application to hard labor, made easier by the absolute lack of tension or of any pressure from the sense of time, and by the rhythmic flow of their motions interspersed with suitable periods of rest. But this existence, they say, is dull and lonely without festivals and celebrations. Luckily their religion provides many occasions for celebration, and at these times the people burst forth in a riot of true *fun*, when all together they adorn themselves, they take part with enthusiasm in the elaborate preparation of offerings and the decoration of the temples, they enjoy to the utmost presentations of dancing, music, and drama, which the religion prescribes. It is significant that the audience for these presentations takes as much delight in them as the performers. Their own arts are to them completely satisfying, a fulfillment in the life of the people for whom they have been evolved. At such festivals one is impressed by the joyousness, the gaiety with which the Balinese seem carried away. And just as these joyous occasions punctuate the dreary round of everyday life, so do the occasions of wild frenzy break into it, affording the individual a necessary release. If it were not for these organized departures from the habitual tempo, it would not be possible for the individual to conform, at all other times, to the rigid order of behavior which is exacted from him. And therefore we must recognize the two aspects, the quiet, relaxed, and peaceful tenor of the private life, and the intense and spontaneous exaltation of group activity, both of which are essential to the Balinese temper.

Interpretation

In conclusion, perhaps it will be well to stress once more the ease and relaxation in the ordinary behavior of the Balinese, so that an impression will not be left that any strain is caused by need to maintain a balanced equilibrium and a perfect orientation in social and geographical respects. On the contrary, the rules by which they abide seem to supply a simplication of behavior. For the Balinese life is divided into two phases quite opposed to those of the modern city dweller in our world; the Balinese works in relaxation, and in his pleasure finds intense stimulation, whereas our city dweller works under a strain of intense stimulation and for his pleasure seeks relaxation. If there should be any doubt of the difference in tension between the two psychological types, let us imagine how the city dweller would react to certain conditions in Balinese life, as, for instance, living in a courtyard shared by ten or fifteen members of his immediate family, divided only by pavilions without walls; or sleeping in such close proximity as has been described, with a number of others; or enjoying a dramatic performance lasting for eight or nine hours, crouched in a press of bodies comparable only to one of our subway jams. These things do not offend nor put any strain upon the Balinese, because of the relaxation of his mood. Likewise he is able to wait for long periods without showing impatience, and to accept with composure frustration of his plans, saying simply, "It did not happen." It may be said that the agricultural way of life, requiring suitable physical exertion, and producing in a direct way the food supply, so that there may be no anxiety about it for anyone, contributes to the mental poise of the people; also that the children are surrounded with affection and given very early a part in the work of the family group, so that they grow up feeling beloved and useful, which gives to them as individuals a sense of security. And because the rules for orientation, posture, facial expression, speech, and so forth are so universally accepted, they soon become habitual and are carried out automatically by the people without any conscious application, without any of the strain which they would cause to us. The immutability of all the laws of conduct relieves the individual of any responsibility except that of obeying them. He does not doubt their rightness, since they have always been so. And since they are his habits, he does not have even to think of them. Beyond this, his only cares are specific misfortunes, which may always occur, but which he considers outside his power to control. Illness, flood, and famine— these are signs of the anger of the gods, and of the dominance, for the time, of the forces of evil. The religious concepts make the cause clear, and they supply, too, the remedy. Offerings must be prepared, purifications and celebrations carried out, for the propitiation of the demons and the glorification of the gods. Although it may seem to us that the Balinese lives in ever-present fear of demons and of evil spirits, the strain is actually not great because the remedy is known and prescribed. Even in some cases charged with much superstitious fear, such as the birth of unlucky twins or the occurrence of certain forms of incest, when the entire village is rendered unclean, tradition takes care of the wrong by requiring temporary banishment of the offenders and elaborate purification rituals. In this way the burden of responsibility is lifted from the offenders and their fellow-villagers who are affected. Tradition tells them what to do in compensation for the wrong. When it is done, no weight of sin or guilt rests on the individual. He has in such matters, as in all other aspects of his life, no choice, no decisions to be made, only the responsibility to maintain the order which he and his society consider established and proved. To judge how suitable and how desirable is such an order, we can only take the evidence of Balinese behavior as it appears to us. If we see in the equilibrated, delicately adjusted, and essentially unstrained behavior of the people the clue to their happy temper, we must conclude that a static traditional culture such as theirs, solving all problems, prescribing every act, does form a desirable background against which well-balanced personalities may be reared.

An Old Temple and a New Myth

GREGORY BATESON

Introductory Note

FOR EUROPEANS and indeed for most of the peoples of the world, the past has some curious smell of romance, some strange enchantment. Not only the poet, the daydreamer, the historian, and the archaeologist but even priests, politicians, journalists, schoolmasters, fathers of families—the very men who do most to shape our thoughts and opinions—are subjects to this same magic which leads them sometimes to dignity and greatness, sometimes to folly, sometimes to revolt. We may without exaggeration say that our attitude toward the past is as fundamental a part of our civilization as are our attitudes toward God, private property, marriage, food, and the rest, and it is interesting to see that when we make "a break with the past" as Russia has tried to do, when we monkey with our religion and our laws of property and marriage, that the same attitude toward the past survives the "break" and we go on pilgrimages to the tomb of Lenin.

It is not my purpose to ask whether this attitude toward the past is "good" or "bad," a question which every reader if he consults his emotions can settle for himself without a moment's thought; nor need we ask whether the stories of the past which we put in books and tell to our children are true—a question which would involve us in a sort

Originally published in *Djawa*, XVII, No. 5–6 (1937), 291–307. Reprinted with permission of the author.

Author's note: "The material contained in this paper was collected by my wife (Dr. Margaret Mead, who is working with me on behalf of the American Museum of Natural History), my secretary (I Madé Kalèr, a young Balinese of Bulèlèng who has had a very good Surabaya education), and myself (working as William Wyse, student of Cambridge University). I therefore owe a heavy debt both to those who helped in collecting the material and to the academic bodies who have financed the work.

of weighing of inadequate evidence more appropriate in a law court than in scientific study. The task of the social anthropologist is not to stand in judgment but to examine social systems and to compare them one with another in order to increase understanding of how they work.

If we compare our attitude toward the past with that of the Balinese, we find at first a certain superficial resemblance; in both civilizations we find ancient writings, scraps of the past, and, especially,

"Our notes, even without the photographs and ciné records, on the events here narrated would, if published *in extenso*, run to a bulk three or four times the size of this paper, and I have therefore omitted almost all details of ceremonial, all technical details of offerings, and all details of the behavior of known individuals except where such behavior illustrated the special subject of the paper; the attitudes of the Balinese of Bayung Gĕdé toward the past, toward trance, and toward sociological symbols.

"Some explanation of the social organization of Bayung Gĕdé is necessary in order to make clear the meaning of some of the native terms. The religious life of the village is regulated by a hierarchy which includes all the full citizens, men who are married or have some woman to cook for them. A man rises in this hierarchy by the death or retirement of those above him, and he is compelled by the hierarchy to perform the ceremonies necessary for his rising. Various disabilities may prevent a man from attaining full citizenship—lack of sufficient children if he is married, incompleteness of his body (for example, a lost fingernail or a torn ear lobe), and so forth. Other disabilities may prevent his rising to the top of the hierarchy. The top sixteen men of the hierarchy are called *dulu* or *guru*, and of these the two highest have the title *kubayan*, while the third and fourth have the title *bau*.

"One other official is of very great importance, and she is a woman with the title *balian*. She is the chief officiant at almost all ceremonies, sprinkling, praying, purifying, and so forth; and at almost all ceremonies she goes into trance, possessed either by deities or by the souls of the dead, according to the nature of the ceremony. She is almost the only channel through which the spirit world communicates with the village.

"Two other groups need mention, the club of maidens, or *da* (called in some parts of Bali *daha*), and the club of youths, or *teruna*. The senior unmarried son and daughter in each household with full citizenship are members respectively of these clubs. The clubs perform certain special ritual functions, and the members have a certain degree of ritual purity.

"Translation: I Madé Kalèr's accounts are all written in Balinese, and he is trained to record the actual words which are used. The language of Bayung has a very terse, clipped syntax, and the texts would therefore be unintelligible without many insertions in the translation. I have therefore put in many extra words in brackets, but I have contrived where possible to make the explanatory phrases fit in with the syntax of the translated sentence. The brackets indicate that what is in them has been *added* to the native sentence by the writer. In some cases, also, translation has seemed inadequate, and therefore the native words are provided in parentheses after the translation, for the benefit of experts in Indonesian ethnology, who may need something more precise than the translation. In the translations, I have taken great pains not to distort the sense of actual spoken words, but I have allowed myself somewhat more liberty in handling Madé Kalèr's descriptions, supplementing them here and there, omitting some passages and changing the order of others."

objects in metal and stone preserved in temples—*peretima* or
relics. The archaeologist, whether in Europe or in Bali, is equally
indebted for his material to these accumulations, and it is interesting
to ask whether it is the same attitude toward the past which leads
both Europeans and Balinese into these magpie habits.

Even the most fleeting tourist in Bali will find that there are
differences between the two cultures in their attitudes toward the
past. A native seller may bring a load of objects which the tourist
must surely want to buy because they are "old." Such collections are
worth a moment's attention and may contain such curiosities as the
rusty bottom of an old "Storm King" lamp. The Balinese, after all,
are not stupid; they know well enough that the European attitude
toward the past is different from their own, and as sellers they try to
exploit this curious freak. The tourist, without realizing how the
blunder occurred, may laugh at it without realizing that his own
desire to buy "a real old piece" is a curious by-product of his own
unique civilization.

It has been my privilege to watch some Balinese in their dealing
with the ancient past, and their behavior was sufficiently interesting
to be worth record and analysis.

The village of Bayung Gĕdé, in the district of Kintamani, is
inhabited by agricultural peasants. They are simple people and poor
by Balinese standards, but they have their own aloofness and their
own customs which they follow almost regardless of the more fancy
customs of the richer peoples in the plains. Bayung, like Tenganan,
has a satellite village outside its boundaries and this is called Pĕludu.
People from Bayung who do not obey the local rules—for example,
men who have two wives—go to live in Pĕludu, and people from other
communities who acquire land in Bayung (generally by lending
money) come to live in Pĕludu to work the land while gradually they
become citizens of Bayung. Pĕludu is a community which has grown
enormously within native memory. Two generations ago there were
only three households in Pĕludu, and now there are many. They live
together on very friendly terms, without any of the stiffness and the
quarrels characteristic of Bayung. They have their own small temple,
complete with *balé agung* (ceremonial meetinghouse), *balé pĕbatan*
(cooking-house), *penegtegan* (central altar supported on living trees),
and a number of other shrines. It is a miniature of the bigger *pură
balé agung* in Bayung itself.

Three kilometers down the road to the south of Pĕludu and nearer
to the richer cultures of the plains is another new village called

Katung. This is a colony from Kayubihi,[1] an important village on the Bangli-Kintamani road. Thus Katung is a recent neighbor of Bayung and Pĕludu and differs from them in having a richer—more varied and more spectacular—culture.

These three communities form the setting in which the old temple and the scrap of new myth, mentioned in the title of the paper, found their place as links between the three communities.

Preliminaries of the God's Visit

On March 16, 1937, a priest from Katung, Pĕmangku Meling, visited Bayung and, after an interview with the *guru*, he came to our house to ask for medicine for his eyes. This was our first intimation of the forthcoming events. He said that he had come to verify that there were no difficulties in the way of a visit from a goddess in Katung; that, if there were no deaths in Bayung which would make the community ceremonially inactive and dirty (*sĕbĕl*), a formal deputation (*pĕjati*) would come from Katung with the appropriate offerings, which he described in detail. We asked him why the goddess from Katung was proposing to visit Bayung, and he said that the talk had come from a woman in a trance at a temple feast (*odalan*) in the *purǎ balé agung* in Katung. The possessing deity was a goddess and gave her name as I Déwǎ Ayu Mas Kĕtut. She said that she was a daughter of a goddess in Bayung and that she had a sibling, *sĕmeton*,[2] named I Déwǎ Manik Tirtǎ in Abuhan. The *pĕmangku* was unable to give the name of the goddess in Bayung.

Later events produced several changes in this list of deities, but there is no reason to believe that the *pĕmangku's* information was inaccurate at the time it was given except for one small detail which he seems to have inserted from some sort of modesty or shyness—other informants told us that the talk had come, not from a woman, but from the *pĕmangku* himself in trance.

After this conversation, we sent our secretary, I Madé Kalèr, to ask Bau Tekek, the village expert on religious and especially calendrical matters, why the god from Katung was coming to Bayung. Madé reports the conversation as follows:

On the day after the *pĕmangku* came from Katung, I went to Bau Tekek to ask him about Katung's bringing their god. Bau Tekek answered: "Yes, the *guru* are talking about that."

[1] For notes on the customs of Kayubihi and the founding of Katung, see "'Kajoebii een Oud-Balische Bergdésa,' door I Déwa Poetoe Boekian," *Tijdschrift voor Indische Taal-, Land- en Volkenkunde*, LXXVI (1936), 127–76.

[2] *Sĕmeton* is a word which means either a brother or sister, without defining the sex.

Madé: What is the reason for bringing the god?

Tekek: Because Katung and Abuhan used to belong formerly to Bayung. The land of Katung used to be Bayung, and it was borrowed by Anak Agung Pekek of Kayubihi. It was given to them but, if there were contributions [levied for temple feasts, etc.], they were to help, and if [we] repaired [our] temple, they were to help too. And at that time they did really help with contributions, and they contributed to the repairing of the temple. But for a long time now they have never helped.

Madé: About the god in Katung—what relative is he of the god here?

Tekek: About that I really don't know—perhaps some sort of a relation (*pesemetonana*).

Madé: I heard they will bring a god from Abuhan too. What relation is the god of Abuhan to the god of Bayung?

Tekek: Abuhan too used to be part of the land of Bayung, but it was a forest. Later Pĕmangku Mual asked for it from the Government, and it was granted to him; so it became Abuhan.

Madé: If people are going to come with a god, what do they do first?

Tekek: They make certain first by asking the *guru* of the place to which they will take the god; and if they have been accepted by the *guru*, then they send a formal verification (*pĕjati*).

We may note that at this stage of the proceedings, Bau Tekek was by no means enthusiastic about the coming visit and that he was quite uninterested in the relationship between the gods, stressing rather the old relationship with Katung, in which Bayung had been in some sort landlords.

In due course, on March 20, the *pĕjati* came from Katung, a delegation of two men but without Pĕmangku Meling. The delegates were expected a little after midday, but they did not arrive till late in the afternoon, after the people of Bayung had finished some other ceremonies. The *guru* of Bayung were a little cross at this, and the meeting was rather strained. The conversation, as recorded by I Madé Kalèr, ran as follows:

Second *guru* of Bayung [tersely and with no politeness]: Yes, and now we have finished offering to the gods. What was our agreement? I thought [you were to come] when the sun just turned to the west.

Nang Ludri of Katung [polite and formal]: It was said that there was a ceremony here, and that was why we came at this time.

Second *guru* [without politeness]: In the southwest [that is, in Katung], what rank have you?

Nang Ludri [politely]: I am already a *guru* but the lowest of them. . . . I submit to you that it is the wish of the god that in going home He visit in Pĕludu.

Second *guru*: As to the *guru* in Pĕludu, they already agree [to that].

Nang Ludri [politely]: The *pĕmangku* [Meling] was to have come, but he went to Manguh.

The fourth *guru* of Bayung then introduced the *guru* of the Pĕludu temple to the delegates from Katung: This is the *kubayan*, and this the second *kubayan* and I am a *bau* [in Pĕludu].

Eighth *guru* of Bayung [in polite language]: The *pĕmangku* spoke about visiting here only.

Nang Ludri [politely]: Just after he arrived back from here, there was talk [from the gods] that the god should visit in Pĕludu.

Eighth *guru*: Bau Tekek said that the god's visit to Pĕludu should be received with a few small offerings only.

The eighth *guru* then went close to Nang Ludri and said [in polite language though his meaning was rude]: The fact is that there is no betel here. Would it not be as well to mention that?

Bau Tekek [a retired *bau* of Bayung and first *guru* of Pĕludu]: Even if you only come here for one night, you must visit in the west [that is, in Pĕludu].

The offerings which the delegates brought were then offered in the various shrines. They had brought a duplicate set of offerings intending to offer also in Pĕludu but the *guru* of Bayung said that they should offer them all in Bayung, and as they were strangers they followed the instructions of the local *guru*.

We may note that at the time of this visit there was still not much enthusiasm in Bayung about the affair, but that Bau Tekek is already changing his attitude. The eighth *guru* says that Bau Tekek had suggested minimizing the connection of the visit with Pĕludu but Bau Tekek is now anxious to welcome the god at Pĕludu.

The Visit of the God

The great day of the visit was fixed for March 24, and in the intervening days the people of Bayung gradually became more excited. They are not an excitable people, and, for the most part, they regard the coming of their own ceremonies with indifference. It is, after all, a little dull to go to a party to meet all the people whom you meet every day and to watch the dancers whom you have already seen rehearse and dance many times before. But this was different. The Bayung people were to be hosts to strangers who would bring with them all their dances—four *baris*[3] clubs and an opera which would play the Sampik story—and they would bring their village orchestra. All the dance clubs of Bayung planned to perform—four *baris* clubs,

---

[3] The *baris* dances of the mountains are formal set dances for groups of men. The performers are generally in square formation and hold some form of weapon, slowly posturing with it in their dance. The *baris* clubs of Bayung dance at all the larger village ceremonies when the orchestra is brought out, but they do not rehearse for these occasions. "If a god is coming to Bayung we rehearse"—that is, about once a year. The village orchestra never has rehearsals because the instruments are never taken out of their storehouse except for ceremonies. The only *baris* rehearsal that I have witnessed was unaccompanied by music.

the maidens' processional dance (*rejang*), the *jangèr* (a purely secular dance of young people), and possibly the little trance dancers (*sangh-yang déling*). Two of the *baris* clubs and the *jangèr* even went so far as to rehearse in preparation for the great occasion.

On the day of the visit, the chopping and preparing of food was all done before midday, and then a party from Bayung went to meet (*mendakin*) the god. The party consisted of maidens and youths and the seventh *guru*, and I Madé Kalèr went with them. The following details of what happened in Katung are extracted from Madé Kalèr's account:

They found the temple of the god in Katung, the Purǎ Sukemerih, almost empty, and of the six men who were there some went off to call the people while the rest went on with their work. One man only came and made conversation with our second *guru*. There was an orchestra in the temple, so—in order to make the Katung people hurry—the youths from Bayung went and played on the instruments. The *guru* from Bayung joined them, the second *guru* playing on the big gong, a dignified and important instrument but very easy to play. He was a fine figure of a man but not musical. The man who came to make conversation played on the cymbals.

Gradually the Katung people gathered in the temple, bringing their personal offerings and the official offerings of the village. They brought also the gods who were to go to Bayung. All the gods from all the temples were to go, and their seats (*tigasanǎ*, shrines built upon carrying poles) were brought to the Sukemerih temple. In addition, one god had been brought from Abuhan, but he had no *tigasanǎ*, only a basket containing a coconut, rice, money, and so forth (*tapakan*). The hamlet of Abuhan lies a little to the east of Katung and like Katung is a newly formed colony. The coming of the god from Abuhan was due to a trance utterance in Katung—that he should join his sibling in visiting their mother in Bayung.

A meal was laid out for the party from Bayung, and they ate there. After the meal, they offered to the gods of Katung the offerings which they had brought with them from Bayung. Then the whole crowd formed a procession which left Katung at 2:55 P.M.

The seats of the gods were càrried by the youths of Bayung, and others of the youths carried silver-bound spears. The *baris* dancers from Katung were all in costume, the maidens from both villages carrying offerings on their heads, men from Katung carrying their orchestra, and others with uncooked food, baskets of rice, a live pig, firewood, and seasoning.

The procession reached Bayung at about 4 P.M. and halted first in the ritual place (*tegal suchi*) to the west (*kauh*) of the origin temple (*puseh*). Here there were already offerings, laid out by the people who had stayed behind in Bayung. The procession formed up facing east, and the seats of the gods were maneuvered into line facing west. A short ceremony followed in which the *balian* of Bayung was the chief officiant. She sprinkled the offerings and offered them, while the *guru* of Bayung and the *pemangku* of Katung prayed beside her. These offerings (*banten pemendak*) were to greet the god, but the ritual of offering them was the same as for any temple feast (*odalan*) in Bayung.

After this short ceremony the offerings were lifted up again, and the whole procession moved on till they arrived, at 4:10 P.M., on the open space (*jaban pura*) south of the gate of the village temple (*pura balé agung*). Here again they found offerings (*banten penyembleh*) and mats ready spread, and again they formed up. This time the gods faced north (*kaja*) toward the temple which they were to enter, and the offerings included a black chicken. The Pemangku Meling chopped off its head, supporting its neck on a coconut; he then threw both the bird and the coconut forward toward the gods.

After this (at 4:15 P.M.) the procession entered the temple and stopped in front of the *penegtegan* (the tree altar). Again the seats of the gods were lined up, and offerings were spread. This time the gods faced south in accordance with the general orientation of the temple, and the same greeting offerings (*banten pemendak*) were offered. At 4:20 P.M. the whole layout was again moved, this time into the *balé paruman*, a building which is specially designed for ceremonial. Along the north wall is a high shelf, the highest place, on which the seats of the gods were set facing the officiants to the south. The mass of offerings was laid out on a much wider shelf below the gods, and the officiants, including the *balian* and the Pemangku Meling, sat side by side with the high *guru* of Bayung on two square platforms. On the floor, between and around the platforms, sat as many of the wives of the *guru* and the rest of the people as could find place. At the entrances to the building small crowds craned their necks to see and hear what was going on inside.

Such interest in ceremonial is unusual in Bayung and was in this case excited by the trance performances of the *balian* and Pemangku Meling. But first there was sprinkling and offering to be done, and, after some delay, Bau Tekek came and politely suggested to the *pemangku* that he should hurry because "the people have to go and fetch their cows" from the fields. Finally at 5 P.M. both the *balian* and the *pĕmangku* went into trance; the *pĕmangku* was possessed by the god from Katung and the *balian* by the Mother of the god. (See Plates XXVIII and XXIX.) The dialogue between the deities was recorded by I Madé Kalèr, as follows:

Pĕmangku [as the god, speaking in subservient ceremonial language]: Speak on, Mother. Yes, now speak indeed in order that your subject under your foot may know.

Balian [as the Mother, in polite but not subservient language]: Now, for the first time, my Child sits in Mother's shrine (*paruman*). Today, my Child brings gifts to Mother; but when my Child goes home to the west of the ravine [that is, to Katung], we shall not be able to make return presents.

And she went on to say that the god should stay three days in Bayung.

Pĕmangku: I humbly obey my Mother.

Balian: If my Child is not really pleased to obey, tell Mother. If he does not sit for three days in the shrine of his Mother, his Mother will not be pleased . . . but he shall decide.

Pĕmangku: Yes, and, whether pleased or not, be kind to me.

Balian: And my subjects from west of the ravine—will they obey or not?

Pĕmangku: Yes.

Balian: My subjects must not fall when they carry my Child.

Pĕmangku: Your subjects are stupid, but I ask my Mother that they may receive when they ask for nourishment. . . . Yes, your Child will humbly obey your wishes. Yes, be pleased, be pleased. . . .

Balian: My Child must visit too in the west [that is, in Pĕludu].

Pĕmangku: Yes, I obey, humbly obey.

Balian: That is all. I am going up [that is, the goddess is leaving and the *balian* will now come out of trance].

Pĕmangku [still in trance, and using ordinary trance jargon to the people of Bayung but subservient language to the goddess]: Do not be surprised, subjects, that I am here now. . . . Be pleased, Mother, to decide for me. I humbly beg for a decision from my Mother. Importunately I beg of my Mother. Mother, Mother, look toward me.

Balian [now out of trance and speaking subservient language to the god]: Lord be pleased, O Lord, be pleased. . . .

Pĕmangku [still in trance]: Subjects do not falter [in obedience]. . . . Mother, Mother [embracing the *balian* and addressing her humbly and enthusiastically] forgive me. I humbly ask pardon. Mother, Mother, where have I ever before had speech with you. Do not look away from me. I and my subjects beg sustenance from Mother. Now my Mother sits, and I obey. Tomorrow we shall speak again, and our subjects will offer libations (*pider buanǎ*). Do not be offended, my subjects . . . and we shall speak again tomorrow, and I shall come to my subjects. If I do not depart for three days, will that be correct, Mother?

Then the *pĕmangku* came out of trance at 5:16 P.M., and the ceremony was shortly after brought to an end.

The whole conversation lasted sixteen minutes, and Madé Kalèr's account of it is of course not complete, because of the difficulties of verbatim recording. He is trained to record the actual words that were said and to give preference to utterances which have some real significance, ignoring the empty phrases. A more complete record would have virtually no more meaning but would be much longer, full of groans, sobs, endless repetitions, and empty circumlocutions of politeness.

Indeed the interest of the trance, for the Balinese audience, lay not in what was said or decided in the conversation between the gods—though the decision that Katung should stay three days instead of merely overnight would put both Katung and Bayung to considerable inconvenience—but in the theatrical qualities of the performance. Much of what was said by the deities was simply emphasizing the fact that the god was son of the goddess and acting out this relationship by exaggerated subservience and affection on the part of the *pĕmangku*. His performance was much more violent than that of the *balian*. With wild hair and facial contortions, he shouted and threw himself about on his seat and beat his head and hammered with his fists on a post of the building. Perhaps not by accident he embraced the *balian* as his "Mother" after she had as a matter of fact come out of trance. Her trance behavior differed but little from that in her regular trances, and she seemed a little piqued by the more showy performance of the *pĕmangku*. She is a spirited and exhibitionistic person and does not like to lose the center of the stage.

The day was finished up by a performance of the Sampik opera from Katung, which lasted till after midnight when rain brought it to an end. The Katung people mostly went back to Katung to sleep and returned next day with a fresh supply of offerings, which were offered in the Bayung temple.

There was more trance. The *balian* (as the Mother) said that the god from Abuhan is a sibling of the god from Katung and that he keeps a switch with a golden handle. The *pĕmangku* (as the god from Katung) asked for this switch, but his Mother's reply to this request was not clear. (This switch is apparently the lightning and not an actual object in the Abuhan temple.) A woman *kubayan* from Abuhan also went into trance possessed by the Abuhan god, who scolded his (or her?) subjects for bringing only a basket (*tapakan*) and not a seat (*tigasană*). Later in the same ceremony, she went into trance again and again scolded for the same reason and said that the god from Abuhan is a sibling of the god from Katung and that both are children of the goddess in Bayung. A *bau* from Katung made a request to the goddess Mother (the *balian* in trance). He said that the temple feast for the *pusĕh* temple in Katung was due in two days, and he proposed that, if she would permit, that the Katung god should return home next day. This was granted.

The God Visits Pĕludu

On the next day (March 26), the Katung god went home, visiting Pĕludu on the way. In the Pĕludu temple the ceremonial was similar to that at Bayung and included an important trance performance by the *balian* and the *pĕmangku*. The trance began at 3:30 P.M. and Madé Kalèr's record of what was said is as follows:

Balian [as the Bayung goddess]: I take care of my Child, Guning Sari. [4] If this is not true, correct me. It is still uncertain what my gift will be, but, if my Child wishes to prosper, my Child will keep silent. [This advice to the god is perhaps the *balian's* reaction to the fact that in the other trance performances the *pĕmangku* had somewhat outshone her.]

Pĕmangku Meling [very humbly and not yet in trance]: I have never [been noisy].

Balian: As to I Bagus who sits in Chekandik, wait for me, father, [5] because, as always in the past, I shall give you [a decision] from above. Whenever I am given offerings, I shall give a share to I Bagus who sits in Chekandik as well as to I Bagus in the temple (*pusĕh*) at Sukemerih [that is, the Katung temple], as well as to I Bagus who sits in Banoa [a small village south of Katung], but my *pĕrbĕkĕl* [6] is deaf and dumb. The Great One of Banoa is male. The Great One in Sukemerih is male, and the Great One in the Kĕhĕn temple [Abuhan] is male. Only the one in Pĕludu is female. . . . How is it that my Child of Sukemerih does not speak? [The *pĕmangku* was not yet in trance.]

A *bau* from Katung: I humbly beseech that my Honored One from Sukemerih may be supported [that is, that the *pĕmangku* may go into trance; the person in trance being the "support" of the god].

Balian: About my staying here—I shall look after the water.

At 3:40 P.M. the Pĕmangku Meling went into trance, and, when he became possessed, his headcloth fell loose and he beat his head.

Balian: Be content to meet with and talk with your Mother. And if you ask for anything your Mother has. . . . Let us talk together pleasantly.

Pĕmangku [as the Katung god]: They are too greedy, my subjects south of the ravine [that is, Katung] are too greedy.

[4] Guning Sari is another name for the Katung temple or for one of the gods in it. The same temple is sometimes called "*pusĕh*" or "Sukemerih."

[5] The gods of Bali are related as *children* to ordinary mortals. Thus when a god speaks to a man he addresses him as "father." This theory is of course the opposite of that usual in Europe. The verb *sayangang* in Balinese means to indulge (a child), to worship (a god), to fawn upon (a prince). The word *dèwă*, which means god, is commonly used as a second person pronoun in addressing children with affection.

[6] A *pĕrbĕkĕl* is an administrative official, a local representative of the Regent. Possession by the great god Deaf-and-Dumb is one of the *balian's* favorite comedy stunts which she performs at the end of her important trances.

Balian: Let us talk together pleasantly. Let us talk today about our subjects, Bagus.

Pĕmangku: Give light to the country south of the ravine, if only you will be kind; and be pleased, Mother, to give me the switch with the golden handle [that is, the lightning].

Balian: It is not in my keeping.

Pĕmangku: Even if you do not keep it, my brother has it.

Balian: Now, if I speak wrongly, my subjects may correct me. And if my subjects are wrong I shall correct them from above. If you offer me a purification [*pesuchian,* here meaning a procession in which the god is taken to the sea or to a stream to "bathe"] let it be together with I Bagus from south of the ravine. How will you receive [this suggestion], subjects from south of the ravine? I Bagus shall receive offerings, a yearly feast (*wali*), and he shall ask for holy water (*tirtă*) from me. I shall sell the holy water to him for 1700 *kèpèng* [Chinese cash].

Pĕmangku: I humbly obey.

Balian: Do you accept that suggestion, Bagus?

Pĕmangku: I accept it, I accept it!

Then somebody asked the *balian* which water they ought to ask for, and she replied.

Balian: That which belongs to me in Pungsu, father.

Pĕmangku: The water in the corner—know this about the water in the corner, that the water on the west side is for bathing the god (*tirtă pĕtaké*) and that on the east is oil (*tirtă lĕngis*); it is for washing the hands (*mĕkobok*). It is not a bathing place for a god (*pesuchian*). It is different and it belongs to me. What else in the quacking?

Balian: The reason why he mentions the web-footed (*batis gempel*) is because I Bagus has charge of that water. [It is said that close to this spring people often hear a noise like the quacking of ducks, but nobody has ever been able to see these ducks].

Pĕmangku [possessed now by the Deaf-and-Dumb god]: Your subject here asks for a food packet (*dampulan*).

A woman from Katung gave him a food packet.

Pĕmangku [beating on his head as if it were a gong instrument and making appropriate gong noises]: Mok! Mok! Pong!

Pĕmangku [talking like a Chinaman]: *Chap chay kongsie.*

The *balian* also was then possessed by the Deaf-and-Dumb god, but what she said was not clear.

Balian: They are laughing at us.

The audience [politely]: No, no.

Another *pĕmangku* from Katung [humbly]: Yes, yes, please talk to us pleasantly and do not talk Malay.

Pĕmangku Meling then took the food packet again and beat on it as if it were a gong instrument, then he put it away and prayed.

The *balian* came out of her trance and offered palm beer to Pĕmangku Meling. Then he also came out of trance (3:59 P.M.) and put on his headcloth again.

This trance was the most important part of the ceremony at Pĕludu, but there was also some dancing by the *baris* clubs. They only

danced for a moment and without their full costume because the
dance was only a sign (*chiri*). After the ceremony the gods were
carried home by way of the water place where they received ritual
washing.

The Myth and the Temple

At this point we may consider the development which has taken place
since Pĕmangku Meling reported on March 16 that a goddess in
Katung was daughter to a goddess in Bayung. The chief additions to
the myth may be listed and commented upon.

1. The Chekandik temple was first mentioned in the Pĕludu trance
as vaguely connected with the Bayung-Katung-Pĕludu-Abuhan-
Banoa complex, and the god of the temple is defined as male and a
son of the goddess in Bayung. The Pură Chekandik is an old deserted
spot in a patch of secondary bush just south of Pĕludu. A few people
had wandered in there in recent times generally in search of stray
cattle, and they had seen a few stone figures lying among the under-
growth. Nobody had stayed long to investigate, because they did not
know whether the place was dangerous or not. Bau Tekek, the
calendrical expert, told us that for a long time he had been intending
to renovate this temple, and he had an idea that the poorness of the
crops might be due to its desertion, and, as will be seen, the Pĕludu
trance led to his carrying out this intention. Previous to the Katung
visit there was no ceremonial done in the Chekandik temple, but
every year offerings were made to it from a distance by the Pĕludu
temple club in the ceremony of *maya-iban* (paying the gods for the
rice harvest).

2. Pĕludu and Abuhan are now definitely included in what was
originally a connection between Bayung and Katung only. Banoa is
also mentioned as having a related god but so far as I know there has
as yet been no ceremonial involvement of this little hamlet, south of
Katung. Pĕludu, which as originally planned "would receive the god
with a few small offerings only," is now in a very important position
thanks to its connection with the Chekandik temple. The god resident
in Pĕludu is now defined as female and as a daughter of the Bayung
goddess. It may be noted that Bayung and Pĕludu, where the *balian*
is a woman, have female deities, while the other villages are all
given males.

3. The myth is now enriched by the inclusion of two older elements,
the switch with a golden handle and the ducks.

4. The names of the deities are still obscure, but the *balian* has adopted the convenient term I Bagus (The Beautiful) for referring to any of the sibling gods. Their relative seniority is still not fixed.

5. The *balian* has suggested that a yearly feast (*wali*) be given for I Bagus of Katung. This would give the whole complex a place in the twelve-month calendar which is much more important that the ordinary 210-day calendar of temple feasts.

Contributory Incidents

It so happened that the ceremonial visit of the god from Katung coincided with the season of *maya-iban*, the only ceremony in the year in which the Chekandik temple receives any attention. The temple land of Pĕludu, in which the members of the temple club share, lies just to the south of the Chekandik bush, and it was customary in the past for the club to offer from the land toward the Chekandik temple. This year, under the influence of Bau Tekek and the trance references to the god of the Chekandik, it was decided to clean up the old temple and to hold the *maya-iban* ceremony actually in the temple instead of casually worshiping from a distance.

Another circumstance also contributed to the interest which was taken in the Chekandik temple just at that time. I was told by Nang Nami, a *guru* of Bayung but not an accurate informant, that a man from Abuhan had felled a tree in the Chekandik bush and had fallen suddenly ill on the spot and in delirium had made some statement or other about the Chekandik temple. Nang Nami believed that this was the reason why they were going to clean the Chekandik temple.

Inquiry of Bau Tekek revealed another (and perhaps truer) version of this story. He said that a certain Nang Saderi of Kayukapas had felled a tree in the Chekandik bush and had fallen ill, not on the spot but some days later. He had *not* said anything in delirium; but a friend of his from Abuhan had thought that the sick man was perhaps being punished by the god of the Chekandik. The Abuhan man had therefore made expiatory offerings in the Chekandik for his friend who had then recovered. Bau Tekek stated emphatically that this incident had nothing to do with the cleaning of the Chekandik, that he (Tekek) had long intended that this should be done "because the crops were poor over the whole area from there to Abuhan," that is, on the whole of the land of the Pĕludu temple club of which Tekek is a senior member. In any case, even if what Tekek said was true, it would seem that for Nang Nami at least the idea of cleaning up the

Chekandik was made more acceptable by the rumor about the delirious man from Abuhan.

Clearing the Chekandik Temple

On the day after the god's visit to their temple, the Pĕludu club had a meeting to share offerings, and from this meeting they went directly to the Chekandik temple to cut down the bush. We and our secretary went with them. Before work could begin, Bau Tekek and Bau Kĕntel, the heads of the Pĕludu club, prayed with small offerings to tell the gods (*matur piuning*) what was being done. Meanwhile the remainder of the club sat in the bush joking and eating a jack fruit (*nangkă*). When Tekek had finished his praying he went forward and cut the first creepers, and the other members then went forward and joined him in the work.

Some idea of their attitudes toward this old and sacred spot can be derived from their conversation during the work. Madé Kalèr recorded the following remarks:

Nang Sayang: The bits of wood—anybody who wants can have them—only strangers don't get any.

Bau Tekek: Oh no, don't let strangers have any. Firewood is dear.

Nang Sayang then cut a liana.

Nang Kendel: Don't cut that creeper.

Nang Sayang: I didn't know it was a *lele* creeper.

Nang Kendel: It's good for yoking oxen.

I Rumă [cutting the creeper]: That's not *lele*, father.

Nang Kendel: Nor it is.

Nang Kendel: Bring a stick and chop down the nettles.

Nang Lokă: Pile up the rubbish here. The part to be cleared is there to the north.

Nang Lintar: These nettles—somebody tell the *tuan* to cut them. His trousers are long, so that it will not itch. [This last sentence was in polite vocabulary.]

Nang Kempel: Well! If this isn't the corpse of a bird here.

Bau Tekek: Ah, that's what was smelling so sweet just now.

Nang Kempel flicked away the dead bird with the point of his grass knife, and it fell beside Tekek's foot. Tekek said "ah!" and Nang Kempel laughed.

Then they found what they thought had once been the lid of a shrine, and Nang Sayang pulled it up on edge. Under the old lid there was a bees' nest, and Nang Sayang got five combs out of it, but they were empty.

Bau Tekek: Offer it to the *tuan* so that he can use it as a vegetable. [This was not a joke, such combs being actually so used.]

Nang Kempel [stung by a bee]: I've been paid for it, but I got no honey. [This was a joke.]

Bau Tekek: Come to think of it, this must have been the *pusĕh* [origin temple of Pĕludu] then. By and by, if the god of Sukemerih will come in trance, I'll ask him who sat here and when the temple feast (*odalan*) is. I expect [now that we are cleaning the temple] that the crops will be better. They've been bad all between here and Abuhan.

Then it began to rain, and, when the rain got worse, the work was stopped.

This account omits a great number of small remarks about the stone figures—suggestions as that the god of Chekandik must surely ride on a tiger, in reference to the stone carving of a tiger which was found—but it omits also a very much greater number of remarks and jokes such as any group of gay people unaccustomed to the bush will make when they go picnicking. Somebody found a millepede, and there was a lot of nonsense about whether it would bite—some thought it would, but some thought that that sort did not. And so on. The person who was most interested was Bau Tekek, and he was content to let the matter go with a vague guess that the Chekandik temple must once have been a *pusĕh* and a resolve to ask the *balian* in trance about the god who lived there.

On the next day, work on the Chekandik was continued, and the figures which had been irregularly scattered on the ground were neatly set up. Two days later the *maya-iban* of the Pĕludu club was celebrated there.

The Finds at Chekandik

It is not within my province to express any opinion as to the age and origin of the stone figures that were found in the Chekandik temple. I therefore sent photographs of them to Dr. Stutterheim and Dr. Van der Hoop for their comments. I give here a list of the finds with the comments on them made by the archaeologists.

(*a*) A figure of *paras* stone, height 55 cm. (Plate XVIII). This object was described by the Balinese as being the figure of a woman, but they also said that it had a headdress like a king (*pĕrabu*). Dr. Stutterheim's comment on the figure is as follows: "It certainly belongs to the youngest class of posthumous figures (*bijzettingsbeelden*) of which the dated ones are placed in the 13th–14th centuries. That, however, does not say that there are none older or more recent, though I must confess that the style of all these hundreds of figures is so much the same that they cannot be much older or more recent. The position of the hands is typical for *bijzettingsbeelden*, i.e., they hold a flower-like object, which likely can be connected with the *puspasarira* or *puspalingga*, of modern *njĕkah* [*nyĕkah*] or *mĕmukur*. Also the crown is composed of petals, which would agree with this identification, opening flowers (especially lotus flowers) being the

proper symbol of the soul's deliverance. There seems to be no doubt
that the figure is an ancestor-figure, put up in a temple or temple
ground at the time the last ceremony for the deliverance of the soul
was performed.

"It is, of course, quite impossible to find out who the deceased was.
Probably it was a king and this figure, one of many smaller posthumous figures, all of which were replicas of some larger figure put
up in the proper place—the king's ancestor temple somewhere in the
mountains. Through the intermediary of figures like these, even the
remotest parts of the kingdom were able to establish contact with
the king's soul after his death. . . .

"There might be a chance that the figure belonged to some small
king in the hills and not to one of the kings of Bali in the plains.
Old-Javanese history shows that after the flourishing periods of central
kingdoms and their hegemony, the dependent regents again and
again tried to become independent and often succeeded. In such a
case one might expect to find a great many of the smaller figures all
over the country, each belonging to one of these regents. Their
style, however, should be different in different regions, for the
structure of Indonesian society implies local tendencies. This not being
the case with the Balinese figures of the 13th–14th centuries, I am
inclined to reject this possibility."

One point in this comment is of special interest in the present connection—the statement that these figures were for the most part
replicas of a larger figure in the king's temple. From this we may
suppose that in its first usefulness the figure served as a contributory
symbol of the link between the village and the kingdom. It is interesting that today the same figure should contribute to uniting the
Bayung-Katung-Pĕludu complex.

(b) and (c) Two figures similar to (a), but headless and badly
weathered (Plate XVIII).

(d) A small head of *paras* stone. Height 21 cm. (Plate XVIII). This
is the only one of the finds which appears to be at all unusual for the
area. Dr. Van der Hoop attributes it to some late offshoot of the
Dong-Son culture and makes the following comment: "Characteristic
of the Dong-Son culture is—apart from the stone images—the use of
the human mask on bronze and stone objects. You find the mask on
some bronze axes, on the kettle drum of Pedjeng [Pèjèng] and the
mold of Manoeaba [Manuaba], on stone menhirs in Central Celebes,
and on big stone funeral urns in the same country. . . . Typical for
the masks on the drum of Pedjeng and the mold of Manoeaba, and

also on the stone menhirs of Central Celebes is the oval shape of the face, with the pointed chin; the curved eyebrows, connected with the straight line of the long nose; and the long, distended ear lobes. This form of mask has a late offshoot in the masks on the "moko-moko," the drums of Alor, and a forerunner in similar representations on funeral urns in Indo-China.

"In my opinion the egg-shaped head is connected with these examples of the Dong-Son culture. This culture came into the Archipelago about 300 B.C. and lasted till Hindu times. Remnants of it may have lasted locally much longer. It is probable that the stone head is from one of these late offshoots, with some Hindu influence recognizable in the more refined shape of the mouth, eyes and nose."

(*e*) A figure of an animal. Length 45 cm. This was identified by the Balinese as a tiger and with this identification Dr. Stutterheim agrees. He says that the figure is probably modern. It is a very crude piece of work, and its crudeness lends support to the theory that it was recently and locally made.

(*f*) Another "tiger," similar to (*e*), but even cruder and more fragmentary.

(*g*) A block of *paras* stone shaped like a square roof and slightly hollowed on the square face (Plate XVIII). This object was at once identified by the Balinese as a *kekereb*, a roof for a shrine; and they set it up. Dr. Stutterheim suggests that it may have been a *pipisan*, a stone mortar for grinding medicines, now turned upside-down.

(*h*) A large number of *paras* blocks of more or less oblong shape.

Various Effects of the Chekandik Incident

The temple feast at Katung, for which the god had to return, took place March 27, and as a return for the visit of the god a number of people went over to it from Bayung. They took offerings, both personal offerings and official offerings from the community. The *balian* went with them, and at Katung she again went into trance and added a little to the growing myth. She is reported[7] to have said that the gods of Sukemerih, Abuhan, Chekandik, and Bijă are all siblings. The last named is some spot in the rice fields of Katung which is now ploughed up. Nobody at the temple feast clearly remembered where it was, but Bau Tekek had heard of it and knew that there was a seat of a god there. In a second trance, the *balian* was possessed by the goddess of Pĕludu and stated that she was the oldest of the sibling

---

[7]Madé Kalèr was unable to get a place from which he could clearly hear her words, he therefore got some of his account from Bau Tekek.

gods, and that Gunung Sari (Sukemerih) was the youngest—and she complained that only the youngest ever received any worship.

On April 2, Bau Tekek told us that the following communities were going to share in the Chekandik temple, all combining to make temple feasts there: Bayung, Susut, Abuhan, Bonyoh, and Katung. He said that of these only Bonyoh and Susut had not yet been told. (It seemed that Banoa, though mentioned by the *balian* in the Pĕludu trance was not now included.)

Asking the Gods about the Chekandik

Following up his original intention, Bau Tekek pushed the village of Bayung to ask the gods (through the *balian*) about the Chekandik temple. A temple feast in the origin temple of Bayung marked a suitable day (April 20) for this ceremony and after the temple feast the *balian* was formally invited to the *paruman*, where offerings were spread. She sat with a big tray of uncooked rice in front of her, supported on a pedestal. She went into trance at 8:38 P.M., and Madé Kalèr reports her utterances and behavior as follows:

The chief *kubayan:* That it may be certain, we entreat for speech about the Chekandik temple.

Then a small tray with betel, and so forth, was given to the *balian*, and she chewed. She was then given leaves of *dap-dap* tree, which she folded into a small cup. Into this she spat her betel. She held this up to god, and then she examined it, holding it under the lamp. She said: Father, here I see: item, a *chatu*[8] shrine; item, a *pĕliangan*.[9]

Then she put down the leaf cup and took up a glass of water into which she dropped three onions. She said (watching the onions): Look, father, they go to the north!

Then she took the onions out of the water and dropped them in again and said: This is the shrine; this is the *pĕliangan*; and this is the outside of the temple. Then she repeated the process a third time, and again pointed out the shrine, the *pĕliangan*, and the outside of the temple.

Then she smoothed the heap of rice in front of her and took up sixty pieces of Chinese cash between her finger and thumb. With the money she tapped the edges of the tray, first on the northeast, then on the northwest, then on the southwest, then on the southeast. Then she threw the money into the rice and inspected the mounds and clefts which were made in its surface. She said: Here

[8] A *chatu* shrine is one with a particular form of architecture. At present there are no shrines of this sort in Bayung—and this is probably the introduction of a new culture trait from the plains.

[9] A *pĕliangan* is an open shrine-like structure on which offerings are put and on which gods are believed to sit when they wander from their own shrines. A *pĕliangan* is not the property of any one god but may be used by any of the gods in the temple.

it is. This is the shrine, this is the entrance. These are steps up and this is the outside of the temple.

Then she put one coin on the east side of the rice and said: This is the shrine of Gunung Agung, at the side. I shall throw [10] again! Be ready. [This last injunction was probably addressed to the gods. They must be ready when she throws.]

Then she picked up all the money and repeated the performance. After throwing the coins, she picked up four of them and laid them separately on the north edge of the rice, mentioning the name of a god, I Ratu Bagus Manik Murug. [11]

Then she said: Because the Great One of Chekandik is said in ordinary speech to be a blacksmith—I will throw again. The Great One of Chekandik must first tell the Great One Who Owns the Village why we are asking—because I already possess a shrine [perhaps regarding the whole village temple as her shrine] and because the Great One of Banoa has always been without a shrine (*peretiwi*), the advice that I give is [to make a shrine for] the Great One of Gunung Agung first. What after that is still not fixed. And because the feast of the Great One of Banoa does not go on [is never held], if you make a feast for the Great One of Chekandik you must give a share to the Great One in Banoa, because [the latter's] domain is in ruins and his subjects do not remember.

Bau Tekek asked about the day for the regular temple feast (*odalan*).

Balian: As to [the day for] the feast, this is it—*Anggară-kasih-medangsia,* [12] because the god comes down first from the west. And about a high shrine for the Great One of Chekandik—he must not have one, father, because he is not the equal of the gods [in the village temple].

Bau Tekek: What then is the reason why the god of Chekandik was provided with a roof of *paras* [referring to the object found in the temple]?

Balian: As to a roof—the seat of the god in Chekandik shall be without a shrine. He may not be equal to me.

Bau Tekek: Yes, I ask pardon. It was because there was a shrine long ago that I asked now.

Balian: Because from the beginning I have always had a shrine [his seat must be] without a shrine, father.

Bau Tekek: Yes, but the reason why there is a roof there now that is what I am asking about.

Balian: Now I shall ascend. Now I shall go to wake up the Great One Ngurah, because all that I do is only a sign [by divination].

Then the *balian* [escaping from an embarrassing situation] came out of her trance [8:53 P.M.].

The son of Bau Tekek: Well, if he is willing, the god of Chekandik will come now.

Balian [at 8:54 P.M., again in trance, possessed by the god of the Chekandik]: Tok, tok! (She beat with hands as if with a hammer as a sign that she is now the blacksmith god.)

[10] The word used for this divinatory throwing was *chontok pulang,* the name of a common Balinese gambling game in which coins are spilled off a shovel and the betting is on which way up they will fall.

[11] I understood her to say that this was the name of the god of the Chekandik temple, but Madé Kalèr thinks that this was wrong.

[12] *Anggară-kasih-mendangsia* is a day in the 210-day calendar. There was no mention of the *wali,* the annual ceremony which was once proposed by the *balian.*

Balian: I sit in Chekandik, father, and my Mother spoke wrongly. The reason why I have no shrine is because I am a blacksmith on the ground. My Mother did not dare to speak of that. That is why I have for my seat a place with no shrine. But my feast day, father, is on *Buda-kliwon.* My Mother was wrong, father. It is *Buda-kliwon-gumbreg,* father. But [make a feast for me] only if it pleases you. If it does not, do not. And likewise I Biyang Sakti Mas Pait. And likewise I Biyang Sakti Gunung Agung. [13] If you wish to try me, father, go on and try me [that is, the god invites Tekek to test by disobedience or experiment the reality of the god who speaks to him].

Bau Tekek: I should not dare. Are we to make a *pĕliangan?*

Balian: Yes, in order that my Mother may sit and, so to speak, watch me while I work at blacksmithing. That is why I am in the middle—so that my Mother can watch me. About the feast day—[it is on] *Buda-kliwon-gumbreg,* and if you make offerings to me I shall pass on a part to the god of Banoa. If you make offerings, [use] a fowl, not a pig, because my subjects to the west of the ravine [that is, in Pĕludu] are only few (*telung katih*). According to my wish it shall be fowls. About bristles, [14] I would not dare [to receive them]. I would be punished by god (*keponggor*) if I were offered too much. Ancestors (*pĕkak-aji*) are not offered bristles.

Bau Tekek asked about the ceremony of consecration.

Balian: The completion [must be done] with a consecration (*mĕlaspas*), father; and, as there is no shrine, [you must offer] a pig, and you should get the holy water from Susut.

Nang Karma [an inquisitive man] told Bau Tekek to ask about the *gamelan* [orchestra] which is buried in Blebu. [15]

Balian: No, no. Not yet, father. You must not ask too much, father. I still have to inquire of the ancestors (*pĕkak-aji*), and if they do not come down [and speak through trance], you must not be cross, father. I have my seat in Chekandik, not with the others; and so you must not ask everything. You must not ask much.

Then the *balian* came out of trance [9:10 P.M.] and, just as she was coming to, she said: Kok! Kok! [the noise of the blacksmith].

Bau Tekek [after praying]: Does that complete the talk [that is, is there anything else we ought to ask]?

Second *kubayan* [guardedly]: I always agree when my children [that is, the other citizens] agree with me.

Balian [now out of trance and nominally knowing nothing of what the god has said]: Will [they] make a shrine?

[13] Both these gods are more usually referred to as masculine. Here the *balian* calls them "Mother Holy Mas Pait" (Majapahit?) and "Mother Holy Gunung Agung."

[14] The words used are "*bulu tĕbĕl,*" literally, "thick hair." This is a metaphor often used in trance speeches for a pig. Cf. the use of *batis gempel,* web-footed, for ducks, above.

[15] Nang Karma explained to us afterward that it was said that, in times past, Pĕludu had been a large village and had had an orchestra. But robbers came to Pĕludu and, in order that they might not take the instruments, the people buried them in Blebu, to the northwest of Bayung. To this day there is a heap of stones in Blebu, and Nang Karma thought that perhaps there might really be something buried under them.

Bau Tekek: The talk is [that they] shall make one *chatu* shrine and one *pĕliangan*. The day for the god is *Buda-kliwon-gumbreg*.
    Balian: Is that the day for the feast?
    Wife of second *kubayan:* [Yes], on *Buda-kliwon-gumbreg*.
    Balian: All right.
    After this the offerings were asked back from god, and the ceremony was brought to an end.

This trance contains the utterances which fix the position of the Chekandik temple in the ceremonial life of Bayung. The date of the feast is fixed, and, since these feasts (*odalan*) are all remarkably alike in ritual and offerings, no further information is required from god beyond the date and statement that the offerings should contain chicken and not pork. The god of Chekandik is now endowed with two attributes—he is a son of the goddess in Bayung, and he is a blacksmith. (He probably owes the second of these attributes to the resemblance of the word Chekandik to the word *kandik*, which means an axe.)

No questions were asked about the stone figures in the Chekandik, and it would seem that no information was required about these. The only relic which was mentioned was the stone roof for a shrine. The *balian* said that the god should have no shrine, and Bau Tekek at once asked about this stone roof. This led to an embarrassing situation, from which the *balian* escaped by coming out of trance. In her second trance, as the god of Chekandik, she repaired her mistake by saying that the blacksmith god should work on the ground and created a diversion by changing the date of the temple feast. Probably there will be no more awkward questions about the stone roof because, fortunately for the *balian*, this roof-piece was actually set up over the ground when the temple was renovated. (See Plate XVIII.) Under this roof the blacksmith god may be supposed to ply his trade comfortably on the ground.

Conclusions

Sociologically we may see the incidents which have been narrated in this paper as the establishment of ceremonial links between the various communities concerned—Bayung Gĕdé, Katung, Pĕludu, Abuhan, and possibly one or two others. First, a little bit of mythical information, that the god in Katung is a child of the goddess in Bayung, leads to ceremonial contact between these two villages; and then, when the god goes to visit his Mother, the link grows stronger and involves Pĕludu and Abuhan. Finally, in addition to the spoken (and perhaps easily forgotten) words of the *balian* and the *pĕmangku* in trance, we now see the link concretely embodied in the Chekandik temple.

Such sociological links, supported by a concrete symbol, are a commonplace of cultural anthropology and may be expected to occur in every country of the world, from aboriginal Australia to modern Europe; but, though the sociological effect of these links and symbols —their "function" in uniting groups of people—may be comparable all over the world, there are very important differences in the way in which the symbolism is handled in different cultures. It is by studying such differences as these that we may hope to get some insight into the psychology that is fostered in any one culture.

Of these different ways of handling the symbols of social unity, that which seems to us most "natural"—because we follow it most often— is somewhat as follows: An event occurs, for example, a battle is fought, or a man is born or dies, or writes a book. Then memory of this event centers later around some relic or, lacking a relic, we set up a tablet or memorial to the past event, and either the relic or the memorial becomes an influence which pushes those who come after to perpetuate the sociological effects of the original event. Thus we invest the past with real authority and set it, like a policeman, to the business of governing the present. Sometimes the precepts of the past do not quite suit us or the past event is not dramatic enough for our taste, then we are compelled to emend or to embellish the story woven around the relic.

An example of this use of the past may be quoted from the culture of the Iatmul, a headhunting tribe in New Guinea. In the village of Mindimbit stands a stone, of which the following story is told: Once, when the village was very weak, two of its men were ambushed and killed by enemies. The men of the village did not dare to go out seeking vengeance as they ought, and so two women went off alone and threw themselves on the mercies of a strange village, Palimbai. The men of Palimbai accepted the challenge and set out. They raided the enemy and used the two women as decoys to attract the enemy into an ambush. So they got many heads and even two captives for the women themselves to spear. Since then Palimbai and Mindimbit (except for a few "unfortunate incidents") have been allies, and the stone which is said to have been set up on this occasion stands as a perpetual memorial of the women's exploit, as a witness of the alliance, and a hint of the shame of the men who did not dare.[16]

[16] For full details of this story, see Gregory Bateson, *Naven* (Cambridge, Cambridge University Press, 1936), p. 145.

The Iatmul in New Guinea and we in Europe look back to a romantic past, but the Balinese of Bayung Gĕdé do not. To us their handling of Chekandik business appears dull—a tragedy of missed opportunities. We might perhaps be able to find parallels to the desertion of the temple; we do sometimes allow our relics to fall into such desuetude that they molder and the stories about them are forgotten. But we could hardly renovate a relic and bring it into active sociological service without knowing and asking or inventing its history—or if its history were quite unavailable we should at least value it the more because its origin was mysterious and unknown. The Balinese did none of these things. They had what would have been an ideal opportunity of weaving history, and trance would have provided a perfect mechanism for the creation of myth and launching it with authority. But they were content to let the matter go with a very minimum of embellishment.

The myth which they constructed contains no reference to the past; it is a bare skeleton of relationships in the present. It says that the goddess in Bayung *is* mother of the other gods in Katung, Abuhan, Pĕludu, Chekandik, and Bijă, and it states that of these sibling gods all are male except the one in Pĕludu who is female and elder than all the others, while Sukemerih is the youngest. This statement of kinship might seem to us to be an invocation of the mythical past, but I believe that in so interpreting the matter we should be doing violence to the material.

It is true that the statement "the goddess is mother of the god" logically implies that in the past she gave birth to him; but in the elaboration of the myth this implication is completely passed over without, for example, any hint (even in this patrilineal culture) of who the father may have been or how the son became separated from his mother. I would see, in the statement of kinship between these deities, a definition only of how one god shall *behave* toward another. Without some such statement of relationship, status, degree of intimacy, and so forth, no conversation between the deities is possible in the Balinese language; but once the matter is settled all is straightforward and the son adopts the vocabulary and tone of self-deprecation when he addresses his mother. Similarly when the *balian* in trance states that the goddess in Pĕludu is senior to the others she is making a statement about behavior and incidentally claiming respect for herself. Her actual words were "*Ragan I Ayu paling duura*" (literally, "I am the highest"), and it is significant that she states the matter in a purely spatial metaphor with no reference to time.

These questions of emphasis are admittedly very difficult to demonstrate, but they are of fundamental importance for the understanding
of cultural phenomena. It is possible that a more convincing test of
whether statements of kinship refer to the present or to the past could
be obtained from the elaborate genealogies of gods and abstractions
which are common in the religious mysticisms of literate groups in
Bali. My expectation is that these documents could be shown to be
symbolic descriptions of the present with only the very thinnest
veneer of historical or narrative form. It is probable too that the
excessively impersonal nature of Balinese deities—their lack of human
character—is connected with the fact that their position is defined in
terms of the present and needs no validation from stories of their past
deeds; that, lacking deeds, they lack personality.

If my interpretation of the scrap of mythology is correct, and we
are right in concluding that the Balinese of Bayung are remarkably
uninterested in the past as a source of romantic validation for the
present, then the problem arises: Why then did they renovate the old
deserted Chekandik temple instead of building a new one, and why
do they accumulate relics just like Europeans?

We know that Bau Tekek was already thinking of renovating the
Chekandik before ever the Katung business and the relationship of
the gods was mooted, and something of Bau Tekek's attitudes toward the
past can be gathered from a remark of his. Mr. Grader and the writer
were asking him why a particular shrine in Bayung had a particular
form of architecture, and he professed complete ignorance. We asked
him about the earthquake which had destroyed most of the shrines in
Bayung in 1917, and he said this shrine also had been broken and he
had had to do with the building. We asked why he had built it like
that and not some other way, and he said simply that he had looked at
the old broken shrine to find out how it should be and had built the
new one on that pattern.

Another sidelight upon his attitude is given by his interrogation of
the *balian* on the subject of the stone roof-piece. He had no reason to
wish that the god in the Chekandik should be honored with a shrine,
but, the moment the *balian* said that the god should not have a shrine,
Bau Tekek spotted that there was an inconsistency; there was a roof-
piece and therefore there must once have been a shrine. The present
as laid down by the *balian* was at odds with the past as indicated by
the relics.

For him, we may suppose, the past provides not the cause of the
present but the pattern on which the present should be modeled; and

he was not interested in narrative reasons for the pattern. This is an attitude toward the past with exactly the sort of negative quality which would explain the whole Chekandik episode, the fact that though uninterested in the past the Balinese did renovate the temple. If the past is the pattern on which the present should be modeled, then it follows that, wherever there are differences between the past and present, it is likely to be the present which is wrong. Evidently in the past there had been a temple at Chekandik, and so perhaps there ought now to be a temple at Chekandik. This is enough, and with this attitude toward the past there is no need to go inquiring into history or inventing stories about the god who sits in the temple. It is only necessary to get a trance statement of the status of the god and the date of his feast day.

To work out in detail all the expressions of this attitude toward the past, in the diverse contests of Balinese culture is of course not possible; but there are many indications that this attitude is not confined to Bau Tekek nor even to Bayung Gĕdé. In many parts of Bali, it is usual to refer to the time before the Europeans came as "when the world was steady (*entèg*)." The modern Balinese is forced to recognize that he lives in a changing world, but that is not his ideal, and he does not think in terms of it. He does not think of the past as of a time that was different and out of which the present has sprung by change. The past provides him with patterns of behavior, and if only he knows the pattern he will not blunder and he need not be tongue-tied.

The Strolling Players
in the Mountains of Bali

MARGARET MEAD

ONCE EVERY 210 days comes the Balinese feast of Galungan, when offerings are made to the souls of the dead, pigs are killed, elaborate cakes are made, people go visiting, and prodigals and wanderers return home. For thirty-five days after Galungan, anywhere on the roads of Bali, but especially on the roads that lead to the mountains, one is likely to meet a *barong*.

The *barong* is a magnificent beast mask, worn by two men who give it a most engaging, lifelike quality, prancing with soft, tripping, carefully synchronized steps, to maintain the four-footed illusion. (See Plate XXV.) The *barong* may be white or black, his hair coat made of various kinds of vegetable fiber, or rarely of crow feathers specially sent by the gods. His great mask is of wood, with a movable lower jaw held in the hands of the man inside—"he who dances in the head of the *barong*"—and manipulated to produce a great clacking and champing of teeth. His protruding round eyes are painted so as "to live" as the people say. The underpinning of basketwork which supports the series of golden leather decorations adorning his spine is so flexible that it is possible for him to turn his head around and contemplate his tail, a magnificent erect structure decorated with many little looking glasses which catch the light of the sun by day and of torches at night. His legs—actually the legs of the men inside the mask, but with the illusion perfectly maintained by the delicate pawing, the mincing prance of the dancers—are decked out in long striped trousers.

Originally published in *Natural History*, XLIII, No. 1 (January, 1939), 17–26. Reprinted with permission of the author.

This is the *barong ketket*, whose magnificence does not correspond to any real animal. There are other *barong*, representing pigs, tigers, lions, and sometimes cows and even caterpillars, but these are usually smaller and less splendid; instead of the shaggy coat they wear cloth, their masks are poorly attached at the neck, and their role tends to be a comic one.[1]

"On the Road"

When the *barong* walks the roads his mask is usually covered with a white cloth, and the men who "wear" him do not wear the trousers which to the Balinese turn their shanks into animal legs. In the little dust-stained procession accompanying the *barong* are tall shallow umbrellas such as are carried whenever gods or princes go abroad; there are lances with floating pennants and, sometimes, banners; an orchestra of small metallophones and cymbals and drums and gongs plays as the procession straggles along. Some of the followers carry on their heads square boxes containing masks; others carry bundles which the children by the roadside know contain costumes for theatricals; others carry double shoulder-loads of dozens of little bundles, each no bigger than a pound of butter, the personal effects and the "presents for the journey" of the members of the club. They are going to *ngelawang*, "to go from gate to gate," showing off their *barong* and their dancing, courting the appreciation of strange villages.

At this season in the mountain village of Bayung Gĕdé, all through the thirty-five days after Galungan, there is continual tension in the air. At any moment may appear a *barong*—a black one or white one, a *barong* that is too sacred to dance and will be set up in the temple[2]

---

[1] I have omitted here any discussion of masks worn by one person. These are also called *barong*, but usually with a qualifying word following, as *barong landung*, *barong berutuk*, *barong belas-belas*, *barong dingklik*, etc. To the children and to the average Balinese, the word *barong* used alone always means one of the four-footed beast masks worn by two dancers. A *barong* such as this is connected with one of the village temples, and there is usually a special group of people who form a "club," and who look after the *barong*, play in the orchestra—which is the property of the club—refurbish trappings of the *barong* when necessary, make him offerings, and accompany him when he goes abroad. This club may themselves give theatricals, or they may confine themselves to dancing in the *barong*, and when they go to other villages, take other theatrical groups with them. In the *barong* group there is someone who acts as the priest of the *barong*, and he, by virtue of his office, is also regarded as sufficient chaperon for the young boys and girls who travel about with the *barong* and who sometimes do not return to their homes for ten days or two weeks.

[2] A Balinese temple consists of a series of one or more walled courts within which stand scattered buildings, shrines, meeting pavilions, and so forth. While almost all strolling *barong* and their followers sleep in the temple, only the more important *barong* are actually entertained by the host village.

like a god, or a *barong* who will wander all over the village selling his hair for a bit of Chinese coin, or who dances with astonishing contortions and tricks, grasps at an umbrella, takes a drum away from the orchestra, or teases and tantalizes the children in the front rows of the audience. And it is usually not only a *barong*, but theatricals also, for in most cases the club does not rely merely on the charms of its *barong* alone, on the catchiness of the *barong* music to which every child has been dandled from birth, on the cleverness with which the men have learned to dance in the mask, or upon the splendor of the gold and mirrors and semiprecious stones with which the mask is adorned. If the *barong* is a very sacred one, whose presence can exorcise the powers and disease and death, then it is true he needs to bring no secondary attractions.

The Troupe

He will be followed by fifty or one hundred men, all dressed in white. The whole company will be entertained in the temple of the host village, the human followers will be feasted, and the sacred *barong* will be given many offerings from which his human followers will also eat. Women whose babies or pigs or chickens are ill, and who hear of his anticipated arrival, will promise special thank offerings—one roasted chicken, two rice croquettes, five pieces of cake, and a quantity of fruit—to be made to the *barong* on his arrival, if only the baby or the pig or the chicken recovers before he enters the village. The rare and most sacred *barong* can command offerings and entertainment from one village after another, on the strength of their power to heal and to consecrate holy water which brings cleanliness and blessing. Most *barong*, although treated with reverence, are said by the people to be made for enjoyment.

The *barong* whose role is to provide enjoyment is associated primarily with dancing. He himself dances, he brings with him dancers who wear grotesque masks and play a mischievous and teasing comedy with their lord, who mauls them about, to the delight of the onlookers. The *barong* may also bring a *légong*, a stylized ballet in which three little girls enact a set and familiar tale; an *arjă*, the popular light opera with its new songs and new turns; a *wayang wong*, in which human actors, masked and costumed like the puppets of the shadow play, stalk through old heroic tales, and perhaps, best of all, they may bring a Chalonarang, a ritual drama in which the *rangdă*, the great witch mask so often carried in the *barong* procession (Plate XXV), is brought out to engage in combat with the *barong*.

Delights of Anticipation

With such possibilities, there is continued anticipation in the village. As the women go to and from the distant spring with their water jars on their heads, as the small boys tend their cattle on the highlands above the village, or the men sit in a solemn town meeting discussing whether the man who arrived late to help chop the pig shall pay a two-cent or a three-cent fine—they listen. Above the steady beat of the women's wooden rice pounders, above the crowing of fighting cocks lined up along the roads in cages, above the incessant barking of the dogs, and, if it is ploughing time, shrill above the mellow thunder of the wooden ox bells, comes the children's triumphant shout: "*Barong! Barong!*" which an American child would take for a cry of "fire" and a South Sea child for the equally excited shout of "mano-war," which announces a ship. For what a fire is to an American child, or a ship to a South Sea Islander, a *barong* is in the monotonous lives of the Balinese mountaineers. For six months they have gone soberly about their business; they have gone daily to tend the cattle, or to their little farms to plant or weed. When there have been feasts for the village gods, they have dutifully made offerings, knelt in the baking sun or played vigorously in the village orchestra. But it has all been terribly familiar, like going to a party where everyone is a member of the same family.

There is no *barong* in Bayung Gĕdé, but, when children are troublesome and fretful, mothers promise them that they will be taken to see one, and they hum over the tunes to which the *barong* dances. Small boys borrow their mother's cloth shawls and play at being a *barong*, or with a smaller piece of cloth covering their faces, with blood-curdling yells, they enact the witch *rangdă*. Their fathers make them bamboo clappers which rattle like the *barong's* champing jaws. Still, life is dull and uneventful, and people say "come Galun-gan" with a light of expectation in their eyes.

With the cry of "*barong*," crowds of children begin to scamper toward the gate from which it came, they tug at their mother's skirts and fret to be taken to see the *barong*, the man whose duty it is to attend such matters this month goes to fetch mats for the *barong* company to sit upon and betel to refresh them. While it is still at a distance, rumors begin to circulate: "It's a white *barong*"; "It's the Lord King from the village of Tiga"; "They have an opera company with them for there are six little girls with them"; "They are bringing two *rangdă* masks"; "They have a *wayang wong*, and they

say they have fifteen monkey masks, but only five tails." Those whose
cattle must be fed before nightfall hurry off to their farms. The *barong*
company marches up to the terrace outside the temple, there to await
a formal welcome from one of the village head priests. They are a
bedraggled little company, dusty, dressed in shapeless faded garments;
except for the shining gold of the *barong*, the paint and gilt on their
musical instruments, the glitter of the lances in the sun, they look as
workaday and dull as the people of the village who gather around with
gaping mouths to stare vacantly at them. No one would guess that
the little group huddled around the *barong* will blossom out into
accomplished dancers most variously costumed in gold and silk, nor
that the sullen peasant spectators will turn, at the drawing of the
curtain, into exacting critics of every turn of the king's wrist and
every swish of the princess's train in the theatricals.

Enter the Barong

Finally, the head priest comes. The *barong* and his followers troop
into the village temple, where the *barong* club places offerings in the
altar made from a living tree, and the *barong* dances a short measure,
"as an offering to the gods of the village." Meanwhile, the dancers
dress outside, on the edge of the terrace, while the village children
cluster about, commenting in low twittering voices on the quality of
the materials and the shape of the elaborate gold headdresses. The
dance troupe comes into the temple and in the wide courtyard they
give a tiny selection from their dance—just a preview. This little
sketch is said to be "offered to the gods of the village." There are only
a few spectators, women with babies, a following of children, half a
dozen men who happen to be about the village. Nevertheless, this
little dance is important, for it gives the village people an idea of
what the *barong* club has to offer, whether the costumes are new and
shining, whether the dancers are accomplished, the clowns amusing,
the kings and queens properly regal. The word goes out, by a child
sent to take a packet of rice to its father, or a boy gone to fetch home
the cows: "The *barong* of such and such a village is here, with a fine
arjă," or "a fair *arjă*," or "a poor *arjă*" as the case may be. And on
the farms people hurry with their work to come into the village, or
grunt and settle more firmly on their haunches to show they are not
tempted by the second-rate.

Meanwhile, whatever the response to the "preview," the village
must order the dance, if only for a hundred pieces of Chinese cash
(about six American cents). The gods of Bayung Gĕdé and the souls

of the dead speak through the mouth of the village trance priestess, an old woman who has been the medium for thirty years. She is a gay and lively old woman, who, no matter how bitter the night air, never fails to watch to the very end a visiting theatrical company. And the gods, speaking through her, have often announced that they so love dancing that no single dance troupe is ever to be turned away, unordered.

On with the Dance

Obediently the village headmen follow the dictates of their gods. There is a long conference between representatives of the village and the head of the dance club, or sometimes with the priest of the *barong*. They speak of the road the *barong* has taken, of the road it will take, and, finally, the village heads say they will offer a *tapakan*, an offering which means "a footstool for a god," which will contain, for example, 1100 pieces of Chinese money. In return for this, the dance club will give so many "characters," if the theatrical form is a long one; so much time, if it is a ballet. If five characters of an *arjă* are ordered, the spectators will see the princess's servant, the princess, the first servant of the prince or king, the second servant of the prince, and the prince himself (Plate XIV), and only so much of the long fairy-tale plot will be presented as can be alluded to in the songs and comments of these dancers.

Once the matter of ordering the dance has been settled and a fair supply of betel offered to the *barong* club, the headmen of the village go home, and the town crier for the month may be sent out to notify the women to make offerings which, after the *barong* has taken the essence, will become the food of the club. The great slit gong, hanging in a high little house in front of the temple, is beaten resonantly so that everywhere, to the farthest limits of the village fields, people know that there will be a performance that night. Meanwhile, if the *barong* is a relatively ordinary and unsacred one, he is set up on two special sticks with umbrellas over him in the courtyard of the temple, or sometimes outside the temple on the terrace, if the dance is to be given outside. (There are always many people who for various reasons, such as a recent death in the family, or a baby not yet three months old, cannot enter the temple, and these make an urgent plea, whenever the news from the preview is very favorable, to have the dance given in front of the temple so that all may watch.) If the *barong* is a sacred one, he will be set up in the special little house in the temple reserved for visiting gods, and later the people will come and make offerings and receive holy water from his priest. Specially sacred or not, he will be given offerings by his own club, and the *barong* priest will ritually lift up food into his very mouth.

If the day is yet young when the arrangements for the dance are completed, the *barong* may go out into the village and, with flags flying and orchestra playing, go from gate to gate, stopping to dance a few measures at the door of anyone who will pay it a little money. The village children troop after it, mothers come to the gate to buy pieces of its hair to make bracelets for their children. (In the mountains the Balinese say they do this because it is the custom, but on the plains they say that this is done so that the children may not have bad dreams after seeing the *barong*, who can be rough as well as playful, threatening as well as lovable.) Village boys who aspire to be *barong* dancers some day follow about wistfully, trying to get up courage to ask to be allowed to dance inside the *barong*.

Open-air Theater

In the evening when the people have gathered from the fields, and the night air is so sharp that the children huddle together and wrap their cloth shawls tightly around their throats, the crowd gathers. If the play is an *arjă*, a curtain is set up and the dancers, no longer the grimy, travel-stained little urchins of the morning but resplendent creatures from a fairy-tale world, file out and sit behind the curtain, to emerge one by one, with lengthy stylized opening and shutting of the isolated curtains, around both edges of which the audience is free to peek at will. The *barong* has no part in many of the theatricals; he stands above and beyond, immense in the dim light, presiding over the festivities which are given under his patronage. But, if the play is one of the many Balinese dramatic performances which culminate in a ritual fight between the *barong* and the witch *rangdă*, then the *barong* is set up ready for action, and the witch's mask-box is gotten out and set up on a pedestal, while in front of it a little house is constructed or curtains are hung from which the witch can emerge.

The long story which precedes the conflict has many forms which center around the terrors of marrying the witch's witch-daughter or the witch who tries to fob off an ugly daughter upon the suitor who loves a beautiful one. Finally, the deception is discovered, and the human witch heroine becomes the *rangdă*, that is, assumes the great witch mask and the supernatural form of the *rangdă*, the human hero disappears and is replaced by the *barong*, and a battle ensues, a battle most frequently ending in a draw. During this climax, either the witch or the *barong* impersonators may go into trance, rush wildly at the deliciously frightened audience, or fall down, rigid or limp, only to be revived by incense and holy water. At midnight, sometimes at two in the morning, a perfect bedlam of barking all over the village announces to the sick and bedridden that the play is over.

Three-a-Day

Sometimes, not one *barong* but three will come in one day, crowding on each other's heels, until the children are hoarse from shouting and the heads of the village weary of ceremonial politeness. In this case, some of the dances may be given in broad daylight so that at least one of the clubs may push on to sleep that night in another temple. During the month after Galungan these remote mountain villages have a taste of all the various elaborate dance forms of the more developed culture of the plains; they hear the new music, the latest witticism, the new songs. For months afterward, the village children will try to stand on their heads as the witches did in a particularly clever dance, and babies born at Galungan will learn in the next six months to dance to the tunes which were brought into the village when they were born. The sluggish imagination of the mountain villages slowly responds to all this stimulation; here a village which has never had a *barong* before decides to make one, there a group of young men form a new club to dance *arjă*. A dance club, weary of its old repertoire, will begin practicing a new set of songs learned from some visiting company. For the mountain villages which are ambitious enough to plan a *barong* and the accompanying dances, next Galungan sets a date toward which they work. The new headdress, the new orchestra instruments must be finished by then, the new dance steps learned, and so the cycle starts all over again.

The Living Art of Bali

Much has been written about the fact that Bali has a living art, that the music, the dance, the theater, despite their high degree of stylization, are nevertheless extremely alive, constantly being recreated in hundreds of performances all over the island. The high standard of the Balinese theater has been attributed to the influence of the old courts, with their Javanese connections. Each of these courts acted as a center which defrayed the expenses of musical instruments and costumes; the kings and their petty princelings who acted as deputy governors, vied with each other in the splendor of the artistic performances they supported. But if the courts were responsible for the standard of elegance and taste, for the selection which curbed, in some degree, the riotous exuberance of the Balinese theatrical imagination, it is to the village dance clubs, and to the *barong* under whose protective aegis they wander the country every Galungan, that we must look for one of the explanations of why the Balinese theater is alive. The *barong* has an honored place; he is treated as a god, and on entering a strange village he and his followers go, as of a right, to the temple. Thus the strolling players who carry from one part of Bali to the other new forms and old forms, newly refurbished, are given dignity and security. The performance, whether ordered by the village or by an individual, is never private; all—the beggar in his rags, the tiniest, grubbiest child—enter the temple or the rich man's court to watch, to learn with their eyes, and later, perhaps, to become actors and dancers.

The Balinese Wayang Kulit
and Its Music

COLIN McPHEE

PERHAPS THE HIGHEST, and certainly the most sensitive form of musical expression existing in Bali is revealed in the music which accompanies the *wayang kulit*,[1] or shadow play. It was during the study of this music and its place in the performance that, lured into fascinating byways, I came across certain information which I have felt tempted to include in this study as throwing some light on the nature of the *dalang*, the manipulator of the puppets, and the conception of the *wayang* as found in Bali. Some attempt at an ethnological background seemed to me to give the musical analysis a richer significance, and I have endeavored to relate the music to various facts concerning *wayang kulit* in such a way as to be of interest both to musicians and to students of Indonesian culture. Before taking up an analysis of the music itself I shall attempt to describe the secular and religious roles of the *wayang kulit* as found in the Bali of today.

For the benefit of those unfamiliar with *wayang kulit* I may be permitted a brief description of the nature of the performance as it takes place in Bali. The shadow play, in which puppets cut from buffalo hide are thrown in silhouette against an illuminated screen, still enjoys great popularity among the Balinese people. The brightly painted puppets are generally articulated at the shoulders and elbows only, motion being thus limited to the arms, which, however, are capable of great expression, punctuating the speeches with tense

Originally published in *Djawa*, XVI, No. 1 (1936), 1–34. Reprinted with permission of Mrs. Shirley J. Hawkins, executrix of Colin McPhee's will.

[1] *Wayang*: literally shadow, but here meaning puppet or, in the broader sense, theater. *Kulit*: skin. A derivative drama in which the parts are enacted by men is known as *wayang wong* (*wong* = man).

nervous gestures. From the head down through the body runs a slender brace of horn, which, pointed at the end, extends below the feet, and serves as a handle. Certain comic characters have in addition movable underjaws, lips, or legs, controlled by strings.

The performance is given in the open air. A raised booth is erected for the event in the outer court of some temple or palace, or perhaps by the roadside, outside the gate of the man who has hired the entertainment. By nine o'clock at night the people have begun to flock to the place. The saleswomen bring their low tables of strange delicacies —fiery curries, arrack, fruits, and sweet fritters—and the soft night air is filled with the heavy scent of flowers which lie, spread out in the light of the little lamps, to be sold to those who may be seized with the sudden desire to make themselves beautiful. The play, beginning late, lasts till dawn.

The screen (*klir*), a white sheet, is stretched tightly between two bamboo poles. At the base is the trunk of a banana tree (*gedebong*) whose pithy texture is easily pierced by the handle of the puppet, which is fixed in this way during the long dialogues. Behind the screen hangs a lamp (*damar*) whose fire, arising from coconut oil, glows through the screen, a mystic flame, disembodied. (See Fig. 1.)

All the figures are operated by one man, the *dalang*, who sits behind the lamp, cross-legged, his puppet-box (*kropak* or *gĕdog*) close by. Two assistants sit, one on either side of him, in charge respectively of the puppets which belong to the right and the left. Back of the *dalang* sit the musicians (*juru gĕndèr*), and a crowd of curious people, who prefer the glitter of the puppets and the sight of their manipulation by the *dalang* to the more abstract version to be seen from the other side of the screen.

We may here call attention to several details in which the Balinese *wayang* performances differ from those of Java. The Javanese tradition, in which the men sit on the same side of the screen as the *dalang*, and the women sit, excluded, on the other side, and in which, for Dr. Rassers,[2] the screen plays such a significant role in dividing the sexes, has, if ever observed, long since disappeared. Moreover, no set time for commencing or ending a performance prevails in Bali. Although generally beginning about 11 P.M., the length of the performance is determined by the *dalang*, according to wages, enthusiasm of the audience, or the wish of the person who has engaged him.

---

[2] W. H. Rassers, "Over den Oorsprong van het Javaansche Tooneel," *Bijdragen tot de Taal-, Land- en Volkenkunde van Nederlansch-Indië*, LXXXVIII (1931), 317–450.

The puppets, too, differ from those of Java, lacking that subtle and fantastic proportion of the human body which the Javanese have developed to such a degree. Their more robust and masculine form and design remain in the style of the figures found, for example, in the stone reliefs of the Hindu temples of East Java, such as Chandi Tégawangi or Chandi Panataran, both built about the fourteenth century.

The many speculations regarding the inner significance of the *wayang* seem to agree to an origin, part religious ceremony, part entertainment, involving the invocation and representation of pre-Hindu deified ancestors and their heroic deeds. Although known to have existed in Java as early as the eleventh century, the shadow play as a dramatic form is assumed, by recent authorities, to be of Hindu origin. This theory has not been allowed to pass uncontested; it is, however, important to note that *wayang kulit* is found in Indonesia only in those places where Hinduism once flourished or still prevails.

Long before the Hindu invasion some dramatic form or other must have existed in Java, in which ancestor legends were enacted. These "originated in old Malay-Polynesian myths, and were first sung in hymns of praise, and later recited in a set dramatic form" (synopsis of Hazeu by Kats.[3] The advent of the Hindus brought the super-imposition of Hindu gods and their legends. The original ancestor-gods gradually became identified with the newer pantheon and their deeds interwoven with those of the Hindu epics. If the shadow play came from India, it superseded at an early date the original dramatic form in the rituals of ancestor worship.

By the time the *wayang kulit* reached Bali, probably around the end of the fifteenth century, when the Hindu-Javanese of East Java finally took refuge in Bali from the invasion of Mohammedanism, it is more than likely that little of the original ancestral significance was still recognizable. Its ritualistic character still survives, however, in Bali, where the shadow play fulfills a role in domestic and religious ceremonies. Along with this goes its profane side, in which it must be regarded as mere popular entertainment. It will be found to have a third and more sinister aspect in its portrayal of the violent legend dealing with witches and black magic, the Chalonarang tale (see Note 1, p. 181).

The plays (*lampahan*) are drawn from various sources. The most generally known legends are modified episodes from the two great

[3] J. Kats, *Het Javaansche Tooneel*. I. *Wajang poerwa* (Uitgave van de Commissie voor de Volkslectuur, Serie No. 387; Weltevreden, 1923).

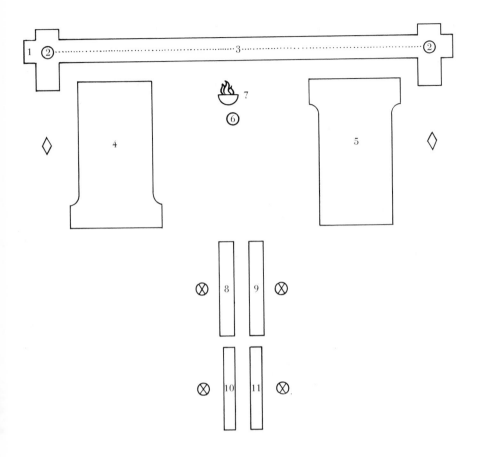

1 *gedebong*, base
2 *lujuh*, poles
3 *klir*, screen
4 *kropak*, puppet box
5 lid to box
6 *dalang*, manipulator
7 *damar*, lamp
8 *gĕndĕr gĕdé (pĕngisep)*, large *gĕndĕr*

9   *gĕndĕr gĕdé (pengumbang)*, large *gĕndĕr*
10 *gĕndĕr chĕnik (pĕngisep)*, small *gĕndĕr*
11 *gĕndĕr chĕnik (pengumbang)*, small *gĕndĕr*
    tututan dalang, dalang's assistants
    juru gĕndĕr, *gĕndĕr* players

FIG. 1

Hindu epics, the Mahabharata and the Ramayana (see Note 2, p. 183). The former is known in Bali as the *astadasă parwă* or the eighteen books or *parva*, but the *lampahan* are usually taken from some part of the old Javanese poem, the *Bharată-Yuddhă* (The Great War), which, based upon part of the Mahabharata, deals with the wars between the two rival houses, the Pandawas and the Korawas. The repertoire includes plays from other old Javanese poems derivative of the Mahabharata, such as Bimaswargă and Ardjună Wiwahă. As a different set of puppets is required for the Ramayana from that of the Mahabharata cycle, many *dalang* specialize in either one or the other group of *lampahan*.

Other plays derive from indigenous, non-Hindu sources, such as the Panji legends,[4] the Chalonarang legend, and the pure Balinese tale of Chupak (see Note 3, p. 183). With the exception of Chalonarang, performances of these plays in *wayang kulit* form are now almost obsolete. For the performance of the Panji plays (*wayang gambuh*) puppets of a different, more Javanese type were used, with the characteristic long neck and slender-waisted body. For Chupak or Chalonarang ordinary *parwă* puppets are used, with the addition of extra ones for the principal characters.

Although it is true that the night performances take place after the celebration of some event either domestic or religious, they must be considered as more or less pure entertainment. The ritualistic side of *wayang kulit* is clearly seen in the performance of *wayang lĕmah* (day *wayang*), which usually takes place between four and six in the afternoon.[5] Here it is one of the prescribed offerings for some religious ceremonies and takes place during the time the priest is officiating. A performance is required for such various ceremonies as tooth-filing (*mĕpandas*); cremation of the dead (*ngabèn*), when it takes place the day before or on the three days preceding the cremation; the consecration of a new or extensively repaired temple or important building (*mĕlaspasin*); for ceremonies attending temple anniversaries (*odalan*); or for the blessing of a child by a priest on one of its first three birthdays (*oton*), 210 days apart. Numerous other ceremonies, occasioned by either personal or community disaster, include a performance of *wayang lĕmah*.

No screen or lamp is used. The absent screen is symbolized by a skein of white thread, stretched, perhaps a foot above the *gedebong*,

---

[4] Panji is the name of a certain prince, the hero of many legends whose scene is laid in East Java. The legends probably derive from pre-Hindu ancestral myths. They are usually performed in Bali in a dramatic form known as *gambuh*, in which the actors are all male, and the motions, very stylized, closely approach dancing. Dialogue is spoken by one man in the orchestra, also known as the *dalang*.

[5] I have seen it in many places; district Ubud, Tabanan, Gianyar, etc. It is still quite common at certain ceremonies. Other villages I distinctly remember were Krambitan (for cremation), Pĕliatan (in the house-temple *pemerajan*) of a prince (the present *pĕrbĕkĕl* of Pĕliatan) while he made a ceremony involving the *mĕlaspasin* (consecration) of new god-statues, in Gianyar and Badung at cremations; in Pĕliatan for the *mĕlaspasin* of a renovated *balé-banjar*, etc., etc.

between two branches of the dap-dap tree.[6] It takes place on the ground, close to the ceremonial offerings. There is no audience; I have seen it take place in complete darkness, on account of the late arrival of the officiating priest. Special offerings, more elaborate than those required for the ordinary performances, must be made before it may be given. The play must be drawn from the "Adi-parwă," the first and introductory of the eighteen *parva*, and is nondramatic, more in the nature of a simple narrative, in which the puppets are mere illustrations to the recited text. It is significant that the *kayon* (see p. 153), once placed in the *gedebong*, is never removed but remains there until the end of the performance.

As a means to circumvent evil forces by what would seem to be sympathetic magic, a performance of the Chalonarang legend is often resorted to. Such notorious haunts of demons as the middle of the rice fields or the edge of graveyards are spots frequently chosen for the presentation of this play. On the anniversaries of the graveyard and the *balé agung* (assembly platform of the village council) this play was formerly given. It is beyond the scope of this study to go into the Chalonarang legend and its significance; I have only touched upon it in this place in order to indicate this third side to the *wayang kulit*.

It is not every *dalang* who is prepared to undertake *wayang lěmah* or who dares to give the Chalonarang tale. Furthermore there exist various rituals which, though constituting part of the duties of the *dalang*, may be performed only by certain *dalang* who have been specially prepared by the priest. Before he is qualified to perform, the would-be *dalang* must go through a prolonged series of studies. His training may be divided into three departments, the scholarly, the ethical or philosophical, and the religious.

His scholarship must include a thorough knowledge of all the classical literature. This demands a knowledge of Kawi, or old Javanese, the language of the classics. He must know the different styles of declamation or chanting of the classics, for there exist numerous metrical forms, each one having its peculiar conventions and requiring infinite variation in delivery and intonation. For the dialogue in the play his voice must be trained and flexible, for the different character-types have each their own special manner of speaking, and the *dalang* must be able to pass easily from the mighty threatenings of demon or

[6]Erythrina subumbrans, the *kayu sakti*, or holy tree. This tree has great significance in Bali. Its leaves are used as a protective charm against *léyak* (Note 1) and evil spirits (Note 6). Formerly, when fire was produced by rubbing sticks together, the *kayu sakti* alone was employed, together with bamboo.

warrior to the noble speech of the hero or the soft seductive murmur of a princess. During the play certain songs occur, and the voice of the *dalang* must be able to deliver the melodies in a pleasing and expressive manner. He must also be able to improvise witty jokes and create laughter in his audience.

The philosophical training includes foremost an understanding of the *Dharmă Pawayangan*, or "Laws of the *Wayang*," an old writing containing a mystic philosophy of the *wayang* (see Note 4, p. 185). It also contains certain directions for the conduct of the *dalang* as well as prayer formulas for his protection, for the puppets, and for the various ceremonies which he is called upon to perform from time to time (see Note 5, p. 186).

As we approach the religious training (since I have chosen to make the distinction), we arrive at the question, what is the true *dalang*? In the *Dharmă Pawayangan* he is given the formal title of *amangku dalang*, but he is only allowed to assume his name when, through preparation by a high priest (*pědandă*), he has reached the stage where he is ready to perform certain ceremonies outside the *wayang*, a stage in which he has priest-like power. Although there is no caste restriction for the *dalang*, and a man of even the lowest caste (*jabă*) may become, through correct training and long experience, one who will be respected with the highest, the *amangku dalang* seems naturally to come from the highest caste, the *Brahmană* caste, whose members only are eligible for high-priesthood. Before the *dalang* has attained this degree he is known simply as a *juru dalang*.

The *juru dalang* must know the correct offerings to make for the various types of *wayang* performances, the various prayers for the beginning and end of the play, and the prayers necessary for the protection of the puppets (see Note 5, p. 187). There are also magic formulas which he must recite before commencing a performance, in order to ensure his success with the audience (see Note 5, p. 187). He is then qualified to perform for the entertainment of others, or when the performance is part of a ritual (for example, *wayang lěmah*).

But the *amangku dalang* is called upon to undertake further ceremonies, which are concerned with the protection of the soul against evil forces. He may free a child born on a certain day of the attending curse (*sudamală*), and he must protect, by means of certain rites, the corpse on its journey from the house to the cremation grounds (see Note 6, p. 187). It will be seen then that the position of the *dalang* is a high one in the social structure, deriving probably from a function existing long before Hinduism.

The beginning of a *wayang* performance is a long ceremony in which offerings, prayers, the taking out and setting up of the puppets, and the opening introductory stanzas have each their own set place (see Note 7, p. 191). It is during the early part of this ritual that a strange figure of deep but lost significance makes its first appearance. This is the *kayonan* or *kayon*,[7] an oval-shaped conventionalized design representing a tree. At the base are mountain symbols representing the Mèru or Mahamèru, the mountain of the gods, or the ancestor heaven, from which the tree springs. For this reason the figure is sometimes referred to as the *gunungan*.[8]

During the play the *kayon* may be used to represent wind, fire, or water, when it is waved about to suggest the restlessness of the elements. But its primary function, which establishes it as a symbol with a far more profound meaning, is to be present at the beginning of the drama, before the puppets are taken from the box, and later to be flourished about by the *dalang* as a prelude to his opening invocation. It may also indicate a change of scene during the course of the play, and is set up at the end of the performance to indicate the termination of the drama. Thus it serves as the curtain of our own theater, opening and closing the play and dividing the acts. It also establishes the scene of the play, the supernatural world of the *wayang*, the kingdom of the immortals (see Note 8, p. 193).

When the *kayon* has first been inserted in the banana stalk, the puppets, one by one, are taken out, sorted, and set up according to tradition, to the right- or the left-hand side of the screen. All, save the demons and animals, must be present, although perhaps only a few of them will be required for the performance. Time is nothing here, and the audience willingly waits an hour or more, gaily laughing and chatting to the soft accompaniment of the music. When all the characters have finally been taken from the box, the stage is cleared of those which are to appear, and the rest remain huddled at either side, a strange and undecipherable forest of shadows. The *kayon* is now taken up and flourished; it is put through a series of fantastic evolutions, twirling, disappearing, reappearing, and spinning in rhythmic sympathy with the music. Seen from behind the screen it takes on the nature of a mystic dance; the *dalang* sways back and forth, carried away by the ritual, and the musical accents seem to imbue the *kayon* with a mysterious life of its own. The *dalang* intones the invocatory stanzas and then introduces the leading characters. The drama is now ready to begin.

[7] From *kayu*, tree.   [8] From *gunung*, mountain.

The lines of the play, inspired by reminiscences of the classical texts, are mostly improvised but interspersed with certain set stanzas, the *peretitală*. These are in the nature of short poems, which serve to illustrate a certain situation by establishing a mood through poetic imagery. They are very fragmentary and often with little logical sequence; the sources of most of them are lost. The greater part of them are sung or chanted by the *dalang* to the accompaniment of music, but occasionally one is delivered by the voice alone. The dialogue is punctuated by a small block of wood, the *chĕmpala*, which, held in the right foot of the *dalang*, is struck smartly against the specially loosened side of the *kropak*, giving a smart staccato sound. During battle scenes the *chĕmpala* creates a terrific din as it accents each blow dealt by the warriors.

The *peretitală*, and also the language of the leading characters, are in old Javanese and are very little understood, if at all, by the audience. Patiently the onlookers wait through the long declamations by the heroes until the time when they are summarized in Balinese by the followers, or *pĕnasar*. For the rest of the time the *dalang*, well familiar with his tale, improvises the dialogue according to his taste, and it is in the spontaneity and wit of the speeches in Balinese that much of his popularity lies.

The *pĕnasar* translate and comment upon the situations with a humor that is both mordant and ribald. The four leading ones, Tualèn (or Malèn), Wredah, Dèlĕm, and Sangut (Mangut) are ever present, no matter whether the play be from Hindu or Indonesian sources. It is held that these characters, unknown in the original Hindu legends, are survivals of a pre-Hindu era and were later incorporated into the newer literature. Tualèn, or Sĕmar, as he is known in Java, the most significant of the four has proved an enigma as yet unsolved, in spite of the many interpretations of his origin.[9] Remote ancestor or god? Embodiment of the early pre-Hindu indigene who accepts with a grain of salt the newer culture, or phallic symbol lauding the flesh? For his mighty weapon is nothing more than a faintly disguised phallus. He is a beloved favorite with the Balinese, whose appearance is always greeted with great enthusiasm. The attitude of Tualèn and his attendant Wredah (according to many his son) toward the principal (Hindu) characters is indeed one of irreverence.

---

[9] In Bali Tualèn is one of the four figures to receive holy water during the *sudamală* ceremony (Note 6a); he forms one of a tetrad of divinities sometimes known as Sanghyang Chatur Lokapală; he is also given a special place when the puppets are taken from the box (Note 7).

Earthly, shrewd, humorous, they represent the eternally material point of view, in sharp contrast to the exalted idealism and nobility of the heroes. Their loyalty and yet lack of respect delight the crowd. Tualèn especially, short, fat, and enormously paunched, is a Rabelaisian compound of Sancho Panza, Falstaff, and Panurge. In the same way he deflates his hero and attempts to bring him down to earth. The allusions in the play to local events do not seem out of place to the audience, and the triumphs of Tualèn and Wredah over Dèlĕm and Sangut, *pĕnasar* of the adversary, afford complete satisfaction. The role of the quartet is always a large one and almost overshadows the original plot.

The *wayang* figures and the general nature of the performance may be less sophisticated than the Javanese, but the music most surely is not. Here no comparison can possibly be made, for the idiom is far removed from that of Java. The music is supplied by four *gĕndèr*, metal-keyed instruments known here as *gĕndèr wayang*.[10] (See Plate XXXI.) The keys, ten in number, are suspended by means of leather thongs above bamboo resonators, which are tuned to the same vibrations as their respective keys, and thus give to the note struck a clear, ringing quality, of considerable intensity and duration. The instruments are played with both hands, each holding a light hammer, whose head is a disk of wood, loosely held between the second and third fingers. The fourth and fifth fingers are thus free to "dampen" the key by resting upon it as the next note is struck, in this way producing a perfect legato. This technique requires great flexibility of hand but is made practical by the fact that skips are rare (as will be seen from the ensuing examples), the melody generally proceeding step by step. Together with the singing quality produced by its resonator, each note has always a slightly percussive, metallic accent, caused by the shock of the wooden hammer.

The instruments are divided into two pairs, a larger one and a smaller one, sounding an octave higher. But in each pair of *gĕndèr* there is a slight difference of pitch between the two instruments. The

---

[10] For the Ramayana cycle, gong, drums, and percussion are added, an inartistic superimposition which completely covers up the delicate music. This combination of instruments is the same as that used in *wayang wong*, which devotes itself exclusively to the Ramayana. It is for this reason that I have chosen to deal with only the *parwă* music, which is complete in itself. The percussion finds justification in *wayang wong* where it regulates the quasi-dance steps of the actors. In *wayang kulit* it merely seems unnecessary, out of all proportion to the miniature stage. For Chalonarang the orchestra is the same as for *gambuh*, the original dramatic form, and consists of *rĕbab* (sort of violin), *suling* (flute), drums, and percussion.

lower *gĕndèr* of each pair, known as the *pĕngumbang*,[11] is almost a quarter of a tone below the pitch of the upper one—the *pĕngisep*.[12] Strange as this practice may sound, it does not make for confusion or dissonance but lends to each note played in unison a peculiarly vibrant and penetrating quality, especially in the lower register. The Balinese reveal themselves possessors of acoustically refined ears when they give as reason for this difference in pitch the desire "to create vibration in the tone." The smaller pair of instruments are used to enrich the tone quality of the lower ones and simply double their parts an octave higher. For this reason it is possible, and often done, to eliminate them. The tone quality, however, suffers greatly in consequence and loses in richness of overtones.

But the tone color of the four *gĕndèr* evades description, and it is difficult to convey in words an impression of the strange beauty of their sound. Sweet, yet acid, soft, yet metallic, the four instruments are in perfect accord with the nature of the performance. The clear-cut design of the music and the delicate arabesques are reflected in the transparent lacework of the puppets, whose gestures, miniature and heroic, nervous and menacing, are in turn retranslated into sound by the sensitive and vaguely sinister nature of the music.

Let us first examine the scale peculiar to the *gĕndèr wayang*, which is pentatonic, and known as *slèndro*. In order to better understand this scale in its relation to the other scales in current use, a brief survey of the Balinese scale system must be given.

If we take the following series of notes, in which occur, after the unison, the following intervals, second, second, third, second, we have the basic formula for all the pentatonic scales. The rest is a matter of pitch and tuning.

EXAMPLE 1:

These notes are given names according to their relative position in the scale, but which can be transposed with the scale, a method similar to the English solfeggio system. The names of these notes respectively are: *ding, dong, dèng, dung,* and *dang.* No matter what the tuning of the notes may be, the name sequence remains the same; the interval

---

[11]From *kumbang*: generic name for bumblebees, beetles, etc. In this case, the "hummer," "droner."

[12]From *ngisĕp*, to inhale, absorb.

between *dèng* and *dung* and that between *dang* and a possible higher *ding* are always the greater ones, and the other intervals the smaller ones. For the purposes of nomenclature, such a scale as the following one is not in its fundamental position; the two lower notes must be transposed an octave higher, in order that the notes and their names may find their true place.

EXAMPLE 2:

U   A   I   O   E   I   O   E   U   A

Now there exists a "mother" scale, a diatonic scale of seven unequal intervals, known as *saih pitu* (series of seven) and which is found only in the most ancient types of *gamelan*. From this scale various modes could be created, by erecting the above note sequence on different degrees of the mother scale. The two unnamed notes, lying between *dèng* and *dung* and above *dang* were known as *pĕnyorog*[13] and *pĕmèro*,[14] respectively, and were treated as passing notes, rarely heard except when the modulation from one mode to another was effected.

EXAMPLE 2a:

Today nearly all the *gamelan* in Bali limit themselves to only one or another of the five-note scales, whose origin nevertheless derives from the *saih pitu*.

We now return to the *slèndro* scale.[15] Curiously enough, this scale does not owe its origin to the *saih pitu* but is entirely independent, complete in itself, tracing back to a very different source. It is claimed by certain musicologues that this scale is the result of an attempt to divide the octave into five equal intervals. Can we say with certainty that this is true? Let us find out just how much it applies to the Balinese scale in theory and practice.

---

[13] From *sorog*, to insert, shove in.

[14] *Pĕmèro* (or *pĕmbèro*), from *bero*, false.

[15] The *slèndro* scale has been traced back as far as the middle of the eighth century, when it is assumed to have first made its appearance, brought by a conquering Cailendra (= *selendro?*) king from the Hindu-Indonesian kingdom of Çriwijaya in East Sumatra.

We must first see what the ideal scale of five equal intervals would be. The intervals would compare with those of the European tempered scale as 1 : 5 to 1 :12. Erecting such a scale on f sharp, the lowest note of the *gĕndèr wayang*, we obtain the following:

EXAMPLE 3:

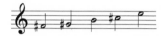

The nearest approach to expressing this scale in our notation would be

EXAMPLE 4:

It is worth noting that if such a scale is played on some instrument on which it is possible, as, for example, the monochord, the European trained ear automatically tends to "correct" the scale by unconsciously raising or lowering the pitch of each note so that it seems to become the nearest note to it of the tempered chromatic scale. Thus the above notation of this scale remains rational. So much for the deterioration of our ears, grown accustomed to tempered tuning.

Now the notes of the *gĕndèr wayang* scale are named in the following order: *dong, dèng, dung, dang,* and *ding*. When this note-sequence is rearranged so that *ding* becomes the lowest note, it will be seen that, although of theoretically equal intervals, the scale, when expressed in our notation, belongs to the regular pentotonic scheme.

EXAMPLE 5:

Now it is beyond doubt that the Balinese themselves consider this scale as composed of unequal intervals, as is shown, not only in the naming of the notes but in general practice. It sometimes happens that *gĕndèr wayang* music is transposed to a *gamelan* with another scale, or vice versa. Such a phrase as

EXAMPLE 6:

becomes, when transposed into the *gamelan gong*

EXAMPLE 6a:

A   U   E   O

and thus proves the relation existing in the minds of the Balinese
between the two scales.

Furthermore, the *gĕndèr* has yet to be found in Bali whose scale is
divided into five equal intervals. Kunst, in Part II of his *De Toonkunst
van Bali*, gives nine different tunings of the *gĕndèr wayang* scale, in
which the intervals of each scale varied in size.[16] The intervals,
however, tend to be greater between *dèng* and *dung*, and *dang* and a
higher *ding*. In my own experience I have found this to be invariably
the case, both on listening to many instruments—making due allowance for "correcting by ear"—and when transcribing music from
gĕndèr to piano. The greater part of the musical illustrations in this
study are from the *gĕndèr wayang* from Kută, district Badung, the
same musicians and instruments recorded by Odeon (see Recordings,
p. 196). The scale[17] of the *gĕndèr pengumbang* of the larger pair may
be described thus:

EXAMPLE 7:

F#   G#   B   C#   E   F#

In this scale such notes heard simultaneously struck as

EXAMPLE 7a:

may be distinctly heard as thirds, fourths, fifths, and sixths, as may
be verified by listening to the records, particularly *Pĕmungkah* and
Sekar Ginotan.

Let us not accept, then, without reservations, the theory that

[16] It is unfortunate that Kunst, noting with accuracy the vibrations of each note,
does not mention whether they were taken from *gĕndèr pengumbang* or *gĕndèr
pĕngisep*, which he has confused as being an octave apart instead of an approximate
quarter tone. Furthermore, instruments are only too frequently out of tune, so that
the true scale may only be ascertained with certainty from a *pandé krawang*, the
maker of the metal keys, and also the tuner, or else from a newly tuned instrument.

[17] The third note, b, is the most noticeably variable to the ear and is found, in the
different places, flattened in pitch sometimes so low as to become almost b flat.

slèndro is a scale ideally divided into five equal intervals. As such it is neither practiced nor understood in Bali today. Were such the case, it would be as colorless and ambiguous as the whole-tone scale; there would be no point in giving the notes of the scale interval-discriminating names; it also could not be used as an accompaniment of the voice, as found in Examples 17 and 19. After four years of listening to the music of the *gĕndèr wayang* I have still to be convinced that this ingenious theory is not unnatural, at least inasmuch as it applies to Bali.

But my objective is not to establish once and for all the absolute pitch of this scale, nor to place it historically, but rather to consider the music of the *wayang* from the standpoint of art, to examine its technique and construction, and to attempt to create an enthusiasm for this form of musical expression.

The music played by the two large *gĕndèr* (doubled an octave higher by the other two) ranges from simple, unison passages to extremely complicated four-part polyphony. The compositions may be divided into two types, one, which serves as an accompaniment to the *dalang* for certain *peretitală* which are sung during the play, and the other, complete in itself, which follows and illustrates the dramatic action. The first type—andante, two-voiced, and irregular in phrase structure—is nonrhythmic, archaic, static. The other type, animated and dynamic, is built upon well-defined forms which are both ingenious and logical. The general construction of this latter type of music, its figuration and style of execution, bear evidence of considerable development during the course of time.

Before proceeding to illustrations of the music which accompanies the voice, several elementary technical details must first be noted. Owing to the irregularity of the intervals of the scale, the following progression of intervals (as expressed in our notation):

EXAMPLE 8:

must be considered as a series of parallel intervals which result when the lower note is separated from the higher by two intervening notes. This would be considered as an argument in favor of considering the *slèndro* scale as built up of equal intervals, were it not for the fact that intervals similarly constructed play a prominent part in all Balinese music, regardless of scale system. Such modifications, even more apparent to our ear, which result by the transposition of this interval from step to step in the following scale, for example, do not in any way prevent it from being considered as having the same context, the same value, and mechanically treated in the same way.

EXAMPLE 9:

When the upper and lower notes of an interval are separated by one note only, we obtain the following sequence:

EXAMPLE 10:

When passages occur in which an effect different from that obtained from consecutive octaves is sought, the first may be employed, but always leading to an eventual octave which terminates the phrase.

EXAMPLE 11:

Series of intervals of the second type are rarely employed, but we shall find them occasionally used in the figuration of the music for *gĕndèr* alone (Examples 30, 44, and 45).

The melodic line will be seen to progress step by step in the scale. The judicious use of a greater interval is allowed from time to time, but rarely do two such intervals follow one another without the intervention of several "step to step" intervals. It will be remembered that this is one of the first demands of our classical counterpoint.

The *ngorèt*, a series of rapid notes approaching or embellishing an essential note, plays a very important part in all the slow music, adding at times to the melodic contour a peculiarly restless and nervous quality.

It is difficult to draw the line where the *ngorèt* ceases to be mere ornamentation and becomes an organic embellishment of some essential note. Many melodic lines, of which Example 25 is a fine illustration, are nothing more than the abstract result of extended

EXAMPLE 12:

embellishment of the essential note, or passing notes between such essential notes.

EXAMPLE 13:

Another characteristic feature is the staccato tremolo, which beginning slowly and pianissimo, suddenly breaks into a crescendo and rushes to the final note, which is allowed to vibrate.

EXAMPLE 14:

Closely related to this is the sharp and immediately deadened staccato, ⨦, so short as to be practically without pitch. The percussive quality of this sound is of rhythmic value; it serves to give a marked accent on an off beat, to break off a phrase or to anticipate a close (see Example 15).

EXAMPLE 15:

EXAMPLE 16:

It may also signal an abrupt change in dynamics. Sometimes it is used as an anticipation of some essential note in the phrase (see Examples 17 and 18). Repeated, it becomes an extended anticipation of a note (see Example 16).

Alas Harum (The Scented Forest), the music which accompanies the opening invocatory stanzas of the *dalang*, seems to me worth quoting in full, for it forms an excellent example of the free, andante type of music. The structure consists of a series of long, attenuated phrases, each leading to a cadence, and recurring in a certain set pattern (see Examples 17 and 18). The music is played with extreme liberty, quasi recitativo, and with practically no nuances. The voice of the *dalang* is noted only approximately, as he delivers his part with great freedom.

Like the dancing, art, and customs, the musical versions differ with the various localities. This is not only to be expected in a land where music is preserved by memory only, for no notation whatsoever exists for the *gĕndèr wayang* music, but also makes possible, by means of comparisons, the fuller understanding of what is musically essential. The two versions come from two villages some thirty miles apart, Bongkasă and Kută. Previous to the facilities in transportation which have arisen within the last decade, their means of communication were slight. The music was learned from two different teachers who, in all probability, had received their own training in points still further apart. Thirty miles still is, for many of the older generation, a great distance in Bali, which represents a great variation in customs and traditions.

We see that the patterns correspond. The phrase sequence may be expressed thus:

Bongkasă   1, (introductory) 2; 3,4,5,2; 3,6,7,2; 3,6,7,2; etc.
Kută   1, (introductory) 2; 3,4,5,2; 3,4,5,2; etc., coda.

The phrase sequence 3,6,7,2 (or the simpler 3,4,5,2) may be repeated, with possible variations, until the termination of the *dalang's* text. The coda (of which the Bongkasă version is lacking) serves as a transition into the following section, the *pĕnyachah parwă* (see Note 7, p. 191), with which the *dalang* introduces his leading characters.

Lack of space forbids illustrations of all the music which accompanies the *dalang*. Much of it is in the style of *Alas Harum*; the mood remains the same, in spite of the difference in texts, and only the voice of the *dalang* changes, varying in pitch and voice quality.

EXAMPLE 17:

EXAMPLE 17 (cont.):

EXAMPLE 19:

etc. (see ex. 44)

However, *Rebong* (see Example 19), the music for love episodes,
deserves to be quoted, for the contour of the phrases is noticeably
different, and the voice of the *dalang*, high-pitched and seductive, is
here florid and gracious, a striking contrast to the hieratic intonations
employed in the preceding illustrations. Here again the voice is free,

this time to embroider with many embellishments the phrase, according to his whim and virtuosity. The concluding sections of *Rebong* will be found in Examples 44, 45, and 46.

These slow movements, freed of any emotion, have a sober and abstract beauty. The almost liturgical cadences supply expressive points of repose, and the free and leisurely way in which the music is performed creates an atmosphere completely static, where all sense of time is lost. Before proceeding to an analysis of the more dynamic music, I cannot resist quoting the following closing phrase from *Bendu Semară*, which has, for me, a peculiar charm (see Example 20). The long, winding phrase uncoils and straightens out like the graceful tendril of a vine.

EXAMPLE 20:

It is in the second type of music, dynamic and overflowing with vitality, that the full imaginative power of the Balinese is revealed. The music is released upon a swift course filled with rhythmic surprises. Complex syncopations succeed one another in endless variety, and the pulse constantly changes through sudden accelerandos and finely calculated rallentandos. A great diversity of sound and color

EXAMPLE 21:

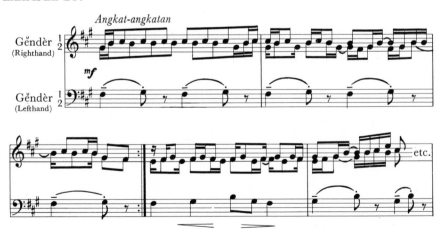

prevails, and all gradations of tone within the possibilities of the instruments are employed. Dry, staccato passages alternate with

EXAMPLE 22:

extended lyrical episodes, fluid and legato, of indescribable grace. The music is like a prism revolving in sunlight, transparent, and glittering with iridescent hues.

EXAMPLE 23:

The pair of *gĕndèr* no longer sounds in unison. Each instrument plays an individual but dependent part and complements the other in such a way that the two are welded together in an indissoluble unity. The music now consists of a repeated motif or an extended melodic line in the bass, with an upper accompaniment which, when heard, may sound as one voice or two voices. The following example may serve as a typical illustration in which the accompaniment, although different in each part, sounds as a single voice. The left hand of each instrument remains the same.

When the accompaniment is truly two-voiced the intervals generally employed are those cited in Example 8, although modern practice admits the use of the second series, as we shall find in Examples 44 and 45.

Sometimes the melodic line is split up between the two instruments.

More sonorous is the following two-voiced variant. The occasional presence of a third, fourth, or fifth in the melody is the result of each part approaching a principal note from opposite directions.

EXAMPLE 24:

Such embellishments as

EXAMPLE 24a(1):

and

EXAMPLE 24a(2):

are frequently employed simultaneously; their characteristic use will be
seen in Example 25.[18] Here the accompaniment is found in its simplest
form but contains the germ of part-alternation whose possibilities of development may be seen in many of the illustrations given in this study.

EXAMPLE 25:

[18] See measures 4, 6, 8, 10, etc.

Through this ingenious dovetailing of the two parts, complicated polyrhythmic passages are executed with incredible speed and smoothness, giving the impression of a single instrument. The two voices meet and separate, intersecting each other with most resourceful variety. An infinite number of patterns are used, ever-changing, sometimes following the contour of the melody, and at other times remaining fixed in a kind of ostinato.

The examples of 26a, b, and c show different instances where the melodic note appears in the accompaniment at the same moment, either in the upper or the lower voice. Example 26c is especially worthy of attention as a carefully worked-out detail in which the figuration follows the descending melodic line and approaches the cadence, dissolving into a simple unison.

EXAMPLE 26a:

EXAMPLE 26b:

EXAMPLE 26c:

A freer treatment of the accompaniment is shown in the following illustrations (Example 27).

Occasionally the accompaniment becomes the center of interest, developing into a melodic line with a direction of its own (see Example 28).

EXAMPLE 27:

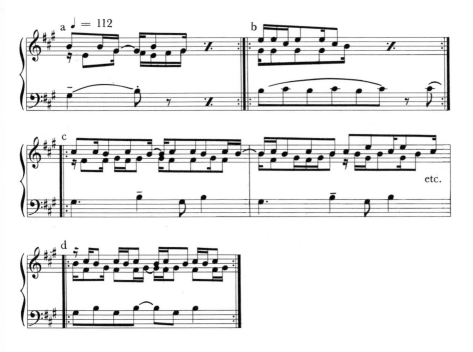

EXAMPLE 28:

A reversal of this procedure will be found in Example 29. Here the accompaniment remains fixed in an upper ostinato, while the melody plays back and forth between the two essential notes, f sharp and b.

EXAMPLE 29:

It is impossible to do more than hint at the wealth of ornamentation which exists in this music. Each district, each group of musicians even, has its style of playing, its favorite methods of procedure which reflect the taste and individuality of teacher and musicians. And as one listens to the music of village after village something more than wonder grows at the endless variety of patterns and melodies. How simple are the following surprisingly Debussy-like figurations (see Example 30); it is impossible to realize without the instruments the charm and delicacy of their sonority.

EXAMPLE 30:

We can better understand where the life and strength of the accompaniment lies when we separate the two parts and find to what an extent each possesses a great rhythmic vitality of its own—a vitality whose intensity springs from a pulse which is essentially syncopated. Although they often seem to negate each other, it has been seen that the two separate parts are actually interdependent; the syncopations, felt rather than deliberately worked out, are so constructed as to form a continuous pattern of notes. The evenness of their execution is made secure by the convergence from time to time of the two voices on the same beat, sometimes at the unison, sometimes at the fifth or sixth. These two intervals create a subtle cross-rhythm of their own, unaccented but clear on account of their relatively greater resonance. In the already quoted illustrations we may find the following cross-rhythms.

EXAMPLE 31:

This inner rhythm may be developed to a point where it dominates the music (see Example 32).

EXAMPLE 32:

Strident passages in fifths, played by each instrument, constitute another element in the music (see Example 33).

EXAMPLE 33:

Occasionally the fifths automatically break into sixths (see Example 34).

EXAMPLE 34:

A fifth superimposed over a lower fifth or sixth is often employed (see Example 35).

EXAMPLE 35:

Sometimes the two instruments become independent and travel in opposite directions. The following example, with its curious seconds, is merely Example 24a carried to the extreme.

EXAMPLE 36:

The next illustrations show even greater imagination; here each part has attained complete liberty. The polyphony has an easy grace and richness of texture which is all the more surprising when we stop to realize that such passages are not the result of some mind trained in the art of counterpoint but are spontaneously conceived during some rehearsal, when some slight deviation or fresh version is sought.[19] How many of these transient details are created from time to time by some musician or group, only to be soon forgotten in the ever-changing and nonrecorded course of Balinese music!

[19] Such fresh variants are developed at rehearsal, usually by the leading spirit of the four musicians. They naturally must be doubled by the two instruments an octave higher. They are practiced until learned and remain fixed until either deliberately changed or ultimately forgotten by degeneration of the group. Time and again I have been told by responsible musicians that the ideal is the perfect doubling at the octave. The results are noticeable in the clarity of the playing of a well-practiced group, and the confusion of careless playing. The Balinese also are critical and discriminating in this matter.

EXAMPLE 37:

In the following quotation (Example 38), from the village of Sayan (Gianyar), the alternating of the independent parts, which resolve into a single melodic line with simple accompaniment, will not at first glance be recognized as an ingenious variant of Example 25 (see measures 18 to 25).

The whole section was worked out and executed in the same way.

EXAMPLE 38:

The two following illustrations may give some idea of the more complex play of the left-hand melody between the two instruments (see Examples 39 and 39a):

EXAMPLE 39:

EXAMPLE 39a:

Before attempting to analyze the musical form, one more element, that of tonality, must be examined. The scale may be divided into five tonal centers, one for each note of the scale.[20]

EXAMPLE 40:

The lowest note of each mode is the point of gravity, a so-called tonic. The third note, forming an interval of a "fourth" with the lowest note, is a secondary point of gravity, while the other two notes have more or less the character of accessory notes. As will be seen, the last mode is irregular, the fourth becoming a third. It is nevertheless treated in the same way as the others. Any motif in one mode may be transposed without alteration to any other mode, retaining, however, the same context. In the following example each group of notes has the same value:

EXAMPLE 41:

The first two modes are the most often employed and form the basis for the greater number of compositions. Less frequent are the next two, and it is rarely that the melody finds itself within the last one. The shorter compositions usually consist of a section in the first mode, followed by its transposition into the second. Back it falls into the first tonality, only to rise once more to the other. These two tonalities are played against each other, each transposition bringing

[20] Needless to say, the Balinese do not consciously consider their scale in this way. I have dissected it thus for the sake of analysis.

EXAMPLE 42:

with it some new variation in the figuration, and the composition nearly always ends on the opening note.

The ostinato is the typical foundation for compositions of this class. Although essentially simple, these ostinatos nevertheless possess, through their syncopation and expressive phrasing, a restless energy which never declines.

Let us take for a basic model *lagu Dèlĕm* (Example 43), whose simplicity furnishes a clear example of a composition constructed on an ostinato which lies within the two lowest modes. The rather broad melodic line, however, which takes the place of the usual figuration, is unusual.

EXAMPLE 43:

The organic structure of the ostinato compositions is, as we have seen, simplicity itself. It is in the figuration of the upper part, continually changing and giving new aspects to the bass, that the form and life of the music generally lies.

The longer compositions are by contrast freer in form, consisting of different sections, often closely interrelated and built upon free development of a single interval or short motif. Sometimes they are divided definitely into two sections, a first, the *pĕngawak* or "body" of the composition, and a subsequent section in a quicker tempo, the *pĕngechèt* or *peniban*. The *pĕngawak* may or may not be preceded by a rather long introduction. Let us examine *lagu Rebong*. The *pĕngawak*, quoted in Example 19, finally dissolves into a melody with accompaniment. The following phrase (Example 44), which now follows the first half of the lower voice of the opening phrase, is obviously a variation of its second half.

EXAMPLE 44:

The second phrase of the *pĕngawak* is now heard, followed by the variation of the second half of this phrase (see Example 45).

EXAMPLE 45:

After several repetitions of the two phases with their variations, a sudden quickening of the tempo leads into the *pĕngechèt* (see Example 46), which is in itself a further variation of the note sequence,

the germ of the whole composition.[21]

---

[21] The construction of *lagu rebong* seems complicated but is simple. The sequence is this: *pĕngawak* (Example 19) consisting of two phrases, the first, repeated with vocal variant, the second (also repeated), but I did not finish the vocal line. The *pĕngawak* can be repeated ad lib. When the change is sought, the first half of the first phrase is played (first line) and followed by Example 44. The first half of the

This music, so clear-cut in form, is in reality program music in miniature, for it is used in love scenes, which it follows with delightful precision. During the *pĕngawak*, at which time only the voice of the *dalang* is heard, the hero woos the princess with gentle caresses.

EXAMPLE 46:

Increasing ardor finds its accompaniment in the transitional music, and the *pĕngechèt*, with its animation and ironic syncopations, accompanies what is often the natural and logical outcome of the preceding tender scenes. This is the moment for Tualèn, inspired by his prince, to approach the female attendant (*chondong*) of the princess and give her unmistakable token of his easily inflamed passion.

Other compositions exist built upon a series of variations of an opening phrase. The variations are then transposed, almost note for note, a tone or two tones higher. Such a treatment has the result of giving (to us) a very satisfactory form, in which the pattern repeats but, by the nature of the change in pitch and interval relation, becomes a further variation. A beautiful example of a composition in rondo form is *Mérak Ngilo*, recorded by Odeon (see Recordings, p. 196). This is one of the many compositions, of great formal variety, which are not connected with *wayang* performance but are played at various ceremonies demanding *gĕndèr wayang* music. They also serve as little overtures to the play, performed before the *dalang* has unlocked his box of puppets.

The integral music commences with the *Pĕmungkah* (see Note 7,

second phrase of *pĕngawak* is played (ninth line up to comma), followed by Example 45. Return to first half of phrase one with its pendant (Example 44). The *pĕngechèt* (Example 46) is introduced on the third measure of Example 44. Its "linking passage" will be seen to correspond in the first measure quoted with the third measure of Example 44.

p. 192), an exceedingly long composition which lasts a good hour. After a short introduction the first tap of the *chĕpală* is heard, calling attention to all. From this moment the music must rigidly conform to the different stages of the opening rituals. No exact time limit is put for the setting up of the puppets, the flourishing of the *kayonan*, or the *peretitală*. Herein lies the explanation for the many musical episodes consisting of indefinitely repeated motifs. These may be extended or contracted at will, to meet the situation. The musicians know all the formalities thoroughly; their tempo only is set, and the cues for changes given by the sharp accents of the *chĕpală*.

It is impossible to give any adequate idea of the *Pĕmungkah* without quoting the music in full. Although one might roughly describe it as a series of episodes, each complete in itself, the relation of these episodes to one another is too complex to be explained without numerous examples. Ostinatos, long lyrical sections, variations and developments of recurring motifs, elaborate transpositions—all these musical elements are exploited to the full. The final section of the *Pĕmungkah*,[22] given in Example 25, leads into a motif which signalizes the appearance of the *kayon* (Example 15a). Developed at great length, with many different figurations, the music comes finally to an abrupt halt, to be followed immediately by *Alas Harum*.[22] The music to the *peretitală* then follows; at its termination the chief music of the play is over. From now on it will be merely incidental, and accompany such situations as warfare, flights, lamentations, and deaths, or fire, wind, and water as represented by the *kayon*.

Angkat-angkatan[23] (for departures and flights) and *Batèl*[24] (for scenes of warfare) belong to the ostinato type of music, which can last one minute or five, according to the occasion.

EXAMPLE 47:

---

[22] Recorded by Odeon; see list of Recordings, p. 196.

[23] From *angkatan*, an expeditionary force.

[24] The nearest translation I could get to *Batèl* is something like the musical term *agitato*. All Balinese dramatic music has some type of *Batèl* or other.

The many musical details which I have given in this study speak for themselves as evidence of the high sophistication of workmanship. Folk art is a too unflattering term to apply to this music. It is non-lyrical, nonexpressive, a complicated antithesis to the simplicity and directness usually associated with folk music. And it is precisely in this abstract formalism that so much of its beauty lies. With five notes a tonal world is created, a small world perhaps, but rich in possibilities which we see everywhere fulfilled. A monotony which might exist through the limitations of the scale is avoided by the extreme rhythmic vitality pervading the music, a primitive and joyous vitality that finds its most complete expression among the Balinese in their drum playing. This coupling of primitive vigor with cultural sophistication gives to Balinese music a great deal of its freshness and distinction. The *gĕndèr wayang* is only one of perhaps a dozen different *gamelan* types existing in Bali today, each with a completely different idiom and combination of instruments. It would be hard to find a parallel of so much musical wealth crowded into so small a space as this tiny island filled with intensely music-loving people.

Notes

Note 1. Many versions of the Chalonarang legend are known in Bali, but the following synopsis has been chosen from a translation from the old Javanese into Dutch by R. Ng. Poerbatjaraka, whose version is clear and dramatic.

The legend derives its name from the widow (*rangdă*) Chalonarang, a sorceress dwelling in Girah, a province in East Java, during the reign of King Erlangga, who ruled East Java in the first part of the eleventh century. Chalonarang possessed a beautiful daughter, Ratna Mangalli, but no man dared to ask for her in marriage, for the mother was too greatly feared as a sorceress. In anger Chalonarang seeks the aid of Durgă, goddess of death, asking permission to spread plague and destruction throughout the land. The request is granted, and so the widow calls together her pupils, and, after plotting at crossroads and in graveyards, they proceed to carry out their evil intentions. The people die in heavy numbers, and the king, after being advised by a famous holy man that the sorceress Chalonarang is responsible for the plague, sends a minister and warriors to kill her. The minister attacks her at midnight, but the *rangdă* springs up, "and from her eyes, her ears, her nostrils, and her mouth fire streamed forth, which, flaming and curling, consumed him." The warriors flee and notify the king, while Chalonarang and her pupils continue their destruction. There is no space to relate the gruesome crimes they perpetrate, disemboweling and devouring their victims, and bathing in their blood. In desperation the king once more turns to the holy man, who sends his foremost acolyte to marry the daughter of the *rangdă* and so appease her. The marriage takes place, but the plague still persists. Finally the holy man himself sets forth and, arriving at Girah, meets with the pupils of the sorceress. These he finally converts to repentance, and dismisses them. And now he confronts the *rangdă*, and the great conflict between good and evil begins. With smooth and hypocritical words the sorceress begs to be shown the way to righteousness. She is told that expiation may be obtained only through death. In rage she replies that, if such is the case, she would rather kill the holy man and gladly expiate her sins in hell. She threatens him and, to show her magic power, blasts a mighty banyan tree, reducing it to ashes. The holy man restores it. The *rangdă* sends forth fire from all parts of her body, and the flames surround the holy man. He remains unharmed, for his magic power is greater, and with a gesture kills her, only to bring her back once more to life. In fury the sorceress reproaches him for reanimating her. The holy one replies that it was done in order to give her a last opportunity for repentance. And so the *rangdă* is calmed and, having been taught the way of redemption, is killed once more, in a state of absolution.

The death of the *rangdă* seems not to be accepted by the Balinese, who still fear her evil powers, and her alliance with the terrible goddess Durgă. In the play she is never killed, and the legend generally proceeds only as far as where she is attacked by the minister of the king. Closely connected with the belief in the supernatural powers of the *rangdă* is the belief in *léyak*, or the metamorphosis into animals, flames, or strange shapes of evilly disposed people who may acquire this power through the means of black magic and incantations involving the aid of Chalonarang.

Now to the special *dalang* who venture to perform this drama is attributed a strange power, the power to summon the many *léyak*, who dwell in the vicinity. During the scene in the play where the sorceress calls her pupils to her the lamp is darkened, and all becomes sinister. In terrific tones the *dalang*, often more than half in trance, shrieks forth: "*Léyak! léyak!*" The suspense is frightening, and the audience grows hushed and apprehensive. According to the Balinese, many a time have the *léyak* been compelled to appear, arriving from great distances, in the form of flickering, blue flames. But only a *dalang* of intense will and magically strong can achieve this feat. And it is accompanied with dire consequences, for in the village next day many people are found dead.

What is the significance of this strange performance, and what is the reason for it? I have asked many Balinese but can get no more satisfactory reply than that it is done in order to prove the power of the *dalang*. It was only with great persuasion that I could get the *dalang* from a neighboring village, an old Brahmană priest, to perform the play near my house, for he claimed to greatly fear the consequences of his powers and did not wish his good name to suffer for any disaster which might befall our village on the following day.

Note 2. The story of Ramă and his faithful wife Sită, whom he won in a contest, breaking the king of Videha's mighty bow. Ramă is the eldest son of the king of the Kocalas (in Northern India) and rightful heir to the throne. But his father is forced to banish him, as a result of an intrigue instigated by Ramă's stepmother in favor of her own son. Accompanies by Sită and his brother Lakshmana, Ramă flees to the forest, where he dwells in peace. The giant Rawană, who rules Langka (Ceylon), becomes enamored of Sită and, sending a golden hind to tempt away Ramă and Lakshmana, abducts her in their absence. Ramă forms an alliance with Sugriva, chief of the monkeys, whom his brother Balin has dethroned. He aids Sugriva to reconquer his kingdom, and in return the army of monkeys is put at his disposal for the rescue of Sită. A series of wars ensue in Langka, between Ramă with his monkey allies and Ravana, in which Hanoman, general of the monkey forces, is the hero of many adventures. Ultimately Sită is rescued. But a stigma rests upon her fidelity, and Ramă orders her death by fire. Sită mounts the pyre, but the flames refuse to destroy her, and, her innocence established, she returns to Ramă.[25]

Note 3. The Chupak story[26] relates the adventures of two brothers, unlike in appearance and in character, vying with each other in the quest to retrieve the stolen Radèn Galuh, Princess of Daha (a province

[25] For a condensation in verse of the chief episodes of this poem, see *The Ramayana and the Mahabharata*, condensed into English verse by R. C. Dutt (London, Dent, 1910).

[26] The version here given is condensed from a *lontar* in the possession of, and translated into Malay, by Dèwă Nyoman Rai of Pĕliatan. He compared it to that of the Kirtya Liefrinck van der Tuuk in Singaraja, saying that the latter was incomplete and included nonclassical innovations (typical of North Bali). The little touches of realism were added after the author witnessed a performance by the *dalang* from Bongkasă who specializes in Chupak.

of ancient East Java). Throughout the tale, the play of their contrasting natures adds a second contest of good and evil to the more common theme, the struggle between heroes and demons.

It is said that Kalǎ (see Note 6a) entered into the elder brother, Chupak, making him lazy, boastful, gluttonous, and cowardly. The younger brother, Grantang, is the gentle and refined type, fair and wise and humble in speech, but strong in battle. The story begins with a trick played on Grantang by Chupak, who sets the mother and father against Grantang, so that they beat him and cast him out of the house. He is forced to go wandering far in the wilderness, but Chupak accompanies him, bringing ample supplies of food which Grantang must carry, although Chupak manages to devour it all. In their subsequent encounters with people on the way, Grantang is forced to do the heavy work, while Chupak's boastfulness and greed are shown at every turn. At last they come to the palace of Daha, where the *rajǎ* asks them to recover his daughter, who has been stolen by the giant Limandaru. Chupak vows to kill the giant, no matter what his strength may be, and the *rajǎ* promises him the kingdom and the princess as bride if he succeeds in his mission. Grantang also says he will try but can promise nothing before he has encountered the giant foe.

After a feast, at which Chupak makes a disgusting exhibition of greed, they set off, well supplied with food, Chupak marching proudly in front and Grantang behind carrying the rice. But at the first sight of the giant's footprints Chupak grows afraid, and gets behind his younger brother. During the battle with Limandaru, when Grantang does the fighting, Chupak hides himself in a tree. Grantang, "like a butterfly," escapes the grasp of the giant and finally manages to kill him. Radèn Galuh is rescued and falls in love with Grantang.

On the way home, they must pass the night in a forest. Grantang and Radèn Galuh go to sleep, while Chupak promises to keep watch. A *raksasǎ* (demon) comes and steals the princess, but Chupak is too terrified to challenge him. Grantang, awakening, starts in pursuit, but he is held back by Chupak, who comes clumsily behind, falling down and calling pitifully for help. At length they come to the lair of the *raksasǎ*, which is at the bottom of a deep well. With the aid of a rope Grantang descends into the well and rescues the princess a second time, while the *raksasǎ* sleeps. Chupak, trembling with fear, pulls Radèn Galuh to the top and then cuts the rope, leaving Grantang at the bottom of the well.

Chupak then returns with Radèn Galuh to the palace, claims the kingdom, and is betrothed to the princess. He spends his time eating and drinking, and pursuing young girls.

Grantang kills the *raksasă*. After a long time of starvation in the well, he manages to construct a ladder from the bones of the *raksasă* and climbs out. He is so thin that people take him for an evil spirit and run away from him. At last he reaches the palace and calls for his brother Chupak. Chupak repudiates him and orders him to be beaten and cast into the sea.

Grantang is picked up by a fisherman, to whom he brings good luck. When he has been nursed back to health by the fisherman, he is discovered by Radèn Galuh in the humble dwelling. She has for a long time put off her wedding to Chupak and now persuades her father to allow her to marry the most skilled warrior. She sends gorgeous raiment and trappings to Grantang, who rides in state to the palace. He does battle with Chupak and, after defeating him, wins Radèn Galuh for his bride.

This popular tale is always performed with great spirit and draws a huge audience. The dialogue is for the most part in Balinese (a rare pleasure for the spectators), and the play abounds in comic situations. The cowardice and greed of Chupak are exaggerated to the point of buffoonery. When he feasts, the banquet is an endless procession of dishes; realistic belchings and worse depict his gluttonous satisfaction. When in terror his bowels vividly turn to water, and his erotic adventures are frankly obscene, graphically illustrated, to the particular delight of the small children in the audience. Such scenes as the episode where the fisherman is out in his boat, angrily pulling up ridiculous rubbish from the sea, until he finally pulls up Grantang, are enacted with a real sense of comedy. As pure entertainment this story seems most suited to the idiom of *wayang kulit* as performed in Bali, the most successfully realized. We are a long way from the noble gestures and deeds of the Hindu heroes.

Note 4. According to Balinese philosophy, each person possesses two bodies, a material body (*sariră stulă*) and a spiritual one (*sariră suksemă*). Within the spiritual body of the *dalang* are many places, which are occupied by the various constituents of the *wayang*. The *Dharmă Pawayangan* says:

The puppet box (*kĕropak*) lies within the bowels.
The gavel (*chĕpală*) lies in the foot.
The puppet handles lie in the fingers.

The screen (*klir*) lies in the omentum.[27]

The poles (to which the screen is laced) lie in the bones.

The cord (which fastens the screen) lies in the sinews.

The lamp lies in the socket of the eye.

The oil lies in the fat.

The wick lies in the marrow.

The fire lies in the liver.[28]

The smoke lies in the voice.

The extinguished fire lies in the gall.

The fire as it bursts into flame lies in the lungs.

The heavy voice (*suară agong, perekasă*) comes from the liver.

The light voice (*suară alus*) comes from the gall.

The brave-serene voice (*suară galak-amanis*) lies in the lungs.

The high voice (feminine voice) (*suară alit*) lies in the thoughts inspired by Sĕmară, god of love (*tengahing hati sĕmară*).

Dèlĕm occupies the place where hang the lungs.

Wredah occupies the place where hang the kidneys.

Tualèn occupies the place where hangs the liver.

Mangut occupies the place where hangs the gall.

The holy *wayang* lies in the lungs.

The holy memory lies in the liver.

The *wayang* figures belonging to the left are situated in the liver; those belonging to the right in the gall; the tree (*kayon*) in the center of the lungs. The "*dalang*-ship" also lies in the center of the lungs.

The god of the *wayang* is Iswară, whose place is within the heart. His direction is east (*purwă*), his color is white, and his syllable is *mang*, in the essence of all sounds inhaled or exhaled.

The gods of the speech of the *mangku dalang* are:

Sanghyang Guru occupying the mind.

Sanghyang Saraswati occupying the root of the tongue.

Sanghyang Kawiswara occupying the audible voice.

(This conveys the idea of the word as thought, formed and uttered in turn.)

In another place in the *Dharmă Pawayangan* the screen is the sky, the banana stalk the earth, and the lamp the sun.

Note 5.a. According to the *Dharmă Pawayangan* the *dalang* must observe certain ascetic rules (*tapa dalang*). He may not eat the heart

---

[27] The fatty membrane that falls in front of and protects the viscera.

[28] In Malay countries the liver as the seat of emotion takes the place of the European "heart." Thus one says "big-livered" instead of big-hearted, "sick-livered" instead of heartsick, and so on.

of any living thing before he understands thoroughly everything concerned with the *wayang*. When eating he must face either north or east. If he should face south or west, he will incur misfortune. The *wayang* stage must also be situated so that the *dalang* faces either north or east. When the *dalang* drinks, he must always do so "four swallows at a time," and his memory will be without fault. There are special prayer formulas for bathing, washing the face, cleaning the teeth, donning flowers, and eating *sirih*. There are prayers for safety to and from the place of performance. He must know the correct way to approach the house where he is to perform. "Let him pause first before the door of him who has called him, exhale deeply from the nose, and detect from which nostril the breath comes strongest; if from the right nostril, let his right foot proceed first; if from the left, his left foot; and if from both nostrils with equal force, then must he proceed with both feet at once."

b. The *wayang* figures demand special attention. Prayers and offerings are required before the figures may be taken from the house of the *dalang*. Further special prayers are required, for bringing back to life those *wayang* figures which have been killed during the play (*pĕngurip*); for putting away respectively the man figures, the *pĕnasar*, and the weapons; for the designing of new puppets, and for their consecration (*mĕlaspasin wayang*).

c. On certain days during the Balinese year offerings must be made for many things which play an important part in daily life, such as coconut palms, domestic animals, books, krisses, and musical instruments. Each one has its special day. The last day of the week *tumpĕk wayang* (Note 6a) is devoted to puppets. Special offerings and prayers must be made by the *dalang*, and the puppets sprinkled with holy water.

d. Certain magic formulas exist which the *dalang* must recite to himself before opening the puppet box, in order to ensure a successful performance, namely:

pĕngegèr, in order that there may be a large audience of "numerous men, women, and hermaphrodites" (*banchi*);

pĕngalup, that his voice may be found pleasing;

pĕngaduh, that the audience may be warm and enthusiastic, that he "holds his audience";

pĕngirut, that every onlooker without exception will be pleased.

Note 6.a. A child unfortunate enough to be born on one of the seven days of the week *tumpĕk wayang*, which occurs once in every thirty

weeks, is under the power of Batară Kală (Shiva[29] in the form of the
destroyer) and must be purified (*lukat*) by means of offerings, a
special holy water (*jehsudamală*), and a *wayang* performance of a
certain legend which relates the origin of this ceremony. It is the
place of the *mangku dalang* to perform both the play and the required
rites. On Thursday (Wrespati *wayang*), October 11, 1934, I witnessed
the following performance.

The performance was given in a high *balé*, one of the many
pavilions within the walls of a Balinese household, at Mas, district
Ubud, and performed by the *dalang* of that village—a Brahmană.
Outside the *balé*, in front of the screen, were elaborate offerings, set
out on a temporary platform. The courtyard was crowded, for many
people besides the relatives had been admitted. A performance of the
subjoined legend was given. At the end, about 3 A.M., the puppets
were put away as usual, with exception of the *kayon*, together with
Chintiă,[30] Siwă, Tualèn, and Bimă.[31] Offerings were brought before
the figures, and, as the *dalang*, a Brahmană, prayed, he took each
figure, decorated it with a flower, and dipped the handle in the holy
water. When this was ended, the *dalang* descended to perform the
nyudamală ceremony, and to liberate the child from the curse.
Offerings were first made on the ground to the evil spirits, and then,
approaching a special shrine made for the occasion, the *dalang* went
through many prayer formulas. The child, held all this time in the
arms of its mother, was then stripped of its ceremonial garments and
stood naked upon the ground in the midst of the offerings to the
demons. Bowl after bowl of holy water was poured over the shivering
infant, and the ceremony was finished. During all the rites special
music, *lagu sudamală*, was played on the *gĕndèr*.

The legend performed for this *sudamală* ceremony illustrates the
cause for the original curse on one born during the week *tumpĕk
wayang*, and how it was first lifted.

After man had been created, he soon grew clever, but was without
morals, and his ways were far from pleasing to the gods. And Batară
Guru (Siwă) saw that the ways of mankind were as those of the
animals and went into meditation on the peak of the mountain
Sangkă Duipă. And it happened that during that time he produced a
drop of semen, and great and lustrous it was. And he called the gods
together and said: "I have called you together because disaster has

---

[29] See Note 7.
[30] See Note 7.
[31] The most valiant of the five Pandawă princes.

occurred here. Who has sent this evil omen, and of what may it be a sign?" And the gods were puzzled and knew not what to think. And Batarǎ Guru ordered them to bring their bows and arrows and shoot at the thing, and as they shot at it with the first arrow it became alive. The second arrow caused it to produce legs and arms, the third a head, and, as they continued shooting, nose, face, body, breasts, and sexual parts appeared. With the ninth arrow it stood up and shouted in a mighty voice. And so he was called Kalǎ. And he went on shouting, calling to his father and mother, for he was filled with an unbearable hunger. And Batarǎ Guru heard him, and went to him and said: "Oh my child Kalǎ, is it that you are hungry?" And Kalǎ answered: "Yes, my lord," And his father said: "Go down to the world to search for food. And if there are people on the road at midday or midnight, those you may eat. And also all those who sleep or work at midday, or when the sun is setting, and those who use wood from fallen trees to build with." And Kalǎ took leave of Batarǎ Guru and set off. And many were the people whom he devoured. Now all the people were sorely troubled, for they knew no better, and they wept and lamented: "O Powerful God! What is our offense, that this disaster should be visited upon us?" And Batarǎ Guru heard them and saw that his people were diminishing. And therefore he descended to earth in the form of a man, mounted on a bull.[32] And with him came his wife, Batarǎ Sri, in the form of a woman. And they appeared upon the earth just at midday and met Kalǎ upon the road. And Kalǎ threatened them saying he would devour them, and, to temporize, the man proposed this riddle: "Oh Kalǎ, what is it that has eight legs, four arms, six eyes, three noses, two horns, one tail, two phalluses, and one vagina. Answer me this before sundown, and we give ourselves to you." And by sundown Kalǎ had not solved the riddle, and the man triumphantly said: "The answer is: Siwǎ, his wife, and his bull. And now it is sundown, and you may not devour us, for we are not on the road at midday!" In rage did Kalǎ reply: "Even so, will I devour you." But suddenly the man disappeared, and in his place stood Batarǎ Guru, brilliant and scintillating as a ruby. And Kalǎ bowed down before him, saying: "Lord, forgive this, your child." And Batarǎ Guru said: "Kalǎ, from this day forward, if there are people on the road at midday and they are singing, you may not eat them; and if they stop and lie down, but do not sleep, even though it be sunset, you may not eat them." And more modifications did he

[32] The bull is the animal sacred to Shiva.

make regarding those whom Kală might no longer destroy. But seeing that Kala was filled with disappointment, he added that all those who made insufficient offerings might be devoured, as well as all those born during the week *wayang*, the week in which Kală had been created. And with that he disappeared.

The legend so far follows almost literally a certain sacred writing, the *Purwan Bumi*, but at this point deviates, taking its plot from another, the *Sundari Bungkah*.

Now there lived a certain Brahmană, of great repute as a holy man, and he had a son named Supradah, who was born on a *sukră tumpĕk wayang* (Friday of the week *wayang*). Kală finds him an important prey, on account of his caste, and sets out in pursuit. But Supradah flees and first hides in a mound of filth which someone has swept out into the middle of the road. Kală arrives, and as he searches the place he sees Supradah escape from the mound and run off. He curses the filth, and all those who from now on may sweep filth into the street, and continues the pursuit. Supradah next hides within a fallen tree, and Kală comes upon it. As he pauses his prey escapes. Kală curses all fallen trees, saying that from now on they may not be used for building houses or any constructive work, but for firewood only (a repetition of the first part). Supradah now hides in the end of one of the bamboo poles fixed to the base of a cremation tower, which are used to bear it to the graveyard. Kală arrives, but Supradah, after darting in and out of pole after pole, once more escapes. Kală puts further restrictions on all bamboo poles not cut at the nodes. And now Supradah enters the house of one who is giving a performance of *wayang kulit* and hides within one of the bamboo resonators of a *gĕndèr*. Kală appears but, fascinated by the performance, forgets his prey. When the play is over, Kală suddenly remembers his objective, but his quarry has long since escaped. In fury he examines the offerings of the *dalang*, but they are correct. Outwitted, Kală admits defeat and announces that from now on, anyone born during the week of *tumpĕk wayang* may avert the curse by giving a *wayang* performance. The father of Supradah hears of this and straightaway gives a performance for his son. Supradah is thus freed of the power of Kală, the feast is called *sudamală* (freed from the curse), and in honor of this his son is given the name of Sang Suda.

We see in this tale certain taboo motifs which probably date from long before Hinduism. There is little in common between this legend and the one published by P. V. van Stein Callenfels in his interesting book on the *sudamală* legend as depicted in old Hindu-Javanese temple reliefs.[33] Whether this latter legend was formerly performed or not I do not know, as all the *dalang* I have consulted have never referred to it but always given some version of the above legend.

b. Complementing this function of the *dalang* at birth is the part he plays after death. On the day of the cremation, he must be present on the cremation tower (*wadah*) from the time the corpse leaves the house until the moment when it is removed from the tower in the cremation grounds and placed on the funeral pyre. To the accompaniment of set music by the four *gĕndèr wayang*, which are mounted at the base of the tower, he must make prayers and throw off offerings of rice, shredded leaves of the dap-dap tree, and money (Chinese cash) at certain moments during the procession. It is of interest to note these moments.

Time or Place	*Music*
When the *wadah* is first lifted from the ground	Batèl
At the crossroads	Rundah
At a fork in the road	Rundah
At a turn in the road	Rundah
If there is a ravine, stream, or footbridge	Rundah
At the edge of the graveyard	Tunjang
When the *wadah* is set down	Mèsem

All these places are vulnerable spots in a progression, points where the road is magically weakened, and where the evil spirits are most powerful. These spots play a large role in the superstitions of Bali. The offerings and money which the *dalang* throws from the *wadah* are to placate the evil spirits, so that the corpse may reach its final destination unharmed. The dap-dap leaves are further charms. It is in these spots that the *wadah* is turned round three times by the shouting bearers (sometimes three hundred in number), in order that any possibly evilly disposed demons may be confused. When the corpse has been removed from the *wadah*, the *dalang* makes a final prayer and throws away the remaining rice and money.

Note 7. The following rites must be observed in their fixed order before the play is ready to unfold.

1. A small offering containing flowers and money (*chanang burat wangi*, with 35 Chinese cash) is placed on the cover of the unopened

---

[33] P. V. van Stein Callenfels, *De Sudamala in de Hindu-Javaansche Kunst* (s' Hage, Nijhoff, 1925).

kropak; two sticks of incense are lighted and held in the hand while the *dalang* prays to the divinity patronizing the performance.

2. The *dalang* recites to himself the various magic formulas to ensure his success with the audience (Note 5d). Up to this point the musicians are free to play what music they choose other than that used in the play.

3. The *dalang* then strikes the cover of the *kropak* three times with the palm of his hand (*nyĕbahkropak*). At this point the musicians commence the long prelude, the *Pĕmungkah*,[34] while the *dalang* opens the box and places the cover to his right.

4. He then takes out the following figures in their set order, inserting them to the right or the left in the *gedebong*, according to their significance.[35]

a. The greater *pĕmurtian* (a many headed figure representing a transcendental state of anger which a benevolent god may assume) is placed to the right.

b. The lesser *pĕmurtian* (with fewer heads, assumed by malevolent gods, demons, etc.) is placed to the left.

c. The *kepuh* tree[36] is placed to the left.

d. Sanghyang Tunggal (Chintiă, the parthenogenetic creator of all) is placed to the right.

e. Sanghyang Siwă (Shiva, the chief god of the Balinese) is placed to the right.

f. Batară Durgă (the wife of Siwă in her destructive form) is placed to the left.

g. Tualèn is placed to the right, on the cover of the *kropak*.

h. The *kayon* is placed in the center.

5. The rest of the puppets are then taken out and set up, either to right or left.

6. The center of the screen is cleared.

7. The *kayon* is taken up and flourished (*mĕbadan kayon*).

---

[34] *Pĕmungkah:* noun derived from *bungkah*, to open up, hence the import, opening music, or prelude. It may have some reference to the opening of the box of puppets.

[35] Right and left, good and evil, white and black, magically, play a great part in Balinese mysticism and superstition. In the *wayang*, characters are thus classed according to their alliance with good or evil.

[36] *Eriodendron anfractuosum*, a large tree sacred to the goddess Durgă. Nearly every graveyard possesses one, and it is taboo to cut them down. In the *wayang* it is depicted filled with demons and evil birds and festooned with entrails. At the roots are bones and skulls. Scenically it establishes the graveyard or unholy ground, the haunts of demons and the goddess of death.

8. The *dalang* chants the invocatory "*Rahina tatas kamantian*" to the music *Alas Harum* (The Scented Forest). This text is a fragment from the Balinese version of the *Bharatǎ-Yuddhǎ* and is used for *wayang parwǎ*. For Ramayana, *Rundah* is substituted.

The *dalang* now recites a stanza on the origin of the *parwǎ* (*pěnyachah parwǎ*), and another stanza introducing the story about to be given (*pěnyaritǎ*). The last stanzas to have a set place in the preliminaries are the *pěngalang*, florid phrases which accompany the *sěmbah*, or bow with clasped hands, which a character must make in coming before his superior. Two forms are used, the *pěngalang ratu*, for nobles and princes, and the *pěngalang pěnasar*, that of the servants or followers. The play now begins. The following compositions have their definite functions but may occur any time during the play.

a. with text sung by the *dalang*:

Mèsem	for lamentation (narrow-eyed type; see Note 10)
Bendu semarǎ	for lamentation (round-eyed type, demons; see Note 10)
Chandihrěbah	introducing demons
Tunjang	introducing demons
Rebong	for love episodes
Rundah	for beginning Ramayana; sometimes for demons

b. instrumental music:

Batèl	for flights and warfare
Angkat-angkatan	for exits, departures to war, etc. (Several versions exist, to fit the emotional key.)
Lagu Dèlěm	for the appearance of Dèlěm (?)
Tabuh gari	closing music (The audience knows the play is over.)

Note 8. It is unfortunate that Kats, in his book on the Javanese *wayang kulit*, should have chosen the *kayon* from the Balinese *wayang* set in the Batavia museum to photograph, in order to compare it with the Javanese *kayon*. This *kayon* is nonrepresentative. Not only that, but its form and design is completely unfamiliar and mystifying to every *dalang* to whom I have shown the photograph. No relic of such a *kayon* has been found in even the oldest sets I have examined in South Bali. The shape is not the graceful oval of the true *kayon* but is

clumsy and awkward. The treatment of the foliage is not classical.[37] At the base of the tree is found a bull and a lion and, beneath these, two entwined serpents (*nagă*).

This photograph, cited from time to time by different authors, when referring to possible variations of the Javanese *kayon*, has proved mischievous and misleading, particularly when it has been used by Rassers to lend weight to his totem interpretation of the animals which are found in the Javanese *kayon*.[38] The true Balinese *kayon* is a pure, conventionalized tree, with a mountain symbol for base, whose foliage harbors neither bird nor beast. This tree design is the most highly developed of an innumerable variety of tree motifs, found over and over again in Bali, and which have a particular place in the design of the *lamak*, festival panels of woven yellow palm leaves with patterns cut from green palm leaves. Together with the *wayang* figures, this tree design in the *kayon* has undergone no significant modification but remains essentially the same as it was at the time of the building of those temples in East Java which contain reliefs in the old *wayang* form. It is not for me to attempt an ethnological interpretation of this figure. The *kayon* is an emblem whose significance and symbolism still await the real explanation.

Note 9. I give a few examples of the *peretitală dalang*. With the exception of *Alas Harum*, they all vary greatly, as they exist in the memory only of the *dalang*. The general subject matter remains the same in the different versions but that is all.

1. *Mèsem.*

Sweet is the fragrance of the *gadung* flower, born on the breeze; sweet is the scent of the *gadung* and the *menuh* flower. Through the open door appears a beautiful person, holding a child. The rain from the east falls upon them. With sorrow she weeps; like the lotus in the center of the lake her sorrow wavers, stirred by pity. A golden tower

[37] The style, that is, the treatment of foliage, animals, etc., is typical of North Bali, but the author does not believe the subject matter is. All is suspect these days, and has been for a long time, from North Bali, where everything in the way of art is nontypical of true Bali. It must be remembered that true Bali is South Bali as far as culture is concerned. The temples of North Bali reveal men on bicycles, airplanes, etc. The *jangèr* dance includes high-heeled shoes and maquillage for the girls; the *légong* dance is unfit to look at, and the *dalang* had to be admonished for the corrupt way in which they performed *wayang kulit*. It stands to reason then, that this *kayon*, coming from there, is a corruption. Even so, I remember showing the photograph by Kats to a prince from North Bali, and he too had never seen one like it.

[38] Rassers, "Over den Oorsprong van het Javaansche Tooneel," p. 422.

is seen lustrous bright, bejeweled at the peak and entwined with flowers. Through the open door a beautiful person appears. The body still remains, but the soul has fled. The soul has gone elsewhere to seek sustenance, for it is overcome with sorrow and pity.

2. *Tunjang*

Hulu-hulu bungbang pinugel ginawé guntang; huniné aketeka-beleng makă gamelaning bungbung; bibi Rangdă siră metu pareng rowang mangigelang; I Lelèngèh tumangală higelé anentenenté (?); ring chatuspată lumekas chalu bukă kéjok-kéjok; bungbung guntang muni ganting merigigih padă ngikikang.

Of thickest bamboo are the *guntang*. "Ketekbeleng" sounds the *gamelan bungbung*. Mother Rangdă comes forth with her dancing followers. *I lelèngèh* appears, dancing in turn. At the crossroads they all turn into chickens, crying "*kéyok-kéyok.*" *Bungbung* and *guntang* sound loud and shrill, laughing and guffawing.

(The *gamelan bungbung* is an almost obsolete village *gamelan*, consisting of thick bamboo tubes of different lengths, each held by a single person, and dropped in turn against a bamboo pole lying on the ground, and thus producing a crude sort of tune. The tone of each bamboo is hollow and macabre. The *guntang* is a small percussion instrument, a tube of bamboo with a snare, which is struck with a stick.)

3. *Sasendon Alas Harum*

(As Dr. Hooykaas has actually localized the text of *Alas Harum* as the beginning of Canto XXVI of the *Bharata-Yuddha*, it is Dr. Gunning's edition and the translation of Dr. Poerbatjaraka and Dr. Hooykaas that is followed here.)

Rahină tatas kămantian; umuning mĕrĕdanggă kală sangkă, gurnitatară, gumuruh ikang gubar bală, sămuhă mangkat anguwuh padasru rumuhun, pară ratu sampu ahiyas asalin, lumampah ahawan rataparamită, nrapati Yudistiră, pramukă Bimasénă, Nakul-arjunagră lumurug.

Thereupon day breaks. With a loud roar resound the drums, cymbals, and conches. The war-cymbals clash, while the people assemble with loud cries. All set forth in procession; the princes have changed their raiment, and journey forth, seated in unsurpassed chariots; King Yudistiră at the head; Bimasénă, Nakulă, and Arjună advance, taking the lead.

Note 10. The principal characters may be divided into two types, the restrained and the unrestrained. The first, the superior type, is the controlled, circumspect one. His actions are concealed within himself, his strength lies in his reserve.

"Such is the content of the smile, which reveals not the heart; at the moment serenity may conceal a troubled mood. Still undetermined, he cares not to make clear his thoughts. His intention he will not quickly tell" (*dadiată săunduk sĕmită*).[39]

This type is denoted by the true oriental eye, self-contained and unrevealing, which is depicted by means of a long, straight underline, and a gently curved upper one (*mata supit*).

With this eye goes the "brave-serene" (*galak-amanis*) voice.

The opposite type is represented by the open eye. At best he is frank, impulsive; at worst, uncontrolled and violent. His thoughts are betrayed, in spite of himself, by his openness. Although often endowed with fine qualities, he is, nevertheless, considered of a spiritually weaker, inferior mold. The "great" or deep voice (*suara agong, suara perekasă*) is used for this type.

Demons and animals also possess this eye (*mata deling*).

Recordings

The following recordings of music for *gĕndèr wayang* have been made:

Odeon A 204764a   Sekar Ginotan (A Pendulous Flower)
         ,,   b   Pemoengkah [Pĕmungkah]
     A 204765a   Alas-Haroem [Alas Harum] (The Scented Forest)
         ,,   b   Slèndero [Slèndro]
     A 204766a   Merak Ngilo [Mérak Ngilo] (The Peacock Spreads Its Tail)
         ,,   b   Batèl (misnamed; should be Angkat-angkatan)
Beka   B 15629   Lagoe Tjoepak [Lagu Chupak] (Batèl type)

References

Callenfels, P. V. van Stein. *De Sudamala in de Hindu-Javaansche Kunst.* Bataviaasch Genootschap van Kunsten en Wetenschappen, Verhandelingen, LXVI, 1. 's Hage, Nijhoff, 1925.

---

[39]One of the opening stanzas.

Dutt, R. C. *The Ramayana and the Mahabharata; Condensed into English Verse.* Everyman's Library. London, Dent, 1910.

Goris, R. "Bali's Hoogtijden," *Tijdschrift voor Indische Taal-, Land-, en Volkenkunde*, LXXIII (1933), 436 ff.

Gunning, J. G. H., ed. *Bhārata-Yuddha, Oud-Javaansch Heldendicht.* 's Graven-hage, 1903.

Hazeu, G. A. J. *Bijdrage tot de Kennis van het Javaansche Tooneel.* Dissertation. Leiden, 1897.

Hooykaas, Christiaan, comp. *Proza en Poëzie van Oud-Java.* Groningen, Noord-hoff, 1933.

Kats, J. *Het Javaansche Tooneel. I. Wajang poerwa.* Uitgave van de Commissie voor de Volkslectuur, Serie No. 387. Weltevreden, 1923.

Kunst, Jaap, and C. J. A. Kunst-van Wely. *De Toonkunst van Bali.* [Pt. I] Welte-vreden, 1925; Pt. II in *Tijdschrift voor Indische Taal-, Land-, en Volkenkunde*, LXV (1925), 369 ff.

Kunst, Jaap, and R. Machjar Koesoemadinata. "Een en Ander over Pélog en Sléndro," *Tijdschrift voor Indische Taal-, Land-, en Volkenkunde*, LXIX (1929), 320 ff.

McPhee, Colin. "The 'Absolute' Music of Bali," *Modern Music*, XII, No. 4 (1935), 163–69.

Poerbatjaraka, R. Ng. "De Calon-Arang," *Bijdragen tot de Taal-, Land-, en Volkenkunde van Nederlansch Indië*, LXXXII (1926), 110–80.

Poerbatjaraka, R. Ng., and Christiaan Hooykaas, trs. "Bharata-Yuddha [Dutch translation]," *Djawa*, XIV (1934), 1 ff.

Rassers, W. H. "Over den Oorsprong van het Javaansche Tooneel," *Bijdragen tot de Taal-, Land-, en Volkenkunde van Nederlansch Indië*, LXXXVIII (1931), 317–450.

Children and Ritual
in Bali

MARGARET MEAD

IN BALI, children are called "small human beings," and the conception of the nature and place of the child is different from that of the West. The whole of life is seen as a circular stage on which human beings, born small, as they grow taller, heavier, and more skilled, play predetermined roles, unchanging in their main outlines, endlessly various and subject to improvisation in detail.

The world of the dead is one part of the circle, from which human souls return, born again into the same family every fourth generation, to stay too briefly—dying before they have shared rice—or for a long time, or even for too long, for it is inappropriate for great-grandparents to be alive at the same time as their great-grandchildren. Such lingerers have to pay a penny to their great-grandchildren, chance-met on the street. The newborn child and the aged great-grandparent are both too close to the other world for easy entrance into the temple. The baby cannot enter until after a special feast at three and a half or seven months, and the very aged enter through a special side gate.

The newborn are treated as celestial creatures entering a more

Originally published in Margaret Mead and Martha Wolfenstein, eds., *Childhood in Contemporary Cultures* (Chicago, University of Chicago Press, 1955), pp. 40–51.

Author's note: "Based on field work done in Bali, in 1936–39, by Gregory Bateson, Colin McPhee, Katharane Mershon, and myself. Bali is now part of modern Indonesia, and many parts of this description would no longer hold. I am using a historical present for the description of old, that is, pre-World War II, Bali." Cf. Margaret Mead, "Researches in Bali, 1936–1939; on the Concept of Plot in Culture," *Transactions of the New York Academy of Sciences*, Ser. II, Vol. II, No. 1 (November, 1939), pp. 1–4.

humdrum existence and, at the moment of birth, are addressed with high-sounding honorific phrases reserved for gods, the souls of ancestors, princes, and people of a higher caste. Human beings do not increase in stature and importance, as is so often the case in societies where men have only one life to live; rather, they round a half-circle in which middle age, being farthest from the other world, is the most secular. There is little acceptance of any task being difficult or inappropriate for a child, except that an infant at birth is, of course, expected to do nothing for itself. Words are put into the mouth of the infant, spoken on its behalf by an adult; the hands of the seven-month-old baby are cupped to receive holy water, folded in prayer, opened to waft the incense offered to it as a god, and when the ceremony is over the child sits, dreamily repeating the gestures which its hands have momentarily experienced.[1]

The Balinese may comment with amusement but without surprise if the leading metallophone player in a noted orchestra is so small that he has to have a stool in order to reach the keys; the same mild amusement may be expressed if someone takes up a different art after his hands have a tremor of age to confuse their precision. But in a continuum within which the distinction between the most gifted and the least gifted is muted by the fact that everyone participates, the distinction between child and adult—as performer, as actor, as musician—is lost except in those cases where the distinction is ritual, as where a special dance form requires a little girl who has not reached puberty.

This treatment of human history as an unending series of rebirths is matched in the treatment of the calendar. The Balinese have a whole series of weeks, of three, four, five, six, up to ten days, which turn on each other, like wheels of different sizes, and there are important occasions when two or three weeks recurrently coincide. These have special names and may be an occasion for festival—like Galungan, a New Year's feast associated with the souls of the dead, and a post-festival season of special theatricals. But, although there is a way of noting the year in a continuous irreversible sequence, it is seldom used. A man who has labored long to recopy a sacred text on pages of *lontar* palm will simply note, when his task of intricate elaboration of a beautiful archaic script is over, that this was finished on the such-and-such, a recurrent combination of days—as we might say, on Friday the thirteenth of September. The principal calendrical unit,

[1] See *Karba's First Years* (film); Gregory Bateson and Margaret Mead, *Balinese Character: A Photographic Analysis* (New York, New York Academy of Sciences, 1942), Pl. 100, Figs. 1 and 2.

the ceremonial year, is two hundred and ten days long. The lunar calendar simply marks the pattern of planting and harvest.

Children, then, are smaller and more fragile than adults, as well as closer to the other world. Their essential personality characteristics— gaiety or seriousness, gentleness or harshness—are recognized early, and those around each child combine to set its formal character in an expected mold. The baby of six months with silver bracelets welded on its tiny wrists, waves and bangs its arms; if someone is hurt in the process, there comes the exclamation, "Isamă is harsh." It takes only a few such acts to stereotype the judgment which will be echoed and re-echoed through its life, setting and defining its ways, but quite forgotten after death as other events—day of birth, experience in other incarnations—combine to give new personality. So, while the people take ritual pains over a corpse—that the individual may be born again fleeter of foot or more beautiful of face—they cannot describe the character or the looks of someone who died two years ago. Personality characteristics are accidents, held gently constant through any given incarnation, that dissolve at death. But the baby who is identified as "gay and mischievous" has a way of life plotted out for it, which again is independent of age. Old men who have been "gay" all their lives still know who sleeps with whom in the fields at night in the brief, wordless first encounters which for the Balinese represent the height of passion; and men and women labeled "serious" may bear many children, but people will comment instead on their industriousness in the rice fields or their faithfulness at the temple.

The child is made conscious of its sex very early. People pat the little girl's vulva, repeating an adjective for feminine beauty, and applaud the little boy's phallus with the word for "handsome male." The child is fitted into words appropriate to its caste, gestures appropriate to each ceremony, and, before the child can walk, it is taught to dance with its hands. Before he can stand, the little boy, who has sat on his father's knees while his father played the *gamelan*, begins to play himself. Peeking over a house wall, one may see diminutive girls of three, sitting all alone, practicing hand gestures. The child learns to walk around a single walking rail,[2] learning that it is safe as long as it holds to this central support, in danger of falling when it loosens its hold and strays out into the unknown. When it learns to walk, its

[2]See Bateson and Mead, *Balinese Character*, Pl. 17, Figs. 1 and 2 (in this volume Plate IV); Margaret Mead and Frances Cooke Macgregor, *Growth and Culture: A Photographic Study of Balinese Childhood* (New York, Putnam, 1951), Pl. XXVI, Fig. 7, and Pl. LII, Fig. 3.

ventures away from support and parents are controlled by the mother or child nurse mimicking terror and calling it back with threats that are random in content—"Tiger!" "Policeman!" "Snake!" "Feces!" —but constant in theatrical affect, until the child learns that undefined outer space may at any moment be filled with unknown terrors.[3]

In the village, in familiar territory, the child learns the directions— *kajă*, the center of the island, where the high mountain of the gods stands; *kĕlod*, toward the sea, the point of least sanctity; and *kangin*, to the right, *kauh*, to the left, when one faces *kajă*. Every act is likely to be expressed in these terms as babies are bidden to come a little *kajă* or to brush a speck off the *kĕlod* side of their face, and little boys of different caste play together happily but learn that the boy of higher caste must get into bed first or sit on the *kajă* side of the food tray.

Children learn the vertical hierarchies of life—that the head, even of a casteless peasant child, is something sacred, that a flower which has fallen to the ground from an offering carried on the head may not be replaced in the offering, that those of highest caste or sanctity must be given the highest seats. As they learn to speak, they learn that the words addressed to them by their elders and superiors are never the words in which they may answer, although sometimes the lesson is imperfectly learned, and a low-caste boy will marvel at the fact that "they say Brahmană parents are very polite to their children, that they say *tiang* to them," not knowing that the children must reply with an exaggeratedly more polite term, *titiang*, in which the pronoun "I" is made more self-deprecating by a stylized stutter.

From birth until long after they can walk, children live most of their waking hours in human arms, carried in a sling or on the hip, even sleeping suspended about the neck of an adult or a child nurse.[4] They learn a plastic adaptation, to take cognizance of the other's movement in limp relaxation, neither resisting nor wholly following the pounding of the rice or the game the child nurse is playing. When there is teaching to be done, the teacher uses this flaccid adaptivity and, holding the hands and body of the learner with vigorous, precise intent, twists and turns them into place or pattern.[5] Verbal directions are meager; children learn from the feel of other people's bodies and from watching, although this watching itself has a kinesthetic quality.

[3] See *Karba's First Years* (film); Bateson and Mead, *Balinese Character*, pp. 30–32 and Pl. 46.

[4] See Bateson and Mead, *Balinese Character*, Pl. 79; Mead and Macgregor, *Growth and Culture*, Pl. XVII.

[5] See *Karba's First Years* (film); Bateson and Mead, *Balinese Character*, Pl. 16.

An artist who attempts to draw a group of men will draw himself over and over again, feeling the image.

The children are everywhere. Very little babies cannot enter the temple, but the toddler is present in the midst of the most solemn ceremonial, attached to parent or grandparent, watching the blessing of the trance dancer, the throw of coins of the diviner, the killing of the fowl as exorcism. Women attending a theatrical performance carry their babies in their arms, and the front row of every performance is given over to the very small children, who watch and doze and are hastily rescued when the play threatens to break the bounds of the, audience square and to involve the crowd in the plot. At the shadow play the children sit in front, and the puppet master increases the number of battles in the plot in proportion to the number of children. As the women kneel in the temple, placing the petals of a flower between their praying fingers, a flower is placed in the hands of the child who is with them. For the temple feast, small children, who at other times may run about stark naked, will appear elaborately dressed, boys in headdress and kris.

They look like dolls, and they are treated like playthings, playthings which are more exciting than fighting cocks—over which the men spend many fascinated hours—or the kites and crickets which amuse little boys. Everyone joins in the mild titillating teasing of little babies, flipping their fingers, their toes, their genitals, threatening them, playfully disregarding the sanctity of their heads, and, when the children respond by heightened excitement and mounting tension, the teaser turns away, breaks the thread of interplay, allows no climax.[6] Children learn not to respond, to resist provocation, to skirt the group of elders who would touch or snatch, to refuse the gambit when their mothers borrow babies to make them jealous. They develop an unresponsiveness to the provocative intent of others at the same time that they remain plastic to music and pattern. It is a childhood training which, if followed here, would seem dangerously certain to bring out schizoid trends in the growing child's character.

But there is one great difference between Bali and the changing Western world as we know it. In the Western world children are traumatized in childhood in ways which are new and strange, for which no ritual healing, no artistic form, exists in the culture. Those who are very gifted may become prophets, or artists, or revolutionaries, using their hurt, their made deviancy, or their innate deviancy

[6] See *Karba's First Years* (film); Bateson and Mead, *Balinese Character*, p. 32 and Pls. 47–49.

exaggerated by adult treatment as the basis for a new religion or a new art form. Those who are not so gifted or who are less fortunate in finding a medium for their gifts go mad or dwindle away, using little even of what they have. We are beginning to recognize how damaging a trauma can be—administered by a parent who is ignorant of the world the child lives in and lived out by the child in a still different world later. The present emphasis in America is on the application of psychiatric techniques—in childhood itself—to undo the damage, take out the false stitches, relearn the abandoned stance. Our conception of life is a sequential, changing, and climactic one. So a trauma in childhood is seen as producing mental damage or intolerable yearning, which must then be solved in later life—and solved alone by the traumatized individuals.[7]

Old Bali is a striking example of a quite different solution, in which the child each day meets rituals accurately matched to the intensities and the insatiabilities which are being developed by the interplay between itself and others. Little children are not permitted to quarrel, they are not allowed to struggle over toys, or to pull and claw at each other—there are always elders there to separate them, gently, impersonally, and inexorably, and so completely that, in over two years of living in Balinese villages, I never saw two children or adolescents fight. When conflict arises, the elder child is continually told to give in to the younger; the younger, responding to the invitation of the older, is jealous of every favor and demanding of anything the elder has.

But day after day, as the child is prevented from fighting, he sees magnificent battles on the stage, and the children are part of the crowd that streams down to the river bank to duck some character in the play. He sees the elder brother—who must always be deferred to in real life—insulted, tricked, defeated, in the theater. When his mother teases him in the eerie, disassociated manner of a witch, the child can also watch the witch in the play—the masked witch wearing the accentuated symbols of both sexes, with long protruding tongue, pendulous breasts, covered with repulsive hair—watch her recurrent battle with the dragon, who in his warmer and puppy-like behavior resembles his father. He can see the followers of the dragon attack the witch and fall down in a trance, as if killed, only to be brought back to life again by the magic healing power of the dragon.[8] These

[7] See Mead, "The Arts in Bali," in this volume, p. 331.
[8] See *Trance and Dance in Bali* (film); Bateson and Mead, *Balinese Character*, pp. 34–35 and Pls. 55–58.

followers of the dragon, like the younger brother, go further than he
will ever dare to go in showing hostility to his mother, in open resent-
ment of her laughter. He sees his possible destructive wish lived out
before his eyes, but in the end no one is slain, no one is destroyed, no
one is hurt. The trancers, who have fallen into convulsions when they
attack the witch, are revived by holy water and prayers, the play ends,
the masks are taken off, the actors lay aside their golden garments for
stained workday clothes; the young men who lay twitching in convulsions half an hour ago go off singing gaily for a bath. Over and over
again, as babies in their mothers' arms, as toddlers being lifted out of
the path of a pair of dancing warriors, as members of the solemn row
of children who line the audience square, they see it happen—the
play begins, mounts to intensity, ends in ritual safety. And in the
villages, when theatrical troupes under the protection of the dragon
mask, patron of the theater and enemy of death, parade about a village
in which they have just arrived, people buy a little of the dragon's hair
as bracelets for their children to protect them from evil dreams.[9]

In this absence of change, the experience of the parent is repeated
in that of the child, and the child, a full participant in ritual and art,
is presented with the last elaborations almost with its first breath. The
people themselves treat time as a circular process rather than a progressive one, with the future ever behind one, unrolling beneath one's
feet, an already exposed but undeveloped film. Here we find a perfect
expression of the historical nature of culture, in which any separation
between cause and effect, any attempt to turn either childhood experience or adult ritual into the cause, one of the other, is seen to be a
hopeless endeavor. The two recur together, at every stage; the teased
baby of the witchlike human mother watches the witch on the stage,
and the teasing mother, even as she teases her baby, also sees the
witch, attacked, apparently destroying, but in the end doing no harm.
The effect on child and mother must both be reckoned in a round of
simultaneous events, repeating and repeating until the child in arms
again becomes a parent.

And yet, in spite of their conception of life as a circle, we may, if we
wish, break the circle—as they are unwilling to do—and, for purposes
of a type of scientific analysis born of our Western conceptions of
time, space, and casuality, ask the question: What happens as babies
born to Balinese parents, equipped at birth with the same potentialities

[9] See Margaret Mead, "The Strolling Players in the Mountains of Bali," in this
volume, p. 137.

as other human babies, learn to be Balinese? How do they make the ritual of Balinese life part of themselves and so become as able to dance the intricate dances, carve or play or weave or go into trance, as did their parents or their grandparents? How do they learn to be Balinese and so perpetuate Balinese culture? This is no question which treats Balinese culture as a mere projection from childhood experience. The themes enacted in the Balinese theater have a long history.[10] On the shadow-play screen there appear the heroes and heroines of the *Ramayana*, the great Indian epic. The witch *rangdă* is also the Javanese Chalonarang, and she is also Durgă, the destroyer. The dragon is found around the world—in Japan, in the streets of New York for Chinese New Year, where he blesses the local merchants whose restaurants may contain a juke box or a cigarette-vending machine. It is only in the particular details of the plots that one can find the distinctive mark of Balinese culture—in the refusal to let the witch die, in the permission to show a violence on the stage which is not permitted in real life, and in the way in which artist, actor, and priest participate in everyday life.

But children in Bali, like human children everywhere, are born helpless, dependent, and cultureless and must be bathed and fed and protected, taught to balance and to walk, to touch and to refrain from touching, to relate themselves to other people, to talk, to work, to become sure members of their own sex, and finally to marry and produce and rear children. We cannot find that which is distinctively Balinese in the mere presence of the witch and the dragon, who recur in many forms throughout the world. It is necessary to look at fine details of difference. For example, the Balinese witch has got hold of a dragon's fiery tongue—and the Balinese dragon has no tongue at all. This can be seen as a part of the way in which the witch combines all the gross overaccentuated aspects of secondary sex characters. In the Balinese ideal physical type, both men and women are slender; male breasts are more pronounced than among us; women's breasts are high and small; hips of both sexes are closer in dimensions. Men are almost beardless, and the muscles of their arms are not developed. The witch's hairy legs and long pendulous breasts accentuate the frightening aspects of highly developed sex differences, and we find, counterpointing her, protecting the people from the illness and death she brings, and presiding with her over the theater, the dragon, a mythical creature, wearing lovely fluffy, feather-like "hair" or crow

---

[10] See Jane Belo, *Bali: Rangda and Barong* (New York, J. J. Augustin, 1949).

feathers sent especially by the gods. Only as the Balinese witch is contrasted with her historical predecessors and as the Balinese dragon is seen in a world perspective of other dragons, is it possible to say what is distinctively Balinese. In the same way, by placing Balinese childhood experience in a context of our knowledge of child development, we can see in what particular ways Balinese children, while repeating universal human experiences, also have special ones.

The Balinese infant has preserved a kind of neonatal flexibility, which in the children who have been studied in Western culture tends to disappear very early, so that both the way a baby relaxes in its mother's arms and the way the mother holds it are sharply contrasting to our patterns.[11] The disallowance of infancy, as adults speak in behalf of the child or press its compliant learning hands into ritual gestures, is again distinctive; and the way in which the child is constantly discouraged from walking, taught to use its right hand rather than the left, which is exposed by the carrying posture, left free to drink from its mother's breast when it chooses, as it is carried high above her high breast, but fed in a helpless prone position as a mound of prechewed food is piled on its mouth—all these details go to build the kind of Balinese personality which will be receptive to rituals danced and acted by others who have been treated in the same way. The constant provocative teasing and threatening which never reaches any but a theatrical climax, the denial of all violence and expressed hostility toward siblings, the serial experience of being the pampered baby, the displaced knee baby, and the child nurse, who, as guardian of the baby, stays to see the usurper dethroned in turn, all these form a background for the plots of ritual and theater to which the child is exposed.[12]

But there is something more here than the correspondence between childhood experience and dramatic plot, something different from the sort of cultural situation discussed by Róheim when a terrifying infantile experience—of a male child sleeping beneath the mother—is abreacted by initiation rites in adolescence.[13] In Bali the absence of sequence even in the life-span of the individual and the absence of discontinuity between ritual role and everyday role seem crucial. The artist, the dancer, the priest, is also a husbandman who tills his rice

[11] See Mead and Macgregor, *Growth and Culture*, Pls. XXXIX–XLI.

[12] See Margaret Mead, "Age Patterning in Personality Development," *American Journal of Orthopsychiatry*, XVII, No. 2 (1947), 231–40.

[13] Geza Róheim, *The Riddle of the Sphinx* (London, Hogarth Press and Institute of Psychoanalysis, 1934).

fields. Occasionally an artist becomes so famous that he lets his finger-
nails grow as he does no other work, and, say the Balinese, he begins
to grow fat and careless and lazy, and his artistic skills decrease. The
priest may stand robed in white during a ceremony, officiating at the
long ritual of inviting the gods down to earth, dressing them, feeding
them, bathing them, presenting them with dance and theater, and
then sending them back again for another two hundred and ten days
in heaven.[14] But the day after the ceremony he is a simple citizen of
the village, only owing the land which he cultivates to his work on
feast days as guardian of the temple.

Nor is there any gap between professional and amateur. There are
virtually no amateurs in Bali, no folk dancing in which people do
traditional things without responsibility to an artistic canon.[15] There
are enormous differences in skill and grace and beauty of performance,
but prince and peasant, very gifted and slightly gifted, all do what
they do seriously and become, in turn, critical spectators, laughing
with untender laughter at the technical failures of others. Between
the audience that gathers to watch the play and the players there is
always the bond of professional interest, as the audience criticizes the
way the actor or actress who plays the princess postures or sings, rather
than identifying with her fate—however lost she may be in some
dense theatrical forest.

Nor is there any gap between rehearsal and performance. From the
moment an orchestra begins to practice an old piece of music, there is
a ring of spectators, aspiring players, substitute players, small boys,
and old men, all equally engrossed in the ever fresh creation of a new
way of playing an old piece of music.[16] Where in Java the shadow-play
screen divided men from women, the women seeing only the faint
shadow on the screen, the men the brightly painted figures, in Bali
people can sit on either side, in front to watch the finished play, behind
—and this is where little boys prefer to sit—to watch the individual
designs on the figures and the deft hands of the puppet master. When
a village club decides to learn a new play—a play in which the main
serious parts are traditional and the parts of clowns, servants, and
incidental characters are all improvised, never set, even in consecutive
performances—half the village attends the rehearsals, enjoys the dis-
cussions of costume, the sharp words of the visiting virtuoso come to

[14] See Jane Belo, *Bali: Temple Festival* (Locust Valley, N.Y., J. J. Augustin, 1953).
[15] See Margaret Mead, "Community Drama, Bali and America," in this volume,
p. 341; Colin McPhee, "Dance in Bali," in this volume, p. 290.
[16] See Colin McPhee, *A House in Bali* (New York, John Day, 1946).

teach a dance step, the discovery of some new talent among the actors. In the rectangular piece of ground which becomes a four-sided stage as the audience gathers around it, isolated pairs of curtains borrowed from a theater with a quite different style of handling surprise may be set up near each end. The actors, their crowns a little askew, sit in almost full view dozing behind these curtains or among the audience, and then, as they make their appearance, part the curtain for a prolonged stylized "entrance," from which they later return to their full visibility offstage.[17] People advance from the audience to pin up a dancer's fallen scarf, and dramatic scenes of chase and conquest will be pursued into the midst of the audience.

Thus in Bali the ritual world of art and theater and temple is not a world of fantasy, an endless recurrent daydream, or a new set of daydreams woven from the desperations of the gifted of each generation. It is rather a real world of skill and application—a world in which members of a dance club scheme to get money for the gold of a new headdress or to buy new instruments for the orchestra; where long hours are spent in the basic work of learning to dance; where disciplined hands and wrists and eyes that click to one side in perfect time to the music, are all the result of continuous, although relaxed, rather dreamy, work. And the temple feasts, where many of these activities combine to make a great spectacle, are called appropriately "the work of the gods."

Children have not only the precocious postural participation in prayer and offering, dance and music, but also a whole series of parallel participations. A little boy will be given bamboo clappers with which to imitate the clapping of the dragon's tongueless jaws and, covered by his mother's cloth shawl—the same shawl with which the witch will dance in the play and which she will carry in her arms as if it were a baby—goes about clapping in imitation of the dragon. In the nonceremonial seasons, when life is a little less crowded, secular dance clubs go about with a tinkly orchestra, which has a hurdy-gurdy quality, and a little girl dancer, who dances with the young men of the village and, in between, dances as the witch, combining the beautiful ballet of the witch's disciples with being the witch herself and placing her foot firmly on the neck of a doll, enacting her role of bringing death.[18]

Children stay in a deep resistant sleep during a childbirth in their

---

[17] See Margaret Mead, "The Strolling Players in the Mountains of Bali," in this volume, p. 137.

[18] See Bateson and Mead, *Balinese Character*, Pls. 60–62.

houses, a sleep from which it is necessary to shake them awake, lest they see the witches which may come to kill the child. But the same children participate with delight in the play in which the witch child, after stealing a doll, born of a man and dressed as a woman, is chased up a tree or into a nearby stream. Children make puppets of banana leaf and parody the puppet master, especially the puppet master who performs with puppets in the daytime, whose screen has shrunk to a single line of thread. They draw in the sand with twigs while master artists work at little shallow wooden tables. And children may form clubs of their own, make their own dragon and witch, and progress about the village, collecting pennies for further finery for the masks.[19]

If one follows these activities carefully, notes the expressions on the children's faces at different kinds of ceremonies, follows the same child on different occasions, and watches the play in which the children think they are reproducing the full theatricals, one begins to get clues to the dynamic mechanisms by which the children, born human like all other human children, become such very different people from other people—as Balinese. The mother who teases her child—who borrows a baby to provoke its jealousy, although preventing any expression of jealousy of a real sibling; who borrows a baby to set on its head, although at the same time protecting its head from real insult—has learned that all this is a safe game. When she watches the witch dance and watches the men and women who have gone into trance and are slow in coming out, she watches with the same relaxed enjoyment or ready criticism for some ritual or technical defect with which she watches the trance dance in which children dance as goddesses. But the child, teased into a violent temper, screaming and clawing to get the borrowed baby away from his mother's breast, has not yet learned that all this is safe. In his intensity and grief, in his fervent acceptance of his mother's theatrical amends for a real hurt, he still shows a capacity for hurt which will not be manifest later. Even as he withdraws from the recurrently disappointing sequences which have no climax, he learns to trust the arts, and he learns to avoid hurting responsiveness to human stimulation.[20]

The faces of the children who watch the trance dance in which little girls replace dancing wooden puppets—and child dancers are indulged by their parents and wilful in their demands—are as relaxed as their parents' faces. But during the witch dance the children's

[19] See Colin McPhee, *A Club of Small Men* (New York, John Day, 1947).
[20] See Bateson and Mead, *Balinese Character*.

faces are strained and anxious.[21] When the witch dances or when some woman worshiper in the temple is possessed by the witch, the fingers are flexed backward in a gesture of fear, spoken of as *kapar*—the gesture made by a baby falling or a man falling from a tree—for the witch is both frightening and afraid, the picture of Fear itself.[22] But when children play the witch, especially when they play her without benefit of costume or music or any of the elements which accompany the finished ritual, their hands are bent like claws, and they threaten an attack in witchlike gestures which can be found in many parts of the world. When the young men, who, as followers of the dragon, fall down before the witch's magic, thrust their daggers against their breasts, they thrust them in response to an intolerable itching feeling in their breasts—a possible reciprocal to the mother's breast during the period when they were so teased, provoked, and given only theatrical climaxes.

When Balinese children are frightened of strangers or strange situations, their elders shout at them, "Don't show fear!" and they learn not to run but to stand stock still, often with their hands pressed over their eyes.[23] In situations of danger or uncertainty— during childbirth in a tiny one-room house, after an accident for which one may be blamed—children and older people also fall into a deep sleep from which it is hard to rouse them.

The Balinese move easily in a group. A whole village may make a pilgrimage of two or three days to make offerings at the seaside or in the high mountains. A troupe of Balinese went to the Paris Exposition in 1931, and a troupe visited New York in 1952. But one Balinese, isolated from those he knows and taken to a strange place, wilts and sickens; people say it is because he is *paling*—disoriented—the word used for trance, insanity, for being drunk, confused, or lost. And the Balinese are mortally afraid of drunkenness, where the clues to the directions, the calendar, the caste system, the framework of life— which gives safety as the walking rail gave it to the little child who learned how dangerous it was to venture away from it—are lost or blurred.

Following the children as they grow up reveals that, even within the simultaneity of ritual satisfaction and individual fear, the capacity to enjoy such rituals, to dance the lovely dances and fill the air with

---

[21] See *Trance and Dance in Bali* (film).

[22] See *Trance and Dance in Bali* (film); Bateson and Mead, *Balinese Character*, Pl. 62.

[23] See Bateson and Mead, *Balinese Character*, Pl. 67.

music, has been—in the case of the Balinese—developed at certain costs. The culture contains—or did contain until the recent upheavals about which we know little—ritual solutions for the instabilities it created, and the people, on their little island, were safe. But it was the safety of a tightrope dancer, beautiful and precarious.

Children and Music
in Bali

COLIN McPHEE

FOR A MUSICIAN, Bali is indeed a special paradise, where music and dancing are not only loved by all but play a most important part in the life of the people. Throughout the year, from one end of the island to the other, hills and valleys relay the echo of gongs, as temples in villages and far-off holy spots hold their annual celebrations in turn. Along the roads drums thunder to the clash of cymbals as chanting processions bear offerings to the sea or follow great cremation towers to the cemetery. From rocky streams rise the voices of singing bathers, while in open fields birds are continually alarmed by the clack of little wind-blown rattles or by the hum of tall bamboo Aeolian flutes that sound with every breeze. In the sky, during the windy months, long kites, furnished with vibrant strings, throb in wiry chorus. Small bells are attached to everything—to oxen's yokes, weavers' shuttles, pony carts, even to the necks of pigeons, along with tiny whistles, to make shrill music when the birds are released to wheel above the trees. Villages ring at night with musical sounds as men, women, and children watch entranced some dance drama or shadow play, while in musicians' clubhouses young men meet each evening to rehearse the swift, intricate music of the *gamelan*, the Balinese orchestra of tuned

This study is a 1954 revision made from an earlier article published in *Djawa*, XVIII, No. 6 (1938), 1–15, and written in 1938 during the author's residence in Bali when the island was still under Dutch rule. The 1954 revision was published in Margaret Mead and Martha Wolfenstein, eds., *Childhood in Contemporary Cultures* (Chicago, University of Chicago Press, 1955), pp. 70–94. In 1954 the author states that "despite many changes under the regime of the Indonesia Republic, Bali, from recent reports, continued to be musically as active as ever." Reprinted with permission of Mrs. Shirley J. Hawkins, executrix of Colin McPhee's will.

bronze gongs, gong-chimes, and metallophones, accompanied by drums and cymbals.

The Balinese *gamelan* owes its more direct origin to the similarly composed, but quite different-sounding, *gamelan* of Java. It is a complex orchestra of separate but interdependent instrumental groups, each with its own musical function. These combine to create an elaborate polyphony, sounding, at different pitch levels, the nuclear theme, fully developed melody, melodic paraphrase, and rapid ornamental figuration. The musical sentence is punctuated by gongs. Large gongs mark the main periods, smaller ones subdivide the phrases or accent offbeats. The pair of hand-struck drums combine in complex interplay to lead the ensemble, controlling tempo and dynamics. Cymbals maintain a steady metallic tremolo, reinforcing the drums on important accents.

While a seven-tone scale, inherited from Java, is still found in certain ancient ensembles, preserved solely for playing sacred music, most Balinese *gamelan* are constructed with the more popular five-tone scale system of which there are various tunings. One type of orchestra, to be discussed in this paper, is limited to a scale of four tones, quite complete in itself. Despite the elaborate orchestration, music survives almost entirely through oral tradition. A rudimentary notation exists to preserve from oblivion the nuclear tones of a composition. It is, however, no more than a bare reminder for the music specialist, not meant to be read from at performance or practice. Balinese musical form shows fine proportion and variety in metric structure, while the underlying rhythm of the drums is highly syncopated. Two-movement ceremonial compositions played on state occasions may take a half-hour to perform. A large repertory of extended suites of contrasting movements exists for the dramatic choreographies of the dance. In the theater, leading characters have each their special theme or leitmotif, and lively, ingenious rondos accompany popular street dances. Modern compositions are tense and restless in their ever-changing moods—free fantasias borrowing from classical repertory with brilliant new orchestral effects. While traditional compositions are kept live through group memory, as young men join the orchestra and older men drop out, new music is taught by the composer through musical dictation. He may be a gifted member of the *gamelan* itself or, famed for his original music, engaged and paid for each composition taught.

The present narrative is an account of how, in 1937, I supplied a group of small Balinese boys in the village of Sayan with a set of *gamelan* instruments, found them a teacher, and how within a period of six months they had mastered the *gamelan* technique sufficiently to make their debut at the anniversary feast of one of the Sayan temples, appearing as a perfectly competent and seriously functioning orchestra. It began as an experiment, for I was curious to see how children who had never played before would learn, if given instruments and a teacher, and how long it would take to produce results. I did not expect that within a year they would become celebrated enough to be called to the local *rajă*'s palace at Gianyar, the head of our district, to play during a great wedding festival, when dancers and orchestras had been summoned from everywhere in the Gianyar district.

But let me first establish the scene. Six years earlier, in 1932, I had built a house in Sayan, a small village in the hills, about thirty kilometers from any large town. The village was chosen partly for its beautiful location on a ridge that overlooked a great valley lined with curving rice terraces, partly for its cool climate, and partly for its quiet and isolation; and when I first came, even the head men of Sayan could speak barely a word of Malay. The villagers were plain farmers, quite poor, and living mainly by a rather leisurely cultivation of their rice fields and vegetable gardens. The Hindu caste system was lightly felt here, for only two or three families had any pretension to rank.

Sayan is relatively new, its inhabitants having settled here within the last century, migrating from the larger village of Pĕliatan, across the valley to the east, where formerly there had been a large court. The village contains three *banjar* or wards, each with its own administration, a half-dozen temples, no school, and a small, crumbling *puri* or noble residence in Sindu, the *banjar* south of mine, intermittently occupied by Chokordă Rahi, a high-born Ksatriyă descended from the Pĕliatan aristocracy. My own house stood in Kutuh, the *banjar* to the north, on the edge of the village.

At one time, Chokordă Rahi, carrying on the tradition of princely patronage of the arts, encouraged dance and music in Sayan by forming a *jogèd* club in his *banjar*. This is a popular and rowdy form of diversion, performed in the open street, in which, to the brittle accompaniment of a small xylophone ensemble, a girl, the *jogèd*, trained both to perform solo exhibition dances and engage in coquettish *pas de deux*, solicits dancing partners from the boys and men who form the main part of the surrounding crowd. But the Sayan *jogèd* had married and retired before I arrived. Chokordă Rahi had also trained an *arjă* club of youths and girls to give the sentimental singing plays so popular today. But this, too, disbanded the first year I lived in Sayan, as members married and no new talent was found.

As for the village itself, it still possessed most of the instruments belonging to the old ceremonial *gamelan gong*, the customary orchestra to supply music for temple feasts and festive occasions. But since the loss through theft, long ago, of the largest and most valuable gong, the instruments had been locked up in the storehouse of the main temple, to rust and rot. The one active orchestra here is commonly called the *gamelan barong*, since it is intended primarily to accompany the periodic appearances of the *barong*, the local dragon, a masked form reverently guarded in one of the temples, which on occasion, animated by two men, emerges to intimidate and rout the local bad spirits. Should the village need other music for its temple feasts and holidays, it engaged, for a small sum, orchestras from nearby villages.

Before coming to Sayan, I had lived in Klandis, a large village near the sea, with dramatic and music clubs of all kinds that rehearsed continually, so that each night I fell asleep to the music of flutes and gongs and soft reverberating drums that seemed to throb in all directions. But Sayan was already in deep slumber by nine each night, with no light showing in any house. In order that there might be some cheerful sound of rehearsing in the evenings, I bought a set of xylophones, drums, and cymbals. With the help of Lĕbah, the young man who drove my car, whom I had engaged because of his wide musical experience, I organized a *gandrung* club. *Gandrung* is merely disguised *jogèd*, performed by a boy in girl's costume, with whom the youths and older men from the ring of onlookers dance at will, demonstrating with varying degree of ironic gesture their awareness of the substitution. Although the entertainment was wildly popular in many parts of the island, in Sayan it was a mediocre success. When I left Bali for America in 1934, to remain away two years, I loaned the instruments to a neighboring village, and on my return did not ask for them back.

Instead, I had decided to organize a serious *gamelan* on a large scale. I learned from Lĕbah that the orchestra used for the *légong* dancers in Tegas, not far away, had only been loaned the musicians by the real owner, my long-time friend, the high-born Anak Agung Mandră of Pĕliatan, and, since the club at the time was inactive, I arranged to rent the orchestra and bring it to Sayan. I had a number of additional bronze instruments made, in order to transform the *gamelan* into a special court orchestra of a type no longer found, romantically called the *gamelan Sĕmar pĕgulingan*, "*gamelan* of Sĕmară [the Love God] of the sleeping quarters," since it was primarily intended to make sweet music of diversion in the inner palace, in the courtyard known as the *sĕmarabawă*, "Place of the Love God," where stood the royal sleeping pavilion. Although I knew the music of this ensemble was rather elegant and classical for simple Sayan taste, I hoped to revive it, at least temporarily, because of its great beauty.

A *sĕkă*, or club, of some thirty older boys and men from *banjar* Kutuh and Sindu was formed, the members chosen by Lĕbah. The club was bound together in the Balinese system through small deposits of entrance money, which would not be refunded if the member dropped out, and various fines for lateness or missed rehearsals. I engaged as teacher an elderly man from the village of Payangan, farther up in the hills, where he had formerly been leading soloist of the *pĕgulingan* orchestra in the local palace. Surprisingly, the group took up this recreation with enthusiasm and, though many had never played before, developed in a year's time a finished technique and had memorized a large repertory of classical music. I then engaged more modern teachers from different parts of Bali, partly to keep up club interest and partly in order that the members (and I) might learn other musical repertories and styles. But all this is another story.

The account I have to give here has to do with the small boys of Sayan, the youngsters of from six to eleven or so, who spend their days half in play, half in herding ducks in the rice fields, tending the placid but unpredictable water buffalos, cutting grass for the family cow, or efficiently performing the other thousand-odd tasks given to the *anak chenik*, or "small man." Met on the road, they are shy and charming, like gentle, furtive small animals whose hearts beat in alternating rhythms of confidence and alarm. Unobserved, they are lively enough, noisily racing about, full of mischief and malice. They scrawl on village walls the latest scandalous gossip about each other and fill them with drawings of shadow-play heroes and diagrams of sex. In the fields you may hear their bright piping voices lifted in song; the words would make your hair stand on end with their sophistication and hilarious smut.

Their early life is based upon imitation of their elders; their play is partly reproduction in miniature of various adult activities, carried out with great regard for detail. They are devoted patrons of the arts, would rather die than miss a play or *gamelan* performance. One would think, watching them, that the performance was given entirely for their entertainment. Naked, they sit in the best places in swarms, lining the edges of the dance clearing like birds along a telegraph wire. They watch intently every movement of dancer or actor and fall asleep against one another when the action drags. Nothing short of a cloudburst can drive them away before the end of the play, perhaps at dawn, when they wander home to work or sleep. It is up to them, for discipline from the adults is mild to the extreme. Perhaps it is for this reason that they have, from so early an age, so unusual a sense of independent responsibility and are, on the whole, so exceptionally well behaved.

In the 1930s, about 2 percent of the children in Sayan went through the inhibiting and disrupting influence of the Dutch-directed village schools. For the privilege of learning that the earth is round and how to draw properly with a ruler, five or six urchins from my *banjar* walked a couple of miles each day to the school in Ubud. The happy rest drifted into adolescence with few cares other than the family ups and downs; they all knew how to look out for themselves in money matters, and some of them would pick up reading and writing Balinese script if they were of studious mind.

A *gamelan* such as the lovely-sounding *Sěmar pěgulingan* that now was heard each night in the pavilion I had built near the road by the garage had probably never been seen by most of the village children. The early rehearsals attracted the small boys from *banjar* Kutuh as honey draws ants. Some even ventured up from *banjar* Sindu. A few begged to be allowed to try the instruments; others simply ran about, disturbing rehearsals with their games. Little by little, as the novelty wore off, they stopped coming. But at odd times of the day, when the club members were off in the fields, I began to hear sounds of experimental drumming and the chime of metallophones coming from the pavilion where the instruments were kept. The imitation was surprisingly good. The number of small men who seemed to grow music-conscious increased, and morning music became a regular thing. But, finally, I had to put a stop to it, for the parchment of one of the drums was mysteriously split, hammers got broken or lost, a cymbal disappeared. The club began to complain.

The *pěgulingan gamelan* practiced nightly, the members meeting at nightfall, after they had bathed in the valley and gone home to eat. From the different teachers I brought to Sayan they built up a widely varied repertory—new music and standard compositions with new orchestration and general interpretation. Each night, from seven to ten, or later, the air was filled with the shimmer of metallophones and gong-chimes, swift drumming, and the soft pulsation of deeper gongs that seemed to float off to infinity. People across the valley said they could hear the rehearsals. It seemed to give them intense pleasure. How nice, they said, Sayan was no longer *sěpi*, dead silent.

Absorbed in this musical activity and daily engaged in transferring what could be transferred of this music to the one notation I knew, I forgot about the children completely. Two of them worked intermittently in the house, polishing knives and spoons, feeding the parrots, looking for leaves and roots the cook suddenly wanted for the daily curry, helping light the lamps at sundown. Between these occupations they would sit down and hammer away at one instrument or another that I always seemed to have standing about the house. They discovered for themselves that certain Balinese tunes could be played on the black keys of the piano, and they improvised astonishing duets. They had that quick, brief concentration one sees in small monkeys, doing one thing for five minutes, only to grow suddenly bored and dart to something else. But every now and then a musical phrase of extremely complicated rhythm would flash out from some metallophone on the verandah, hammered out with neat precision and quite unaccountable virtuosity.

What went on in the inner life of these two, what they were thinking or absorbing, was an utter mystery to me. In true Balinese fashion they were completely uncommunicative, at least as far as I was concerned, about their real activities. They went home at night; they returned in the morning. What they did when not around was not withheld from secrecy, for we were old friends. It merely did not occur to either one to mention anything about himself or anything which might be happening in our *banjar*.

Knowing this, I ought not to have been surprised, as I was, when sudden proof was given that a number of small boys in Kutuh had been engaged for some time in an occupation invoking the aid of nothing less than the muses of music and drama. This was most unexpectedly brought to my attention one sunny morning at Galungan time, the big yearly festival when the gods descend to earth for a visit, officially a week, but exuberantly celebrated by a month of plays, music, traveling dragons, and sociable gadding-about. As I sat at the typewriter, I grew aware of a gradual crescendo of noise, which seemed to indicate that a procession of sorts was passing through the village. Sounds of strange and lively music drifted down from the road above, in which I could distinguish the vigorous beating of a drum, the crash of cymbals, and the deep jangling rattle of a gong, which sounded badly cracked.

"What on earth?" I began, when Lĕbah, coming down from the road, announced it was the children's new *sĕkǎ barong* making its public debut. They had organized a *gamelan* of their own, got up a play with masked actors, and made their own *barong* to patrol the roads during the Galungan holidays.

At this point, before reporting further on the children, I should describe the *barong* more fully. It consists of the formidable mask of a mythological beast—lion, said some; bear, said others—and an elongated body covered with fiber or feathers. An elaborate gilded headdress, studded with little mirrors, crowns the mask, while the tail rises high in the air to end in a tassel of tiny bells. It is danced by two men, concealed within the body so that only the lower legs are seen. The front man controls the mask, snapping the movable jaws in fine simulation of demoniac frenzy. Though generally housed in the temple, these creatures are often used in plays to represent the supernatural form of some transformed king or saint. At Galungan, accompanied by the *gamelan*, they travel from door to door throughout the village, giving a short performance for a small sum of money. They are the Balinese version of the Chinese New Year's dragon.

I went up the road, to find the children's *barong* gathered at the gateway, surrounded by a small but admiring crowd of adults and children, including tots of two or three. The *barong* proved to be a fine imitation, with a body of straw, paper decorations, and a small, rather worm-eaten, but authentic mask. The *gamelan* was reduced to bare essentials, a heavy-keyed metallophone for the melody, a drum for rhythm, cymbals, a large gong (showing a very great crack indeed) for main punctuation, and a small gong to beat time. These, I was told, had been salvaged from various houses in Kutuh—the club was formed of Kutuh boys only—where they had been lying idle and forgotten for years. In addition to the *gamelan*, there were several youngsters, two of them with masks, who formed the acting cast, for a formal *barong* performance often precedes some plays. I let it be known that I wished to engage a performance, and the crowd settled down in agreeable anticipation to witness once more a show they had seen only ten minutes before, a little farther up the road.

The performance was quite astonishing in its general integration and continuity. The musicians played with great spirit, and the drumming, done by one of the older boys, who may have been eleven, was incredibly good in its imitation of the strong, dynamic accents, rapid and syncopated and beaten out at one end of the drum with a drumstick, which marks the *barong*'s entrance. The *barong*, operated by two boys of nine or ten, danced with the ferocity of a puppy playing big dog, snapping its jaws in rhythm to the music. When the dance was over, it retired to the background, and the play began.

The story presented was from *Chupak*, the well-known adventures of two brothers—Chupak, the elder, a demonic type, a bully, lazy, boastful, sensual, and cowardly, and Grantang, the younger, gentle, wise, outwardly delicate but inwardly strong, and in the end winning all, of course, after harrowing trials. I have published elsewhere[1] the outline of this tale, which, when played at normal Balinese tempo, can be spread out to last from four to five hours of heroics, romance, and clowning. The children had neatly contracted it to a series of tabloid episodes which reduced the plot to its essence. Poor Grantang! Awful Chupak! The amorous saleswoman (played by a giggling boy of seven) and the lustful farmer who makes uninhibited advances, and, above all, the beloved scene where Chupak makes a revolting exhibition of himself, feasting in Gargantuan fashion on roast pig, sausage, and other delicacies (the stage property here was a small empty basket), gasping, whining, belching, and breaking wind. The actors performed the more ribald moments with great gusto, to the intense satisfaction of the youngest members of the audience. When all was over, I presented the drummer, who seemed to be club manager, with a *kitip*, a Dutch dime (6 cents American, 1938), about the equivalent of 75 Chinese cash. The club cheered at the windfall; they had been taken seriously and engaged! Off they trooped, followed by the crowd, to play at intervals down the road until they reached the edge of the village.

I wondered at the time whether the little club would have been formed without the inspiration of the large *gamelan* which they could hear practicing at the house each evening. I felt certain the primary impulse for the children in organizing their club was one of imitating the older boys. They, too, would have their *sěkă*! As for the music, they must have learned it by ear from the large orchestra. For since the *barong* in our village was rarely seen except on ceremonial occasions, I had, in order that I could write it down, the *gamelan* club learn the complete musical repertory connected with the *barong*, whether it was presented with offerings, marching in the streets, or appearing in some drama of sorcery. For the most part, the music is wild and somber; its violent accents are intensely suggestive to Balinese, pregnant with imagined movement and dramatic situations. Such music, after a silence in the village long beyond the life of these youngsters, was bound, I thought, to stimulate them, and it was indeed shortly after the *gamelan* had been learning the *barong* music

[1] See McPhee, "The Balinese *Wayang Kulit* and Its Music," in this volume, p. 146.

that the children's *barong* made its appearance. They were, of course, familiar with the method of presentation, for they had seen many *barong* in nearby villages.

Chupak they had also seen, either in shadow-play form or given by strolling players, and the music here was reduced to standard theatrical set pieces which also were in the larger *gamelan*'s repertory. It was the initiative of two or three boys, I learned, which started the group, and I was not surprised to find that Kantin and Kayun, the two musically minded youngsters who worked now and then at the house, were among the leaders. The others followed with varying degrees of enthusiasm, while a few simply trailed along in order not to be left out. Strangely enough, it was in this condensed performance by the children, in their choice of material and their direct portrayal of the various characters, that I felt the essence of the play for the first time and, through it, caught a new glimpse of the lively Balinese theatrical sense. The love for broad comedy, the sensual delight in being frightened by the supernatural, the gift for creating a vivid general impression (at the expense of a finished performance), and the special talent for exuberant dramatic and musical expression—all this was present in miniature in the performances of these children. Most amusing and impressive of all were the continuity and complete assurance with which everything was done. They were very serious. When an actor suddenly grew self-conscious, lost his *élan* and fluffed his lines in an unreasonable access of shyness, he was sternly reprimanded on the spot by the musicians with, "Go on! What's the matter with you? You're simply rotten!" while the audience laughed unfeelingly at this unnecessary yielding to temperament, which broke the spell.

The club amused themselves in this way for several months, adding to their stock of plays and improving considerably. The drumming grew surer, and a couple of instruments were added to the orchestra. But the Balinese temper is strongly colored by sudden enthusiasms and as sudden reactions. I was therefore not surprised to hear, right after an unusually successful performance, that the *sĕkă barong* had broken up. They were, to use a word one heard a hundred times a day, *mĕd*, bored, fed-up, and through!

I now can turn to the real object of this report and tell of the deliberate organization on my part of this group of children into a regularly practicing *gamelan* club, with a complete set of instruments of their own. This idea, however, did not occur to me all at once, and before the *gamelan* was finally formed, the group had passed through several phases of musical development. Hating to see the *barong* club break up, I suggested they form a *sĕkă gènggong*, a jew's-harp club. This diverting instrument, cut from the rib of the sugarplum leaf, is heard everywhere, strummed by children and men alike, in quiet solitude or in a companionable little group. The repertory of simple folk tunes known as *gending gènggong*, "jew's-harp pieces," is endless, with amusing titles such as "Yellow Snail," "Croaking Frog," "Golden Dragonfly," "Fighting Cats," "Crow Steals Eggs," and "Monkey Looks at His Reflection in the Water." This idea of a jew's-harp club met with Kantin's and Kayun's instant approval, and they banded the others together again. Lĕbah suggested for teacher a man from the next village, who had a local reputation for remembering countless jew's-harp tunes. He agreed to come to the house each night, but when I asked him about finding the instruments, he answered in an unexpectedly professional manner: "There's no hurry. They must learn to sing the tunes before they can play them."

Each night the children sat in a ring on the verandah, the teacher in the center, chanting as they learned the wordless tunes. Most of these were brief, repeated over and over without a break. They then began to learn longer pieces, composed of two sections—the first, the *polos* or plain, sung in unison, and the more animated finale, the *chandĕtan*, a syncopated two-part affair, in which two separate but interlocking rhythms are combined to create an unbroken musical continuity. It sounds complex, and it is, but not to Balinese, who throw themselves into such passages with sheer delight. The children sang the tunes and figurations to a few different syllables, mostly, it seemed, *na* and *no*. I give a purely rhythmic sample of *chandĕtan* here; a musical example will be found on page 237 (Example 2).

EXAMPLE 1:

From the composition "Rearing Horse"

It was only after a month had passed, when the chorus knew a dozen or more tunes and had gained some precision in ensemble, that the *gènggong* were produced. The instrument, a short thin strip of pliant fiber in which a tongue is cut, is held before the mouth by the left hand. The right hand holds a string attached to the right end. A quick tug of the string causes the tongue of the instrument to vibrate, and, if the mouth is open at the right degree and you breathe against the tongue, a faint humming tone results. It is a trick any Balinese child knows, one which I could not master. A kind of "breathing" the tune, rather than singing it, against the vibrating instrument is important in amplifying the tones. Within a night or so the *gènggong* orchestra was producing a charming sound, transforming the familiar chanted tunes into an elfin chorus of softly twanging harmonics.

It was another month before I began to notice the well-known signs of waning interest. "What's the matter?" I asked Kayun, "Is the club growing fed-up?" "*Mĕd*," he stated briefly, and that was the end of the *sĕkă gènggong*.

It was about this time that I discovered, while exploring several remote villages to the far east of the island, the survival of an archaic, certainly pre-Hindu, bamboo musical instrument known as the *angklung*, a species of tuned rattle. Three open bamboo tubes of different lengths hang within a light upright frame and fit loosely into separate slots in the transverse base of the framework. (See Plate XXXVI.) When the instrument is given a quick sideways jerk, the tubes knock back and forth in their slots and produce, if correctly tuned, a short musical tone. Continued shaking of the instrument produces a steady tremolo, but the preferred method is to agitate the frame briefly, to produce a single note at a time. The three tubes are tuned to sound the same tone in three different octaves. Since the *gamelan* in which the *angklung* is used has a four-tone scale, a set of four instruments is needed, one for each scale tone. Four players are required, each operating a separate *angklung*. They sound their instruments in irregular turn, following the melodic continuity of the rest of the *gamelan*. In *polos* passages this is not too difficult; in the syncopated *chandĕtan* sections it requires considerable alertness and practice.

In eastern Bali these instruments are still included in a small ceremonial orchestra known as the *gamelan angklung*, since it includes these instruments, whose traditional function in this part of the island is to play only for temple feasts and cremations. In central Bali the special village orchestra bearing the same name, which plays for temple feasts, processions, weddings, and cremations, has not included these ancient instruments for so long that no one has any idea of the origin of the name *gamelan angklung*.

I was fascinated by the tone of the *angklung*, their special use, and by the unusual tuning of the four-tone scale in the orchestras in which they were found, which lent a further antique tonal color to the music. By chance, I came across a newly made orchestra including these instruments, which was for sale in one eastern village. Although I had no idea what I should do with such an orchestra, I could not resist buying it then and there and had the instruments sent back to Sayan by bus.

I placed the *gamelan*, for the time being, in a small open pavilion near the kitchen. The instruments aroused the greatest interest in Kayun and Kantin, who soon, with several friends, were daily occupied with making experimental music, trying the drums and other instruments, and improvising a little ensemble. The *angklung* they ignored completely as utterly strange and absurd.

It was on seeing once more the eagerness of these children to make music whenever they had free access to musical instruments that I suddenly had the idea of forming a *gamelan angklung* of small men only. The orchestra I had just acquired all at once seemed ideal for this. The scale was reduced to four tones only, the instruments were all unusually small, and the tone of this ensemble was high-pitched and sweet. Even the drums were miniature in size. One day I told Kayun to call all members of the defunct *sĕkă gènggong*, for I had something important to say, and at sundown some fifteen small boys entered the verandah with polite little bows and sat down on the floor, all attention. I asked them how they would like to form a *sĕkă angklung*; that if they would, I would lend them this *gamelan* and find a teacher. But this time, I said, it would have to be in earnest, and, if they learned to play properly, I might let them have the *gamelan* to keep.

My words created an immediate sensation. A *gamelan*! A *gamelan* of their own! They discussed it with each other excitedly. Yes, they would learn. No, they wouldn't grow tired of it. They would practice every day, only give them a teacher! I said the orchestra needed perhaps twenty-five players, and, since there were only fifteen present, should we call some boys from *banjar* Sindu? This produced a quick and violent opposition. No, it must be the boys of *banjar* Kutuh alone. They would guarantee more members.

I told them they could take the instruments, all except the fragile *angklung*, away that night, and keep them in Kayun's house, where they could try them out for themselves. Left alone and under Kantin's and Kayun's direction, they could learn how to hold the hammers, how to strike the metallophones and little gong-chimes. The brightest ones, I knew, would quickly seize the more difficult instruments. They bore off the *gamelan* with joyful shouting, and later that evening I heard sounds of wild and confused music in the distance. This went on each night for a week, when I left for Java and was gone a month.

On returning, the first thing I did was to call the group to the house, to find out what had developed in my absence. I do not think I expected anything in particular, other than to see whether the children had found the instruments they preferred and had perhaps learned to play them well enough to go through a simple tune or so. Every child knows from observation the basic method of playing the *gangsă*, a special form of metallophone used in the *gamelan angklung*. (See Plate XXXVI.) You hold the hammer in the right hand, strike the key smartly, and damp its sound by grasping the end with the left hand as you strike the next key. At slow speed this is easy enough, but at modern Balinese quick tempos it requires great dexterity and quick thinking. The children also know by observation how the *réyong*, a set of four small gongs mounted in a horizontal frame, are played. They also have some ideas concerning the technique of the other instruments, with the exception, of course, of the *angklung*.

The youngsters file in, carrying their instruments, set them down, and arrange them in proper order: two rows of small *gangsă* in front, flanked at each side by a large metallophone; behind these the *réyong* and two xylophones; behind these again, the large gong, the cymbals, and two drums. There is a little noisy quarreling on the distribution of the hammers—which belong to which instrument, who gets the best—but finally there is silence. Kayun is in the middle of the front row of melody-sounding *gangsă*. Kantin is one of the two at the *réyong*. All look at each other gravely, catching each other's eye. A swift signal is given by Kayun, who raises his hammer a little way and quickly brings it down on the key; with the same seriousness of intention, quite absurd in a group of such small children, they proceed to play a complete and decidedly intricate composition of considerable length, with sparkling *chandĕtan* toward the end and filled with rhythmic complications, such as syncopations and shifting accents. All this is done with complete assurance, even with style. The music is polyphonic, and there are at least four separate melodic lines, two of which would indeed worry a Western musician. These children, however, sail through all this with ease. True, the tempo falters once or twice, and the drums get out, but the general sound is clear, for there are amazingly few false notes. Changes of tempo are managed smoothly, and some attempt is even made at contrast in dynamics. They finally come to an end with a well-controlled rallentando. I am about to speak, but before I can utter a word they start again. A second piece, shorter this time. And after that a third.

It seemed that they could not wait for my return, when I would call a teacher, but had found one for themselves, the father of a friend from a nearby village, who belonged to the village *gamelan angklung*. Lĕbah also helped train them. The pieces they learned were not entirely new to them; the tunes were familiar, and the form was fairly simple. But there were various technical hazards which required both practice and natural musicianship. What they had accomplished so far could only have been done through ardor and determination and a youthful precocity peculiarly Balinese.

I learned that the club was now organized on a sound basis. A system of fines had been instituted: one Chinese cash for being five minutes late and more severe penalties for missing rehearsals. They had hung their own *kulkul*, or bamboo signal drum, in a tree near their regular place of rehearsal in Kayun's house (the other club also had a *kulkul*), and they had elected a treasurer and a *klian*, headman and manager. In short, there was to be no nonsense about this undertaking. I began to note emerging personalities, which I will discuss presently.

I had nothing but words of praise for the performance, which they accepted with composure. After such a fine beginning it was indeed up to me to find them a teacher without further loss of time. They firmly demanded a *good* teacher, one who knew plenty of new, up-to-date pieces, saying that the *gènggong* club lost interest because the teacher came from too nearby and that his music was out of date. I promised to find them one from Selat, sixty kilometers to the east, famed for musical innovations. I had had this in mind from the start, first of all because the *angklung*, which the children continued to ignore, were still employed there, and I intended, gently but firmly, to insist that the children learn to play them, and also because the *gamelan angklung* of Selat had a wide repertory of both very old and very new music.

A few days later I fetch the teacher from Selat, I Nengah, a commoner, perhaps forty, shy, gentle, a man of few words, and rather alarmed at the idea of traveling so far from home to a completely strange district. "I have never been to Java," he says, using the one name he knows for the great unknown. He has never taught a group of children, for a *gamelan* composed exclusively of small men is unheard of. To be called to live for some time in the house of a foreigner is stranger still, although we are old friends. His nervousness, however, will wear off in a few days, and he will become very popular with the children.

The first lesson takes place on my verandah, after sundown. The children arrange their instruments in accustomed order and sit down, quiet for once. I notice that the brightest boys, led by Kayun, are in the front row of *gangsă*, which play the leading melody, and in the second row, which sounds, according to the orchestration, the melody or performs ornamental figuration. Most of the children seem to be about Kayun's age, around eight. Some are younger, and only a few may be several years older. I have already suggested the music I would like them to study first, which I know very well, for I once wrote it out in full while staying in Selat, and later published it in an article on *angklung* music.[2] It is *Jaran Sirig*, "Rearing Horse," and consists of two parts, a first, at moderate speed, in simple unison for everyone but with several tricky syncopations, and a second rapid movement, with melody accompanied by two-part *chandĕtan* figuration. This last section is complicated, perhaps too complicated for the children, for Selat figuration is difficult. Nevertheless, they asked for it, I thought, and we would see.

Nengah's teaching method in this first lesson seems strangely oblique. He says nothing, does not even look at the children. Without so much as an opening word, he begins by dreamily playing through the melody of the first movement on the *gangsă*, softly, almost to himself. He plays it through again. Then he plays the first phrase only, with more emphasis. He now indicates with a glance at the *gangsă* that they are to begin. Two or three make a tentative attempt to follow him. I notice at once that they do not seem to listen so much as watch the direction his hammer takes along the keys. The phrase is repeated, and they try again. Another joins in, then another. Those instruments which do not play the melody are forgotten for the present, for the melody must be learned first; the neglected players, however, tap out the rhythm of the tune to themselves as they grow familiar with it. Bit by bit the children who are learning the melody are able to extend it, phrase by phrase, forgetting, remembering, gaining assurance. I Nengah remains silent, unless to point out a repeated mistake; generally he is gazing into space. At the end of an hour, however, several can play through the whole melody correctly, and it is a long one, continually going back to the beginning and then taking a new turn. All the children learning it are using the utmost concentration, and I am astonished at their seriousness and patience. But some at least show signs of tiring; the idle ones begin giggling and pinching.

[2]Colin McPhee, "*Angkloeng* Music in Bali," *Djawa*, XVII (1937), 322–66.

It is time to stop. They all go home to eat, although those in the front row can hardly tear themselves away and come racing back almost immediately to try things out for themselves. One by one, the others return, and the lesson is resumed, to continue until almost ten, a late hour for Sayan people. It is now time indeed to go home and sleep, and the lesson is declared over.

Let us now examine the leading personalities of the group, those who will surely form the backbone of the club and hold it together. The youngest of these is Kayun, about seven. He is quiet, lovable, and popular (his name, Kayun, "Désiré," fits him perfectly). He is remarkable independent and goes about the house, industriously putting things in order, doing little things which no one tells him to do but which he thinks need his attention. He has an unusually quick ear, musically, and the keenest rhythmic sense of the group. He has been sitting next to the teacher, watching every hammer stroke and listening with every indication of complete absorption in what he is doing. He is the first to get the melody correct; he never forgets it, and Nengah has already recognized him as a star pupil.

Luar,[3] perhaps a year older, is almost as quick. He also is a serious one and runs Kayun a close second in learning the melody. Lungsur is about nine; he hasn't quite the endurance of the first two, but he is eager and willing and learns quickly. Kantin is still older, eleven, I imagine, rather grave and phlegmatic. It was he, however, who gave such spirited drumming to the *barong* performances, although he is considered much slower than the other three. Kreteg, about ten, goes to school, so he is treasurer and writes down fines in a small notebook. Two new tots, one hardly five, have appeared tonight for the first time, so inexperienced that they came without a stitch of clothes, to the indignation of the others, who sent them home for their sarongs. But they have managed to take possession of two *gangsă* in the second row, and in no time at all I will find them hammering out syncopated *chandĕtan* passages with all the nonchalance in the world. There are two older boys, around fourteen, who don't quite fit in but are needed to fill the quota. They are good-natured but definitely slow at learning, and the younger children have assigned them the easiest instruments to play. The cymbals have been pounced upon by Jati, aged eight. He is a lively, prankful child, not too quick at rhythms, but intensely enjoying what he is doing. He was one of the actors in the *Chupak* cast who forgot his lines. But the cymbals seem to be his true medium;

[3] Drawings by some of these children are reproduced in this volume, Plates XXXII–XXXV. See Belo, "Balinese Children's Drawing," in this volume, p. 240.

he delights in their continuous and animated clashing, smiling gayly in the loud parts.

During the first lesson, there were several children who sat around rather vaguely, the untalented ones for whom the less appealing instruments had been left to choose from. At the second lesson they still have not made up their minds and shift from one to another. These are the ones to grow bored first and start small scuffles during rehearsals. Their interest is intermittent and passive; they might easily drop out but for their desire to remain part of the group. They will finally settle down and turn out to be quite good enough for secondary instruments.

The second lesson begins where it left off the night before. Nengah runs through the melody again, to be sure the front row has not forgotten the melody, which they haven't, and is about to turn to other instruments. But I am anxious to introduce the *angklung* as soon as possible and have them assigned right away rather than waiting until later. The four boys finally chosen to play them must be made to feel that their role is important and a privilege. As Nengah has no idea whatever of how to begin demonstrating their use, I take a hand.

I first ask the club to play the shortest piece they learned while I was away, in order that we may have some already known music to which the *angklung* accompaniment can be fitted. They play "Hibiscus Flower," a short tune with *chandĕtan*, which repeats over and over. But since Nengah does not know this tune, the club must teach it to him. This is a simple matter, however, for before they have repeated the tune five times, he knows it. We can now turn to the *angklung*, which I now bring out. The children are inclined to laugh, but they are also curious. Kayun and Luar, as the quickest to learn, are each given an instrument. Nengah takes a third and gives the last to Lĕbah, who, although he, too, had never seen an *angklung* before I took him to Selat, is willing to try, to help me on with this project.

The four *angklung* are tuned to produce, collectively, the *gamelan* scale and to sound in turn a series of tones which are, approximately, f-sharp, g-sharp, b, and c-sharp (see musical examples on pp. 237–39). In unison passages the *angklung* follow the melody. In passages with figuration accompaniment, the *angklung* either follow the *chandĕtan* or the special filling-in patterns played on the *réyong*. As each instrument produces one tone only, the trick is to wait one's turn until the proper melodic note must sound, then play it by giving the *angklung* a little shake. Generally f-sharp and c-sharp are sounded together, g-sharp is often sounded with c-sharp, while b is always heard alone.

In simple melodic passages this method is not too difficult, but in fast syncopated parts this seems to me a hopelessly impossible task.

It isn't, apparently. The children begin the piece again, while Nengah sounds his *angklung* in the right place in the tune. Lĕbah, quick to get the idea, joins in as the tune repeats. Before long, Kayun and Luar have begun to follow, rather awkwardly. They listen intently, their heads cocked to one side, for their turn. As the melody repeats, Kayun suddenly gets the feeling for his instrument. He smiles delightedly, looks around, and starts boldly playing, introducing syncopations of his own. On they go until the music has been repeated a sufficient number of times, and the gong is struck on the closing note. Everyone laughs and cheers. This is new and amusing; the *angklung* aren't so bad after all! They continue to practice "Hibiscus Flower" for a time with the *angklung*, and then return to "Rearing Horse." I feel I have won my point. Later we can decide who is to play these instruments. Not Kayun or Luar, of course, for they are too important in keeping the main melody steady and the *angklung*, after all, are secondary instruments.

It was not too surprising that Kayun and Luar succeeded as well as they did on this first attempt. The melodic outline they were following was already fixed in their minds, since they had already learned it on the *gangsă*. Furthermore, each note in the fast-moving *chandĕtan* recurs in such a way as to create a special rhythm of its own. With four *angklung* you have four separate rhythms sounding on the four different scale tones, which, combined, form an unbroken chain of mosaic-like patterns. Rhythm, then, and especially highly syncopated rhythm, forms the basis for their integration.

These four-part *angklung* patterns offer only one instance of the special Balinese feeling for polyrhythmic integration. A dozen boys in bathing will beat out different rhythms on rocks with pebbles and stones, to produce an exhilarating hail of organized flinty sound. In the larger *gamelan*, especially in the older forms, one may find as many as seven cymbal players, similarly integrated. And, it seems to me, it is precisely this exuberant rhythmic sense which, above all, made these rehearsals go, made these children coherent from the very start. And when the second lesson was over, I had the feeling that the *sĕkă angklung* would be a success.

The third night, Nengah begins work on the difficult second movement of "Rearing Horse." Melodically, it consists of a straightforward tune of eight measures, ending with a gong stroke, repeated many times without pause, with various changes in speed and force, sometimes soft and calm, sometimes loud and agitated. The *chandĕtan* accompaniment is intricate. Before it can be studied, the melody must first be learned, which should not take long, since it is so short.

As on the first night, Nengah begins by playing the tune through. It has a short introduction, which will later be played solo and which he takes far too fast. Although I know it well, having once written it down, I cannot recognize it, for he seems to upset the rhythmic balance of the phrase by hurrying one or two essential notes which should have the same time value, thus making it impossible to realize where the strong beats of the phrase lie. For the first time during these lessons Kayun and the others are puzzled. They cannot fall in together on the right beat after the solo, and there is a complete muddle. I tell Nengah to take it slower, more evenly, but he apparently can play it only the way it is inflexibly fixed in his mind. Finally, I take up a *gangsă* hammer and play the solo myself, slowly, distinctly, so that all can hear its correct time values. Nengah's rubato can come later, if the soloist wishes it. The melodic group grasp the time values at once and, from now on, can't possibly be put out by Nengah. The following tune is now quickly learned by the front *gangsă*, and Nengah can now proceed to the *chandĕtan*, played by the second metallophones, the *réyong*, and the *angklung*.

Nengah's *chandĕtan* is essentially the same as that which the children learned in the *gènggong* club, only far more intricate in syncopation. The *chandĕtan* playing instruments are divided into two groups, one playing the *molos*, simple (!) part, the other playing the opposing *nyangsih*, differing part. To me, one seems as complicated as the other. The rhythms, however, are mother's milk to the children. The *molos* part is taken first, since it follows the melody more closely. This takes up most of the lesson. The rest of the time is spent in intermittent rest, with exaggerated complaints from the players of *kéwah!* (difficult). The next night Nengah runs the *molos* part through, to be sure they have not forgotten (they have been practicing it at home), and then turns to the *nyangsih* players. He also does not forget to run through the first movement, to reassure himself it has not been "lost." The next night is spent mainly in fitting *molos* and *nyangsih* together and playing them along with the melody.

In five days more the club is playing the whole piece through, without teacher and without a break. During this time they have begun to learn another piece. The rhythm now gets out of hand less often, the front rows are less inclined to race. The cymbals are not yet steady, the drumming is still sketchy, and the gong, played by the oldest boy,

often comes in at the wrong time. When this happens, the children
shout at him in exasperation. They are sharply impatient with one
another's mistakes. But the amazing thing in their performances is the
freshness and life and the general musical effect, far superior to many
gamelan I have heard that had been playing together for years. This
comes partly from the natural agility of Balinese children in general
but more especially from the eagerness of these children to learn and
the enthusiasm with which they play. What seems to me most remarkable is this quickness, the rapidity with which they have learned a
long, difficult, and completely new piece at the very outset, and the
authority and precision with which they already play, especially those
in the front rows.

It is now five weeks since the club started lessons. I no longer watch
them, and they now rehearse in one of the pavilions near the kitchen.
Rehearsals start regularly after sundown, after they have all returned
from the fields, bathed, and eaten. The *kulkul* is beaten first, warning
tardy ones to hurry. But not one rehearsal has been missed, no one has
been absent, and they average about three hours' practice each night.
In this time they have learned nine completely new pieces. Nengah
has gone home, and another musician from Selat, Purni, a boy of
nineteen who is a specialist in new *angklung* compositions, has replaced him. All work together harmoniously. The drumming is better,
the cymbals steady, and nuances of shading are being mastered. As
they play, I hear, farther off by the garage, the *pĕgulingan gamelan*
rehearsing, in another key and tempo, and feel well surrounded by
music at last. The next temple anniversary is due in a few weeks'
time, and the children have been asked by the priest to add to the
program of ceremonial music. (The older club has been furnishing
most of the music at the temples for some time.) This will be their
public debut, and they practice more intensely than ever as the day
approaches. But I know from experience that afterward some fresh
stimulus will be needed to keep them going at this pace.

Here I would like to stress certain points which can be made from
this report and which apply to the general study and practice of music
in Bali. It will be seen, first of all, that the teacher here does not seem to
teach, certainly not from our standpoint. He is merely the transmitter;
he simply makes audible the musical idea to be passed on. The rest is up
to the pupils. It is as though, in teaching drawing, a complex design were
hung up and one said to the class, " Copy that." No allowance was made
here for youth; it never occurred to Nengah to use any method other
than that which he uses when teaching an adult group. He explains

nothing, since for him there is nothing to explain. If there are mistakes, he corrects them, and his patience is great. But even from the first lesson he played everything too fast, and it was up to the children to follow him as best they could, quite the reverse of our own method of practicing difficult passages slowly at first, then gradually increasing speed.

Yet Nengah's system produced swift results. Perhaps it was because of the alertness of the leaders, though the group as a whole learned more quickly than the older club. This I not only saw for myself but was told by Lĕbah, who watched their progress with delighted admiration. As for Nengah, he called them, at the start, "sharp as needles." In all fairness, however, let it be said that their music was far simpler than that of the other *gamelan*. The scale had only four tones; no instrument extended in range to a second octave, and pieces were relatively short. But the orchestral fabric was just as complex, and tempos were generally twice the speed of those in the other music.

Then again there is none of the drudgery of learning to read notes in this music or, worse still, of counting time values; no one to say, "Use the fourth finger." "Did you practice your scales?" The children produced music from the start, in an orchestral group. Learning was fun. Each child took pleasure not only in what he was doing but in the fact that he was doing it in company with his friends. (Hence the opposition to including members from another *banjar*.) And again, no heavy demands were put on any single player. No part was too difficult to be learned with a reasonable amount of application. Each instrument presented a single problem, to which the player could give his whole attention. Combined, the parts produced a full orchestral effect, sparkling with life and movement. This was not children's music they were learning, no mere bong-bong of some progressive rhythm class, but adult music, which, when learned, was fitting to be performed in the temple or at festivals. As a group, the children would practice willingly a far longer time than they would have as isolated soloists. And when a sufficient number had lost interest for the night, they all stopped and, saying they were "very tired," went home. Their teachers accepted this as perfectly reasonable.

While these children are considered to be unusually bright, I do not feel that they were exceptional for Bali, where all over the island one finds boys of eight, nine, and ten taking responsible positions in adult *gamelan*, even playing leading parts. It might be mentioned in passing that girls are never seen in the *gamelan*, since music-making, at least in public, is traditionally man's occupation. In music and in the theater, the role of girls is confined to singing, acting, and dancing.

One last point remains to be made here which concerns both the children's *gamelan* and Balinese *gamelan* methods in general. There is a popular idea that *gamelan* playing is largely improvisational and that the musicians are free to elaborate on a basic theme as they please. This is partly true in Java, but even there to a lesser extent than is commonly imagined. While in older Balinese *gamelan* the leading solo instrumentalist was allowed considerable leeway in melodic interpretation, in modern Balinese music, where the soloist is replaced by a melodic group, increasing emphasis is placed on precision in unison playing. This applies to all sections of the orchestra, where the parts are doubled or redoubled. As for the punctuating gongs, their places are firmly fixed in the metric design. Only the drums seem free, but these, too, are controlled by the metric structure. Ordinarily, the two drums lead the orchestra, urging it forward or holding it back, but in the *gamelan angklung* the tiny drums merely fill in with background rhythms, and the front row of *gangsă*, sounding the melody in unison, are the true leaders. The only time that solo playing is heard is in the free melodic introductions which sometimes precede a piece, and here the performer is at liberty to play as he pleases, as long as the theme is sufficiently recognizable.

The composition is firmly fixed at rehearsal and from then on must be played exactly as learned. Individuality of expression comes into play only at this time, when either teacher or one or two musicians of the group have some new idea, melodically or in figuration, which they would like to introduce into the music being practiced. This is the time when new effects are sought and tried out, with which to surprise and impress some rival club on public appearance. The children of the Kutuh *gamelan* finally accepted the *angklung* I gave them as something sufficiently new and different to make them worth learning, and later, when they played, as they frequently did, in the large centers of Pĕliatan and Ubud, they could swell with pride of monopolized possession when they heard the admiring comments on these absolutely novel and therefore utterly desirable instruments. They could hear other clubs' envious declaration to form similar *gamelan*. What, for the moment, could be sweeter. As for me, I was amused to find these ancient instruments, long since discarded in most of Bali as too primitive, suddenly creating a sensation which could possibly restore them to popular use.

It is the opening day of the temple feast, and the children have assembled at the house to carry their *gamelan* to the temple. I give them each a cloth of large black and white check for a headdress, which will mark them as a club, and they all proceed to pick bright red blossoms from the hibiscus shrubs and put them in their hair. They then take up their instruments and go out in dignified single file, while I follow behind. On the way to the temple someone suddenly remembers that the *gamelan* has never been blessed and purified. This is a bad start, but, on reaching the temple, we find that it can be done on the spot, for there are both priest and holy water, and we may have the benefit of offerings already prepared for other purposes. The arrival of the *gamelan* has caused much excited comment. The other club is already there, and the two *gamelan* are set in opposite pavilions. The ceremony of blessing the instruments is performed, and the children are told to play one piece as termination of the rite. They sit down, and people eagerly crowd around, their curiosity aroused by the size of the children and the presence of the surprising *angklung*. The priest asks them to stand back. It is the children's hour; they dominate the scene. The women pause in their offerings and stand by; the big club watches from the pavilion. The priest says, "*Enggèh, tabuhin!* (Well, strike up!)" and the children begin, while everyone listens in silence, smiling with pleasure. Suddenly, for once, the Balinese seem almost sentimental. There is no doubt that the children are a success.

But the music is soon over, and the program of rituals must proceed. It is now time to go in procession to a distant sacred spring to bathe the gods. The children pick up their instruments as though they had been used to doing this all their lives, and sling them on carrying poles. There is much shouting about getting started. They go out of the big gate, followed by the women bearing the god figures on their heads. The *barong*, which is kept in the temple, follows, and the procession is brought up in the rear by a reduced *gamelan* of gongs, *réyong*, drums, and cymbals. The children strike up "Rearing Horse" (their instruments hang before them, from the poles resting on their shoulders), the women chant, and the animated sound of gongs and drums is heard in the rear. Across the fields we go, with waving banners and gilded parasols, through a rushing stream, up the banks, down again into a deep ravine, to wade through one more stream, and up steep rocky slopes. It is getting dark as we approach the next village. At the crossroads everyone has turned out, drawn by the sound of unfamiliar music, to watch the procession. We pass through in triumph and finally reach our destination. An hour later it is pitch dark, and torches are lighted. Home we go, the children playing gaily on, losing the rhythm as we step over a fallen tree or scramble down a narrow slippery path. As we return to Sayan, people rush to the door-ways with more torches, and children and adults alike join the procession back to the temple. There is a blaze of light in the outer court, where a crowd of men and women move about, gossiping, smoking, eating, and drinking around the refreshment booths, while men and boys are seated about the little gambling tables. Rites have begun in the inner temple, and I decide to go home. I am told the next day that the new *gamelan* club is now famous, people coming from many villages to listen, and that the *angklung* proved a great success, every-one remarking on their "very sweet" tone. I am also told that the children, apparently drunk with success, could not stop playing but went through their whole repertory several times, until dawn finally announced the end of the first day's celebrations and they suddenly realized they were very sleepy indeed.

Postscript One: 1938

At the time I originally sent this article in for publication, I learned that both Kayun and Luar had been admitted to the big club. This they had wanted for some time. In spite of their youth, the club was glad to have them, for extra musicians were needed in the figuration section of the *gamelan*. Kayun and Luar were already able to play figuration parts, *molos* and *nyangsih*, to most of the big club's reper-tory. They simply picked them up by listening, then tried out the passages when the older boys were not rehearsing.

Postscript Two: 1954

When I left Bali in 1939, I formally presented the *gamelan angklung* to the club, with a paper, signed by village witnesses, stating that it was theirs to keep. In 1952, when the Pĕliatan *gamelan* and dancers, under the direction of Anak Agung Mandră, from whom I had once rented the *pĕgulingan gamelan*, arrived in New York for their famous appearances. I asked Lĕbah, who was one of the group, news of the *sĕkă angklung* in Sayan. "Oh, the boys are all married and have small men of their own," he said, "but they still hold the *gamelan* you gave them. They have added many instruments and play every-where." He went on to say that *angklung* became quite the rage after I left and that many clubs include them these days. Even Pĕliatan had brought a set to New York. "The club," he added, "still like to remember and laugh about the time you first asked them to play those old-fashioned things."

EXAMPLE 2:

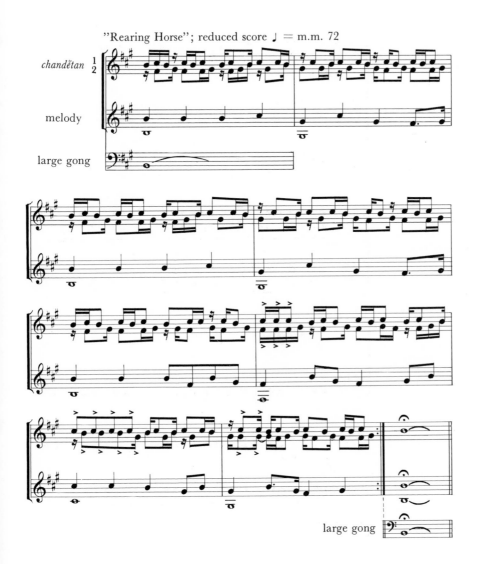

EXAMPLE 3:

"Crow Steals Eggs"; full score

Balinese Children's Drawing

JANE BELO

BALINESE ART has a style and a character of its own. The artists are numerous and prolific, distinguished by the patience and efficiency of their craftsmanship and by their extreme faithfulness to an artistic tradition. Unlike Western artists, they seem to try to produce works conforming as nearly as possible to the patterns used by their fellow-artists. Any individuality in the artist is not stressed, as it is with us, but rather the contrary. If any works which show an unusual vision, a touch of originality, are produced, it would seem that they have come about through the agency of an artist's particular gifts, not by intention, but, as it were, in spite of his effort to make them like everyone else's. In all the aspects of the plastic arts in Bali, in painting, in sculpture, in the design of the puppets of the shadow play and the carving of masks, the similarity to a traditional form is strikingly apparent.

From the past there remain a sufficient number of objects to show that, although the classical styles changed from century to century, each period was characterized by a set of conventions to which the artist adhered, much as they did in Europe during Gothic times—and not since then—without showing any desire to make each his statement in terms which he might call his own. And even today, when various "modern" movements are growing up in the Balinese arts, the tendency of the great mass of the artists seems to be toward perfecting themselves in the technique of the new conventions rather

This paper was originally prepared for the Cultural Congress organized by the Java Instituut, the first conference to bring together in Bali scholars from other specialized areas of Indonesia. The congress was held in October, 1937. The paper was published in *Djawa*, XVII, Nos. 5–6 (1937), 248–59. Later it was reedited for a Western audience and published in Margaret Mead and Martha Wolfenstein, eds., *Childhood in Contemporary Cultures* (Chicago, University of Chicago Press, 1955), pp. 52–69.

than in any effort to create a personal idiom. Although the motivation for the artistic production of these modern schools appears radically at variance with that of the classic periods, the same tendency toward uniformity rather than toward differentiation is to be remarked. The talented Balinese of modern times seems as willing to turn his abilities into those of a craftsman, who copies and recopies the accepted motifs in the accepted manner, as were his grandfather and his great-grandfather who dwelt under the rule of the *rajă*.

Where there exists this readiness to follow a set of conventions, the artist is provided with a short cut in the learning of his trade. Very possibly the great number of Balinese artists and the quantity of their output are due to the simplification of their problem by the very rigidity of the artistic tradition. It would seem that less talented individuals can make more presentable pictures, and more of them, under such a scheme. We are not here concerned with the ultimate aesthetic value of the product but with the fact that the arts thrive in Bali. And whatever their starting point, whatever the influences acting upon them, they turn out to be characteristically Balinese.

Because the artist in Bali functions under conditions which are foreign to the Western world, it should be of interest to investigate the beginnings of the effect on him of his cultural tradition. The Balinese child is already subject to the conditions of his culture; he is learning the meaning of the symbols, learning to adopt a special attitude toward the arts. He will grow up into a Balinese adult, who practices the arts or who is audience for them—in Bali the arts are everybody's business, not the affair of a restricted few. Through the medium of children's drawings, I would inquire into the manner of transmission of the tradition. How does the child absorb its influences? How does he learn to wish to draw things, not as he himself would like to draw them, but as his society is accustomed to seeing them drawn?

Some years ago I was asked to collect a number of drawings by Balinese children of from four to ten years, to be shown in an international exhibition of children's drawings. In those days, before the movement for free drawing in the schools had been instituted, the school children were directed to draw tables, cupboards, and lamps. I was therefore forced to seek out children who had never had paper or pencil in their hands. Nevertheless, the drawings which these children produced, when they were exhibited in New York in 1934, attracted a great deal of attention from artists and educators. There were numerous notices in the press, stating that the work of the Balinese children, with that of the Mexican children, outdistanced in interest the work from the various European and American countries represented. The qualities in these drawings which made them stand out from the work of other children were the strict stylization of the forms, the dramatic portrayal of demons, witches, and mythological beasts with gaping mouths and glaring eyes, the decisiveness of the line, and the free and spontaneous recklessness of composition, combining uproarious action with a balanced, if rudimentary, sense of design.

In comparing the work of Balinese children with that of Western children whom I have observed (working under free conditions, outside the old-fashioned schools), my impression was that the drawings of these children did not differ up to about four years of age, but that very soon after this the tendencies characteristic of the culture began to show themselves. Very little children, the world over, like to draw. When they are undirected, they take the pencil in their hands and let it run over the page, describing mysterious shapes meaningful only to the child himself. At the same time they may tell themselves stories, whose content is not to be recognized from the representations on the page, yet which will often be found to be reducible to common terms. To the child, the lack of representational value of his drawing seems to matter not at all; the pleasure is in the drawing and the telling of the tale. As the child's skill develops, the forms which he draws assume a likeness to the subjects of his story, but the affective basis for the symbolism strongly persists and remains the most significant part of the drawing to him. Later, among children whom I have observed, the child began to be conscious of his drawing as a thing-in-itself, a symbolic rendering of a certain content, which should be interpretable by others as well as himself. At this time, if his advancement in skill had not kept pace with his development of social consciousness, the richness of his fantasy was cramped by his inability to render it. Still later, certain children found their results so unsatisfying that they stopped drawing altogether. Then they had lost the joy of creating with which they began.

I should suppose that, in any culture in which the arts are practiced and which therefore possesses a standard for a modicum of skill, it would be at this time in the development of the child or in the development of any artist that the traditional conventions come most forcibly to his aid. They would provide a key to his problem of representation. The ready-made symbolism, already significant to his audience, can be a mold into which he pours his fantasy. It is probable that this assistance helps over an obstacle a great many potential artists who would have dropped out of the race, had they been required (as they are in Western culture) to find a symbolic language of their own. Does a culture possessing such a tradition produce for this reason a more uniform art and a greater number of artists than one which demands individualism? To throw light upon this question, I instituted an experiment dealing with the drawings of Balinese children, in order to ascertain at what point and in what way the effects of the artistic tradition begin to make themselves felt.

The subjects of this experiment were a group of children, twenty in all, ranging in age from three to ten years. They lived in the undistinguished village of Sayan (district Gianyar), Banjar Kutuh, which possessed neither a professional puppet master nor a professional painter. Not one of the little boys who drew—and, true to Balinese custom, they were all boys—had a father or an elder brother whose business it was to paint or to carve or to cut out in leather the *wayang* puppets. They were therefore not in a position to observe directly the practice of Balinese techniques or to serve an apprenticeship from an early age, as do the children in the households of master craftsmen. They were not more closely in touch with the Balinese cultural background that the children of the average village, unrenowned for elaborate temple-carving or for wall decorations. But they shared with the rest of Bali the all-pervading artistry of Balinese life, which underlies and makes coherent all the varied manifestations of the arts. The same stories which are depicted in color or in relief are acted out in the plays; they recur in formal dancing and, most important of all, in the representations of the shadow play, from which a preponderance of the conventions are derived. When there are temple festivals or private rituals celebrated with a dramatic performance or when at New Year season the streets are gay with roaming dragons and bands of wandering players, the children attend en masse. And especially at shadow-play performances, the children constitute the most devoted and enthusiastic section of the audience. Certainly for the children of the village in question, the shadow play was the chief medium through which they were initiated into their heritage, a knowledge of the legends and the distinctive characterizations of the major roles.

The shadow play is the form of visual entertainment which the children see most often, a form of storytelling which has a special intensity for them. It takes place at night. In the darkness of the village, a screen of white cloth is set up, and behind this screen an oil-burning lamp is lighted, which illuminates the oblong of space upon which the pictures performance will take place, and yet which flickers, flares up in a passing breeze, and sends out eddies of light which lend to the picture a magical quality of life. Upon this focused rectangle of light the figures who are to enact the play appear as shadows, cut in sharp silhouette as they are held by the performer between the light and the screen, or wavering and flowing in outline and in movement as he passes them to and fro in such a manner as to indicate action upon the stage which the screen defines. The figures which cast the shadows are small in scale, a foot to eighteen inches or so in height, and cut out of stiff leather to a sharp and highly stylized outline. Perforations in the leather allow the delineation of the features, the details of the dress, and especially of the elaborate headdress, which, with the character of the features, serves to identify the figure. Quite a number of the figures recur in different series of plays: various heroes of the Hindu mythology, some well-known demons, monkey princes, and other fearsome forms and, with these, some well-beloved stock characters who belong to and speak the language of the people, translating for the audience the sense of the more abstruse passages, and lending an earthy commentary to all that transpires. All these characters become in time familiar to the playgoer, and the children quite early learn to distinguish the finely drawn and delicately noble heroes from the large-mouthed, threatening demon figures and the more robust, crude-featured outlines of the comics.

The shadow play is called *wayang kulit* throughout Indonesia, *wayang* meaning "shadow," and *kulit* meaning "leather," referring to the material of which the puppets are made. The word *wayang* in Bali may refer to the performance itself or to the figures. An individual figure drawn in the characteristic style of the *wayang* is spoken of as a *wayang* and is distinguished from figures drawn with a more realistic intention, which are spoken of as representing "men" (*jelema*). Historically, the shadow play had a ceremonial significance and served to portray the stories from the Hindu literature, recounting the epic episodes believed to have actually occurred in the past and in this manner ritually bringing to life the ancestral personages of the Hinduistic genealogical line. Thus, though the connection of present-day men with the events of this early past was remote, it was nonetheless of a piece with their history and their religion. And perhaps the word "shade" as it is used in English to refer to the departed spirits, and especially to the spirits of departed heroes, comes nearest to a translation of the word *wayang* in Indonesia, with its manifold connotations. The shadow puppet and the shadow play are the mediums through which the invisible world is made tenuously visible; the *shade* itself, without the interposition of the dramatic medium impossible to visualize, becomes formalized in the mind's eye as a characteristic shape.

To the children this conventionalization of the forms of the heroes, the demonic figures, and the favorite clowns offers an acceptable patterning for their developing fantasy. It is a parallel influence to that which picture-books have had upon our children in the past and that television is having upon them at the present time. The Balinese children show evidence in their drawings of the influence of shadow play in three major directions. The *wayang* characters themselves are the subjects of the drawings, selected as more lively in the imagination and more technically precise in pattern than ordinary "men." The scene of the drawings is very often an action picture, as if there were an attempt to fix upon the page a scene of battle or the climax of a dangerous situation, taken from the more animated passages of the shadow-play performances.

In the mass of the children's drawings[1] it is possible to point out a great number which portray a "typical *wayang* scene," that is, a scene in which the two sides in a contest are set in opposition to each other. Although the child's drawing freezes the moment of action, it is a scene of animated combat or of the opposition of the forces of good and evil in a moment of confrontation which is selected for representation. The action itself is rendered by means of certain conventions derived from the structure of the *wayang* puppets, the elongated arms (which are movable in the puppets) appearing at full stretch, caught in the hurling of a weapon or in a threatening gesture. The feet of the puppets are immovable, placed one before the other and in profile, and in this feature also the children's drawings reproduce the puppets, rendering considerably less movement of the feet than of the arms. The puppeteer's custom of bringing the puppets in from the side of the screen and across the scene, either at the base or halfway up the screen, to represent walking or flying, also finds its counterpart in the children's rendering, and the figures in motion may appear in the child's drawing anywhere on the page, from the base line to the upper corners. Because of this carrying-over from the dramatic into the plastic medium, a certain turbulence is to be remarked as a characteristic of the children's composition; there is balance, often a marked symmetry, a tendency to fill the page, and beyond this a tendency to compress into the picture the action of a heroic scene, at times the sequence in a saga leading up to and including the moment of climax. It is as if it were not possible to put in the

[1] For examples of children's drawings see Plates XXXII–XXXV.

picture all the action of the moment portrayed without including a bit of what went before. There is no sense of the static in these pictures, and, in so far as the composition itself is concerned, it is from the influence of the *wayang* play that this attribute of the drawings is derived.

I estimated that the children saw an average of eight to ten *wayang* performances a year. Attendance begins when the child is still a baby in arms, and I knew many a three-year-old who could stay awake throughout most of the night watching the play. From this, most magical of storytelling means, the children learned to recognize Arjună, Bimă, Tualèn, Merdah, Sangut, Dèlĕm, Hanoman, Rawană, and so on, and to associate with each his characteristic headdress, profile, shape of eye, and stretch of mouth. As the familiar characters appear and reappear upon the screen, the sharp lines of the silhouette fix themselves in the child's mind, the more easily remembered because of the rigid conventional forms to which each puppet must be cut. The motion of the puppets is limited and also stylized. Their only movable parts are the jointed arms, which may be extended or bent at the elbow, and the lower jaw of the most talkative characters. Often, to create an illusion of action, the puppet master passes the puppets rapidly across the screen or slaps them back and forth against each other, for a fight, in good old Punch-and-Judy style. The children evidently become accustomed to this manner of representing action in a simplified way and to the sudden appearance of mythical serpents, giant birds, gods, or nymphs flying in the sky and the hurtling to and fro of the strange-shaped weapons.

If one is familiar with the shadow play, one can trace many of the compositional elements in the children's drawings to scenes and arrangements occurring in the *wayang*: the position of the arms, the setting of two figures in opposition to each other, the appearance of others hovering in the air, the filling of space with weapons in flight. The special attention given to the headdress is due to *wayang* influence, since it is chiefly by the headdress that a great many specific characters are identified, while others are recognized as belonging to a certain category, "holy men," "demon," "warriors," etc. From *wayang*, too, comes the children's disregard for feet, which they often leave out of the picture, just as in *wayang* they are off the screen— strikingly out of accordance with the usual precise *mise en page* of these children's drawings. If the course of the play were consistently as violent as in the battle scenes, no one would have much chance to concentrate upon the conventional forms. But they include many long and rather static passages in which nothing much happens. Through these the child sits patiently, at times dropping off to sleep without leaving his place in the audience. Possibly the long hours of attendance, sometimes lasting throughout the night, serve to impress upon the child the outline and the detail associated with each character, the names of heroes, demons, and evil spirits, and the roles attributed to them. We will see later how the little children begin to give *wayang* names to the figures in their drawings even before they are able to attempt, in line, the depiction of their favorites. And this mythological infiltration into their fantasy occurs at a stage when Balinese children, like other children anywhere, are still drawing, in vague amorphous shapes, puppy dogs with little ones inside, snakes, "men," or birds with droppings.

The world beyond reality, the world of the supernatural and of creatures of the fancy, seems to be present with intensity to the Balinese child. A world of unreality exists for him, and the conventionalized figures of the shadow play offer a visible model for these creatures of the invisible world. Supernaturals, heroes, witches, and animal forms, handed down to the child by his culture, become easily mixed with those which his own fancy may spontaneously call up, and the culturally stylized patterns offer him a symbolic language for expression. The mythological characters are loved, feared, and thought about, I believe, with the same sort of feeling as our children have for Cinderella or for Peter Rabbit. But, because they have a very definite, unalterable, concrete shape, because they may actually be seen, time after time, against the magic screen and be heard to speak, they take on a conviction of reality with which no story-book character is imbued. Perhaps the nearest rival of Bimă and Merdah in the Western world would be Mickey Mouse, who also lives upon a screen and every detail of whose fascinating anatomy is delightfully familiar. If Mickey Mouse meant to the adults what the *wayang* characters mean to the Balinese, if he were a figure believed to have existed in the past which their ancestors knew, who conversed in those not-so-remote times with the gods they honor to this day, if he appeared again and again in the paintings and bas-reliefs which decorate the temples, if, in short, he were a character as closely integrated with the life of an entire people as the *wayang* characters are with the life of the Balinese, then he might be expected to take hold on and to dominate with steadily increasing persistence the artistic trend of the child's development, as do the *wayang*.

And in Bali there is not one "Mickey Mouse" but a score or more of figures familiar to the children—some brave, some fierce, some

jolly, and some beautiful to behold. There are heroes and demons,
horrifying enemies who burst out at one in dangerous places, and
brothers who come to the rescue when one is in a difficult situation.
Thus the *wayang* provides the Balinese child with a whole gallery of
puppets for the play of his own fantasy. Later I will show with what
freedom the young child adapts these characters to his ends; for, if he
introduces them fully formed into his picture, he does not by any
means remain faithful to the plots and situations which classic purity
would require. It is, however, not unusual for adults in Bali to take
great liberties with their classics, to revise and extend the well-known
tales, and a lively and not very erudite puppet master or a group of
actors often play out an unorthodox story with the stock characters.
The child shares this tendency with his elders. But little by little, as
his knowledge increases, he makes his characters more true to their
traditional prototypes and to the roles assigned to them in legend.

The vivid unrealities of the Balinese child's world are taken not
only from *wayang*. There are also hordes of evil spirits, the witches,
malevolent spirits of trees and rivers, the frightful beasts which infest
lonely places and whose pleasure it is, everyone knows, to devour the
defenseless *jelema* ("person," "human being," in contradistinction to
wayang, "gods, demons, and spirits"). The life of the little boys keeps
them a great deal of the time outside the safe limits of the village.
They drive the cattle out into the fields, cut grass for them in lonely
places, lead them for their bath, perhaps, to some deep and gloomy
ravine, where the water flows mysteriously out from the ground and
in under the choking, tangled foliage, to disappear in a dark cave.
These are the sites which Balinese fancy has peopled with a host of
grotesque and fearsome spirits of whom even the adults stand in dread.
Grown men whisper to one another that a tiger is not a mere tiger but
a sorcerer who has taken that form, the better to eat up his prey.
Young mothers carry charms to protect themselves and their newborn
infants from the evil spirits which might attack them when they go
to the river to bathe. The adults are genuinely afraid for themselves.
But they also cheerfully use fear of these bugaboos to frighten their
children into caution, to keep them in order. Fear of the supernatural
can be so intensely felt by the Balinese that he is rendered speechless
and turns greenly pale. But when the danger is not imminent, he likes
to play with it, to summon up a Grand Guignol situation, to laugh and
shudder at once, like a child saying "Boo!" to himself on a dark stair.
The Balinese, as a people, love to make fun with fright. They love to
relate, to re-enact and dramatize, some terrifying episode from their

own experience or from some legendary or factitious source. That is why the little boy's fancy will dwell with persistence upon strange creatures, and why the big-mouthed, long-toothed monsters, in demonic or in animal form, devouring or anxious to devour, recur again and again as the subjects of his drawings.

It is possible that the whole feeling of the Balinese toward these exponents of the powers of evil is condensed and crystallized in the masked figures of the *barong* and the *rangdă*—the former commonly representing a gaping-mouthed lion, tiger, or wild boar, the latter a witch, whose wild hair reaches to the ground and from whose tusked jaws dangles a long red tongue. They are dancing figures which may play alone or may take part in a drama. They exist in thousands of Balinese villages, honored often as demigods, and performances by them may be interpreted as an exorcism of the powers of evil. Here again we find a concrete and stylized form given to what we would term "unreality," turning it into visible reality. So that when *barong* and *rangdă* appear in the drawings of the children, we must consider that they may be, not representations of the reality of a performance, but a repetition of the symbol for all that is mysterious and magical and frightening in the dream world of the child. Indeed, in some cases it is impossible to distinguish a child's rendering of a *rangdă* from that of a *tonyă*, an animistic spirit, not a "character" of the plays. The child has never seen a *tonyă*, but he has heard much of them. Therefore, when he draws one, he may give to it the formalized shape of the *rangdă*, as an equivalent. (It may be noted that adult Balinese do likewise in their drawings.) Apparently, the child responds in the same way to the performance of *rangdă* and *barong* as he does to the *wayang*, taking over from them a stylized pattern for the representation of some underlying emotion for which they also stand. In other words, when he witnesses a performance, he may be said to be verifying with his own eyes the existence, the living aspect, of that in which he already believes.

My observations of the drawings of children were undertaken with the idea of clarifying the way in which their style develops, the way in which they adapt the ready-made symbolic patterns of their culture for the expression of their own fantasies.

Controlled Observation

It was necessary for the children to draw at my house, so that they might be observed and also to prevent cheating in the form of assistance from their elders. My observations covered a period of three months. One hundred and seventy-three drawings were made by a total of twenty children. For purposes of convenience I have divided them into groups according to approximate age as in the accompanying table.

	Group A	Group B	Group C	Group D
Age (years)	9–10	7–8	5–6	3–4
No. of children	7	5	4	4

They were all boys. (The girls of this village persistently refused to draw.) The children in Group C had just lost their first teeth, those in Group D were a year or so younger. They did not draw separately according to these groups, for they came to draw when they pleased, with greater or less regularity. One child made fifty-four drawings, another twenty-five, others no more than two or three. As a rule, the more talented turned up more frequently; but there were also two bigger boys who drew with no more skill than a six-year-old but who were most devoted in attendance. Two of the children had been to school, but, as they had no particular talent, the school influence had not spread over from them to the other members of the group. Rather the contrary was the case.

No pressure was put upon the children to draw, other than the attraction of the pennies, which they received for their pains. The work was done on a commission basis. I provided the materials—pencil, pen, or brush, occasionally colors. The paper given them was of big size, 60 × 80 cm., and they were allowed to subdivide it if they wished. The subjects were not suggested to them. They drew what they pleased, and when they were done, they told me the "story," often more remarkable than the drawing. The artist then received a penny or two and departed to cut grass for his cow. Rarely did he ask to see again one of his former works.

The children took an interest in one another's drawings at the time of making them, admired the more proficient, but often admitted that they liked their own the best. We pinned up on the wall, from time to time, examples of the work of all ages, done in various media. New boys, who were strangers to the house, often came to see what was going on. They stared for a few moments at the children's drawings on the wall, then asked for paper and popped themselves down with utter confidence to make drawings of their own. I did not observe any instance of the direct taking-over by the new boy of subject matter from the drawings on the wall. Subjects already treated by one boy might recur days later in the drawings of another, but in quite a different style so that it was not clear how much of their influence on each other was carried over through time. On the wall hung two works by adult Balinese, the one a modern drawing of two warriors, the other a painting of mythological beasts in classical style. Neither was directly copied by the children in any of the four groups. I will describe later how one of the children seemed to learn an anatomical point from the old painting, indirectly, through the intermediacy of another child.

Contagion in subject matter often occurred from one work in progress to another. This applies to decorative motif as well as to content. If one child had introduced a wavy line along the edge of his picture, several more working at the same time would take up the idea and add a similar motif to their own drawings at the top, the bottom, or the sides of the page, afterward interpreting them variously as "mountains," "sky," "road," "coral in the sea," "the edge of the grass," or "irrigation dams in the rice fields." A child of Group B, Gandir, when he had drawn one threatening figure on his page, looked over at Lungsur (Group A), who had balanced such a threatening figure with a demon and placed a tree in the center of the battle. Gandir's drawing, when finished, contained a witch (equivalent to a demon) and a tree arranged in the same pattern as Lungsur's, worked in with his own material, a fisherman, dogs, pigs, etc. In the design the relation of the witch and the tree to his original figure is similar to Lungsur's, although in technique and in content the drawings are dissimilar. Again, three boys simultaneously produced drawings unlike in design and in characterization but representing the idea *mětapa*, ascetic meditation. Two of the nine-year-olds took to pinning their papers on a single drawing board, the edges contiguous. In this position they several times produced drawings so nearly identical, in design, subject, and style, that had I not seen them at work, I should not have known to which child to attribute either drawing. As the skill of these two when working individually was equal and as each seemed to work with equal concentration and attentiveness, without stopping to inspect the other's drawing, one can only consider the influence they exerted upon each other as reciprocal and wonder at the harmony of their common effort. (It is not uncommon to see adult Balinese working in unison on a decorative motif, as, for instance, when two carvers begin at either end of a strip of wall to cut out, without the use of any preliminary sketch, a conventionalized pattern which will join and be continuous when they meet in the center.)

In the interplay of influences between the children, we had cases where the form had been taken over—with or without content—

content without form, or the two in combination, producing, when the children had reached the same level of technical development, an almost identical result. Another sort of infectiousness ran through the series, that of purely verbal association, without regard either to form or to content. Dr. Margaret Mead called my attention to this occurrence in her observations of Balinese mountain children, who say "this is a *barong*" when another child announces that he is drawing a *barong*, even though the form may be the same as that which was called a "cake" on a former occasion. Among my children this sort of association occurred most noticeably in the naming of the characters, so that if one child had drawn a more or less recognizable Sangut, Hanoman, or Bimă, well-known characters from the shadow play, a number of amorphous figures on the pages of other children would be dignified with these names from *wayang* when the time came for telling the story. Again, a child who was dissatisfied with his drawing might affirm that his not very successful tiger was intended to be a pig. The story told afterward was for this reason not a fair reflection of what the child had in mind during the actual drawing.

Taken all together, the reciprocal influences between the children produced a "style" to which new members entering the group tended to conform. The children had a common background of experience, and to all of them the materials they used were unfamiliar. Under these conditions, certain individuals stand out as more talented than others. But no one or two could be said to dominate the group, to exert an influence upon it with a force comparable to that of the trend toward uniformity which came about through the interaction of the whole group and which bore upon all its members.

It was evident, as the number of drawings piled up, that shadow-play subjects would be found to predominate. A count of the drawings of Groups A, B, and C over the three months showed 65 per cent which could fairly be classified as *wayang* drawings because of the clear attempt of the child to depict a *wayang* scene. The proportion of *wayang* to non-*wayang* varied with the individual child; one member of Group A drew 72 percent *wayang*, another only 43 per cent. Of those in Group B who drew sufficiently frequently to make a proportional count of value, one drew 75 percent *wayang*. Not included in this count are the pictures which attempted realistic representation, into which a single *wayang* figure or detail has crept, or those in which no formal representation of *wayang* has been attempted but to which names of *wayang* characters are given. I have included, however, the pictures predominantly of *wayang* scenes, to which have been added subsidiary motifs from real life. It is to be noted that, except in the cases of unusual children, even the realistic figures approximate *wayang* drawing and differ from it chiefly in the lack of a crisp decisive pattern on which the forms are modeled. Whenever possible, the children seemed to find it easier and more satisfactory to represent their subject through the use of a convention already fixed by the culture, and they often drew rocks, trees, even the familiar kris, in a manner taken over from the *wayang* "properties" or from paintings or temple-carvings which they had seen.

The smaller children, Groups C and D, were more likely to mix indiscriminately *wayang* with a rendering of real life. A five-year-old drew a motorcar with a full-fledged *wayang*, complete with crown and trappings, at the wheel. The car is being "stopped" by another *wayang*. Below this scene appear four other figures, three mortal and one *wayang*. Two are doing battle between themselves while the other two, said the child, are forbidding the car-stopping *wayang* to stop it! The dramatic motif is the same as that in the picture of a nine-year-old, in which a *wayang pĕdandă* (high priest) is held up by a beast. Compare another subject from Group A: Batară di Luwur (ancestor god) confronts Batară Suryă (the Sun as a god), and causes him to stop. In the center are symbols for the sun, moon, and stars, standing still in their courses. If we recognize this "arrestation motif" as a common one in *wayang* compositions, we do not know whether to take the motorcar picture as an incident from real life into which *wayang* figures are introduced, or as the child's idea of a *wayang* episode in which a motorcar plays a part. The two planes are not clearly distinguished; in fact, they are thoroughly mixed.

The small child brings to the making of his picture an impetus, a desire to create, which carries him over the difficulties of such confusions. Nothing is impossible, and his fancy could fill a dozen pictures. In the work of Groups C and D one generally finds a whole saga crowded onto a single page. In Group B the frame is already closing in, the subject matter is limited to as much of the story as can conveniently be got on the page. Group A, by comparison, has reduced it still further, so that it seems to focus on a single incident, a single moment, in the tale. For this reason, perhaps, the liveliness and activity of the composition reaches a higher point in the drawings of Group B. They have mastered the technique sufficiently to be able to coordinate it with an integrated section of the content of their fancy, but have not yet become so technique-conscious as to restrict the subject by the limitations of the style. Where a member of Group B cheerfully draws "little brother" with the crown of a hero, a nine-year-old says, "I can't draw a man"—and sits down to draw a pair of struggling demons, sure of line and complete in detail of physiognomy and trappings. Tradition supplies no accepted "model" for a man, but for a demon it does.

The battle motif, whether of *wayang*, beasts, men, gods, or spirits, is the favorite among all these children. We have over and over again a battle scene in which the participants brandish stylistically drawn weapons, the air is filled with flying arrows, enemies transform themselves into strange beasts, and heroes "emanate," through their magic powers, as serpents or fierce birds of prey. I found an average of 66 percent of the drawings representing a flight or some form of attack. This is not surprising in a group so strongly influenced by *wayang*, for the battle scenes are indispensable in every *wayang* performance and constitute the recurrent climaxes up to which less animated passages lead. In some cases the children interpret these scenes as representing themselves. One seven-year-old explained his drawing, "This is me hitting my father, over here I'm hitting my uncle." But in most cases it is difficult to trace an identification. The hero Arjună today defeats with magic weapons the giant demon, but tomorrow we find he's had his head cut off. Often the children state of a battle scene, "Nobody wins. They're still fighting." The contest is the subject of the picture, chosen as a dramatic moment.

I shall set down the title and content of a few of the drawings which it is not possible to reproduce, to give some idea of the flexibility with which the stock characters are treated and the variety of protagonists who may take part in the struggles. Animals, both domestic and imaginary: the king fights a *kuplak-kaplik*, an evil spirit said to resemble a goat, but whose ears are so long that they make a sound "kuplak-kaplik" against the ground as he walks; a battle between a mythological bird and a mythological lion, the bird, Garudă, the lion, Rawană transformed; a cow ridden by a man encounters a *léyak*, a human being transformed into fiendish shape, with wild hair and long projecting teeth—in the center the child of the cow, crying for its mother. A *tonyă* pops out of a tree while Arjună fights a demon. A *tonyă* appears in the river, where an ordinary man is taking his ducks to water; the *tonyă* steals a duck. Here is a pair, done by a child on a single day. Scene I: The monkey prince Hanoman comes to tell Bimă that his little brother is lost. Bimă weeps. Hanoman is very angry. He flies through the air, but he does not find them. Scene II: A follower of *rangdă*, the witch, hurls herself into the picture from one side, offering in her outstretched hand the head of Bimă's little brother, which *rangdă* is about to devour.

Or, if we have as a subject the stealing of a bride, one man with his allies is endeavoring to wrest the girl away from the men of her family. Unrequited love: a lady, almost twice the size of her admirer, refuses to wed him, while he threatens her with drawn kris. A hunting scene: two men with their dogs give chase to a deer, the deer disappears, the dogs mistake their masters for the prey and eat them. In the picture the two men are lying dead, their weapons fallen beside them, one with his leg bitten off. Above are the dogs showing their long-fanged jaws, and all about are the great trees with monkeys in the branches, a common Balinese symbol suggesting danger in a lonely and deserted spot.

What are the scenes not based on fights or acts of violence? The purely pastoral have not occurred—the cows and ducks with which the little boys spend their days are only drawn in combat, perhaps with a mythological lion or threatened by some evil spirit. The nearest approach to lyrical feeling is expressed when two of the children draw temples, with carved gates and decorated walls, over which show the multiple roofs of the little shrines, unprofaned by any human presence. Generally when the children take as their subject a scene from real life, they choose, as from the *wayang* material, a dramatic moment, a cockfight in action, the communal slaughtering of a pig, a dancing performance at which a crowd has gathered—a *gandrung*, a *jangèr* (favorite dances) or, most popular, a *barong* (dragon). When it is a performance, the orchestra, which adds so much to the gaiety of the actual scene, has always been represented. Two children drew a cremation at its most turbulent point, when the crowds of shouting men mill around the tower in a frenzy to get at the corpse. Only once did a child attempt to depict an actual masked figure of *rangdă* which he had seen perform the day before, flanked by trance dancers pressing krisses into their breasts. In this picture, as in all other attempts at "real life," the execution of the child-artist fell far below the level of his more formalized legendary drawings. This same child had drawn *rangdă* many times, with great conviction, after the model of the *wayang rangdă*. It is curious to note that *barong* have appeared twice in his pictures, not as masked figures supported on the legs of men but with the legs of beasts.

In the discussion of the subject matter of the drawings, I have not made a distinction between the groups according to age, for it seemed to me that the difference was one of treatment rather than of choice of material. I have stated that the field of content narrows as the child grows older, bringing it into line with his skill. Let us see now how the littler ones begin to master the special technique which makes their drawings Balinese. Of the four children in Group D who had not yet lost their first teeth, three did not yet show any signs of the formalized technique. They made round heads, lumpy bodies, and stick-like legs, seen from in front. Their animals were only slightly longer shapes, with four legs to distinguish them from men. The fourth child of this group began at once to draw the head of a man in profile, with the characteristic long nose and slanting eye of *wayang*. Of eight figures in his picture, seven were drawn in this way, and the eighth, at the bottom of the page, was given a round eye and the rounded horn of a *wayang* headdress—perhaps a miniature Bimă? Also in the picture are three very large ducks. A child in Group C, who lost his first teeth during the period of the experiment, I was able to catch at his first attempt to draw a *wayang*. He had been drawing in the manner of the tiny ones when one day he began to put in minute compact *wayang*, with horned headdress and extended or bent-at-the-elbow arms, interspersed among the figures of men and beasts drawn in his usual manner. I have reproduced this drawing here (Plate XXXIV) so that the aspect of the germ of a style may be known. A month later this child was drawing *wayang* with considerable freedom —it was he who put one to drive a motorcar. The other members of Group C were all drawing *wayang*, as they had done from the beginning, to the exclusion of all other subjects. They had already attempted a number of complicated headdresses which distinguished the characters (see Kresna and Salyă by a six-year-old in Plate XXXIV).

It is not often that the observer can put his finger on the exact point which marks a step forward in any given child's development. These children were not seen all day long, nor had any one of them been seen every day. They themselves said that, lacking paper and pencil, they drew only upon the walls. And the walls bore witness to the fact that they did. Except for spatial limitation, the equivalent of a frame, which the edges of a piece of paper provide and which an expanse of wall lacks, I could see no appreciable difference in the style resulting from the change of medium. If the line is looser when the child uses a brush on paper rather than a bit of charcoal on the wall, it is relatively tighter when he uses a pen. Therefore, when a six- or seven-year-old child begins at once to draw recognizable *wayang*, one assumes that he has practiced his craft on the walls.

According to the data collected during this period, which cannot be conclusive because of the limited number of children studied, it would seem that the children began to draw in the culturally dictated manner between the ages of five and seven, varying with the precocity and special aptitude of the child. Only two children came under my observation who were over the age of seven and who yet made no attempt to draw in the classical style. Both children were very aberrant types, in all their ways quite unlike their fellows. There are probably many children who do not draw at all, but it seems that those with a touch of ability try very hard to master first the accepted technique. In my Groups A and B, only those who stand out as the most talented ever attempted the more difficult task of portraying a realistic scene. They themselves considered it more difficult and probably less rewarding.

Another point in learning was noted in the case of a nine-year-old when he passed from drawing the hindlegs of animals with knees in front like a man's to hocks in back like a beast's. Kantin had been drawing very regularly for a month in the shadow of the wall where hung the classical painting of mythological beasts mentioned earlier. From April 21 to May 14, he had made eight separate drawings containing animals, all with their knees in front. On May 14 and 15, a child of twelve years was seen by Kantin to make a copy of some of the beasts on the wall painting, reproducing their classically drawn hind legs. On May 16, Kantin attempted an animal, was dissatisfied, turned over the page, and drew men. On May 22, he again drew an animal, with knees in front as before. On May 27, suddenly the legs of his animals were changed, forever after to be drawn with the "knees" where they belong. The curious fact is that he did not himself attempt to copy the wall painting, nor did he learn by looking at it. Through the medium of the older boy's drawing, his attention was brought to this problem of animal anatomy, and he seems to have carried the problem in his mind until he had it solved. I have observed children in America becoming concerned with and meeting this problem at very nearly the same age. In spite of the marked conventionalization of Balinese children's drawing, a certain underlying course of their development can be correlated with that of children living under very different conditions.

The drawings themselves bear witness to the fertile imagination which the children bring into play when left to draw what they please. Note with what freedom of treatment the most significant elements have been made to stand out in the *barong* and the cockfight pictures here reproduced (Plates XXXIII and XXXV), simply by magnifying them out of proportion to the scale. From the drawings, too, one can better judge the spontaneous sense of composition and balanced design than from any written description. It is true that whether the composition "comes off" or not depends a great deal on accidental factors. These Balinese children often achieve what seems a masterpiece of design and spoil it afterward by the addition of a wealth of decorative detail—not an unfamiliar trait in the art of adult Balinese. Similarly, the frequent filling-in of space with "mountains," "greenery," "rocks," etc., must be taken over by the children from the decorative conventions of the adults in painting and in temple reliefs. When the children were first given colors, they used them decoratively, not conventionally or realistically. The specified colors of even the most familiar *wayang* figures—Hanoman, white; Bimă, black; Baladéwă, red; etc., which may be seen in Bali by anyone who wanders around to the side of the screen where the puppet master is manipulating them—were completely disregarded by these children. They began by applying the colors in stripes along the sides of their lines, a red and a blue stripe down one side of a leg, a green and a yellow stripe down the other side, a purely decorative device. After a month of using color, the children came to painting in solid sections, occasionally even backgrounds, but the leaves of a tree were still likely to be red and the feet of a man sea-green.

As the work progressed, as the child's interest in and mastery over technique increased, the field of content tended to be reduced. Compositions once overflowing, spilling over the margins, became more constricted, the subject matter was limited to what could be adequately handled on a page. There was a loss in compositional dynamism, a widening of margins, and a more meticulous attention to detail. The bold individual expression in the design seemed to diminish, the design became more set, dry, and static. It is only fair to add that early drawings of these children are often their best and that perhaps the lure of the pennies led them to draw at times when they had "nothing to say." It is quite possible that some of these children had drawn too much. I am reminded of the statement of Mr. Bonnet (artist and collector of modern Balinese paintings) that in his experience the work of the young adult painters tended to go down after the first year or two and that their best work was done while they were mastering a new technique. Gregory Bateson and Margaret Mead have told me that in collecting the woodcarvings of adults who were just beginning to make statuettes, the first piece of any individual was usually his most effective, that it often had a quality lacking in his later work. These observations, which corroborate each other, would seem to show that, although the Balinese, adult or child, is never at a loss for a subject, the rich background of legend and the tricks and conventions of a traditional style cannot be depended upon to produce "art" by a formula but that the whole mechanism must be fired from within by some intense feeling of the artist.

Dance and Drama in Bali

BERYL DE ZOETE and WALTER SPIES

THE MERE FACT of isolating one aspect of Balinese life involves an arbitrary distinction which does not exist in Bali and makes that one activity stand out in an artificial way. In Europe we have subdivided our activities as we have subdivided our day into a regular series no one of which encroaches on the other. A dancer is a dancer and not a carpenter, he must not even be confused with an actor. In Bali the reverse is the case; our disciplined march of hours corresponds to nothing in Balinese feeling, and just as one hour does not stand out from another with insistent individuality, nor does the activity which we call dancing. A dancer may be a fisherman, a wood carver, a goldsmith; he will almost certainly work on the *sawah* [rice fields]. There is, however, an obvious excuse for devoting a special study to dancing, for their movement, even more than their physical beauty, is the first thing that strikes one about Balinese people. The Balinese are plastically gifted to an extraordinary degree, and their power of rendering movement, whether in stone or pencil or the evolutions of the dance, is equally astonishing and rare. Wherever he may be, idle or at work, sitting at home, in the market or the temple, or walking on roads or devious footpaths, squatting naked on a rock in the river in the act of making offerings to the stream, carrying heavy burdens, or playing under the waterspout, cutting down a palm tree or perched without support on its narrow crown still trembling from the shock of decapitation, the Balinese is so perfectly in harmony with his surroundings and so graceful in his poise that we almost have the impression of a dance.

Reprinted with permission of Faber and Faber from the authors' *Dance and Drama in Bali* (London, Faber and Faber, 1938), the first part of the essay being from the Introduction, pp. 5–28, and the second part from Additional Notes, pp. 262–70.

Certainly the Balinese child has from infancy its limbs trained and persuaded to become perfectly pliant, and daily work in the fields makes them strong. But there is a surprising tact and refinement in the everyday movements of the Balinese. A peasant who holds your hand down a steep and slippery path gives exactly the right support, and relaxes it at the right moment. Perhaps the Balinese has few thoughts in our sense, and few intellectual perceptions. But he has a vast store of physical perceptions. Somewhere diffused in his limbs are images of movement appropriate to each person and each situation, images of style which are both instinctive and remembered. The subtly graded scale of values which exists in the physical behavior of the community plays of course a great part in the dancing, but it is not itself dancing. It is indeed only because the trend of our civilization has been in the direction of obliterating forms and ritual behavior that perfect tempo, measure, and modulation in ordinary movement appears to us to have a choreographic quality, the quality of a design with conscious balance of parts. The Balinese would be amused at the idea that women carrying offerings or six-foot piles of coconuts on their heads had anything to do with women dancing; for dancing is to them something quite different, another mode of being. One must indeed have lived in a strange disorder before coming to look on the harmonious body as a dancing body, and the mere presence of measure in movement as a dance. The Balinese is part of an inherited order governed by a most complicated system of laws, which are natural to him because they are innate in the conscience of his community. Within this pattern he seems to find perfect satisfaction. And just as the energy of the village finds harmonious expression in the order of the village law, so the energy of the individual passes through the sieve of his body in perfect distribution.

It is natural that such a genius for movement as that of the Balinese should find expression in the art of which movement is the only body —in music. Music permeates their life to a degree which we can hardly imagine; a music of incomparable subtlety and intricacy, yet as simple as breathing. Like every other expression of Balinese life, it is easily accessible and at the same time inexhaustible in its interest and variety. "Day and night the air is vibrant with the golden metallic sounds of the *gamelan*—the orchestra peculiar to Java and Bali—accompanying either religious ceremony or the performance of dance or drama for the celebration of some domestic or religious event. Here is a music which has successfully achieved the absolute, impersonal and nonexpressive, with a beauty that depends upon form and pattern and a vigor that springs from a rhythmic vitality both primitive and joyous."[1] Like all the other artists of Bali the musician may be of any rank, age, or profession. At the head of one of the finest *gamelan* in Bali is a chauffeur who is also a composer of bewildering fertility, and his principal collaborator is a boy of about five, who a year or two ago used to be carried off to bed under his mother's arm. Children sit between their father's knees in the *gamelan* before they can walk, and their tiny hands strike the cymbals or metal keys or hold the drumsticks, enclosed in their father's. It almost seems that they absorb directly into their bodies the melody and the complicated rhythms, just as they absorb the rhythms and postures of the dance. There is not *one* music in Bali; there is an appropriate music for every occasion, and an appropriate type of *gamelan*:[2] for birthdays, tooth-filing, weddings, cremations, for temple feasts and processions to the sea with the holy images, for purifications and the driving away of disease and demons. There is naturally also an appropriate music for every kind of dance, and it is only to these that we can refer in the course of this book. But it is impossible to approach the subject of dancing without allusion to the unfathomable world of tone and rhythm which is continually being revealed in the rare and complicated texture of the Balinese *gamelan*. It is the most direct yet mysterious expression of the Balinese temperament and genius, as impersonal as nature and as sensitively alive. One has the feeling as one listens that something of the brilliance and depth of the infinitely varied Balinese landscape vibrates in the resonance of metal, cowhide, and bamboo, by some intense sympathy which becomes articulate in rhythm.

Though Bali is thought of as a place where everyone dances, because dancing forms an integral part of the Balinese scene and is an essential element in the endless series of private and public festivals, nowhere in the world is dancing more specialized. We shall return later to the singular fact that though dancing accompanies every stage of a man's life from infancy to the grave, there is no spontaneous communal dancing, and among a people of peasants practically no seasonal dances. It may be that temple service and processions are an

---

[1] Colin McPhee, "The 'Absolute' Music of Bali," *Modern Music*, XII, No. 4 (1935), 163–69.

[2] There are a number of gramophone records of Balinese music which give at least some idea of its texture. The American composer Colin McPhee has written about it, with singular clarity, in monographs devoted to particular *gamelan*. (See Bibliography, pp. 404–5.) Miguel Covarrubias's *Island of Bali* has an excellent general description of Balinese music and musical instruments.

important substitute. It is as members of age groups that unmarried boys and girls perform ceremonial dances of offering and dedication in the temple, where also old women renew the religious dances of their youth. These dances are often performed perfunctorily and without any of the grace which distinguishes the most casual movements in ordinary life. Outside the temple, however, the dancer or actor, for the same word applies to both, is differentiated from others by the fact that he dances, whether he be of high caste or low, *rajă* or priest, gold or silver or iron smith, wood carver or fisherman or simple worker in the rice fields; for dancing needs special gifts and training and is not everybody's business, though, as we have seen, nothing but inability or lack of desire could possibly stand in the way, and the fact that he is a dancer does not interrupt his normal life in the village unless he is so famous as dancer and teacher that dancing and teaching take up the whole of his time. The dancer in Bali is simply another of those anonymous artisans who are continually renewing its cultural life.

* * *

But for the purposes of this book the most important origins of Balinese dancing are in Bali itself, in a certain richness of temperament which has been able to transform what came to it from elsewhere and to make it into something purely Balinese. About this one can transmit certain facts, certain stories and a certain impression of the scene on which dancing takes place, and of its social and religious character. There is a continual process of developing, blending, modifying, going on in Bali. Fashions change rapidly; much that could be seen ten or even five years ago can now perhaps be seen no more. *Perhaps*; for one knows by experience that a little investigation may bring something to light in one corner of Bali which has ceased to exist or perhaps not been known elsewhere, and which even in its own neighborhood no one would trouble to tell one about. Again, a little stimulus may often revive an almost forgotten form, and the sudden interest of a *rajă* or even of a European in an old-fashioned dance drama may restore it to its former vitality and splendor.

* * *

The Balinese Attitude toward the Play and the Story

Watching dancing is not for the Balinese a matter of such concentrated attention as with us. It is almost a state of being, a feeling rather than an action. We gaze and gaze with an earnestness of purpose which fatigues us long before the dance is over. The Balinese, like other orientals, enters into the atmosphere of the dance and remains there as in a familiar landscape. Of course he expects the figures to appear which people his traditional landscape, just as we expect the landmarks on a familiar walk, or at least should be much surprised if they were not in their usual places. But like us on the familiar walk, he is not at a stretch of expectancy, what the Germans call *Spannung*, from the image of a stretched bow. His attitude towards the performance at which we gaze with such rapt and fatiguing attention must be a good deal like that of the fashionable world who had their boxes in the Italian opera; noticing now and then, criticizing technical points, enjoying the improvisations and topical jokes of the clowns, admiring pretty girls on the stage and off, flirting, talking to their friends, and then watching again.[3]

Nature does not make perpetual demands on one's attention, nor does a dance performance on the Balinese. It is just there to be enjoyed in a variety of ways. Someone has said that dancing in Bali is not there to be looked at, nor music to be listened to, but both only to be seen and heard like trees and streams in a wood. The story, which so much interests us, does not trouble the Balinese in the least. He does not mind at what point it is taken up, nor at what point it is left. The success of a play never depends on the story. There are no good or bad stories, any more than in our ballets, though there may be some which are not suitable—even dangerous to put upon the stage, from some quality of magic they possess. In any case the story is only comprehensible to the unlettered Balinese who form the greater part of the audience in the passages where the obsolete language in which it is played or sung is rendered in Balinese by the courtier who acts as interpreter. The characters, whatever their name, are dressed in the traditional manner for the type they represent, and the range of interpretation for every part is very small—except for the clowns, who on every popular stage from time immemorial have enjoyed almost unlimited scope. The conversation of the clowns, who are also courtiers, consists, besides the necessary information they give us about the main characters and the fulsome homage they pay their masters, of a long series of witticisms as good or as bad as those of our own music-hall stage, with all kinds of improvised comments evoked

[3] In Balinese drawings of dance performances the attention of the audience seems to be chiefly devoted to love-making; but perhaps this is a wish fulfillment rather than a portrayal of what usually happens.

by the occasion. Judging it from the point of view of a play, it might seem to us strange that people should be content to sit for hours without knowing what they are looking at. But this is quite a wrong way to look at it. We listen for the story while looking at the action. The Balinese are absorbed in the rhythm, in a general not a particular action. And about the general action no one is in doubt, for everyone on the Balinese stage has his traditional, generalized style of dress and movement. This style is so deeply rooted from infancy in the plastic vision of every Balinese that any departure from it strikes him as comic, and part of the comedy of the *kartală* (secondary attendant) lies in his dancing without dance style, that is, almost casually, with unstylized movements common to ordinary life, with knees not turned out, with swinging arms and legs, a drooping head, etc. It lies in the conception of the clowns that they should show a certain lack of style in relation to space. The vulgar gravediggers, market women (danced by female impersonators), peasants in general, tend to move round in rapid file or procession rather like a drill class. A vulgar character, even if he has become ennobled and changed his headcloth for a grand headdress, will keep his styleless movement, as well as his comic mask. His deportment at court is indeed deplorable; he even touches the prime minister's dress, and cannot be taught obsequiousness. I have imagined the reaction of an ordinary unlettered Balinese to the dance-drama. But naturally all Balinese do not look at dancing from the same standpoint, any more than we do here. Those who are versed in the details of the very exact science of dancing will notice a thousand things which the ordinary man does not notice. But the skeleton of dance-drama is ceremonial behavior, of which the dance is a floreation, and the general lines of ceremonial behavior are known to everyone, just as the rules of a game of cricket are known roughly to all the spectators at a village match, though the fine flower of performance only finds an echo in the hearts of a few connoisseurs. The atmosphere is indeed rather similar to that of the village green. Everyone knows everyone else, for it is your own village; and every type on the stage is equally familiar, for there is no individualization, and no one could possibly have his own thoughts or his own manner of producing himself, unless, as we have said before, he is a clown. Every feature is traditional, and every character can be recognized, or rather every type of character, by dress, manner of movement, order of appearance. The presence of all the right types seems to be the important thing quite irrespective of what they do; in fact the working out of a plot seems to interest no one, except in the type of play known as *arjă*, where the sequence of events is shown at enormous length. We shall deal with this subject again in reference to each individual type of play but would suggest in passing that, all the stories being familiar, the whole action is perhaps conveyed in any fragment of it, just as often in our poetry a single word or turn of phrase may allusively summon up a whole situation, or complex of events. A Balinese artist once brought me a drawing of a humble interior where a wedding was going on. It was soon clear, though there was no graphic indication of the fact, that it was not *any* wedding, but a quite particular one, on which hung a whole sequence of events. All these events—the ceremonial bath of the bride, her theft by a water sprite, her husband's descent to the world under the river, his victory over the water sprite and the winning of great riches—were contained for the artist in that first picture.

Balinese pictures are, however, far more documentary than plays. Pictures are a narrative. We seem to have reversed the role, and bring to the stage requirements which they bring to the picture. Drama is not the telling of a story, but action, *dancing*; the same word applies to both, for drama is only conveyed through the heightened rhythm of dance, never at the flat pitch of actuality. Thus a character will belong to an imaginative type which will quite outweigh the actual circumstance of his situation as depicted in the story. A classic example of this is the stage presentation of *Grantang*. Grantang, though actually the son of Vishnu, had as earthly father a poor Brahmană who worked in the rice fields, and was certainly a very humble person, according to this world. But he belongs essentially by nature to the most refined type of character and could therefore at no point be shown in any other way than as the most refined and elegant prince. For as there is no décor, so there is no change of costume. A character wears what his type should wear, and if he disguises himself the disguise remains in the story and does not show outwardly on the stage. The heroine Sentai, in the *arjă* play *Sampik*, from a Chinese original, dresses up as a boy and goes off to school in her motorcar; but on the stage she is dressed and dances like any refined heroine, which indeed she becomes later in the play. A headdress does occasionally serve as a quite effectual disguise. It seems not to matter at all that the voice and gesture remain the same, as well as the rest of the costume. Rawană, in *wayang wong*, has only to put on a priest's hat for Sită to be completely taken in by him, though his demonic voice and violent gestures would, one supposes, have at once betrayed his real nature to her. But the world of dance is a spiritual world governed by its own laws, which are indeed much more appropriate to it than those of the so-called real world.

It is fitting that in such a world the quality of characters and not their acts should be the criterion by which they are judged. The *topéng* story of Ken Arok is a striking example of this. Ken Arok, in order to attain to power and win the queen for himself, committed the basest of crimes; he was a traitor, liar, and murderer, and by a long-delayed fatality was finally killed by the weapon with which his crimes were linked. But there is no hint of a judgment on him. He was of divine birth and worked miracles in his infancy; and he had seen an inner fire lighting the body of the queen whom he desired. He possessed *sakti*, magic power, the all-redeeming quality for which we have no equivalent. *Virtue*, if we divest it of all moral connotations, all idea of "good living," and leave it only with its strength, is the nearest we can get. "The virtue has gone out of him." The Chinese *tê* exactly expresses it; so does the Sanskrit *guna*, energy. In the *Ramayana* Subali the monkey could not be killed till he had voluntarily given up his "flower of magic," his *tê*, to Sugriva. The *rajă* of Nusă Pĕnidă was undoubtedly a "wicked" person, but he was magically powerful, he had *sakti* and could only be killed by a special magic weapon. In the story of Chupak the *raksasă*-like, braggart, greedy elder brother of Grantang seems to win all the points against his magically gifted younger brother, but only so long as Grantang does not put forth his power against him. When that happens he is at once proved inferior.

Dance Style

If the innumerable sculptured figures of kings and queens, princes, courtiers, and servants of all degrees, demons, monkeys, and the great goddess Durgă herself, which posture in the temples of Bali were to come to life, they could take their places without arousing any comment in the dance-dramas of today, when they had shaken a few time-flakes from their limbs. For they are already in dance attitudes and the dress which befits their rank, whether on the high stage of the temple or the dust of the village dance floor. In fact, reversing the situation, there is one delightful play in which a prince and his two attendants slip into the place of their own images which the lovesick princess had set up in her garden, and at once deceive her, so easy is the transition from stone to flesh. In Bali where wood and stone are always in dissolution, tradition is permanent and alive. It is not from any desire to perpetuate the *past* that the style of centuries ago is renewed again and again in stone or in dance, but because, despite their love of novelty, the Balinese have not really learnt any new attitudes and cannot imagine a present which does not clothe itself in those which are immemorial. The gesture-language, the attitudes of the Balinese stage today, can be paralleled in the oldest stone figures in the temples, because the ritual knowledge which created the one still directs the other and is still the eye through which the Balinese view behavior in the dance world where artists and spectators are equally at home. The imagination of the audience as well as the skill of the dancer animates the forms and lives in the familiar ritual which is bound by indissoluble links to the ritual of their own life. A "well-bred" knowledge of behavior is perhaps always the basis of enduring dance technique. It necessarily excludes the idea, which is after all quite a new one even with us, that the dancer should express "himself." Such an idea has something of nakedness about it, such as an Arab woman would feel if she went with face uncovered into the road, or a film star if she wore no eyelashes but her own. In Bali, as elsewhere in the East, the dancer is possessed by his role. He lets the dance *dance*, and functions only as a vehicle of the dance, and the measure of his success as a dancer is no doubt the degree to which he is possessed. But this fusion of the dancer with his role naturally does not operate directly, or by a kind of subjective inspiration. Dancing is Bali is as exact a science as in Java or in the other countries which inherited the Dramatic Code (*Natya Çastra*) of India. Javanese dancing may appear more "classical," because of its extreme restraint and infinitely fine shades, and an almost pedantic measurement of angles; the *Kathakali* of Malabar may seem to possess in its still living sign-language (*mudras*), a more precise and powerful medium of expression; the art of dancing is in Bali as definite a science as either of these, and at least as eloquent. The abounding life of the Balinese stage tends so to floreate the structure that it gives an air of spontaneity to ritual proceedings; but the ritual is there none the less with all the minutiae of technique which ritual demands. One might almost compare the apparent freedom of Balinese dancing to that of Chinese cursive writing, which, though apparently very free and willful in its flourishes, none the less always conformed to some particular type which everyone could name, and would otherwise be thought to be low, unclassical, hugger-mugger. In the same way, if to the question: "Is there this poem?" meaning "Is it a subject for poetry?" the answer was given: "There is not such a poem," a well-bred Chinese would no more have thought of writing on that subject than of moving his knight straight down the chessboard. In Bali, the deplorable stylelessness of the new form known as *komedie* or *stambul* is no doubt due to the fact that this important question was not asked or that the answer was ignored.

It is true that the few *mudras* which outside the ritual of the Sivaite priests still remain in Balinese dancing seem to mark a punctuation of a phrase, or a posture, and to have no expressive significance in the sense of being a sign-language. But the technical science of the dancer is worked out with the utmost exactitude, and one could fill a chapter with the ritual of entry of a single character in one style of play. For just as every character enters with his or her own melody, so every character who has passed the degree below which behavior is merely "natural," up to the most exquisite prince, has his own shade of dynamism in gesture and step, and exact correspondence of every movement with the rhythm of the music. And naturally every movement has a name, descriptive generally of itself, not of any expressive significance. We have noted at least sixteen kinds of accents (there must be many more), foot accents of many kinds, accents at the end of a phrase, accents with or without weight, touching the headdress, catching up the dress, head accents, hand accents, halting accents. There are many kinds of obeisance, many manners of dropping to the ground, of lifting or touching the dress; every method of progression, smooth or violent, a style for every character with many shades in each; standing on one foot or both, at what height from the ground, whether still or with moving hips or knees, swaying, bending forward, with bowed head and body listening to spoken words. There are countless movements of the feet, in combination with arms and hands, movements of the head in all positions, and for every type of character; movements of cheeks and mouth; and many, many glances of the eyes. There are wide, angry glances, violent glances up and down, fixing an imaginary foe, impelling fear, eyes which look into the distance, sweet looks, sleepy glances, lazy glances from side to side. There are manners of eying the ceremonial umbrellas, which change their nature according to who eyes them, for the eye creates the function; symbols of state or palace gates to the courtier, they are transformed by the intent and agitated scrutiny of the *baris* hero or the mythological *barong* into some mysterious symbol of the unknown.

There are all the relations of the hero with the heroine, from the touch on her shoulder giving her an order, reasoning softly with her, inviting her to make love, to the *pĕngipuk* (love-making) itself, when in slow or rapid dance the two faces, very close together, even rubbing

noses, glide to and fro in front of each other and arms sometimes
encircle necks. There is provision for kicking the beautiful lady, or
whipping her with leaves, if she is temporarily out of favor. There is a
whole category of women's movements, drooping of head and eyes,
"with weeping and a sad face," shedding real tears, sniffing, shading
the eyes with her hand; and provision for her just to dance exquisitely,
showing herself off, winding with many steps and curves and beautiful
balance of arms and hands. There is an immense variety of fancy foot
movements, proper to every kind of person and animal; shuffling,
side-stepping, circling, turning, beating of the ground, and rapidly
leaping off it, as if one had stepped on fire, or only a swift drawing up
of the foot without the leap; there is even a classified movement for
throwing water over cows with the foot. A simple walk round will of
course be different according to who walks. The *baris* dancer will
walk differently from the *jauk*, who is, nevertheless, very close to him
in style; for the latter must shake his long-nailed gloves as he walks,
and this modification affects his whole motion and gives his walk a
different name. The coming out of a *manis* king will be different from
that of a *kras* king, and there is a mingling of two styles, halfway
between the "fine" and the "rough." The naming of the many
styles of entry in *gambuh* alone would fill several pages.

Then there are the many *lagu* (styles of talking) for each person.
The *pĕnasar* has an imposing voice, with considerable compass and a
certain accentuated violence of speech. He has a slow, loud chanting
manner, varied with high, hoarse cries and laughter. Each play has a
different *lagu*. In *arjă*, which is largely sung, the intonation is very
characteristic, with extraordinary variations of pitch. There are also
specially to be mentioned the softly curving, affected speech of the
refined characters, male or female, the rippling laugh of the *baris*
dancer, the uncanny scale of sounds uttered by *rangdă*, the witch, and
all supernatural apparitions, a high-pitched cockcrow which sometimes strangely breaks from the most refined throat.

The application of some of these many manners of moving and
speaking will be shown in the attempted description of passages in
various dances. Obviously they can only really be rendered in a sound
film, for the relation of each step to the rhythm of the music is of the
utmost importance, and only this can really bring the dance to life.
As an accompaniment to this, a dictionary of the movements in their
manifold combinations and nuances of style would indeed have some
point. It is only possible here to give a faint indication of the enormous
wealth of this grammar of movement which does not exist as a

language till it is danced. It is perhaps worth while to analyze a little more completely just the opening phrase of Rama's entry in *wayang wong*, which is more generally described in a later chapter.

His dance is called *igĕl sambiran*, from the word *ngambir*, meaning to play with a *kain*, which is a general name for the unsewn material folded in various ways to form the lower part of a man's dress. In his opening dance he moves forward in a slow walk, flicking the ground with a very much turned-out foot, before taking a step. His hands are held with a slight accent at his sides. Between each step, and as if anticipating it, is an accent called *angsel buang*, which literally means an accent which has been thrown away—discarded, dropped, rejected —clearly only the step itself can describe it! It has the effect of having miscarried, and the result is a hesitating, postponed step, as if the dancer were feeling his way.

He comes to a pause on the *angsel batis*, a foot accent coinciding with and underlined by the *chèng-chèng* (cymbals). His arms, stretched at the sides, rise in a wide curve to shoulder level, then bend inwards to touch his forehead with his fingers, as if adjusting his headdress. It is indeed called *pĕnakas galung*, "touching the headdress." He then continues in a wide downward curve backward, with the palm facing back.

His right hand grasps his *saput* (special word for a man's *kain*) and holds it stretched at an angle in front of him. This is clearly the central feature of the *igĕl sambiran*, from which it takes its name. At the same time he makes a twisting movement of the hand, as if peeping out of a hiding-place, his *saput* forming a curtain. This move-ment is called *awasan* (to see), describing its "look-out" character. A movement of the head accompanies it, called *engotan*, a very charac-teristic side-to-side movement of the neck, used in all degrees of speed in Balinese dance; sometimes it is so swift that it is more like a very rapid vibration than an analyzable movement. Every one who has seen Uday Shankar's troupe will be very familiar with it; it is used by them, as by the *Kathakali* dancers of Malabar, with a nuance of seduction. In Bali it perhaps also has that meaning, but more generally I think it implies an intent vision, and is said to represent a bull looking from side to side!

A gong beat ends the phrase, which is of considerable length. Dur-ing this phrase Rama sings *Kĕkawin* (text in Old Javanese). He makes a *selyog* (an arabesque of head and shoulders), a winding, shy evasive movement, accompanied by a *pĕnarek*, the curious high-pitched cock-crow alluded to above. He alternates his balance from one foot to the other, more or less on the spot, but his winding body movements continue, with half-closed eyelids, after his speech. The right arm does arabesques of movement, while the left hand catches up his dress under his armpit. This is a very partial analysis only of a single phrase of a single dancer, who was not dancing alone. It is only a hint of the immense complexity of the task before anyone who should attempt to limp in words after the living beauty of the dancer, and without the music that is so inseparably linked with his passage.

When an eminent Chinese was shown the famous Ku Ka'i-chih roll at the British Museum the highest praise he could give to this masterpiece of painting was: "It is statutory." To us who are so free with the word *expression*, and who always look first for some *expressive* quality in a work of art, this seems rather chilling praise; but the only measurable quality in a work of art is indeed its conformity to a certain standard or tradition which is in the minds of those who look at it. The rest is personal appreciation, which in a highly traditional art plays as secret a part as the personality of the artist. We have underlined the tradition of the technique on which the marvellously vital dance of Bali is built because it is certain that the Balinese connoisseur, who is of course the Balinese dancer, will judge a performance first on its "statutory" side, just as a connoisseur of classical ballet would in Europe. No doubt the difference between a good and indifferent dancer is actually less when, as in all great periods of art in the past, the individual, if he be not great, is at least submerged in something greater than himself; for if he is great nothing will submerge him. There is obviously a very great difference, none the less, between one dancer and another in Bali, and it is a difference not only of proficiency in the traditional technique without which he cannot begin to manifest his powers, but in his capacity for identifying himself completely with the *attitude* or appearance of his part. The whole point of a play or dance is that it should live a new life. The human beings on the Balinese stage do not show individual emotion on their faces, which are stylized to an expression typical of the character represented. But the ordinarily calm Balinese face is so infinitely flexible that it can literally be molded afresh by the "other thought" or concept of the dancer. If one stands beside a *baris* dancer as he advances from behind the umbrellas on to the scene, one sees his cheeks quivering, contracting and expanding, his eyes intently focused. His face has changed shape, something within is molding it.

The extreme impersonality of Balinese dancing is disconcerting to some people, and it is perhaps all the more striking because it is accompanied by every conceivable aptitude for expression. But personal temperament, as we have seen, has been translated into another medium. Something stands between it and the spectator, the dancer's body strangely modified and rarefied. This passage into a new medium, into the "other thought," as the Balinese call it, certainly happens to every great actor or dancer, and is perhaps what we mean by "great." But in Bali, apart from the masked dramas, no make-up transforms the actor. An ugly old man becomes a young woman in every line of his dancing body; a short-nosed, spotty-faced youth a supremely elegant and noble hero with a lovely profile; and this entirely without make-up. The great *kĕbyar* dancer Mario when shown his own photo in Covarrubias's book exclaimed: "That man is a good dancer. How is it I have never seen him?" and laughed with amazed delight to discover it was himself; no doubt because he has never seen his own face when it has become the vehicle of the "other thought." He only knows his ordinary face, and nothing could be more retiring and unobtrusive than the dancer Mario in the street, or even up to the last moment of his appearance, before his mind has assumed the attitude of the dancer. Covarrubias also tells how, after seeing Mario dance night after night, he still did not recognize the very quiet and ordinary young man who one day walked in to see him. One has had a similar experience again and again. It is hardly credible that the dancer one has just seen as the very embodiment of demonic power should really be the inconspicuous little peasant who a few moments after the play is over sits chewing betel and chatting with his friends.

Someone remarked on the melancholy expression of two *légong* dancers; they were "*wehmütig*," he said. It is true that joy never finds expression on the Balinese stage, except among the clowns, though sorrow does in the conventional forms of weeping and lamentation and anger, with beating and violent gestures. Passion except as anger has no place at all. The absence of joy is certainly striking. It is really only *shown* by monkeys, and in a monstrous way by supernatural beings like *rangdă*. The usual impassive face of the *légong* dancer is sometimes lit by a smile, but it does not therefore become more personal. The great *bută*[demon]-like, staring eyes of the *légong* dancer would indeed be horrible if they expressed anything but a dynamic state. Even the *kĕbyar* dancer, who most nearly approaches an individual relation to the music, expresses nothing personal in his changing face. Only the moods of the music live through him, he reacts as an instrument, not as a person. The occasional violence of his reaction would be hideous or insipid if it expressed *himself*. He simply becomes a new musical medium. There is no doubt a very great difference between the capacity of one dancer and another to become possessed by his part, even in Bali, but it must, I think, in some degree happen to all. Is not the assuming of an "attitude," without which both in ritual and in dance we may suppose the action to be incomplete, a substitute for real possession by a demon or a state of being, whichever we choose to call it? The Japanese have an expression *kokoro-no-oni*, "demon at the heart," and sometimes one really feels that it is not the dancer who has assumed the attitude but the demon who has assumed the dancer, and that one is in direct contact with a state of being which in us is either entirely submerged or only rises to the surface in the fantasy of a madman.

Animal Movement in Balinese Dance

In certain Balinese dances we find movements which not only remind us of animals but which have animal names, showing that the resemblance is a conscious one. In *wayang wong*, which dramatizes the *Ramayana*, there are the *igěl-igěl bojog*, or monkey dances, in which monkeys, birds, deer, dogs, and all the variety of animals which figure in the masks worn by Hanoman's monkey host, gambol, hop, frolic, and coil according to their kind. In *baris polèng* there is a definite imitation of birds, and we find a "feather-ruffling" movement when the dancer is making himself magnificent for battle, a swooping movement named after a bird which is wheeling in search of prey, a "flying bird" movement and a particular manner of walking which is named after a crow and which occurs in many dances. The familiar movement of the neck from side to side, called *engotan*, which we find in every dance, is said, as we have seen, to be that of a bull looking from side to side. The *Kechak* is called by tourists the Monkey-Dance because at a certain point the dancers become monkeys with remarkable realism of sound and movement. Could their dances in a general way be said to imitate birds or animals? Probably not. Yet if one watches the love dance of a turkey cock one is vividly reminded of a *baris* dancer, as the Balinese also were when first they saw an imported turkey. The bird, ruffling his feathers, and treading in slow portentous rhythm with each deliberately lifted leg, is doing a definite love dance of display just as the *baris* dancer balancing in turn on each widely turned-out foot, beneath his splendid stoles, displays his human beauty in a battle dance. We read of men and birds and animals who make themselves as splendid as possible for love, for battle and for death.[4] And part of the beauty in which primitive man dresses himself is surely his beauty of movement.

But if one watches kittens at play or the exquisite evolutions of tropical fishes one is also reminded of many dance movements of the Balinese. We may even feel that the kitten's play is like a dance, though it is obviously very far indeed from the elaborately artificial dance of the Balinese. Yet the kitten's play in its delicate complexity of springs, withdrawals, glancings, pouncings and ambushes seems to cover a world of possible emotions. There is a great element of play in Balinese dance, not only in the war play called *Pĕnchak* and similar martial "dances," but in that *other world* of dance. If the evolutions of tropical fishes, their smooth spells and sudden accents, turns and doublings, infinite lightness and grace, their flickering fins and the rippling life of their glowing bodies seem to us to bear some real relation to Balinese dancing, it is perhaps because the perfectly coordinated Balinese is the human exponent of a world where motion and emotion merge even more completely than in our vocabulary. The Balinese let the dance *play* as trees and tendrils, kittens, monkeys, birds, and fishes play.

Relation of Music and Dance

Dance, melody, and the accentuated rhythm of gong, drums, and cymbals form together an indivisible whole. The music is indeed danced, but in a different and far more intricate way than we understand it in the West. It is easier to suggest by negation the relation of the dance to the melodic line. It is never a literal transposition of the melodic line into bodily movement.[5] Nor is there any eurhythmic balance of phrases, as little as in nature. Nor is Balinese dancing a pattern going on and on without kinetic change, like some folk-dancing. The path of *gamelan* and dancer is at the same time one and different. One might almost say that they move in two different temporal dimensions which are yet inseparable.[6] Common to all

[4] See Gregory Bateson, *Naven* (Cambridge, Cambridge University Press, 1936), p. 158.

[5] There is really no "up and down" in music, and it is rather bizarre to translate varieties of speed in vibration by raising the arms for a high note and depressing them for a low.

[6] In one figure of the *légong* the dancers also move on two different time-schemes, the course of one corresponding to the space covered by the end of a pendulum near its base, where its swing is shortest, the other to that at the end, where its swing is widest; both movements being interdependent and indivisible, for both are indeed one.

dances is that the dance is connected not with the continually recur-ring unemphasized melody, but with the rhythmic structure. The melody may perhaps be compared to a pattern repeating itself indefinitely on stuff or wallpaper. Upon this background the dance winds about, taking its own course. When, as sometimes happens, dance and melody coincide one becomes conscious of the undercurrent of melody with a shock of delight.

The melody of the *gĕndèr*,[7] which uninterruptedly keeps time, depends on the prompting of the drum which stands in intimate and indispensable relation to the dancer. The cymbals also are in constant attendance on the dancer. The great difference between the classical music of *légong* and the newer music of *kĕbyar* is that the melody in the latter sometimes abandons its quadrangular cage and joins the drum in the restless activity of its abounding accents. The familiar *chondong* melody has two parts, a sequence of two bars in *andante* tempo, the melody being in crotchets, and two bars in *andante*, of which the melody is in quavers. There can be as many series of these two bars as are necessary to the dance.

There is a difference in intensity between these two groups. The second is more *mouvementé* both in dance and music; their succession depends on the construction of the dance, the figures of which take place within this framework, and are differentiated by accents of drum and cymbals which have an existence independently of the melody. The rhythmical accents of the *chèng-chèng* (cymbals) and in part of the drums are solely related to the dance, not to the melody. Visiting dancers always bring their own *chèng-chèng* and drums. A very good dancer would be able to dance up to a certain point in the style of the *gamelan* in the village to which he had been invited. But the drummers naturally vary in musicality and in the power of following an unfamiliar dancer. Once when for some hidden reason a *baris* dancer suddenly inserted himself into the middle of a *topéng*, the drummer and hence the whole *gamelan* made no effort to follow him. In vain he turned his head and made various signals while dancing, as if soliciting their support. They cheerfully continued in their own lively tempo, though it was very evident that he required a slow music.

The leader of the *gamelan* is the drum. Certain accents of the drum are fixed points in the musical framework. The drum may be regarded as a kind of *souffleur*. To make the instruments fall in their right

[7] Instrument with metal keys, placed transversely on upright bamboos.

place, or the dancers enter, the drum has to make signs, and every kind of sound or combination of sounds forms as it were a very complicated language of traffic signals. Without the drum the whole structure of music and dance would fall to pieces. The language of the drum is very rich and varied. Pitch and quality of sound and timbre vary according to the touch of the drummer's fingers or hand; one, two or more fingers, the whole hand, the muting or striking of the cowhide. It is an exceedingly complicated language in which varieties of rhythmical elements combine with all the varieties of tone. For not only are all degrees of accent indicated by the drum, but also all nuances of time and degrees of tone; accelerando and rallentando, crescendo and decrescendo. The Javanese *kĕprak*, a kind of wooden clack operated by the leader of the *gamelan*, which indicates the sequence of movements to the dancers, has certain functions of the Balinese drum but is concerned only with the dancer, whereas in Bali the drum is part of the *gamelan* and may itself participate in the accent it has announced and induced. The indications to the *gamelan* serve also as indications to the dancer if their accents coincide.

The *chèng-chèng* (groups of small cymbals) which, in North Bali especially, often take a very complicated form, translate into sound the flow and accents of the dance. They are illustrations of movement in sound. They too depend wholly on the indications of the drum, but their orientation is towards the dancer, and in the "pure music" of the *gamelan gong* they play the part of the dancer, with their exciting and varied rhythms. They may be compared to the hanging decorations of a temple superimposed on the structure, or the carved festoons on a door. The dancer can dispense with every instrument except gongs, *chèng-chèng*, and drums. The *ostinato* melody goes on and on but is not danced; it is the changing pattern of the rhythm underneath its regular flow which is danced.

* * *

"Possession" during a Temple Feast

The temple courts were slimy with trodden mud, every *balé* filled to overflowing with people: flower-decorated women, white-robed *pĕmangku*, children; and behind them the glittering masks of *barong* and *jĕro gĕdè* and *jĕro luh*, both brilliantly lacquered, he with his black grinning demon face and huge white teeth, she with subtle curves of gold on her ivory cheeks, and enigmatic slanting slits of eyes. Both were splendidly dressed, for the occasion of this visit, in scarlet cloth-of-gold; he also in black velvet military-looking coat and sash, with gold and scarlet epaulettes. Besides them on the same *balé* were tiny shrines, filled by masks of the *barong landung* in miniature, two of *jĕro gĕdè*, one of *jĕro luh*. These are called *pajegan*.

A few women were dancing *mendét* round the principal shrine, on the only narrow strip of dryish ground. All the ceremonial umbrellas and spears stood in front of this shrine, which was hung with splendid palm-leaf panels. Suddenly there was an excited rush towards the *balé* of the *barong landung* and *barong bangkal*. A man was entering a *barong bangkal*, already in trance. Women screamed. The *barong* came streaming magnificently down the steps with glorious ribbed golden snout and leather wings, golden shoulder-pieces and tail-pieces, and wound his enormous black length round the shrines, clacking and threatening with his jaws, prying into every corner. He trotted round again and again and got involved in the cortege of *rejang*, which swelled more and more, till about a hundred women old and young, and tiny children, were dancing round, densely packed in several circles, and with them a few isolated individuals whom the *pĕmangku* shepherded into the ranks. The very slow *rejang* had taken on a quicker movement more like *gabor*. A few *pĕmangku* joined in. This procession gave way to half-circles of kneeling women making their *sĕmbah* (obeisance), regardless of the mud. The dance had a more informal character than usual, owing to the mud; for no one had put on the proper long-trained dresses, but just wore their ordinary *kain*, often with the favorite bath towel wound round the waist. Now there was a fresh stampede. *Jĕro gĕdè* began to disappear; he was being pulled from behind. I must mention that during all this time, ever since the appearance of the *barong bangkal*, men and women had been "krissing" themselves with shrieks and ecstasy, and a young man had been dancing and gesticulating in front of the *barong landung*, trying apparently to leap up on to the *balé*. As during the last feast I saw at this temple, any attempt of the *barong ketket* to climb on to the *balé* was strongly repressed. The young women standing by me were obviously in great distress and anxiety as *jĕro gĕdè* was brought out, together with the mask of *rangdă*, which was put on a man, who descended the steps to join the large crowd round the possessed and the *barong bangkal*. *Jĕro gĕdè* swaggered about round the shrines, looking very martial and magnificent, his stomach well stuck out, an overpowering figure, grotesque and splendid. Men were now dancing a desultory *mendét*, mixed with the women; there was a good deal of confusion, especially round the *balé* of the *barong ketket*. Women were moaning, girls whimpering with fear, as they strained towards the dark mass of figures lying on the ground or crowding round the *barong bangkal,* who stood with *rangdă* beside *jěro gědè.* There were prayers, incense, dense kneeling half-circles, the thin peep-peeping of the sacrificial chicken. A woman lying back in the arms of her neighbor talked continually in a high strange voice and was answered by the *pěmangku.* A shrill uncanny laugh broke from somewhere in the temple as someone else went for a moment into trance. Gradually all become quiet; everyone was blessed and sprinkled. All the time, during the excitement of possession, and the lovely calm procession of the dancers, through the kaleidoscope of moods, *jěro luh* looked on from her *balé,* leaning slightly forward, with nodding head, under her golden tiaraed headdress. Gradually all become quiet; the crowd separated into little groups, the *wayang* screen (for the shadow play) was put up. Lights became scarcer; people drifted away under the stars. Children peered out of the curtains where they had been sleeping below the altars. Everyone was preparing for an all-night sitting of *wayang.* An extraordinary feature of every ceremony or preparation in Bali is the alternation of noisy confusion and order, chaos and exquisite design. It seems impossible that the dreadful unrest and disorder of a house-court where a cremation is preparing should yield in a moment to the lovely and perfectly designed procession, which will form as soon as the people, carrying an apparently heterogeneous collection of refuse and untidy offerings, have come out into the village street, as if an invisible hand guided every detail. It is perhaps not design at all, but an inevitable instinct for rightness, and for the alternation of order and disorder.

"Possession" during Temple Feast at Nuhtěběl

We saw as we hurried up the lane a solid mass of red spears closing the horizon. The men, dressed in scarlet, with yellow collars and white headdresses, were grouped behind the village square, empty save for a great table of offerings. They burst shouting down the lane on the way to the *pură pusěh* (the holiest temple of the village), and taking a short cut we got there first, in time to see the army come swiftly up the street and burst into the temple with their spears and banners. They placed their banners in the upper court and dispersed, after prayers, to feed. These are the *daratan* of the village, the men into whom the gods will enter. Then they began to reappear, each in a short, bound-up *kain* of various colors, carrying on their shoulders, wrapped in a banana leaf, the checked scarf they would wear in the kris dance. The *gamelan* played continuously while the young men dressed and were blessed and made their prayers in the upper court, where no one else was allowed. Their spirits grew more and more boisterous. They challenged each new entry with loud cries and danced posturing within the gateway, flourishing their weapons. Now they come down, one by one, into the lower court, exultantly kicking up the dust so that the wildly dancing bodies and their brandished krisses were half lost in the swirling clouds. It was less a fight than an exhibition of fighting men dedicated to the temple. Some sawed at the bamboo pillars supporting the *balé*, some turned their blades upon themselves in an atmosphere of indescribable excitement. A few seemed definitely in trance, and these had their weapons taken away from them. The *daratan* were always reappearing at different points of the temple precincts, sometimes pouring down side stairways and bursting again into the fray with challenging cries, as if they really saw the phantom invaders invisible to all of us. While they were in possession no one else ventured into the upper court of the temple; but they melted away at last as suddenly as they had assembled, and the offerings began to be carried up to the many altars. Always a fresh group was kneeling before some fresh altar and offerings being made. Every stone shrine and every bamboo table was soon filled to overflowing with offerings, and in an endless procession the women still brought more, meeting the counterstream of those which had been blessed and might be carried away. The ground was strewn with *měcharu*, the offerings to baleful spirits, and with kneeling girls and women being blessed by a priestess. The *barong's* small latticed house in the lower court had a continual stream of visitors, sitting on the doorstep or circulating in the small space round his body, or praying at his feet.

Pak Sěbali near Klungkung

The temple lies a little way from the road, high above the river where the gods go to bathe. The wide river spread out in the sunshine among great rocks, at the foot of the steep cliff down which, by a narrow winding path, the gods were carried, their litters covered with great sheaves of rice straw. Two gongs sat at intervals to accompany their passage with music. I caught glimpses of *rejang* dancers preparing in the courtyard of a house. They were dressed in cloth-of-gold, sleeveless, and wore amazing headdresses, like *jangèr* in shape, but built up tier upon tier with frangipani flowers, whose petals were cut and curled; a magnificent impression of gold and white, on a foundation of glittering fragments of painted wood. The backs of their crowns were also entirely made of flowers. They came out to kneel in the path

of the gods as the procession wound out of the narrow lane which led
up from the river and passed into the open space, divided from the
temple court by a low wall. Already the gods' attendants were in
trance. A man or two came dancing before them with a kris, doing
wide stylized steps, and immediately behind these came the litters,
the young men who carried them being harnessed, as it were, between
bamboo traces. Frantic scenes took place. They swerved about with
their burdens, driving the long poles of the litters among the onlookers, so that the gods were tossed from side to side as if on a rough
sea. They were guided one by one down the lane into the temple,
while the *rejang*, screened by a few older women, sat in a flowery
group against the wall of the inner temple court. Soon all the litters
were in the big outer court of the temple, including one on which a
regally dressed small boy was enthroned. The crowd was driven
helter-skelter by the long poles; even those on the raised platforms
were in danger of being prodded. The confusion was indescribable and
continually increasing in violence. Wild soloists rushed about dancing
and "krissing" themselves; the air seemed to bristle with kris blades.
One man streaming with blood from many self-inflicted wounds
pranced furiously among the ecstatic litter bearers. Another supporting his chest on his kris blade, the hilt planted in the ground, danced
round on it almost prostrate, like some orgiastic flapping bird. And all
the while the gongs beat wildly in the midst of the tumult. Sometimes
men were trampled under the litters and had to be dragged out by the
assistants, who now began to move about, sprinkling water and
removing daggers.

At last all had passed unsteadily with their litters into the inner
court, guided through the narrow gateway and down the steep flight
of steps. The *rejang* followed, and the crowd began to move off home.
Soon the most unyielding of the possessed *daratan* had been restored
in the darkening inner court by offerings and water, and sat eating
together on a *balé-balé* (table on covered platform). Some of the older
women began a *mendét* round the table of offerings, and then in the
dark court the twelve *rejang* formed in file and very slowly danced
round the principal altar, led by the older women. There was a wild,
rather unfriendly atmosphere, very unusual in Bali, and one left
feeling that one had already outstayed one's welcome.

Mendét *and Trance at Kĕpaon*

On a clear space down the middle of the temple, between the *balé*, like
a wide nave, the *mendét* was being danced by three women, one with

a fan, one with fire, one with wine or water in a bottle or vessel made of leaf. These three, winding about together with curving arms, dipping or rising, meeting and glancing off, were joined by a maze of others, all older women, variously dressed. An old woman with flowers in her hair stood above them on a high *balé*. She was the *dèwă* of the village, a kind of priestess presiding over all the rites. She did not on this occasion actually go into trance, but, in her silent session throughout the night, she seemed to contain all that happened within herself. Offerings were meanwhile being made on a wide loggia in front of the main shrine, by *pĕmangku* and elders from several villages who chanted continually. Over these also the *dèwă* presided. There was always an undercurrent of movement in the darkness of the court, fires lit, groups reforming, offerings, music. At last all the old men sitting motionless, intently waiting, with a few old women among them, on a wide bamboo bed (*balé-balé*) with fire offerings between them and a large group below them, chanting.

Suddenly two men leap and shudder and rock to and fro, one convulsively springing into the air, though still keeping his place among the others on the bamboo bed. Now two women twine their arms and cry, and soon the whole platform is swaying and surging with old men and women in trance. Only the *dèwă* sits upright and motionless in her corner. They moan and howl and weep, and fling themselves about, talking incessantly. One leaping to his feet beats violently against the bar above his head and has to be captured and lowered. All around the *balé* are shuddering forms, a heap of possessed bodies writhing and coiling. Only one man, with a splendid headdress and long, flowing hair, sits very still, his hands crossed, bending forward, and never stirs from his meditation even when an old man sitting by him begins to howl and shiver, leap and dance, and finally collapses on his knees, supporting himself against him.

Loud laughter breaks from the group on the high bed; there is a continual undertone of crowing, barking, clucking. Different currents of speech seem to be moving at once, as at a new Pentecost. And all the time the *dèwă* watches and presides unmoving. A few minister to each other, tying up draperies, replacing head cloths, removing rings. Against a background of heavy breathing a few individuals hold long monologues. Then the chorus begins to sing, and immediately all become quiet, entirely recovered from their trance.

The old *dèwă* is borne on men's shoulders through the gateway into another court and lifted onto a high *balé*. A few men group themselves below the bed on which she sits sideways fanning. The *gamelan* is brought, and a great crowd forms below the temple gate. Women carrying offering bowls kneel or stand with them beside the *dèwă's* bed, then break into a *mendét* and dance away.

Suddenly there is a group of old men with spears, and a moment's great excitement, shouting, and clapping of hands. A very brief *biasă*, with lowered spears as if really fighting; then the spears have disappeared, and the old men are "krissing" themselves before the *dèwă*. This also was very brief, and the main crowd went trooping out of the temple with spears and banners, while the *dèwă* was carried back through the high gateway into the inner court and lifted again onto her original high seat. A row of men on the ground below, a bigger group before the offerings, sing and pray, clapping their hands at intervals, persuading the gods with shouts and cries, sometimes almost with catcalls, to return to heaven. There is an atmosphere of hilarity, a relief from strain. Men have become normal human beings again.

Early Morning at Sindu

It had poured with rain all night and when we went up to Sindu at 7 A.M. the temple courts were a series of lakes, and it seemed impossible that any feast could be held. But gradually a few small islands emerged, and on each sat or knelt a group engaged in prayer or offering, like the souls saved from the Ark or the survivors of a shipwreck. (On one of these islands Gusti Rakă danced the *kĕbyar* he should have danced the night before.) The tide receded; an old woman led a *mendét* with a priest, an orange sash bound over her black *kain*. One by one, through the long hours, the dancers appeared and joined in a *gabor* or *mendét*. Again and again we were told that the kris dance was imminent, that the *rejang* must begin. Then suddenly, just before midday, the head of the orchestra fell into trance, and his fingers strayed aimlessly over the metals of his instrument. A kris was pulled out of the roof and given to him. Soon he was dancing wildly in the mask of *rarong* (a minor manifestation of the supreme witch *rangdă*). The kris in his hand was bent in two in a moment but could only be straightened again by the whole strength of a man leaning on it. Another man fell violently into trance and had to be forcibly lifted into the *barong's* front legs. A third was led off up the steps of the high gateway and reappeared presently in the mask of *rangdă* herself. All were unusually exhausted afterwards and took a long while coming to. The old woman who had led the dancing procured two krisses and leaped frantically about, her mouth wide open, an ecstatic expression on her face. She seemed to hear the remarks of another old woman

who remonstrated with her, but she was enjoying her escape from
reality too much to come back so soon, and it took the *barong's* beard
and the prayers of the *pĕmangku* to pacify her. Then she quickly
became sober and joined in the normal prayers.

Pĕngrebungan *at Kĕsiman*

This was one of the most moving and antique shows I have seen in
Bali. Of unusual splendor, it was to celebrate the opening and dedication of the new gateway, which is immensely tall and tapering, built
of a pale coral brick. At 3:30, when we arrived, there was already a
great crowd outside, and the cockfight was still in full swing. An
endless procession of holy images moved down the steep steps of the
gateway and across the courtyard to their place on a high, long, altar-
like table, or small separate shrine, each under its own umbrella, and
accompanied by flags and the slender banners called *umbel-umbel*.
There were gilded women's faces, white cows, winged dragons, deer,
a *nagă* gay and twisty, with a glittering red tongue. Some wore the
high golden Ramă headdress; all had round their necks a colored silk
sash, and flowers stuck jauntily behind their ears. More and more gods
streamed in; old and young women, men and boys, carrying lances
with dangling peacock feathers. Rows of women, in gay sarongs,
emerald green with yellow sashes, and flowers on their heads, knelt
before the high table and the various shrines, waiting to be sprinkled
with holy water. They prayed with beautiful gestures, each with a
flower between her fingers—hundreds of brown shoulders and gleam-
ing black heads, studded with flowers. The pattern of the crowd was
continually and imperceptibly changing as they moved from shrine to
shrine. The mass of people was unusually splendid because the
punggawă had given orders that everyone must come in Balinese
dress, and all the men and boys belonging to Kĕsiman and its *banjar*
(wards) had naked torsos. Two *barong* were splendidly outspread on a
high *balé* waiting to come into action. The umbrellas and spears grow
thicker and thicker, and now a huge crowd is sitting on the ground in
front of the table before the large closed shrine where the *rangdă*
masks are kept. The open door is covered by a curtain, drawn aside
from time to time as a white-robed priest passes in and out. Now the
masks come out and are laid on the table, five in all, each under its
umbrella. Three *barong* lie on the ground, prostrate before the table
of masks, heading the huge crowd. A man who is to wear the *rangdă*
mask sits among them, already dressed in white trimmed with fur,
rangdă's pendulous breasts attached to his costume, the long-nailed

gloves of *rangdă* on his hands. The *punggawă*, in an ivory brocaded *kain*, with a gold-worked border and pale gold sash wound among the deeper gold, a long white *kanchut* falling in front, sits gravely watching on a high *balé* among his wives. One sees a few of the decorative old Bali *kain*, with beautifully disposed stripes of red, blue, green, yellow, and white. An old man in golden tissue, priests in short white *saput*, mingle in the stream of color ceaselessly flowing down the steps under the high coral gateway.

Now the first *rangdă*-bearer is in trance. Among shrieks and cries, waving krisses and long-nailed fingers, the *rangdă* mask is put on. The *rangdă* are led out shaking. Men and boys leap with high shrill cries, defying each other but attacking only themselves. The *rangdă* and *barong* pass up the steps and through the gate among streaming banners. Now the great procession of "*exaltés*" moves round the booths which edge the *wantilan* (cockfighting place) in the outer court. The *kul-kul* (Balinese *tam-tam*) towers and the boughs of the huge banyan tree are full to the top of boys, and the high *balé* are filled with women watching. One *rangdă* after another dances forward with subterranean cries, as the mad cortege goes round and round, and collects continually new-formed groups of entranced "krissers." A very old man, supported on both sides by his attendants, goes trembling round, murmuring to himself, while the purple end of his splendid headcloth flaps on his forehead, and clusters of gold pendants, hanging from pear-shaped ornaments above each ear, dangle on to his great square ceremonial collar of black and gold. The court is full of waving palm pennons, umbrellas of all colors—magenta, blue-fringed, red-fringed, white, black- and white-check—slender banners, green and yellow flags; and among them the rearing golden tails of chattering *barong*. Drums and cymbals keep up an exciting, insistent beat.

Meanwhile, in the inner court many old men, also magnificent in black and gold, sit on the ground before the *rangdă* shrine, making offerings and prayers; among them is a woman, a *pěmangku's* wife, holy and very beautiful, in emerald and gold. They are led to the great *balé* where all the notables sit, and take their place cross-legged, while women weep and shudder before them on the steps, their faces twisted in an apparent simulation of grief, for they do not seem to squeeze out a tear. A man in a black-and-white check scarf, headcloth, and *kain* of purple brocade, very grave and with half-dazed expression, stands motionless by the steps, holding up a drawn sword. One by one the *barong*, the *rangdă*, the banners come down the steps from the outer court, and the next procession sets out. Wedge-shaped, spiked maces, large fans, circular shields—two of each—are brought, krisses are held up. The guardian, still holding his sword erect, is now in trance and weeps with puckered face, feebly howling. The women carrying the fans, and all the praying elders, climb the steps and pass through the gate. They stand motionless, each supported by two attendants, and slightly trembling all the while, just outside the gate, looking down over the outer court, the beautiful priestess among them, also supported on either side. A great procession streams round and round once more. This time a number of women, chiefly old and very skinny, dressed in white, dance vaguely with tragic faces, linked together by an endless length of checked cloth which passes over their shoulders and is carried, wound in a thick roll, by a man behind them. The weapons are borne round. As they pass the group of the elders at the top of the steps, each man in turn stops and addresses them and passes briefly into trance, "krissing" himself. They watch, remote and unmoved, except that the muscles of their face tremble slightly. A strange-looking man, curiously like an Indian ascetic, and the guardian with the sword go into occasional ecstasies. There is huge press in the crowd, an impression of old women's puckered faces, of recurring ecstasies, of drums and cymbals, of waves of intense emotion. One has the feeling all the time of some great and ancient tragedy which is being commemorated, the significance of which is entirely lost but not the emotion connected with it, which is sacramentally evoked whenever the rite is enacted. The great blood sacrifice of the cockfight is of course in some way intimately associated with it.

Now back to the inner court. The masks are again in their baskets. Old and young women, about twenty in a group, wind slowly forward in a *rejang*, with beautifully curving arms, while the ancients behind them tremble and weep. An old priest leads the emerald priestess up onto the high *balé* where the women sit fanning. Now the oldest women take up the *rejang*, and wind forward, ten in all. When they reach a certain point in the temple court, they suddenly break off their dance and go and kneel in a group. The guardian, who just before the *rejang* was shaking and laughing, now stands again impassive, with a purple bow drooping over his ear, and beside him the curious ardent man (Indian ascetic), in striped black and white *saput*, with long, black, tapering beard.

Two men with entranced faces dance weirdly forward, mount the *balé*, and begin an orgy of "krissing" on the steps, while the guardian stands impassive with empty gazing eyes.

Now the elders, five in number, come forward and stand in a row in their gorgeous drooping headcloths. Before them a man exultantly "krisses" himself. The holy woman is led down and stands before the elders, saluting each in turn. The guardian with the great Semitic nose walks briskly forward, swinging his arms, and circles in front of the priestess and the elders, "krissing" himself.

Four huge spears are brought out, black with silver bands. The priestess and three man grasp them and dance slowly in two pairs, crossing each other with slanting spears. This is the *biasă*, inseparable from temple ceremonies, but always very fragmentary. The woman wears a man's headcloth and a woman's skirt. Instead of the woman's earplugs she wears, like a man, a pear-shaped gold ornament and golden pendants.

A very aged man in an amazing headdress of cloth-of-gold, with a pointed flap of rose and gold, sprinkles the dancers and then is led back to his seat. Now all come out by twos and fours and go and pray in rows. The guardian, holding a leaf in his right hand, does a quick graceful dance. A man does a *mendét* round him, filling the leaf with *tuak* (palm beer). They meet and evade, circle close and separate. The guardian, with closed eyes, continues his dance alone, then suddenly strides down to a shrine, seizes a sword, and begins to dance with wide swinging movement in front of the *gamelan*, his arms making great circles in the air. He is disarmed and quieted. The temple slowly and imperceptibly empties. The moon is high; night has fallen suddenly. All the gods are carried away on women's shoulders. Long after, one meets along the road fragmentary processions with gongs and singing and waving banners; for many have far to go.

Pĕlausan *at Pură Beji Sangsit, North Bali*

It is the night of the full moon. A vast crowd is seated before the offerings below the sun altar, the smoke rising round them from fires of coconut shell. The offerings are all quite low but very pretty and crowned with fan-shaped palm leaves, which with the hibiscus flowers make patterns of red and gold. An immense tongue of white cloth hangs from one of the side temples all the way down the steep high flight of steps. The pinnacles and traceries of the huge baroque temple rise dark and fantastic against the moon. Two *gamelan* are playing against each other at the far end of the great court: the *gong gĕdé* and the *chumbang girang*, with old instruments played by old men. There is an extraordinary confusion of sound. For an age nothing happens.

The ground and the different *balé* are covered with sleeping children, lying in close rows like sardines. The waiting people sit on and on, joined occasionally by priests, who make a diversion with their prayers and sprinklings. Suddenly a man in the front rank begins to go into trance. He is the scribe of the headman of Kubu, a village along the coast, and famous as a *permadé*, or medium. Immediately there is a great crying and shouting and clapping of hands, firecrackers are set off, and hands wave wildly upward, calling on the god to descend into the medium. The medium too lifts his arms and rocked to and fro. Then he is raised up and dressed in white-and-black check, with a headcloth of the same, and a scarf crossed over his chest. Supported by two men, he is carried round and round the table of offerings, tottering along, his outstretched arms waving to and fro. A procession moves with him, with loud noise of *gamelan* and voices. Now the crowd has formed again in the center of the great court, this time in a hollow square. The *permadé* on trembling feet dances irresolutely forward with outspread arms into the middle of the space. The offerings are handed to him one by one, and he swings forward, throwing them to the crowd, who rush toward him, especially the little boys, to snatch at what they can. (This is called *prang kětipat*.) If the offering is too heavy to be thrown he gives it intact, and it is distributed. Next he is helped up the steps of a high *balé*, on which sit the *pěmangku*. He is sat leaning against a pillar and remains with his arms outspread during what follows. Along two sides of the square, offering bowls are spread, called *pělausan*, from the ginger-like root which must form one of the ingredients. From them the dance which follows is called *pělausan*. A man takes a palm leaf at one end of the row and dances with it with great agility to a perpetually recurring melody in the *gamelan*. The point of the dance for which everyone waits is to mark the recurring accentuated pause in some particular way, generally by dropping on both knees. When the dancer replaces his palm-leaf fan on the corresponding opposite offering bowl, the person sitting behind it must rise and do a similar dance. There is a great deal of laughter at each fresh invention. Some are nervous and hurry over it as fast as possible. One only walks across brandishing his fan, to place it on the next bowl. Some dance with leaps and springs and frantic dashes. A small boy dances with great grace and skill; an old woman with tripping steps and wriggling hips and sweet smiles. She gives the true character of the dance—a *mendét* (offering dance) parodied. A fat man and a small frisky comic make further amusing variations. Some anticipate the accent and are ridiculed. If any cheat by replacing the fan

too soon, they are headed off and obliged to begin again. When every
offering has been treated in this manner, the ceremony is over. The
medium comes out of trance and is undressed, the women are sitting
again in prayer before the shrine of Suryă, the Sun god, under the
full moon.

Dance in Bali

COLIN McPHEE

UNTIL THE LAST WAR, Southeast Asia was a legendary region where dance and music of the antique Orient had been miraculously preserved. Travelers returned with fabulous accounts of dance schools in Cambodia and Siam and the spectacular dancers of the courts. In the palaces of the Javanese Sultans in Jogjakarta and Surakarta, dancers moved with a perfection and purity of style, a grace and mystic serenity that once seen could never be forgotten. In the temples and villages of Bali, the small island to the east of Java, dramatic dances and colorful plays and mask ballets took place throughout the year. In palaces or beneath the trees, the highly trained dancers and actors moved in perfect synchronization to the resonant music of orchestras composed of gongs, gong-chimes, drums, small flutes, and ancient cymbals. Travelers to more remote regions—Sumatra, Celebes, or the innumerable small islands that dot the Indonesian Archipelago—brought back precious films of archaic ritual dances, fertility, courtship, animal, wrestling, and weapon dances that were still performed on festive occasions. Here was a complete history of the dance of antiquity—the simple magic rite, the luxury performance of the court, the formal offering in the temple, and the popular entertainment of the village.

Surely it was here that the dance as a pure, impersonal art of significant gesture and movement had reached a final stage of perfection. While in the more remote villages dance was simple and almost primitive, in the palaces there was an apparently endless variety of historical plays and dance pantomimes with elaborate choreographies,

Originally published in *Dance Index*, VII, Nos. 7 and 8 (1948), 156–207. Reprinted with permission of Mrs. Shirley J. Hawkins, executrix of Colin McPhee's will.

whose performers were reared under princely patronage and court supervision in the best Oriental feudal tradition. Here the past survived astonishingly intact. Gestures and poses of dancers carved on the walls and columns of thirteenth-century Hindu-Cambodian temples at Angkor were still taught in Cambodian and Siamese dance schools. Balinese and Javanese dancers still assumed the postures of dancing figures in Hindu-Javanese temple reliefs of the same period. Hindu culture, penetrating these lands a thousand years before, had brought, along with the new gods of Buddhism and Shivaism, a wealth of literature and legends. These supplied the source material for plays and dances surviving through the centuries. Principles of the dance set forth in ancient Hindu treatises formed the basis for later dance developments. In the courts, generations of performers had refined the dance into a subtle and abstract art of restraint, exquisite balance, harmonious movement and gesture, so that dancers now moved with an almost literary perfection, a stylistic idealization of the gods and heroes as they were portrayed in sculpture and in poetry.

Yet even the simplest farmer from the fields could admire and enjoy the dance plays of the court, with their casts of gods and demons, fairies, magic birds, noble monkeys, princes and princesses. Stylized as the choreographies were, the movements of the dancers were not unfamiliar. Over and over they reflected the more archaic dances of the village, the countless ceremonial dances that went back to pre-Hindu times, when life was governed by the worship of ancestor souls and divinities of forest, lake, and sea. Even in the modern courts, the dance retained a magic and ceremonial character; dramas were a blend of history, legend, and religion, with the moral atmosphere of a medieval Mystery. The dancers themselves, in their remoteness and perfection, seemed half shadow, half incarnation of the gods.

Closely related though they are, the dance styles of Cambodia, Java, and Bali create three entirely different impressions. Both Indian and Chinese influences have been absorbed and combined in different degrees of intensity; each country, depending on its contacts, has long since evolved a dance and music unmistakably its own, with its own elusive atmosphere and mood. Cambodian and Siamese dancers move with a peculiar elasticity and almost serpentine suppleness; curves are emphasized in the apparently jointless back-turned hands, the flexible arms, the rounded postures of the body. The dancers are trained to dazzling, almost mechanical perfection, smooth as a tight-rope act; they move with bright alertness to the rapid, brittle music of small, percussive orchestra pitched high in the treble, animated in speed, and filled with little glissandos and tremolos that sparkle like the costumes.

The Javanese dancer moves with a slow and wonderful muscular control, a dreamlike gravity that recalls the classical Nō plays of Japan. All is pure technical *tour de force*, yet there is no display of brilliance. Motion is spacious and fluid, but at the same time there is a certain angularity; the joints of the arms and legs are emphasized structurally rather than concealed. While Cambodian dancers seem forever on the verge of springing into the air and vanishing, the Javanese rest firmly on the ground, slowly shifting the weight of the body from one foot to the other as they proceed. In their composure and detachment, their aristocratic bearing, they create an indescribable atmosphere of mystic serenity. They translate into movement the soft, shockless music of the *gamelan* (orchestra of gongs, keyed instruments, drums, and cymbals), stately in tempo and constructed in long phrases that are punctuated at intervals by the deep, vibrating gongs, struck always a fraction *after* the beat, as though to intensify the mood of timeless calm.

Against these two opposing styles the Balinese stands out dramatically in its freedom, its exuberance, and almost feverish intensity. Although the ritual dances of the temple and the ancient dance plays of the court have the grave serenity of the Javanese, the trained dancers of today, who appear in plays or by themselves, give theatrical, dynamic performances, wild, moody, filled with sunlight and shade like the rushing, shimmering music of the Balinese *gamelan*. Rhythms are taut and syncopated throughout, and filled with sudden breaks and unexpected accents. Gongs and metal-keyed instruments are struck with small, hard mallets so that tones are bright and incisive. Dance movement is not conceived in a single broad, legato line but is continually broken by fractional pauses that coincide with the breaks in the music; on these the dancer comes to a sudden stop, and the eyes of the spectators focus momentarily on a motionless, sharply defined pose. These breaks are not endings but phrase accents, like brief "rests" in music; they last no longer than a flash, and serve as starting points for renewed and vigorous movement. Unlike the almost inaudible drumming in Javanese music, Balinese drums throb continuously in agitated crescendos and diminuendos that forever urge the dancers onward or hold them back.

Cambodian, Javanese, and Balinese dancers all use their hands in brilliant, crystallized gestures that add the final significant accent to the body in motion. Hands never relax, are never vague, casual or forgotten. All dancers use as basic leg technique the turned out thighs, knees, and feet typical of Hindu sculpture. In each country dancers move to music based on quadruple rhythm. Triple rhythm, with its contrast of strong and weak beats, is inconceivable. Dance is without climax, proceeding from sustained, even tension throughout. With these features in common, each country has solved in its own way the plastic movement of the dancer, his projection into space, his method of covering the stage and reaching his audience. Cambodian dancers are fanciful Emperor's nightingales, Javanese the mystic reincarnation of the gods. The Balinese combine something of the nature of both with a fresh vitality and irresistible personal charm.

Bali, Past and Present

Hinduism reached Bali in the early centuries of this era, both directly and by way of Java. Traders, followed by priests and princes, arrived on both islands about the same time, to introduce Indian culture and impose the feudal system on a purely communal society. During the great Javanese empire, which flourished until the fifteenth century, Bali was sometimes a vassal state, sometimes free. As Mohammedanism began to spread through Java, many Javanese princes migrated to Bali, bringing with them their court entourages of dancers, actors, musicians, sculptors, poets, craftsmen, and warriors. With the final Islamic conquest of Java, all cultural exchange between the two islands ended. One by one the other islands were converted, but the Balinese held firmly to their religion and way of life. Until the Dutch conquest in 1906, which brought in its train schools, hospitals, taxation, Boy Scout clubs, and tourists, a medieval world had survived intact.

Today,[1] the dance as sacred rite or theatrical entertainment for gods and mortals still flourishes. No temple feast, no reception in any of the larger palaces, no village holiday is conceivable without a long program of traditional dances, plays, and music, performed by highly skilled dancers and musicians. In even the smallest mountain village untrained girls and women perform the simple but beautiful ritual dances they learned watching their mothers during annual temple ceremonies. Special magic dances still take place to protect the villages from sickness.

During the month of New Year holidays, the even routine of village life is broken by the appearance of traveling actors, dancers,

---

[1] The author left Bali in 1939. According to reports received since the end of World War II, the situation has not greatly changed.

and musicians from the more animated lowlands. In the daytime tall masked figures dance grotesquely and sing erotic songs; the *barong*, the great masked, four-footed dragon, dances from door to door, snapping wooden jaws to drive away all demons. At night along the road, the *jogèd*, the public dancing-girl, draws a crowd of youths and men who step forth in turn to dance with her. Balinese operetta companies with casts of singing actors and actresses bring romantic plays in Malayan-Chinese style, while men, women, and children gather under the trees to watch from midnight to dawn the classical plays performed by little shadow-puppets shown against a lighted screen.

The large and prosperous villages of the lowlands from whence the dancers come present a very different picture. Villages are divided into wards, each with its temples, music clubs, and societies that specialize in one form of dance play or another. Some groups exist for purely ritualistic events; others solely for the pleasure of rehearsing, and performing in public. Musicians, dancers, and actors live for the most part by farming or fishing; some are goldsmiths, wood carvers, makers of masks or shadow-puppets.

The Clubs

To be a dancer or musician and not belong to a club or society is unthinkable. In Balinese village organization no one lives or works independently. Each man owes labor to the village in the upkeep of roads, field irrigation, and temple repairs. Each helps the next with his rice harvest; for temple feasts the women unite in preparing the offerings, while men do the elaborate cooking. Dancers, actors, puppeteers, and musicians all contribute to the festival of programs arranged as much for the entertainment of the village as for the pleasure of the gods.

The club system sets the pattern for all activities, from road-mending to music-making. Clubs range from serious to frivolous, from the group that has inherited the task of playing for temple ritual to the carefree Kite Flyers' Club, Palmwine Drinkers' Association, or the society devoted to cricket fighting. In the village where I first lived, with a population of perhaps two thousand, there were at least ten music clubs to play for the different rituals, processions, dances, and plays, each specializing in *légong*, *kĕbyar*, or *gandrung* performances. There was the society that performed the Chalonarang witch drama, a shadow-play group, a Dragon Society, and two rival operetta companies. Each club has its special *gamelan*, or ensemble of gongs, metallophones, xylophones, and other percussion instruments. Each club had its special musical repertoire, depending on the dance or drama the members had decided to present.

The club is largely a male organization. Musicians of the *gamelan* include boys of ten and men of fifty. Classical plays are performed by men alone, youths taking feminine roles. The casts of modern operettas include boys and girls in their teens and a few older men. The accent is on youth in most dances today, and clubs find nothing strange in training and presenting as the star attraction gifted small boys or girls of seven or eight. The object of these clubs? "A little pleasure, a little profit." "To please the gods." "So that the village may have a good name." Since most performances are free, there is generally little profit.

Club members are fined for absence from rehearsal or performance, and repeated absence may bring expulsion. Successful professional clubs, hired by other villages, invest their money in coconut or rice plantations and divide the profits annually. Star dancer and least musician of the *gamelan* share alike in dividends. Less ambitious societies spend their money on music- and dance-teachers, handsome gold-leaf costumes, and expensive musical instruments. Like ballet companies everywhere, Balinese dance societies and clubs have their sudden quarrels and reorganizations, their periods of brilliance and decline.

Against the village activity stands the palace or smaller residence of the prince or noble. Once important cultural centers with their troupes of actors, dancers, and musicians, the courts no longer can afford these luxuries. Today nearly all creative activity occurs outside the palace. Yet the best trained dancers, the finest *gamelan* are found in those villages which once came closest to palace influence. Balinese princes still pride themselves on their dancing and acting, appearing in traditional plays and heroic mask dramas; a few still train their own dancers and musicians. They continue to follow the pattern outlined in an old Javanese treatise on the conduct of a prince: "A man of condition should be versed in the history and literature of the past. He must know how to play in the *gamelan* and understand the *kawi* language (ancient literary Javanese). He must be clever in painting, wood carving, gold- and iron-work, needlework, the making of shadow-puppets and musical instruments. He must also be skilled in horsemanship and the management of an elephant and have the courage to destroy all wicked men and drive away all women of loose character."

The Gamelan

The swift, aerial music of the Balinese orchestra, or *gamelan*, fills the open air with chiming resonance. Innumerable little gongs, large and small xylophone-like instruments with ringing bronze keys blend in an intricate polyphony that floats above the throbbing drums and periodic accents of deep and vibrant gongs. The air is shattered with a continuous shower of bright, percussive sound as the difficult music is performed by thirty or forty carefully rehearsed musicians. The music itself is based on a five-tone scale; beneath the complex ornamental patterns lies melody of unique grace and charm, constructed according to metric forms that have mathematically balanced proportions.

The tone color and instrumentation of the *gamelan* varies with the nature of the performance. Small flutes, a pair of drums, cymbals, and a bamboo gong are enough to accompany the dancing and light, delicate singing of the *arjă* operetta. The popular *jogèd* street dance (see Plate XX) takes place to the gay, staccato sound of an orchestra of xylophones. The large *gamelan* that accompanies historical mask plays and the heroic *baris*, or warrior-drill dance, has a brilliant, heavily metallic sound and an almost barbaric splendor, while the music for the swift, humming-bird movements of the little *légong* dancers is filled with an indescribable, sensuous iridescence. In and out of the glittering figuration the melody weaves, stressed softly from time to time by gongs of different pitches, while from beneath, the restless, agitated drums rise and fall, their syncopations intensified by the thin clash of tiny cymbals.

The dancer is aware of all these separate strands—the melody, figuration, metric accents of the gongs, and rhythm of the drums. All of these are danced; the melody is phrased by the hands, arms, and body; the sparkling figuration is reflected in the faintly trembling hands; the progress of the dancer, the tempo, and tense inner movement forever impelled by the rhythm of the drums.

The two drummers lead the orchestra. They are at the same time the vital link that connects the dancer with the music. Without them the musicians cannot play, the dancers cannot move. They sit in front of the other musicians, their eyes fixed on the dancers, bending forward tensely over the drums held crosswise in their laps. The drums are "male and female" and are pitched differently, the former having the higher, more penetrating sound. They interlock in intricate patterns of which there are many formulas, depending on the nature of the dance. The male drummer, leader of the two and guiding spirit of the whole performance, is frequently the teacher of the dancers. He must at least have rehearsed with them many times, to know their movements and changes of tempo. A performance can be ruined by a sluggish drummer or a lack of perfect sympathy between him and the dancer. So important is this relationship that dancers engaged to appear with other *gamelan* will bring along their own leading drummer and cymbal player. Musicians can take their tempos easily enough from a strange drummer, but the dancer feels ill at ease, for dance and drumming fit like hand and glove.

The Audience

Everyone goes to dance performances. At night, when by the village market or in the clearing before the temple some performance is taking place, the houses of the village are dark and empty.

Children see dances and plays from the time they can walk. No audience is complete without its front row of naked tots who line the edges of the dance clearing like birds along a telegraph wire. They watch intently, with absorbed interest, napping intermittently as the night approaches dawn. Small boys are so familiar with the stories of the plays, the details of dancers' gestures and costume that village walls are covered with drawings of actors, dancers, and shadow-puppets. They organize dramatic societies in imitation of the older boys, rehearse, and give their own plays for other children.

Audiences are critical. People will leave their village and walk fifteen miles to see a famous dancer or cast of stars. Their interest quickly wanes at dull performances; uninteresting or imperfectly trained dancers and actors frequently find their audience melting away long before the play is over. The play is of far less importance than the performance, and actors are admired for their appearance, style, declamation or the florid ornamentation of "flowers" in their singing. Dancers appeal through their technical perfection, their personal charm, and above all their hair's-breadth synchronization of movement with the rhythmic syncopated music. Adverse criticism of a performance will point out that the musicians were not sufficiently together, while the dancer "lacked suppleness," his gestures "lacked clarity," and the timing of his movement with the music was "always a little late."

The Plays

The ancient Hindu and Javanese epics and romances which form the substance of Balinese literature and theater are translated in endless different ways. The same heroic figures recur in temple sculpture and shadow-play, painting, mask drama, and dance performance. The audience watches with equal pleasure puppet, masked actor, or dancer, lost in a legendary world where gods and heroes are perpetually engaged in conflict with demons and the dark forces of the underworld.

The characters of the play are flat and two-dimensional. "Good" or "evil," divine or destructive, they are allied once and for all with one side or the other, irreconcilable as the opposing forces of *Paradise Lost* or a Western movie. Heroes are divided into two fundamental types, the *alus*, or fine, and the *kras*—the stronger or violent. Prince Arjună, delicate of limb and feature, exalted in motive, reserved in attitude, is the *alus* hero *par excellence*. He is the abstraction of all noble qualities. He moves with feminine, almost catlike grace. His expression is one of mystic serenity, eyes half closed "like a rice grain," mouth set in a "brave-sweet" smile. If he speaks, his voice will be pitched high in artificial falsetto. If he sings, he will use the upper register of the voice. His strength is spiritual; it comes from within, magically acquired through ascetic meditation. "Even in battle he remains tranquil."

A *kras* character stands in sharp contrast. His strength is purely physical, and he moves with impulsive energy. The eyes are round and staring, the mouth turned down at the corners. The gestures of the dancer are wide and vigorous, his advances menacing. His voice is loud and deep, and if he sings he uses resonant chest tones.

There is, of course, infinite variety in character types, each with its special stylistic variations, from *alus* prince to demon king. The more romantic plays have casts that balance and diminish in importance like a set of chessmen. Priest opposes witch; prince, minister, and attendants of the "right" side are matched with prince, minister, and attendants of the "left"; princess and lady-in-waiting are balanced by false princess and stepmother. Actors and dancers fill the roles most suited to their physical appearance. A graceful youth, small boned and finely featured, will play both *alus* hero and princess; a robust, muscular physique is needed for *kras* types. Dancers specialize in one style or another; an audience will accept without comment the appearance of an elderly man with drooping moustache, famous for his elegance and *alus* style, in the pathetic role of abandoned princess.

Character types in the different plays closely resemble each other in appearance, costume, and movement. The same *alus* mask or the same *alus* facial expression is used for the princes Ramă, Arjună, or

Panji, and the chief distinguishing differences lie in the stylistic detail of costume, crown, or headdress. An audience may watch for an hour the formal dance-entrance of a dozen princes, ministers, and attendants, but only when the dialogue begins and some name or clue word has been dropped will the characters become persons and the plot "emerge." Yet even now there can be considerable confusion. Gods, kings, priests, witches, and demons speak in old Javanese, understood only by the scholars in the audience. Every speech must be translated in turn into colloquial Balinese by an attendant, who confirms each statement in something like the following:

Arjună (chanting in Javanese): I now step forth and bend my magic bow.

Attendant (translating): Yes, my Lord, indeed yes. Just as you say. Do deign to step out, right over this way, and draw your bow. [*Aside, to second attendant*] Good Lord! How terrible he looks in his anger! How frightened I am! I really can't stand it much longer.

Arjună: I place a golden arrow in my bow.

Attendant: Ah! The beautiful golden arrow. It will surely kill the boar. . . .

etc., etc.

Only in the comedy scenes that alternate with heroic episodes is the audience brought down to the world of reality. Now is the time for improvised puns and farce, sly parody and rough humor. Boorish peasants are frightened by demons; drunken priests have altercations with Dutch colonial officials or tourists. All is fantasy and escape from the rarified atmosphere of the heroic action. These scenes have only the slightest connection with the main plot. The audience breaks into loud, delighted laughter at the jokes, and the episodes can be prolonged indefinitely.

At this relaxed tempo, plays may last all night. Many performances are engaged "from midnight to three," or "from midnight till dawn." I once asked two boys of my household about the play they had seen the night before.

"What was the story?"

"The story never emerged."

"But how could you possibly stay till morning?"

"Oh, the costumes were all new. There was an excellent new dancer. And the clowns were so very funny!"

Yet, with their free, half-improvised construction, the plays can be neatly telescoped to a rapid end, should a sudden downpour of rain make it necessary. Then, in a flurry of activity, wrongs are righted, princesses rescued, and in ten minutes the performance ground is deserted.

The Ritual Significance

The performance of plays and dramatic dances in Bali is still something of an ancestral rite, in which the hereditary gods are evoked and their deeds enacted.

Worship of ancestor gods forms the core of Balinese religion. The objective of any temple feast is to renew contact with the departed village forefathers. They are ceremonially invited to descend to the shrines prepared for them, to be feasted and entertained. Before they depart, advice and favors will be asked of them; they speak through the voice of a medium fallen in trance.

The protective gods inhabit the mountains. In the earth, lurking at crossroads or in ravines are the demons, a retinue of dangerous sprites to be constantly propitiated. No village is without its two main temples, one for the village ancestors, the other by the graveyard for the yet unpurified dead and all destructive forces.

Ancient Hindu gods and heroes have long since been incorporated into a purely Balinese pantheon. Shivă, Lord of all, inhabits the highest mountain of Bali. Durgă, goddess of death and the underworld, is patroness of all Balinese sorcerers and practitioners in black magic. The shadow play or stage play is in essence a symbolic conflict between god and demon, light and darkness, life and death.

The masks and shadow-puppets are holy objects. It is a ritual to take them even from their box. Before they can be shown, offerings must be made, magic verses chanted. Once a year, on the day dedicated to them, puppet-figures and masks, along with dancers' costumes and headdresses and all musical instruments are purified with holy water and blessed anew in each village by the local priest.

Thus the individuality of the dancer is of no importance. His performance may have unusual finish and personal charm, but with these he does not seek to express himself. These are assets that contribute to a more elegant performance of a traditional role or dance. He is admired for his technical perfection and charm as a shadow-puppet is admired for the delicate workmanship and gold leaf. His performance, however, is exactly as it has been learned from the teacher, or worked out at rehearsal with the musicians. Masked or unmasked, he seeks only to present a character already known, or translate into stylized movement the music of the *gamelan*.

Sometimes, in ritual dance or on the stage, a dancer may fall suddenly into a state of trance. Then he is no longer accountable, no longer under control, for he is possessed by the god itself.

Dance and Dramatic Forms

Dance in Bali can be divided into three distinct categories: the rehearsed, the improvised, and the uncontrolled performance in trance. The dancers themselves may or may not have received any formal training. The trained dancer moves in strictest accordance with the music; gesture and movement are controlled by the musical form and inner rhythm. The half-improvised steps and gestures of the untrained dancer are still stylized and traditional, learned through observation and imitation. The ritual processional dances of the temple are limited to a few uniform gestures and movements. Only in the spirited performance of the *ngibing*, where a youth steps out of the crowd to dance opposite the trained dancing-girl, does the dance become a pleasurable and spontaneous act of self-expression. This dance is one of courtship, a game in which the boy attempts to get as close to the girl as possible. She, however, is skilled in evasion, deftly retiring or slipping her fan before her face when the face of her partner has come too close. In the sequence of youths and men who dance with her a great variety of moods can be seen, from the ardent and erotic to serious gravity or ironic self-caricature. There is still another type to be found in every crowd. His interest in the partner is purely formal. Withdrawn into himself, he dances as far off as possible, lost in the rhythm of the music or the pleasure of self-display.

Yet all these dancers, trained or untrained, move with the same restraint, the same sharply defined articulation of the limbs and awareness of the separate units of the body. Only those muscles immediately involved in the gesture are used; the body is always under complete control, from formal design of the hand to carefully placed foot. The dancer in trance moves very differently, either limp and dreamily swaying back and forth, from side to side, or with wild abandon, tossing and writhing convulsively, the arms flung out in full, free movement. Music is forgotten in the agonized, ecstatic release, and the dance becomes involuntary, no longer technically interesting. I shall return to the trance dancer later; it is the choreography and technique of the trained, dramatic dances of the stage that first demand attention.

To give a complete list of the dance and dramatic forms that existed in Bali in 1939 is not my purpose here. The catalog is endless, and an analysis of the many transitional variations from ritual to secular dance is a study in itself. We must limit ourselves, therefore, to a brief outline of the principal forms of dance and drama, as they were practiced and performed in the more densely populated part of the island.

The *baris gĕdé*, or warrior-drill dance, originally performed only in the temple and now incorporated into dance plays, is a dance of great tension—a controlled but dramatic display of physical vigor performed by youths or young men. The dance is based on a slow advance, thighs, knees, and feet turned out, the body swaying slightly from side to side as the weight is shifted from one foot to the other. The hands tremble rapidly throughout; the expression on the face is *kras*, with wide-staring eyes, giving an effect of menace and defiance. The hands are bent back at a sharp angle from the arms, with fingers spread, taut and quivering as they gesture in the dramatic style known as *rajă singă*, "king of the tigers." *Baris gĕdé* is danced to a single repeated motif, with an undercurrent of loud, agitated drumming beaten out with drumsticks in rapid alternation (Example 1).

EXAMPLE 1:

Ritualistic forms of *baris*, performed by a group of older men, are still presented in mountain temples. These dances, however, have none of the dramatic tension of the *baris gĕdé*, and consist chiefly in posturing with weapons or in stylized imitation of animals. *Baris goak*, drill of crows, is based on bird-movement; *baris kĕkupu*, butterfly-drill, is performed by four young boys; *baris irengan*, drill of black apes, and *baris chină*, Chinese drill, are fantastic variants. Other performances include dances with spears, swords, or shields. *Baris pendét* is a ceremonial dance with burning incense.

The *barong*, or masked "dragon," is performed by two dancers concealed within a framework covered with horsehair, or chicken or peacock feathers. (See Plate XXV.) The mask, with movable jaws, has the form of a mythological "lion." In plays the *barong* frequently represents the magic transformation of a dangerous character. Often the *barong* performs alone, especially during the month of New Year celebrations. The dance is a capricious blend of moods; the beast is formidable, shy, playful by turns. There is beautiful coordination between the two dancers, whose ankles and feet alone are visible. The footwork is light and delicate; here for once the Balinese actually dance with their feet.

The *barong* is sometimes accompanied by masked dancers. Four boys, the *sandaran*, with delicate, *alus* masks and four men, the *jauk*, with fantastic, round-eyed masks, weave in and out in a four-square choreography. Stories are mythological or mystic. I can't resist outlining one of them here, a strange ballet connected with the five points of the compass—north, east, south, west, and center.

The sorceress Chalonarang (who does not actually appear in the dance) wishes to destroy the scholars of white magic in her village, for she fears they can become dangerous to her, a practitioner of black and harmful magic. In order to protect herself, she "splits herself into five parts," four guardians and a center, and thus is able to control opposing magic forces coming from all four directions, and remain in the center at the same time. To protect herself still further she divides her now five-fold form into pairs, five watery (or female) and five fiery (or male). The ballet is a dance which symbolizes the mystic conflict between the two elements. The four boys are the female, watery guardians of the four directions, the four men the male or fiery. These eight figures dance in an intricate series of formations, intermingle, separate, and end by pantomimically merging in reconciliation. Sometimes the sorceress herself, represented by the *barong*, joins the dancers; the performance is utterly strange—a ritual whose mystic meaning is only half grasped by the spectators.

The *gambuh*, the formal, slow-moving theater once fostered by the courts, is seldom performed today. Only a few companies remain, appearing on great ceremonial occasions. The plays are based on an old Javanese romance-cycle, in which the legendary prince Panji is the central figure. The cast of kings, princes, knights, ministers, and squires is large. It takes all afternoon for the main characters to make their formal appearance, and the play may not advance past the opening scene before nightfall. The faces of the actors are immobile, and their voices rise and fall in the strange, artificial declamation of the shadow play. The actors move with elegant and incredible slowness, their gestures unfolding one out of the other with the leisure of something taking place in slow-motion film.

Yet the *gambuh* play still sets the style for more recent dances and plays. Gestures, movement, character types, and music are all borrowed and translated into the swifter-paced dances and operettas that are popular today.

The *topéng*, or historical mask play, deals with ancient kings and princes of Bali. In the highest courts a performance has something of the nature of exhibiting the family portraits. It is above all a ceremonial spectacle. It may be developed into a play with spoken dialog, but in its purest form it is a silent performance by a single dancer who impersonates in turn one character after another. With his back to the audience and a cloth over his head he changes masks, removes the cloth and turns suddenly round. Each dance is different; each interprets the character of the mask. There is no other dancer, unless perhaps an attendant to kneel at his feet.

Many clubs specialize in the Chalonarang play, a spectacular dance-drama based on sorcery and black magic. The story tells of the Javanese king Erlangga, in whose reign the witch Chalonarang and her pupils brought disaster to his land. She is finally killed by a powerful holy man. The music is of violent and somber beauty, and the performance of the witch among her pupils, young girls who execute an intricate, whirling dance, has a heavy atmosphere of sinister enchantment. Most popular of all, however, is the *arjă* operetta, with its Cinderella and Frog Prince stories, its heroes who fall in love with a portrait, its princesses who are led astray in the forest by a golden deer or dragonfly. There is also the popular shadow play, or *wayang kulit*, in which little figures cut from hide are shown in silhouette through an illuminated screen. The performance takes place late at night, and in the dark the screen is a luminous rectangle across which the shadows come and go, mysterious as moths flying across a beam of light. The plots are mostly from Hindu-Javanese literature; the puppets are managed by a single operator, the *dalang*, a scholar well versed in the classics and trained in the art of improvised dramatization.

There remain the two most brilliant performances of all, both danced by highly trained children. The *légong* dance is performed by two small girls, with a third, the *chondong*, or lady-in-waiting, in attendance. The *kĕbyar*, a recent innovation, a free, rhapsodic dance performed in seated position, is danced by a youth or small boy. Both dances require infinite rehearsal and great technical skill. Music clubs are eager to include one type of dancer or the other. Their charming appearance and brilliant movement give life and meaning to the music. They are the "flowers," the final embellishment to a performance, youthful and alert, of the more leisurely dances and plays which Bali has inherited from the past.

Dance Movements

The Balinese dancer moves within a narrow frame, out of which he never steps. It is in the narrowness of this frame, and the amazing life and freedom created within it that the beauty of his dancing lies. With the exception of those dances which take place in trance, dancing is not an ecstatic, emotional expression. It is a formal, detached, and carefully worked out art based on traditional gesture and movement. It is always a refined and sophisticated understatement, reserved and stylized in even the most dramatic moments.

The heroic male pose of the *baris*, thighs and feet turned out, knees bent, spine erect, arms extended, head held proudly, recalls the classical pose of Indian dancing figures in bronze. (See Plate XXII.) It is interesting to compare the position of the *baris* dancer with a thirteenth-century sculpture from South India of the Dancing Krishna, a figure unknown in Balinese sculpture.

The fundamental female pose, which even untrained ritual dancers assume, is a modification of the *baris* pose. The knees are bent, but not turned out so far; the feet are close together; the spine curves outwards and the buttocks protrude. In the *légong* dance this position is intensified; the body curves in an arc which becomes more pronounced in the animated passages. (See Plate XXI.)

The dancer never leaps, never reaches out or upwards in open gesture. He remains firmly on the ground, moving across the surface by a controlled shift of weight from one foot to the other, the free foot raised an inch above the ground or grazing it as it moves to the next position. The normal slow advance is accomplished by the free foot moving out in an arc and returning to center ahead of the other.

Male characters of the vigorous type use a walk or stride keeping feet and thighs turned out in basic position. The females' pace is short; light shuffling steps (*segseg*) or runs carry the dancer sideways across the width of the stage in arcs, zigzags, or circles. An occasional swift, tiny spring may raise her momentarily off the ground; these are rare, however, and serve merely to emphasize the energy of a rapid passage. In the *kĕbyar* dance, performed in a seated position with feet tucked under, the dancer moves in a curious gliding hop on one foot, while the other, serving as *point d'appui*, drags behind. The feet are concealed in the folds of the sarong, and the dancer manages to perform this difficult step without altering the basic position. (See Plate XXIV.)

The hands are the "flowers" of the dance. In simple ritual dance or intricate, studied performance they embellish all movement. In rhythmic passages they move alertly to the syncopated accents, or vibrate rapidly from the wrist with nervous, brilliant effect.

For more energetic dances, the hand may be open, with fingers spread, or used in closed formation in a number of elegant, set designs, known in *légong* as *nawǎ sari*, "nine flowers." Strongly reminiscent in style of the *mudras*, or symbolic ritual gestures of the priest, these hand positions as used in the dance are purely ornamental. Unlike the technique of gesture in Indian dancing, they tell no story; they are purely abstract and never intrude upon or mar the significant outline of the dance. A few of them have dramatic meaning. Shading the eyes with the hand (*mĕpawasǎ*), fingers curved back and body drooping, indicates sorrow and weeping. First and second fingers pointing at the end of a stiffly extended arm form a gesture of anger or denunciation (*nguding*). But the names of the complete series of set positions, if they ever existed, have long since vanished.

Facial expression remains set in one of the basic representations of serenity or physical energy. In dramatic moments narrow eyes grow still narrower, round ones more staring. Eyes are slewed first to right and then to left to stress certain rhythmic accents. Accents may also be marked by a slightly raised eyebrow. In softer moods the lips may curve in a "sweeter" smile, but generally the face preserves a mask-like immobility. Only in the modern *kĕbyar* does facial expression become fluid. Here quick changes of expression follow and reflect the changing moods of the music—dramatic, mysterious, serene, coquettish in turn.

The rapid shoulder quiver (*engejen palǎ*) and slight rhythmic shifting of the head from side to side with neck erect (*engotan*) are a feature of many dances. Arms extending sideways in a straight line from the shoulder have the elbow pointing up, the forearm bent back as far as possible, the hand turned at a sharp angle. Such a position is typical of Balinese dance movement in its emphasis and articulation of each separate joint. Dance technique calls for complete muscular control in all parts of the body and an incredible degree of physical endurance.

The Trained Dancer: Theatrical Projection

While Javanese dance retains much of the two-dimensional character of the bas-relief or shadow play, the Balinese dancer emerges boldly onto the stage, becomes dramatically plastic, with three-dimensional movement which must be interesting from all sides, for his audience surrounds him.

The stage is a long rectangle on the ground, within an open-air theater pavilion (*taring*), or merely an improvised clearing in the open, its boundaries marked by bamboos decorated with leaves and flowers. At one end sit the musicians; at the other, the stage entrance is marked by a pair of ceremonial lances or parasols thrust in the earth or held upright by a pair of boys. The entrance may also be marked by gilded standards, baroquely carved in Chinese style; for dance dramas and operettas with a large cast, the entrance is concealed by a pair of curtains hanging from a wire.

Special melodies and motifs are played as cue for the entrance of each personage. So closely related to the character is the musical theme that even the smallest child knows in advance who is about to appear from behind the curtains—god, priest, lady-in-waiting, princess, prince, witch, or dragon.

The effect of an actor or dancer entering the stage is that of someone approaching from a great distance. It is very much like the slow and ceremonial entrance of actors in the Japanese No theater as they move down the descending runway that leads onto the stage. In the Balinese theater this entrance, this emergence into full visibility is delayed as long as possible, as though the dancer could not bear to cross the magic line and step out upon the stage. If there are curtains, the only hint of the actor behind them is his voice, or the twitching folds gathered in his hands which move in time to the music. This is the dance of the curtains, a prologue to a prologue, for, when the curtains finally part, the dancer remains framed in the entrance, to continue the preliminary dance that delineates his character. If no curtains conceal the entrance, the dancer approaches from an indefinite point behind. At night, as the figures slowly emerge from the darkness into the light that brings to life the gold and bits of glass in crowns and costumes, the illusion of gods manifesting themselves is complete.

These entrance dances, perhaps the most beautiful of all in their delay and abstract elegance, take a long time to perform. The dancer, finally leaving the entrance, steps out. The slow advance downstage is begun, with its sudden animated detours to right or left in the form of circles, spirals, or loops. After each detour the dancer winds up in the center of the stage to resume the gradual advance. The strong feeling for balance which is fundamental in Balinese music and dance can be seen from the diagrams (Fig. 1), one of which represents the entrance of a minister, the other the dance of the *chondong* (lady-in-waiting). Heavy lines indicate the slow advance, light ones progress at twice or four times the speed. The dancer faces front during the forward progression, and in the direction of movement where indicated by dotted lines. The basic beat of 2, 4, or 8 remains unchanged; only the drumming takes on a sudden animation, "drawing the dancers forward" in the loops and spirals.

The final point once reached, the minister turns and kneels as the prince steps out upon the stage. The *chondong* may continue her dance as the princess enters, or simply walk off stage to sit among the musicians and await her next cue.

Each character in the play has his special entrance dance that expresses in traditional, stylized movement his inner nature, his rank, his physical appearance. Within the narrow frame of the dance there is room for unlimited characterization. Audiences appreciate even the slight difference between the bearing of a prince and that of a minister or minor official. The princely hero is poetic; his subordinates are delicately ironic caricatures of the eternal official conscious of his own importance. In the sequence of love scenes, abductions, flights, or fights, dramatic emotion is expressed in terms of dance movement and revealing but stylized gesture. Dancing and acting are so closely interwoven that it is impossible to say where one ends and the other begins.

Teacher and Pupil

There are no dance schools in Bali. Instructors are professional or retired dancers who have specialized in some one form of their art. The dance teacher is usually a man of considerable Balinese cultural background. He is sure to be a musician; he is frequently skilled in the arts and crafts, a painter, costume designer, maker of masks or puppets. Familiar with both literature and the stylized pictorial arts, he preserves the traditions of the past and hands them on to his pupils. Teachers with creative imagination now develop stylistic innovations for their pupils; others insist on a rigidly classical technique. Clubs seeking to train new dancers will choose a teacher famous for whichever style they prefer.

Dancers begin training at an early age. Children are chosen for their grace and physical charm. The two little girls who perform the intricate *légong* dance must match "like two peas." The third child, who plays the role of attendant, should contrast in appearance. Small boys selected for the modern *kěbyar* exhibition dance must have a natural suppleness; for the heroic *baris*, a robust physique is needed. Slender, graceful youths are chosen for the masked *sandaran* dance, or to take the place of a girl in the popular *gandrung* street dance. Training is severe; the best teachers rehearse their pupils relentlessly for hours each day.

Before the first lesson is given, a week or more may be spent in daily massage and exercise to "soften" the body. Only when the teacher has decided the child is sufficiently limp and passive does the real work actually begin. There is no preliminary verbal explanation. It is taken for granted the pupil already has some idea of the dance—

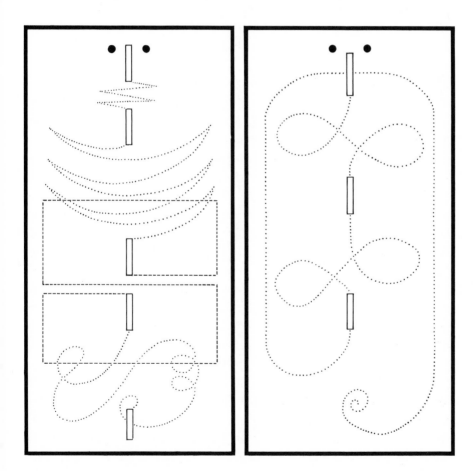

FIG. 1. The *chondong*'s dance is shown at the left, the minister's entrance at the right. These diagrams were made partly from notes, partly from memory. They do not indicate the full choreographic design.

he has seen it performed so many times! Instead, the teacher walks behind him and, lightly holding his wrists in either hand, draws out his arms in the opening pose. Humming the music of the dance, he propels the small body forward, inclining it this way or that like a puppet. For days the teacher continues to lead his charge as though he were playing a fish, but the time finally comes when, with a sudden release of the hands, he launches the dancer off into space. Now at last criticism can begin, and gesture and posture be rectified through patient correction. Over and over the teacher steps out to lower an arm, straighten a shoulder, bend a hand at a sharper angle or mold the body into a more sculptural unity. Sometimes the little dancers are slow to relax. One small boy, the son of a mountain farmer, who later became famous for his brilliant performances, was the despair of his various teachers. Yet in spite of a peasant stiffness which was never completely overcome, he succeeded in giving performances of such dynamic and rhythmic precision that he drew large crowds wherever he appeared.

The little girls who learn the difficult *légong* dance work hard. They begin at the age of six or seven, while their fragile bodies are still alert enough for the lightning-swift dartings and turns, the jointless backward bends. Only after a year, when hands and feet, head, shoulders, and arms, accents of eyes, and innumerable details have been timed to perfection with the music will they be allowed to appear in public. By this time they have learned several hour-long choreographies, the most intricate in all Balinese dancing. For two or three years they dance at temple or village feasts, for palace or private celebrations. At the age of ten, with the approach of adolescence, they have become "too heavy." Their haunting, sexless charm, their swift, miniature virtuosity suddenly vanishes. The club looks about for new dancers, and, as these become expert, the older ones retire. They never appear again, unless as members of the operetta company. But no girl dances after marriage, except perhaps as one of the group of ritual dancers in the temple.

From the beginning, the dancer learns movement and music together. These are inseparable, the expression of a single impulse. The dancer *is* the music made visible; he bears the same relation to the melody as the words to a song. At the first lessons, the melody for the dance the pupil is learning is hummed in his ear by the teacher, while the important gong and drum accents are verbally expressed as his body is suddenly jerked into different poses. But after a few days two or three musicians of the *gamelan* are called in to give a skeleton musical accompaniment, a drummer—-without which no dancer can move a step, a *gĕndèr* player for the melody, and someone to supply the main metrical accents of the gongs. Here are the musical essentials; these three things the dancer must know by heart—rhythm, melody, and metric construction. When movement and gesture reach the point where they coincide with these like well-conditioned reflexes, the dance has "entered" the dancer.

Musical Form

Balinese musical form may be described as circular. Each section of a composition returns to the opening note and repeats immediately, the final note generating a new beginning. Long sections may repeat only once or twice, shorter ones more often. Brief four- or eight-note motifs or ostinatos may be repeated indefinitely, serving as mere rhythmic background for the more dramatic dances. Dances end, *not* on the closing tone, but on the sharply accented *upbeat* before it. On the final tone, which could also be the beginning of one more repetition, the dancer has already begun to relax. His closing pose is that of the beginning. In this continually recurrent music, with no conclusive ending, no true beginning, the Oriental conception of timeless, endless melody is revealed, revolving in smaller or larger cycles but never advancing to a climax.

Yet, in spite of this perfection of abstract form, the dance itself is filled with events. The circle is divided into inner sections which are marked by different systems of gong punctuation. The music itself is animated by the warm pulsation of drums which create an inner rhythm that is tense and restless, filled with disturbances and sudden agitations. Many of these disturbances are created by the metric structure; they are intensifications of accents which mark the division of the circle into quarters or eights. In Java the dancer may indicate his awareness of a metric accent by a mere turn of the head or slight pause of the hand in the middle of a phrase; the Balinese dancer dramatizes these accents by surrounding them with brilliant, turbulent movement or by coming to a sudden, momentary stop.

One may observe two quite different relationships between dancer and music. In extended metrical forms all movement is impelled and controlled by the metric structure, the divisional accents, the inner phrasing of the melody. Here the dance is purely abstract; it tells no story. A mood is created or a character presented as the dancer scans the music with gesture and movement. This is especially true of the long dance prologues of the *légong* dance. But as the story "emerges" the dancer is freed. A new relationship with the music is established. The dancer occupies the foreground, the music recedes. It is now an eight- or sixteen-note ostinato that repeats again and again to ever-changing rhythmic patterns of the drums and little cymbals. There are no longer involved metric accents to be taken into account, and the dance now has direction and wide unbroken sweep.

A beautiful example of this may be found in the dance of the *chondong*, whose progress downstage has already been described. Her entrance and slow advance is accompanied by the short *chondong* melody, repeated over and over against animated and constantly changing drum accentuation. In the following example I give the melody (without figuration) together with basic gong punctuation (Example 2). Below the melody I have indicated the rhythm of the drums. The five lines should be read separately, one after the other. They represent the rhythmic continuity that keeps changing with the dance, while the melody continues to repeat.

EXAMPLE 2:

But as the dancer begins moving with rapid, shuffling sidesteps to right and then to left, the melody changes to double the speed, while keeping the same fundamental beat (Example 3).

In the shorter detours, four notes are sufficient to carry the dancer to the outer point, four back to center, four out to the left, four back to center; with a repetition of the pattern the dancer is brought back

EXAMPLE 3:

to center, to resume the slow advance. The second detour, in wide sweeping arcs, is twice as broad; it takes a full sixteen notes to swing from one point of the arc to the other. In their contrast to the slow advance, with its little gestures and inner accents, these wide, pendulum-like figures have a sensuous charm and grace impossible to describe. These are the interludes, of which there are many variations. The dance ends in the center, downstage, the music returning to the opening theme.

These two contrasting dance styles, the abstract and the dramatic, are frequently combined. A complete *légong* performance begins with a dance prologue, followed by a series of dramatic scenes that tell the story in the condensed formal terms of the dance, and ends with a dance epilogue that returns to the mood of the opening. One of the most popular *légong* dances during the time I lived on the island was based on the story of Lasĕm, a legendary-historical prince of medieval Java.

The prince of Lasĕm has carried off the beautiful ward of his vassal Mĕtaun and married her. But the princess shuts herself up in her apartments within the palace and refuses to admit the bridegroom. Lasĕm hears that her brother is on the way to rescue her. He prepares for battle but, before leaving, begs the princess to admit him, for he is desperately in love. She opens her door, only to repulse him. On his way to battle, Lasĕm meets with evil omens. He injures his foot against the wheel of his chariot; a raven flies across his path foretelling his death. He is killed, and the princess is taken home.

The performance opens with the entrance of the lady-in-waiting who, after a long entrance dance, turns and presents the fans to the two dancers who stand waiting to begin. There is a short episode by all three dancers, after which the lady-in-waiting retires, to sit down by the *gamelan*. The prologue proper now begins. This is a long and formal episode in two contrasting movements, a slow section, grave and very elegant in style, and a light animato, in which the mood changes and the dancers seem to come to life. So far, however, they represent no one.

The choreography of this dance prologue is intricate (see Fig. 2). At first the two dancers move as though, by some optical illusion, they were the double projection of a single image. From the carefully formed design of the hand, the tilt of the head, down to the position and angle of the foot, their movements are identical. Suddenly, at an accent in the music, they break away, to go off in opposite directions. They return, but now their gestures reflect, as though one were mirroring the other. The stage is covered in the most elaborate interweaving patterns as the dancers cross and recross each other. Wide, oscillating arcs overlap at the inner points, and spirals coil and uncoil in opposite directions.

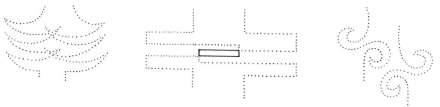

FIG. 2. Dance prologue of *légong* performance of story of Lasĕm.

The prologue finally comes to an end. There is a fractional pause, and then the musicians sound in loud dramatic unison the cue which marks the transition from prologue to story (Example 4).

EXAMPLE 4:

A soft prelude is heard from a single instrument, while a voice in the *gamelan* sings a brief synopsis of the story. There is a light introductory passage on the drums to set the tempo, and the *pĕngipuk*, or love music, begins. To this accompaniment the dancers perform a lyrical *pas de deux* in which Prince Lasĕm's advances are repulsed by the princess. The mood is one of sensuous melancholy. The melody repeats again and again, each time with more intense drumming. As Lasĕm's advances become increasingly ardent the drums swell in throbbing crescendos which are periodically broken by sharp accents that coincide with every gesture of refusal (Example 5).

EXAMPLE 5:

The dance ends, and the lady-in-waiting returns to kneel before Lasĕm. She is his first wife and is bidding him farewell as he leaves for battle. Lasĕm droops, his body suddenly limp. The scene is brief and filled with sorrow. There is only the free, half-improvised solo by a single musician for accompaniment.

The scene changes, and the child who played the first wife retires. As the lively *pangkat*, or departure music, begins, Lasĕm followed by the second dancer who is now his attendant, prepares for battle. They cover the stage in a series of slow advances, spiraling detours, and rapid marching steps against a background of quick, syncopated drumming (Example 6).

EXAMPLE 6:

Now comes a pause, and the dancers leave the stage. While a solo musician improvises quiet melody, a voice from the *gamelan* sings of the approach of the raven, and the child who danced the lady-in-waiting attaches a pair of golden wings to her arms. There is a sudden,

sharp signal accent from the drums, and the musicians begin the
stormy *garudă* music that repeats over and over above an undercurrent of agitated drumming (Example 7).

EXAMPLE 7:

Kneeling, the raven starts her dance. The body inclines from the
waist to one side, then the other, while the fluttering wings tilt at
angles like a bird soaring in a high wind. This is really the climax of
the performance—rhapsodic, fantastic, somber, and filled with brooding mystery. The dancer covers ground with curious little hopping
steps performed while still kneeling. The music grows more violent,
and she rises to her feet to sweep about the stage in arcs and circles.
Lasěm reappears and begins to dance, while the bird crosses and
recrosses his path. Suddenly it vanishes, as the second dancer, now the
rescuing brother, approaches. There is no break in the tension of the
music as the two dancers confront each other. In gestures of anger
they slap their closed fans against their left hands and advance, left
arms extended, two fingers pointing together. They engage in a duel;
the closed fans wave in circles but never touch. The music has grown
still more tense, a single note is repeated over and over (Example 8).

EXAMPLE 8:

At last, in the death struggle, the brother places both hands lightly
on Lasěm's hips, dragging him this way and that. The little figures
sway like reeds in a stream. Lasěm is killed with the tap of a fan and
falls to the ground. His opponent continues to dance. The *gamelan*

now modulates without a break into the "epilogue music," and the dancers return to the formal choreographic style of the prologue. Their dramatic identities have vanished; once more they scan the music with abstract gesture. The performance ends as it opened, in the same mood of calm and timelessness. The closing phrase of the dance, the *tanjĕk*, leads to the final pose—right hand and fan held close to the body, left arm extended level with the shoulder and palm turned back—the pose with which the dancers began, an hour earlier.

If I have perhaps described at too great length a single choreography, it is in order to show the relation between dancer and music and how an extended ballet is constructed. I am only able to describe the metrical structure, the tempo, and the basic plan for movement. Some idea of gesture, position, and fluid movement may be gathered from the drawings of *légong* by Covarrubias,[2] which catch with wonderful accuracy the swiftness and grace of the dance.

Ritual Dances

The slow-moving ritual dances of the temple, performed by the older women of the village or by a line of serious-faced youths or maidens, are beautiful in their simplicity, their grave, untroubled serenity. One notes two separate types of ritual dance; in one the dancer ceremonially presents symbolic offerings—incense, oil, wine, holy water, bearing in the upheld palm a cup, a small bottle, or smoking brazier; in the other it is the dance itself which is the offering. Dressed in finest clothes, the women with elaborate headdresses of flowers, real or golden, the men in golden headcloths, the dancers present themselves in the dance as an act of devotion.

Ritual dances vary so with the occasion and region that it is difficult to describe them in any set order. The slow, processional *rejang* is performed by the group of unmarried girls of the village. The dancers advance in single or double line, arms extended and moving up and down, hands posturing in a simplification of the complex gestures of the trained dancer. The most attractive girls, the best dancers, lead the line. In the rear are the shy, smaller girls who have just joined the group and are learning the dance by following the girls ahead of them. Movements and gestures are relaxed and simple; the important thing is uniformity.

Gabor, performed by the older women, is generally more animated and tense, and may lead up to some of the dancers falling in trance.

---

[2]Miguel Covarrubias, *Island of Bali* (New York, Knopf, 1937), Pl. preceding p. 227.

The women dance in pairs of fours, in a more intricate choreography in which they weave in and out, cross and recross. In this dance, offerings are presented before the shrines, and the dancers are frequently led by priest or priestess. The quick shuffling steps of the *légong* and frequent breaks in the movement on a syncopated accent place the performance somewhere between the simple ritual and the studied, professional dance. The music has considerable variety, based on definite dance impulses. I give one motif here, a rhythmic ostinato, which may indicate the animation of the dance (Example 9).

EXAMPLE 9:

Mendét, a variation of the *gabor* dance, is performed by women and girls, sometimes by youths and men. In a few older villages the *tĕrună*, the group of unmarried boys, perform a stately processional dance, baroque and elegant in style, known as *namiang*. All ritual dances, handed down from generation to generation, are learned without the aid of a teacher, through observation and imitation. In the more remote mountain villages ritual dance retains its simple archaic character but tends to become involved and elegant in those regions where there is much dance and musical activity.

Performances in Trance

Trance frequently forms the climax to the ritual dances of the temple. The women or youths who perform the ceremonial *gabor* or *mendét* may arrive at this state quite suddenly, having literally danced themselves into trance. The transition is abrupt, for there has been no cumulative rise in ecstasy in either dance or music. What induces this change is hard to determine, but the monotony of a brief musical phrase reiterated at the same tone level, neither loud nor soft, is a powerful hypnotic agent. Along with the dancers, musicians frequently play themselves into a state of trance. One after another, boys and men collapse among their instruments, are helped to their feet, to step out from the *gamelan* and join the other dancers. At this point each dancer may be given a *kris*, to perform the ritualistic *ngurek*, the hysterical self-stabbing—a violent suicidal pantomime that rarely ends in a wound, for the dancers are closely watched and disarmed before they can injure themselves. (See Plate XXVI.) With some, the state of trance is brief and transitory; with others it is intense to the point of utter exhaustion. But when, by means of holy water and incense, the dancers are revived, they rise and calmly walk away as though they had never lost consciousness.

Dancers may also be brought into trance by means of incense smoke and the chanting of special magic songs. In times of epidemic (now rare), special ritualistic dances are performed nightly in the infected village, as a means of dispelling sickness. Once in trance, the dancers, possessed by a protective divinity (*sanghyang*), can consecrate water and give it the magical power of disinfection. As such it is sprinkled on the ground by the officiating priest and distributed among the people of the village.

The dancers in trance perform all sorts of feats to demonstrate their divine possession. In the dance of "sacred horses" (*sanghyang jaran*), men dance astride small bamboo sticks with little horseheads and horsehair tails. They neigh and prance jerkily, dart through burning coals scattered about the courtyard. In the dance of "heavenly nymphs" (*sanghyang dĕdari*), two small girls in dancing costume and elaborate headdresses dance on the shoulders of men who carry them around the clearing, their eyes closed and bodies loosely swaying. (See Plate XXVII.) Sometimes a ladder of bare kris blades is prepared for them, leading to a high platform. Dancing and posturing, their naked feet on the sharp edges, they mount step by step to the platform where, with eyes still shut, they continue dancing, miraculously avoiding a false step which would cause them to fall from the narrow ledge.

Though the chants that lull dancers into unconsciousness are sung in a slow, almost dreamlike manner by a group of women, once the dancers have fallen in trance the music changes. A group of boys and men now perform the *kechak*, a lively, rhythmic chorus consisting of explosive syllables half shouted, half muttered. In recent times the *gamelan* is used instead. While *sanghyang* societies boast their dancers are not trained but enabled to dance through possession by the gods, this is not always the case. Rehearsals *do* take place; a few steps and positions recalling the *légong* style are practiced by the little girls for the *sanghyang dĕdari*. Margaret Mead notes that in the village in which she lived, after a visiting *légong* performance the little *sanghyang* dancers added to their repertoire new steps which they had copied from the *légong*.

Dance performances in trance demand a special study. They have nothing to do with set choreographies and musical forms. The performance of the two little girls lies on the borderline between dance and somnambulistic pantomime. In more remote parts of the island one may still find *sanghyang* "dances" in which youths or men in trance "become" deer, monkeys, serpents, or even swine. Their performances have nothing of the dance in them but are fantastic and hysterical transformations, executed with violent and at times quite terrifying realism. They are mentioned here since they are a necessary though psychopathic detail in the picture of the dance and its function in Bali.

The Kĕbyar: *Escape from the Past*

With the popular modern *kĕbyar*, a brilliant exhibition dance performed by a youth or small boy, we reach the end of our survey. Here we come to the breakdown of traditional forms in both dance and music. Composition is free in structure—a loosely connected series of melodies in different moods that are given a new and glittering orchestration, while the dancer, seated in a square surrounded by the musicians, translates the changing moods into movement. He dances from the waist only, half kneeling, half sitting, moving from one part of the square to another in a smoothly gliding hop. Great emphasis is laid on animated articulation of the hands and mobility of facial expression; the face is no longer a mask but a screen which shows a succession of expressions that match the temper of the music—dramatic, serene, vivacious, or seductive. Movements from *baris*, *légong*, *topéng*, and *sandaran* are all incorporated into the dancer's performance, selected purely for the sake of effect and contrast. Although the dance appears highly dramatic, the story is no longer important; both dance and music are an exuberant display of fireworks that show off the skill of the performers to the delighted audience.

The word *kĕbyar* itself means a sudden release of forces—an explosion, "a flower bursting suddenly open," the crash of many cymbals. It indicates to perfection the explosive energy and liberation of both dance and music. Musicians and dancer alike find exhilarating freedom in the rhapsodic music and choreographies that are composed, in a spirit of creative enthusiasm, for approaching festive occasions.

Dance and music are constructed together—the combined effort of the dance teacher and leading musicians of the club. Sometimes the club will buy a dance and its music from a star dancer, after permission to use the composition has been obtained from the dancer's own organization. The dancer then teaches both choreography and music to the club that has engaged him, adding, perhaps, a few novelties in the process. Most clubs, however, prefer brand new compositions in which they can make something of a sensation. They may engage a well-known *kĕbyar* composer to create new music and outline a new choreography; or they may prefer to compose both dance and music themselves, in which case dancer and musicians all participate, contributing ideas for gesture, movement, melody, and orchestration. The composition grows from night to night as the club meets for rehearsal until, after a series of trials and rejections, it reaches, a month later, its final, definite form.

With a *kĕbyar* a significant phase in the evolution of Balinese dance is reached. The dancer is still closely linked with the music; he is still its visual projection; his movements are still in traditional style; his facial expression, while no longer immobile, is still colored by the stylistic conventions of the mask. But there is now a strong personal appeal in his performance; individuality begins to assert itself; the dancer establishes a closer, warmer contact with his audience. It is he himself they are watching, no legendary figure from the past. They react strongly to his personal charm, his sense of the dramatic, his little innovations in hand movement, play of the eyes, manipulation of the fan. Through a long transition the dancer has emerged from sculptured stone to youthful, breathing mortal.

References

Bateson, Gregory, and Margaret Mead. *Balinese Character: A Photographic Analysis.* New York, New York Academy of Sciences, 1942.

Covarrubias, Miguel. *Island of Bali.* New York, Knopf, 1937.

McPhee, Colin. *A House in Bali.* New York, John Day, 1946.

Ridgeway, William. *The Dramas and Dances of Non-European Races.* Cambridge, Cambridge University Press, 1915.

Van Lelyveld, Theodore B. *La Danse dans le théâtre javanais.* Paris, Floury, 1931.

Zoete, Beryl de, and Walter Spies. *Dance and Drama in Bali.* New York, Harper, 1939.

(For music see list on p. 407.)

Form and Function
of the Dance in Bali

CLAIRE HOLT and GREGORY BATESON

To an anthropologist, next to the question of who, when, how, and why certain members of a given society dance, arises the problem of the relationship of the peculiar character of the dance to the character of the people concerned, and to the whole pattern of their culture. What is the relationship between the movements characteristic of a given dance and the typical gestures and postures in daily life of the very people who perform it? Gesture and posture in daily life are certainly expressive of a people's character, but how are their gestures and postures in a stylized, heightened, and intensified form, as they appear in the dance, related to their particular character?

Why, for instance, is the Balinese dance so totally different from the dance forms of any people in the Western hemisphere? And why, moreover, while having quite a number of affinities in the basic technique with other Indonesian dances, are some of the Balinese dances so strikingly different from the dances of even the Javanese, who are their closest neighbors, only a few miles to the west? The introduction to the dances of Bali given in films in the seminar demonstrated a few of the points raised here.

As a point of departure, the first film showed a Balinese wood carver at work. He sits cross-legged and relaxed on the ground, and his nimble hands carefully manipulate the chisel, chipping away the yielding wood bit by bit. An Iatmul wood carver who is seen next tensely hacks away at his woodcarving while crouching. And while

Originally published in *The Function of the Dance in Human Society, a Seminar Directed by Franziska Boas* (New York, The Boas School, 1944), pp. 46–52. Reprinted with permission of Franziska Boas.

obviously the work of the Iatmul does not require the precision and fineness of that of the Balinese, one can state from experience that a Balinese working at an even larger and cruder piece would still proceed with much greater and more meticulous precision that the Iatmul, and with none of the Iatmul's rapid, intense gestures.

Examples along similar lines could be multiplied. People at work in Bali will be observed to use the minimum of effort. They have developed a peculiar separateness of their limbs, and do not engage the body, chest, back, when they have to do things with their hands and arms. Often only the arm, the hand, and the individual fingers will move, without engaging the rest of the body. It was clear in the film of the Iatmul wood carver that while he worked he was straining to an undue extent the muscles of his whole body.

A feeling of relaxation and detachment characterizes the movements of the Balinese in daily life, whether they are cutting rice or carving a temple wall, preparing a meal, or arranging fruit in the market place. A similar but even more cultivated form of detachment can be detected in some of their ritual dances. So, for instance, the stately processional temple dance, the *rejang*, which was shown in films next, demonstrated the slow circular progress of a series of female figures with trailing skirts who, at intervals, between a series of stately steps, paused to incline their bodies while slowly swinging their fans. One by one they complete their round in almost spellbound tranquility in which there is no climax, no variation, but a seemingly endless chain of repetitious movement; then, suddenly, as casually as if she had just finished an errand, a dancer walks off across the court at an ordinary gait, while her companions continue their calm circling.

In contrast to the stately and slow *rejang* processional is the *légong* dance performed by two small girls aged about eight or nine. With a swiftness and agility that is amazing to any dance expert, Balinese *légong* dancers move and flutter over the open dance space, in small, rapid, staccato steps, jerking their heads, twisting their arms, and swaying their incredibly nimble little bodies with a precision rivaling that of our robot Rockettes. Their dance can last for an hour or longer. It is supposed to depict a story. But the plot is almost undiscernible, and serves only as an outline to determine the pattern of the choreographic figures and dance gestures which typify *légong* dances no matter what part of the legend is being played.

The girls, like our ballet dancers, are puppets par excellence. There is not a trace of individuality in them. The only variation is the degree of perfection to which they have mastered the stylized movements, and a trace of difference due to the fact that of two identical dancers, one is made to perform a "male" and the other a "female" role in the story. *Légong* dances are performed on festive occasions, usually in the temple court and, like many other dances or dance plays, are regarded as an offering to the gods.

The next dance shown on the screen was *jogèd*. A dance girl, also preadolescent, is the center of attention. She is a skillful and trained dancer, wears an elaborate and beautiful costume with a special type of dance crown decorated with flowers, and plies the indispensable fan. The style of her dance is similar to that of the *légong*, but the movements and pattern are simplified and slower. From the audience male dance partners come out in turn to dance opposite her. Unlike the dance girl they are not specially trained although some of them are very skillful. With varying degrees of accomplishment and grace they posture and circle near the girl dancer, sometimes moving away only to turn back suddenly and approach her again. At no time do the partners touch each other save for an exceptionally daring pat on the arm or shoulder which an extravagant or flirtatious partner will permit himself. This provokes laughter from the audience. To the Western observer there is not a trace of emotion visible in the dance girl, and he may wonder how such a completely detached figure could possibly attract the male dancers. Her whole bearing is *noli me tangere*. This *jogèd* is the most popular form of social dancing in Bali, and it is natural therefore that, when a Balinese or, for that matter, any other Indonesian sees our manner of social dancing, with the forthright sexuality and closeness of its contact, he thinks it indecent and crude. On the other hand, our young males are not attracted to, and do not dance with nine- and ten-year-old girls.

It should be added that sometimes the role of the female dancer in the *jogèd* is filled by a young boy who takes the place of the dance girl, is dressed exactly like her, and is correspondingly feminine and detached in his movements.

A purely male dance is the *baris*, representing the exercises of warriors. In recent times stories have been woven into the *baris* and thus a kind of dance drama evolved in which the stylized movements of the actual dancers closely followed the style of the old war dances. Upon *baris* one can hinge a few of the underlying principles of Balinese dance. Imagine a dance in which no jumping, leaping, steady whirling, running, bending of the torso from the waist occurs. Legs and arms form angles in the air; the only emphasis is provided by the hands with spread fingers and by the sharply turning head.

It seems at intervals as if something forces the dancers into startled jerks. There is no suppleness or continuity in any of the dancer's movements. Quite different from *baris* and its stilted style, is the comparatively modern *kĕbyar* described as a flirtatious solo dance by a man or boy, the moods of which closely follow the moods of the music. The dance is performed in a seated position. The film showed one of Bali's renowned dance masters giving a lesson in *kĕbyar* to a young boy. The method of instruction consisted mainly of the teacher leading and pushing the limbs and the body of the pupil into the proper positions until the pupil could get a proper feel of the postures. From time to time the teacher dances before the pupil so that the latter can imitate his movement, but again and again he kneels or crouches close behind the boy and, getting hold of his wrists, forces him to bend and undulate his body—teacher and pupil becoming, as it were, one.

Despite the supple grace and soft sways which occur in the dance, it is always punctuated by very precise and marked accent of the head or the hands. Long phrases are brought to a stop with a sharp accent. There was for that reason a curious comparison between the Balinese boy, a novice at dancing, and a skilled professional Hindu dancer who tried to learn *kĕbyar* from the same master, and whose efforts were also shown in the film. For the Hindu dancer the greatest difficulty was to master these very neat, precise accents, sudden jerks and stops, which punctuate the Balinese *kĕbyar*, for his native art, compared with that of Bali, has a much greater continuity of softly flowing movements.

In recent years *kĕbyar* has become one of the favorite dances with which the Balinese entertain foreign tourists. Its gay and flirtatious mood, combined with high technical accomplishment of the dancer, who always stays close to the ground, half sitting and half kneeling, and only from time to time changing his place by peculiar hops without actually rising, appeals to foreigners.

A peculiar feature in Balinese life is the widespread phenomenon of trance which in the religious life as well as in the dance has become a regular occurrence. Bali's famous trance-dancers, the *sanghyang*, who are very young girls, become divinities, or possessed by spirits of god. When in a state of trance they dance in a manner similar to the *légong*. There is a regular procedure to put these little girls into presumably autohypnotic trance and again to bring them out of it, by means of incense, chants, rhythmical movement, and so forth.

These ritual preliminaries, however, are quite different in the case of kris dancers—those who bear a dagger called a kris. Usually kris dancers are men or boys who appear in a group as supporters of the *barong* (a mythical animal figure associated with "white" or positive, benevolent magic) and as antagonists to the traditional figure of the witch *rangdă*. After stepping about in stylized dance manner, with the kris upraised, each dancer in turn attacks the witch. A short fight ensues in which the dancer is very tense and the witch completely relaxed. She only waves her magic cloth. The dancer then falls backward to the ground in a state of trance. He is aroused from this state by the *barong* and arises in a somnambulistic state of entranced fury, amok against himself. He directs the dagger against his own chest now. Repeatedly, with convulsive movements, he pushes the kris against his own body (oddly enough without actually wounding himself, as a rule) until he falls down in a cramp or in convulsions, writhing on the ground. At a given moment a number of the kris dancers can be seen entranced, jerking their bodies backward and fitfully pressing the kris against their chest, then falling to the ground. They are then carried away and brought to by means of sprinkling of holy water and other established means.

A variant of the kris dance, one performed by women in a certain village of South Bali (in response to European suggestions) was shown in the next film. It took place at a great festive occasion in the temple court where all sorts of ritualistic dances were performed. The female kris dancers appeared in a stately procession, slowly advancing with upraised kris. After having reached the dance space, the files broke up, and each individual dancer began to move about until at a given moment, to the accompaniment of accelerating music, one after the other, as if affected by a rapidly spreading contagion, they began, with a short leap, to swing up their daggers and push them against their chest, bending forward over the dagger point pressed close to the collarbone. It was observed that these climax movements of bending forward and downward by the women during the kris dance were in peculiar contrast to the climactic posture of the men, who jerk backward when pressing the kris against their chest. Aside from the possible symbolic eroticism of this difference, it is noteworthy that the entranced individuals are able to remember to observe this formality at the height of their paroxysm. Before long the whole dance space becomes a scene of wild ecstasy. All over the place, figures of women with long streaming hair leap and sway, boring their krisses, as it were, into their chests, bending over the weapons. In one corner a male kris dancer writhes in convulsions on the ground while the priest, sprinkling holy water out of a beaker, moves between the dancers. Villagers carry off twisting bodies of other dancers who have reached a dangerous state of entranced ecstasy, and wrest the daggers from their cramped fists.

This brief description of a few of the Balinese dances cannot, of course, evoke a clear vision of the dancers' appearance and of their movements in space and time. However, one can state that among the typical features characterizing Balinese dances, the following can be observed:

1. Complete lack of visible emotional expression. Even in dance drama, where emotions are enacted, they are conveyed through a traditional pattern of stylized gestures which, effective as they may be, leave no room for interpretation by the personal expression of the individual dancer. In short, complete detachment reigns throughout, whether it be a ritual, a social dance, a drama, or a pure dance spectacle. The only very important exceptions are the grotesque and comic characters. In delightful burlesques they indulge, during their roughhouse scenes, in violent emotional reactions which, however, are often either startled surprise or fear. Supplanting emotion is a tenseness of a strange detached kind, which in our terminology can be likened to a state of trance, or possession, as the Indonesian would term it.

2. All dances, whether male or female, with the exception of ancient ritual processionals, are characterized by intermittent sharp accents. These can be a sequence of precise, sharp, staccato steps, little taps occurring at intervals, or sudden jerks of the dancer's head which punctuate a dance phrase, or a sudden stop and pulling up of the whole figure as though the dancer were suddenly startled.

3. The fundamental posture in female secular dances involves a markedly outcurved spine with the buttocks pushed out. The torso of the male dancer is comparatively rigid. The pubic area is never pushed forward, nor do undulating movements prevalent in Indian and Polynesian dances occur. In both male and female dances the limbs form angles, and there is a tendency to pull up the shoulders with upraised and outturned angular elbows pointed upward so that the head sinks between them and the neck disappears.

4. The technique of Balinese dancing calls for extraordinary control of the limbs, for endurance, and in many cases for meticulous precision.

5. The Balinese, like all Indonesian dancers, never tend away from the ground. They do not dance upward and away from the earth but move on it, along its surface, in slow circles or lines, rapid semicircles

and serpentines, and in a sudden zig-zag of short duration. In some cases they dance seated on the ground. Elevation above the ground occurs, as an exception, only when the *sanghyang*, the little girl trance dancers, mount upon the shoulders of the men who then carry them, unsupported, through the dance space. Standing on the shoulders of their carriers the *sanghyang* continue dancing with their bodies, arms, and heads, high above the ground.

6. In Balinese choreography, sudden changes of direction are a marked feature. With a sharp accent, semicircles or lines are reversed. Intermittently the dancer checks her swift progress with a jerk and proceeds in the opposite direction. Again the old processional dances are an exception.

Perhaps an attempt could now be made to relate some of the peculiarities of the Balinese dance to the Balinese character and temperament, inasmuch as these have been a subject of anthropological study. To a foreign observer the striking feature of the Balinese scene is the seemingly subdued and even tone of social relations among the Balinese. There is an outward equanimity bordering on indifference. Even friendly gaiety or sullenness do not carry any feeling of pulsating emotions of the order we know. Rarely does one discover any passions given expression at village gatherings or courts, at cremation ceremonies, temple feasts, or in the market place. It has been stated that, owing to an observed pattern of frustration which the Balinese undergoes in early childhood, his emotions or emotional expressions are suppressed or even paralyzed; as is, to a lesser degree, similarly achieved in England. The detachment which characterizes Balinese dancing would thus not be a departure from normal life but an extension and intensification to further the cold passion of everyday Balinese behavior.

Institutionalized trance, which finds an outlet in the dance, can be traced to the strong autosuggestive forces at work in every animistic society, where possession by spirits and deities in a formalized manner plays such an important ritualistic role. It is suggested that certain Balinese trance dances, especially the kris dances, are relevant to the Balinese character structure. Frustrated impulses of a violent nature, which in childhood were compensated by tantrums, find sublimated parallels—in an adult society where imitative pressure requires an outward equanimity—in the self-directed violence of the kris dance. This is, however, not even symbolically a total expression of the suppressed stresses, for the witch in the kris dance (possibly a mother symbol representing the social environment) is not touched or harmed by the dancers' attacks; she only waves, and through her magic the dancers must turn the weapons against themselves until in frenzied convulsions they roll on the ground—in itself, no doubt, some release from inhibited tensions, whether the trance is autosuggestive and intense or merely a dance pattern.

Like most Indonesians, the Balinese dislike wide open spaces. They will never build a house without hemming it in with trees and walls. Fear of spirits pervades life and all activities. The "happy islanders" are really a fear-haunted people, and endless precautions are always taken to prevent or counteract the ever-lurking but undefined dangers. One must be on guard always. Perhaps these fears are reflected in Balinese dance as well as in its repressed life. One could venture the suggestion that leaving the ground is dangerous, and one must bend toward it and move along it; and only such chosen and semi-divine beings as the *sanghyang* in trance may soar for a moment and stay above the ground for any length of time.

Angularity, precision, and clean-cut details are characteristic not only of the dance but also of traditional Balinese pictorial and plastic art. It may be pointed out here that spirits always travel in straight lines. They are misled by change of direction. One confuses them by turning cremation towers in the middle of a procession and does not build a house in a straight line with the entrance gate.

In the course of their history the people of Bali learned many things from other people, among them the Hindu-Javanese and the Chinese. Many features of Balinese art, including the dance, bear unmistakable traces of these influences, yet none of them were completely decisive in the molding of Balinese art forms. The peculiarities of Balinese character were a factor in the selection and adaptation of foreign elements, and in the final shaping of their creations, whether of stone, cloth, or motion; painted, chiseled, or danced.

In searching for this cultural temperament, this mass character, the anthropologist can find in the study of the dance corroborative material for his observations, as well as clues which will direct his research toward new aspects. One field which still awaits exploration is the question of how far a dominant kinesthetic awareness of certain parts of the body is related to psychological factors. If posture and movement of an individual are closely interdependent with his psychological state, would not stylized posture and gesture in the dance of a people be relevant to a general psychological trend in their life?

Other questions, too, still await an answer from future study and research. For instance: Are peoples who have belly dances, with rhythmic, rotating movements of the pelvic region different in cultural temperament from those whose torsos and hips are rigid in dancing? If so, wherein does the difference lie, and is the mass character of the people to be considered similar to that of their dance and expressed by it, or opposite to it and compensated by it? As, for instance, in the case of the above-mentioned belly dance versus the rigid pelvis. Or, for another instance, are peoples whose dances call for high leaps and jumps more aggressive, braver, or more cruel than peoples who only step or shuffle along the ground, or are they less so? Does a predilection for soft, continuous, undulating movements disclose a particular psychological feature or total character different from that of peoples whose movements in the dance are abrupt? What is this difference?

PLATE I

Main gate to the village temple in Sanur (South Bali) on a feast day.
Sanur, December 13, 1937

PLATE II

Small boy bringing his water buffalo back from washing it in the stream.
Batuan, February 21, 1939

PLATE III

Woman carrying home sheaves of rice from the fields at harvest.
Karangasem District, February 23, 1939

PLATE IV

A small boy learning to stand and walk. His father has set up for him a horizontal bamboo supported on two posts. The boy learns to walk by using this as a support.

Bayung Gĕdé, March 26, 1937

PLATE V

A mother suckling her baby. The child is dressed up for its 42-day birthday, wearing a golden fontanelle ornament and a flower in the hair.

Klandis, Denpasar, February 28, 1939

PLATE VI

A father playing with his daughter.   Bayung Gĕdé, March 21, 1937

PLATE VII

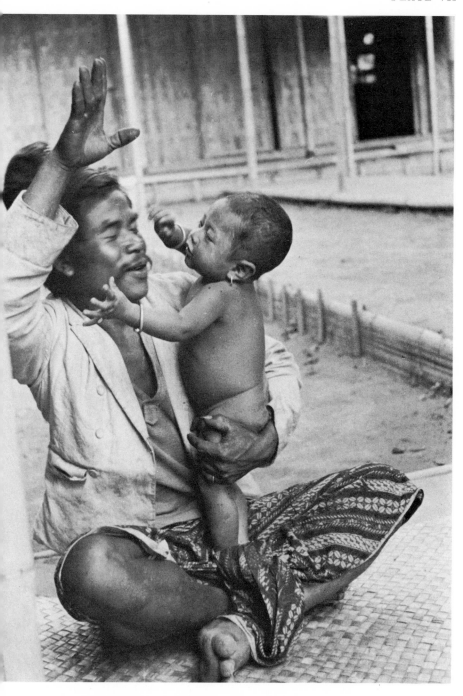

A father teaches his son to dance, humming a tune and posturing with his hands.
Bayung Gĕdé, October 1, 1936

PLATE VIII

A Brahmană artist working on a pencil drawing for a picture.
Batuan, October 6, 1937

PLATE IX

Two children participating in the ceremonial sweeping of the courtyard during the cremation ritual.   Batuan, October 5, 1937

Little girls playing at prayer in the midst of a dramatic reenactment of the cremation ceremonies.   Batuan, October 7, 1937

PLATE X

A baby girl with her sister as child nurse.   Bayung Gĕdé, March 30, 1937

PLATE XI

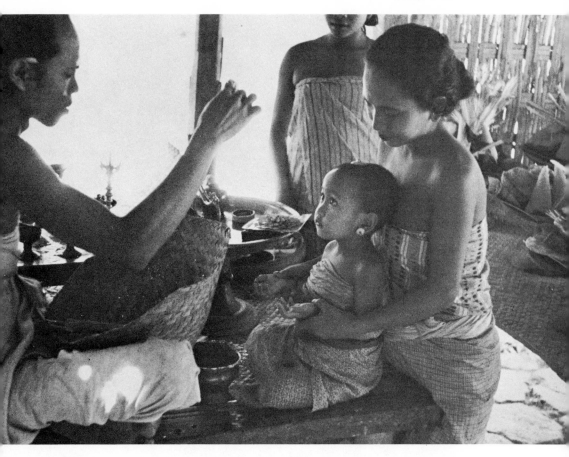

A Brahmană priest (*pĕdandă*) blessing a baby Brahmană girl, on the fourth celebration of the 210-day birthday (that is, the 840th day).

Batuan, August 4, 1937

PLATE XII

High shrine for offerings at a girl's puberty ceremony. It is decorated with a *lamak*, a palm-leaf cut-out pattern.   Batuan, December 8, 1937

PLATE XIII

The adolescent daughter in a Brahmană household making an offering to the shrine outside the entrance to her house, at the feast of Galungan.

Batuan, December 1, 1937

PLATE XIV

A prince (*mantri*) and his two servants in an *arjă* play.
Bayung Gĕdé, May 12, 1937

PLATE XV

A mountain audience watching the *légong* dance from the women's and children's side of the temple.   Bayung Gĕdé, May 30, 1937

PLATE XVI

The bride and bridegroom and the bridegroom's father praying, holding flowers
in their hands, while a priest intones the final ceremony of a wedding.

Batuan, January 9, 1938

PLATE XVII

Carrying a *wadah* (cremation tower) to the cemetery.
Sekahan, September 19, 1936

PLATE XVIII

Finds at Chekandik, showing (*top*) the stone figure with headdress and the two similar but headless figures; and showing (*bottom*) the small stone head and the block of stone (possibly the roof of a shrine, *kekereb*), with part of the figure with headdress in the background.

Pĕludu, March 30, 1937

PLATE XIX

An offering (*chanang rebong*) made principally of flowers supported on a central core of banana stem and with a fan-shaped headdress (*chili*).

Batuan, August 23, 1937

PLATE XX

Jogèd bungbung, a ceremonial dance performed by women.

PLATE XXI

Légong dancers. The *légong* dance is performed only by highly trained little girls.

PLATE XXII

Ceremonial *baris*, a warrior-drill dance.

PLATE XXIII

Baris jangkang dancers.   Pĕlilit, Nusă Pĕnidă, 1933

PLATE XXIV

Kĕbyar dance by I Sampih. The *kĕbyar* dance is a solo dance performed in a seated position by a youth or a small boy.

PLATE XXV

Rangdă, the witch.

The *barong*, the dragon.

PLATE XXVI

Self-stabbing by kris dancers in trance.　　　　　　Village of Denjalan

The kris dancers falling down before the *rangdă* (witch).
Pagutan, December 16, 1937

PLATE XXVII

Sanghyang déling, a small girl in trance dancing on a man's shoulders.
Bayung Gĕdé

PLATE XXVIII

PLATE XXIX

Jero balian (the village priestess) in an official trance ceremony in which she speaks as a god. The first picture (*upper left*) shows her at the beginning of her trance; she has already taken on the facial expression usual in her trances, an expression of mixed agony and ecstasy with the eyebrows drawn together, forehead wrinkled and corners of the mouth drawn down. The second picture (*lower left*) shows her speaking in trance. In the last picture (*above*) she has come out of trance; she starts to look around her but is apparently still not fully oriented.   Bayung Gĕdé, June 23, 1937

PLATE XXX

Gamelan bebonangan, musicians in procession. The *gamelan* is an orchestra of gongs, keyed instruments, drums, and cymbals.

Gamelan gong gĕdé, a large orchestra possessing a scale of music that differs from the usual *gamelan*.

PLATE XXXI

Gĕndèr limolas (a keyed instrument) in the *gamelan pelègongan.*

Gĕndèr wayang ensemble, the group of four *gĕndèr* (keyed instruments) used in the performance of the shadow play.

PLATE XXXII

By I Lungsur, age 9. *Artist's title:* "Subali and Sugriwă fighting. They exchange blows and bite each other. They are brothers, Sugriwă is the younger brother." Two monkey princes from the Hindu epic, the *Ramayana*. Note the symmetry of the design.

By I Kantin, age 9. *Artist's title:* "On the right Chupak and Nang Komun below him, and above, a *kuuk*, who eats people. On the left is Nang Sĕdahan stabbing Chupak, with Paksi [great bird] and Chélèng Lelingsen [person transformed into a pig]." Composition in a circle, overflowing the margins. Chupak is the chief character of a cycle of folk plays presented in the shadow-play theater.

PLATE XXXIII

By I Gandir, age 7. *Artist's title:* "A *barong* dancing in the road. People carrying flags, banners, and ceremonial parasols. They are playing *gĕndèr* [musical instruments], and cymbals and gongs." A performance of the dance of the dragon is represented. Note the magnification of the size of the dragon mask in relation to the size of the players. (Cf. Plate XXV.)

By I Lungsur, age 9. *Artist's title:* "A Chalonarang story. Pandung stabs the *rangdă*, but she does not die." The Chalonarang is the story of the witch, performed with the sacred mask, which is the well-known prelude to the ceremonial trance with krisses. The composition renders the balance between the forces of good and evil, in the same manner as the shadow play. (Cf. Plate XXVI.)

PLATE XXXIV

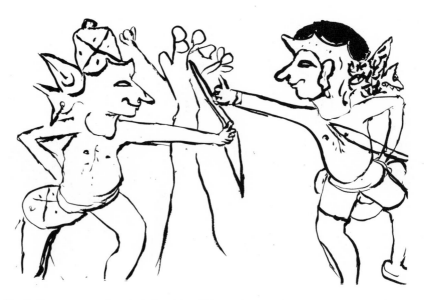

By I Lanus, age 6. *Artist's title:* "Kresna fighting with Salyă." The god Krishna and the hero Salyă, known to the child from the shadow play, are represented in stylized rendering strongly influenced by the shadow play, in the attitudes of the personages, the balance of the composition, the distinctive detail of the headdresses, and the delineation of the features.

By I Dapet, age 5. *Artist's title:* "A cow lying down, a man, a bird, a man, Arjună, Malèn, Sangut, a man, a pig, a bird. . . ." Here the figures of ordinary men and animals appear with *wayang* figures, which are given the names of heroes from the shadow play.

PLATE XXXV

By I Langsur, age 9. *Artist's title:* "A cockfight."

By I Langsur, age 9. *Artist's title:* "Food and drink are brought to Chupak by his followers, Panak Saté, Tuă Dayă, and Nanang Sedahan." A typical shadow-play scene from the Chupak cycle.

PLATE XXXVI

Child players in a *gamelan angklung*, an orchestra featuring the *angklung*, an instrument made of bamboo pipes as seen in the first row. The *gangsă* players are in the next two rows.   Sayan

The Arts in Bali

MARGARET MEAD

SINCE CIVILIZED MAN first began to speculate about uncivilized man, the Noble Savage, the Red Man, the South Sea Islander—one after the other—have been daydreams of succeeding generations. When serious scientific study of primitive peoples replaced travelers' story-telling which had lent itself to this romancing, it became the fashion to disparage these daydream images of primitive peoples, to point out that the Indian was not so "natural" as Rousseau had dreamed and that the classical picture of the South Sea Islander lying on his back on a delectable stretch of white beach waiting for breadfruit to drop into his mouth was untrue and described neither the real activities of the South Sea Islander nor the properties of breadfruit—a good fruit, but edible only when scraped and roasted. This sort of debunking was necessary if anyone was to come to understand the importance of primitive societies as experiments in different kinds of social forms, forms so different from our own as to be incomparably valuable material on man's potential handling of his world. As long as civilized people continued to imagine primitives wrapped in mysterious auto-matic armor called taboos, or stripped of all clothing, even a G-string, being "natural," ethnologists could not get a hearing for their findings that the institutions of uncivilized peoples were comparable to our own and were of genuine importance in our thinking.

But necessary as this change in emphasis was and is, in a good and very important sense the ways of life of simpler and different peoples can serve as symbols for the nostalgia or the dreams of civilized spec-tators; they can mobilize longings, sharpen social perceptions, crystal-lize attitudes toward change. The French academician reading a

Originally published in *The Yale Review*, XXX, No. 2 (December, 1940), 335–47. Reprinted with permission of the author.

Jesuit missionary's account of the Red Indians, the English theorist enchanted with Captain Cook's voyages, the American schoolteacher or stockbroker fascinated by Frederick O'Brien or James Norman Hall —all seize upon something in these accounts which has symbolic reality for them and for their periods.

It has twice been my accidental fortune to make ethnological expeditions to islands which, besides presenting an ideal setting in which to investigate certain theoretical problems of the relationship between heredity and environment, have also been current daydreams in the Western world—the South Sea Islands in 1925, and Bali in 1935. In both instances, the announcement of my destination to a group of listeners at home caused the same breathless stir, as if I had said I was setting off for heaven. People crowded in as if to touch me; others moved a little away, as from one already set apart for more than earthly delights. From their longing "Oh, take us with you!" to their fervid "Oh, tell us what it was like!" the daydreams of the two periods were registered, accurately and sensitively, as by a needle moving on a smoked drum.

These daydreams were essentially different, and the difference reveals, I think, a significant and hopeful change from the outlook of the 1920s to the outlook of the 1930s. In the 1920s there were people who wanted to go to the South Sea Islands as a personal escape from their postwar world, from a dull and empty routine, from the denial of spontaneity, and the trammeling of individual passions. They wanted to escape to a kind of divine nothingness in which life would be reduced to the simplest physical terms, to sunshine and the moving shadows of palm trees, to bronze-bodied girls and bronze-bodied boys, food for the asking, no work to do, no obligations to meet. They wanted to go to the South Sea Islands and never come back, and the fiction of the period emphasized that one did not come back; the divine, sensuous inactivity was too alluring.

The steamship companies which advertised Bali, in the 1930s tried to make Bali the lineal descendant of the Tahiti of the romantic 1920s, with the slim figure of a high-breasted, scantily clothed girl as the symbol. But they failed. The average tourist—the business man from Milwaukee, the college boy from California, the schoolmistress from New England—came away from Bali talking not of undressed maidens but of happiness and art. They asked in wonder, "What makes the Balinese so contented?" They did not, like the escapist, moan, "Oh, why can't I live here forever?" For even the cursory three-day tourist visiting the Dutch East Indies in the 1930s recognized in Bali the very opposite of the pleasant, sensuous idling away of life which the romancers had imputed to the South Sea Islands. Here was an almost incredible busyness; day and night, the roads were full of people walking with a light and swinging step under heavy loads; the air was never empty of music, even in the small hours before the dawn; and it was not mere woodland piping but complicated orchestrated music which bore witness to many hours of concentrated rehearsal. Upon the hundreds of stone altars of Bali, there lay not merely a fruit and a flower, placed as a visible prayer to the many gods, but hundreds of finely wrought and elaborately conceived offerings made of palm leaf and flowers, twisted, folded, stitched, embroidered, brocaded into myriad traditional forms and fancies. There were flowers made of sugar and combined into representations of the rainbow, and swords and spears cut from the snow-white fat of sacrificial pigs. The whole world was patterned, from the hillsides elaborately terraced to give the maximum rice yield to the air which was shot through with music, the temple gates festooned with temporary palm-leaf arras over their permanent carved façade to the crowd of people who, as they lounged, watching an opera or clustered about two fighting cocks, composed themselves into a frieze. The most casual and unanalytic tourist recognized that these people were contented and gay not because they lived in a salubrious climate, where they could find food without work and love without responsibility, but because their lives were packed with intricate and formal delights. And the tourist wondered. For wasn't his own life full, crowded with striving and effort?—yet he was not content. What difference was it between the Balinese way of packing the hours and our way that brought them contentment and relaxation to which music and dancing and gay laughter are the natural accompaniment, while we had so much strain and fatigue, grumbling and discontent, and weariness of living?

The South Sea daydream summed up one view of life—that it was complicated organization, multiplication of needs, and demands at the expense of the simpler satisfactions that made man unhappy. If only we could return to a world in which man made few demands upon the universe and could find a soft and sunny climate—it was the climate and not the social order that was to make life satisfying—all would be well.

But when we look over a whole series of primitive societies—and primitive societies are good material on this problem because there we can study whole living social systems meeting the needs of their members in traditional and slowly changing ways—we find societies with a minimum of symbolic forms and societies with a maximum. We find people like the Lepchas of Sikkim, whom Geoffrey Gorer described so vividly in *Himalayan Village*,[1] who have virtually no symbolic life at all; the children play hardly any games and the adults' idea of a festival is an occasion on which to eat and drink to repletion. Like the Balinese, the Lepchas are a quite well-fed people, although both have to work hard to produce a surplus. This surplus, however, the Lepchas simply eat up and drink up in conviviality, while the Balinese consume their surplus in far more complicated ways, in rice cakes which the village women have shaped into a goddess, in gold leaf spread in square yards over cremation towers which will glitter for an hour above the treetops and then are dismantled and burned, in feeding the members of five orchestras to play at once for one ceremony. The great emphasis upon artistic expression in Bali immediately raises the question: What sort of people are the Balinese artists? Is their excessive preoccupation with symbolic activities the result of neurosis? What sort of society is Bali? Is it the sort of society in which people escape from the miserable realities of their everyday life into the arts? Are we, then, to conclude that the Lepchas are all normal, happy people, and the Balinese all maladjusted neurotics suffering from maiming during childhood?

For if we have been tutored by some forms of psychoanalytic thought, we associate the arts with neuroses; if by economic determinism, with drugs and opiates which keep the minds of the oppressed from their wrongs and the minds of the oppressors from their sins. From either of these points of view, art, and religion, and the whole symbolic structure by which man has made his universe meaningful, are definitely dated and will pass away in a better world. When hiatuses in his own soul, the result of faulty education, or hiatuses in the social order, the result of a faultily organized society, are remedied, the man of the future will face reality without crutches and blinders and eyeshades; he will see life sanely and see it whole, stripped of the trappings of unreality with which his ancestors have found it necessary to bedizen it. Both these views—that which sees the artist as a maimed personality and that which sees the arts as softening the harshness of an unfair social system—condemn the arts, especially the arts with "escape plots" as over against the arts which are merely patterned stimuli to sensuous experience.

But in Bali it is impossible to regard every contributor to the arts

[1] London, M. Joseph, 1938.

as a deviant, a misfit, a maimed individual who seeks to heal his diseased soul through artistic expression. My husband and I made a collection of casual carvings from a mountain village, carvings which in the cleverness and resourcefulness with which they express, in outrageous and grotesque forms, fears and attitudes toward the human body, can be paralleled only from children's psychotic wards or the purposely disassociated products of the Surrealists. Yet these carvings are not the work of one or two specially aberrant or specially gifted individuals but of some sixty male inhabitants of a village of about eight hundred people; and the carvers ranged in age from seven to seventy, and in physique and character they ran the whole gamut of Balinese personality. They differed from their fellow citizens in that they knew how to carve rather better, and perhaps gave less time to dancing or to music—that was all. Otherwise they were simple Balinese peasants working within a flexible tradition which allows fancy free play.

In the same way the Balinese dancer, with tranced expression, going through his intricate and highly patterned dance; the clown, improvising with inexhaustible fertility among well-worn clichés; the priest, every movement of whose delicate, jeweled hands is a prayer— these have not different characters from the members of the audience who watch their performances and comment critically on a false step, turn away from an inept pun, or kneel at the tinkle of the priest's bell. There are exceedingly gifted Balinese, dancers or musicians who stand head and shoulders above the rest. But, although the difference in standard of artistic performance is so great, there seems to be no more reason to believe that the proportion of genius in Bali exceeds that in any other country than to assume a difference in structure of character between the performers and the spectators.

The arts are practiced in some small part by all, for there is no girl so unskilled that she cannot construct offerings and no man so inept that he can play no musical instrument. These are part and parcel of the daily life of the average Balinese. They are as much a part of it as the structure of his self-governing village community, or the efficient system of irrigating rice fields. This puts a different color upon the various theories that have condemned the arts.

It is necessary to ask over again, in other terms, what is the difference between the society in which the arts are an integral part of everyday life, enriching it and enhancing it, and the society in which the arts are almost wholly dispensed with? Should we assume in the Balinese a sixth sense, an aesthetic sense, which the Lepchas lack, or should we regard the whole Balinese personality as essentially maimed and so needing escape, or the whole Balinese social system as rotten and needing a panacea? Should the play to which the people flock be regarded as Cinderella meeting the dreams of the little shop girl, or as "bread and circuses" for the people?

It is true that the aesthetic sensibilities of the Balinese are developed far beyond our own, that in flexibility and skill of performance, in interest and appreciation, the simplest peasant approaches our idea of connoisseurship, muttering with disapproval over a false note or a badly turned step. It is also true that the potential artistic ability is very high, that with very little encouragement or training, orchestras and dance clubs can be made to flourish in villages which have not known these special forms within the memory of the present generation. The Balinese child is exposed from infancy to a gesture, posture system, to a way of walking and a type of attitude which makes him early susceptible to the more formal patterns of movement and sound which are characteristic of his culture. The style of the Balinese arts is imbedded deep in the form of the simplest acts of everyday living. From the point of early determinative experience, everyone born a Balinese may be said to have a high aesthetic capacity, both as potential performer and as critical spectator.

We can, furthermore, add the obvious fact that enduring and beautiful artistic expression demands style; it demands a rich and living artistic tradition upon which the gifted can be nurtured, that they may provide food for the ardent but less gifted spectators, listeners, readers. And artistic styles develop slowly, with deep roots in the social life of a people. The history of European arts has demonstrated over and over again how dependent the great artist is upon his period, how helpless he is when there are no living forms ready to his hand. It is possible that there are very basic ways in which the arts may be integrated into social life, so that there is a sturdy, deep-rooted tradition upon which genius can feed. And it is to societies like Bali that we may well turn to examine this question.

And although we may say that the Balinese artistic abilities are learned with the gestures of everyday life combined with early exposure to the rich traditional forms, as children fringe the front rows of every audience, as the small boy sits on his father's lap while his father plays in the orchestra, or the small girl cuts out simple palm-leaf designs while she watches her mother cut out intricate ones —that is to give an account of the *how* but not to answer the question of the *why* of the hypertrophy of artistic expression in Bali. It does not explain why the Lepchas are content with meat and drink, while the Balinese have an insatiable appetite for an elaborate patterning of the world. To explain this difference, I think we must turn to the experiences of childhood.

Let us assume that the human child is born into the world with a primary system of already patterned and defined needs and with a capacity for taking on further series (or systems) of acquired needs, which may also be patterned. Each human society meets the needs of the child's developing individuality in different ways. Those societies which, like the Lepchas, display slight symbolic forms, subject the child to few strains, and, by definition, expose him to few complex and patterned stimuli; they neither deny nor overemphasize the child's early needs, so that no one of these needs becomes so intensified that it can be satisfied only by more intense and elaborate means, and therefore none remains relatively insatiable. They do not present new stimuli to ear and eye and touch with which to arouse and pattern the child's developing sensuousness. And such children grow up with no need for and no capacity to enjoy symbolic forms, either as performer or as spectator.

But in societies like Bali, where an unusually large part of human energy goes not into eating and drinking, sleeping and making love, but into the arts, children are brought up differently. Each need of the developing child is not satisfied simply and inevitably, as it appears, but instead there are areas of understimulation and areas of over-stimulation which so pattern the developing organism as to make it demand other satisfactions than food and drink and sex. One of these special needs which is developed in Balinese children is the need for symbolic activity—playing a musical instrument, cutting out offering designs, titivating a fighting cock, or watching a play (for the attitude of the Balinese spectator differs from ours in that the spectator identi-fies himself not with the character but with the acting, not with the prince lost in the wood, but with the technical accomplishments of the actor who performs the role). This emphasis, this need for symbolic activities, is different from the familiar picture of the puritan goaded by an uneasy conscience to more and more industriousness, or the housewife who is never contented with the polish she has given to her household gods. These things are not done as a propitiatory offering to some grim, introjected sense of duty. They are done because in the performance of these rhythmic, sensuous actions the Balinese feels safe in a world which his training has made him feel to be undifferen-tiatedly full of vague terror. The tone in his mother's voice, the tensing of her arm, her use of terror words—*tiger, wildcat, scorpion, witch*—whenever she wishes to deter him from any act, have intensified this fear. He may later learn that there are very few tigers in Bali and that wildcats only scratch, but he does not lose the fear which, in his mother's voice, was as deep and intense as the choice of her words was casual and random. From playing upon such human potentialities as these, the impetus toward symbolic activity is developed—to a greater degree in some individuals than in others.

And for every intensified sensuousness, every need for rhythmic expression, the culture is ready with a dozen available answers. The Balinese, who might be miserable without his orchestras, his rituals, his theatricals, never realizes his misery, any more than the shut-in child of an inventive mother will never know boredom as long as his mother can produce a new and diverting toy. If his culture has developed needs and desires which can never be satisfied on the simple biological level, it has also generously provided forms which meet these needs and give satisfactions of another order also.

We see this not only in the rhythmic activities in which the Balinese take timeless delight but also in the plots which their artistic forms embody. In looking at any people's arts, it is possible to consider them primarily as intricate patterns giving sensuous satisfaction only—as is the case with pure design, or with Balinese music—or we can see them as the statement of some basic plot which generations of that people have found so meaningful and relevant that it has become embodied in literature and drama, in painting and sculpture, and by its continued appearance there has continued to feed the need which originally stimulated its embodiment in artistic forms. So the primary plot themes of Bali, the struggle between mankind and the witch who brings death, who is so powerful that she can turn the daggers of her attackers back against their own chests; the rivalry between the elder and the younger brother; the tragedy of the man who finds he has married not the beautiful princess of his dreams but her ugly and ill-favored sister—these plots are grounded firmly in the childhood experiences of the Balinese, in his experience of a remote, faintly teasing mother who will not meet the responses which she has mischievously aroused but turns unconcerned from the child's impassioned pleas; in the reiterated admonitions to the elder child to give in to the younger and to the younger to defer to the elder; in the fear that the woman he marries will be a familiar and unfascinating cousin, forced on him by the bad mother, the witch, instead of a glamorous stranger, a princess. These childhood fears and agonies are sharp and poignant; left to fester unexpressed, they might easily lead to maladjustment, to deep unhappiness, and perhaps, in the rare and gifted individual, to some artistic expression. But in Bali they are not left to fester but are given continuous expression in the traditional art forms. At festivals the witch mask is brought out; in the shadow play the same drama is enacted; in the dance forms, in the religious trance, in the children's mimetic play, the fear of the witch is relived but never completely exorcised—for, another week, the play goes on with the same spectators, the same actors, so as to give satisfaction to a people whose common childhood experience is being reenacted, to lend contentment to their faces and unstrained gaiety to their laughter.

The Balinese material, placed side by side with material from other primitive societies and from our own society, suggests a number of possible ways in which man may develop his relationship to his world. He may construct a culture which puts few special strains on children, develops no deep unsatisfied longings, no insatiabilities, but permits them to grow up in an uncomplex world. In such a world, children will be happy if the very simple needs which they have developed are satisfied; if there is food and drink, a bed and an available sex partner. Such a society will be good, in the sense that it satisfies the needs of its members, but it will be poor, dull, and impoverished when compared with those societies which have developed rich and intricate symbolic systems. Or, man may shape his culture, as the Balinese have done, so that there is a symbolic answer for every need which is patterned in the growing child. The young child may be taught to know terror and frustration, bitterness of rejection and cruel loneliness of spirit very young, and yet grow up to be a gay and light-footed adult because, for every tension of the threads which have been twisted or double-woven in the delicate mesh of the child's spirit, the culture has a symbolic relaxation ready. And so Bali is a good society, meeting the much more elaborate needs of its elaborately patterned members.

If these were the only alternatives, the two theories which condemn the arts would never have arisen, and the problem would be as simple as the choice between clothing and no clothing; some would perhaps choose a society in which children, taught to go barefoot in the snow, went barefoot gladly as adults; others, societies in which the growing foot was fitted to ballet shoes in which it would later take intricate dance steps. But, unfortunately, there is another path open to man. He may construct a society in which the human beings grow up to demand more than meat and drink, in which the frustrations, the excitements, the high points of childhood experience have made them, too, insatiable, but in which the symbolic answers take another form. We in America and in Europe have followed neither the simple ways of the Lepchas nor the complex ways of the Balinese. More and more children have grown up, insecure and frightened, clutching at any support, frustrated and embittered, until symbols of power and conquest and destruction have become frighteningly congruent with their needs. Totalitarian states have capitalized these needs, have built symbols so relevant that they have been able to turn out armies of youth marching willingly to destroy and be destroyed. Today, even the Balinese on their tiny island, with their good society, are no longer safe; their *rajă putri*, their white queen under whose rule their way of life was respected and conserved, is in exile. Tomorrow destruction may come to their terraced green valleys which yielded food enough for all, just as destruction has come to so many small countries, each in its own terms seeking for the good society.

Many Americans in the 1920s sought for an escape as single individuals from a society which denied them self-expression. Many in the 1930s sought for a formula by which we could build our society into a form which would make possible, on a firm economic base, both simple happiness and complexity of spiritual expression. Of such a dream, Bali was a fitting symbol. We in the 1940s face two new problems. If democracy is to survive, we must develop a set of symbols which will be meaningful and fulfilling for all those born within our gates, symbols of life instead of symbols of death. This is no mean task in a society where so many have known and are experiencing extreme poverty and insecurity, and in a world where the number of the homeless is increasing by thousands every hour. Yet, if democracy is to prevail, we must meet this challenge, and with a set of symbols which are better than those the totalitarians have to offer. As our second problem, we must face the knowledge that it is no longer enough to plan a good society, here in America, but that any plan we make must be part of a world picture; for the borders of our lives have widened until they include the fate of the whole world.

Community Drama, Bali and America

MARGARET MEAD

"I HAVE A NICHE in my house at home," the tourist visitor to Bali told me. "I had it made ten years ago when I built my house and I have been waiting all these years to find just the perfect statue or carving to fill it. I want you to find me, here in Bali where they make so many beautiful things, something to put into my niche." She didn't believe my answer—that although I should have no difficulty at all in finding her a dozen charming, delicate carvings, I could not find her "one perfect carving" for her niche. Yet in her request and my answer was summed up the present difference between art in Bali, in which everyone from the poorest peasant to the proudest prince or priest can share, and art in America which is practiced by the few and ignored by the many. In the comparison there may lie some clues to the problem which concerns and perplexes all who are interested in American culture.

A Balinese village or palace court or temple has something of the quality of a sculptor's studio with its half-finished and just-begun statues standing about draped in wet cloths. Here a gateway is just receiving the finishing touches; there an old gateway, carved long ago, is finally sagging to the ground; somewhere else a third gate presents the solid crude surfaces of blocks of tufa which may not be carved for another twenty years. Nowhere does one find a dwelling unit or a temple which can be said to be complete, in perfect repair, and finished. In such a place a Balinese would feel uncomfortable; there

Originally published in *The American Scholar*, XI, No. 1 (January, 1942), 79–88. Reprinted with permission of the author.

would be nothing for the dozens of extra hands to do when three times too many people are gathered to prepare for a feast, no uncompleted work for the gods to chide gently about during routine trances, no new work for the gods.

A theatrical club may have, you think, a fine set of costumes—beautifully woven textiles and resplendent headdresses of golden leather set with semiprecious stones. But the members of the club will tell you that these costumes are just a beginning—really the princess's headdress is very inferior and they always have to borrow the kris that the prince carries. Long before the costumes attain anything like the level the club members regard as desirable the club will have dissolved or changed its form of expression, slipped away like the unfinished gateway that sags to ruins before it is completed. Nothing is ever finished. There is no goal toward which an individual or a group work intensively, sinking into anticlimax when it is attained. The Balinese, whether they be musicians or actors or carvers, are primarily interested in the process, not in any fixed result.

When the young men or the young men and girls or the small children of a Balinese village decide to form a club to play some particular type of music, dance a ballet, or give some special type of play or opera, the interest of the rest of the village fastens not on the final performance, as it does in America when a group of amateurs decides to attempt a play or a concert, but on the rehearsals. While the principals laboriously practice and practice, sometimes under the tutelage of a teacher especially imported, sometimes under the casual guidance of the visitor to the village who is known to be skilled, the other members of the community stand about in rapt attention, enjoying the mild commotion of the rehearsal and meting out untender laughter to mistakes and clumsiness. Some day the club will have attained enough skill to make a formal debut at a temple feast or a birthday party but this will merely mean that the club is "out," performing in the clear as it were, and not that it has reached its climax. Instead there will be more rehearsals, more schemes to acquire costumes or musical instruments or skilled teachers. And in every such club there are members who never perform, who neither sing nor dance nor act, whose only function it is to attend rehearsals or be fined, and finally to share, when the club breaks up, in the division of any funds that may have accumulated. When a new club is being formed —which is spoken of as "the x-club is looking about for members"— no question is asked as to the special skill or accomplishment of prospective members. You get your group together and see what you have.

If any special skill is lacking it will be necessary to search further. You may have to import a teacher to train your dancers from the start. Those among the group who are least good at any art will practice it least often and then only when those who are better at it are tired or ill or ceremonially incapacitated from participation. Club practice might be summed up as being "from each according to his ability and to each the same sense of participating," including fines and shares of fines.

This interest in rehearsals, and the tendency of nonperformers and slightly-skilled persons to cluster into clubs on an equal footing with the performers, work to transform the participation of the audience. Every audience is composed of individuals interested in how it is done, the way the dancer is moving her hands, the way in which the actor is singing, the skill with which the comic servant is punning, the gaiety and daring of the drummer's improvisations. When the shadow play is given, part of the audience sits in front of the screen to enjoy the shadows as they flicker against the swinging light; but another part, including most of the boys, are seated *behind* the screen, watching how the puppets are manipulated and how the puppeteer makes a thunderous noise by tapping on his box with a plug of wood held between his toes—both his hands being occupied with the puppets. And the puppets, theoretically supposed to be seen only as shadows, are carefully painted on both sides, every detail executed with minute delight.

This delight in the art of acting rather than in the play, in the way in which the music is played rather than in the music, in the mechanics of the greenroom rather than in the play itself, is essentially Balinese and depends of course upon the Balinese character, with its preoccupation with activity for its own sake and its studied avoidance of climax and of identification.[1]

The interest of a small American community in the theatrical arts can take several forms. The members of a community can band together to pay companies of professional actors to give in their community, in one-night stands, plays that have been successful on Broadway. This happens continually in Bali. Traveling players—sometimes players who have been received with acclaim at a court and must be paid a very substantial sum for their services, sometimes just boys and

---

[1]For a more detailed discussion of this point see Margaret Mead, "The Arts in Bali," *Yale Review*, XXX, No. 2 (December, 1940), 335–47, and her "Researches in Bali, 1936–1939; on the Concept of Plot in Culture," *Transactions of the New York Academy of Sciences*, Ser. II, Vol. II, No. 1 (November, 1939), pp. 1–4.

girls of the next village on tour—come for one-night stands, presenting at least part of their repertoire for the local community. Subsequently, especially after the forty-two days following the Galungan, Feast of All Souls, held every 210 days, new steps, new twists and turns and sophistications, appear in the performances of the local actors. And here lies the difference. In America, after a good play has been presented by a good company, the drama club may discuss the plot, the club's recording secretary will include the event in her report of the club's activities for the year, somebody's daughter may become stage-struck and start off for New York, two or three schoolgirls may set the actor's picture up on their dressing tables—otherwise the artistic life of the community remains unaltered. The simplest Balinese peasant, standing in his earth-stained clothes after a day of backbreaking labor in the rice fields, watches a highly trained dancer with a cool and critical eye, withholding praise and approval if it is at all possible, appraising, judging, practicing in imagination, whereas the members of an American village audience feel an unbridgeable gap between the actors and themselves, however easy they may find it to see themselves as the heroes and heroines of the theatrical story.

The play-reading group was another form of community interest in the theater which once flourished among the women's clubs of America. In this the very life of the play was destroyed, all emphasis on presentation vanished in a discussion of the fine details of plot construction by people who never, even in their imaginations, hoped to become playwrights. Here again there was no connection between the group and the dramatic material they were handling. Their sole aim was to demonstrate erudition in identifying elements in the plot which literary criticism had found it convenient to label and catalog.

We come next to the "Little Theater" movements, the setting up of clubs by people actually interested in putting on plays—in acting, costuming, or stage setting. These, for the club members, come closer to the Balinese position. Interested in performance, they try to achieve a standard of excellence that will successfully measure up to some professional standard, at least to the standard of an older, larger, richer little-theater movement. But here again there is one great difference —the rehearsals are secret. Interlopers are thrown out, actors and actresses are overcome with embarrassment if any nonparticipant intrudes upon the rehearsals, and a line is drawn between the cast and the rest of the town. The latter are supposed to serve as audience and as such must have an ignorance of the details that will render them passively astonished and admiring. To the extent that the community "supports" its Little Theater it cuts itself off from active participation in the theater. Usually, also, the bulk of the community is cut off from the little-theater performance by the type of play selected. The members of the little-theater club are looking for the Drama; they want to experiment only with the sort of plays written for the intelligentsia of the cities. Their desire to act is born in most cases not of their pleasant contentment with life in their communities but of their scorn for their narrowness and littleness, their provincial, corn-belt quality. But this scorn, which might be transmuted into a lively irony or scathing caricature of the local population, is instead used to create distance between the community and the play, and finds expression in a choice of plays which almost no one will understand or enjoy. Yet it will be objected, with some validity, that the older form of community drama—in which a school or club group purchased some atrocity called "Three Kisses" or "Her Second Husband" in little pamphlets and performed it to the great joy of the local audience (a joy based mainly on the *double entendres* provided by the coincidences of casting and plot)—never produced any real community theater; its aim was too low, its material too cheap.

So we come to the final alternative: that the local group members write the play themselves—the dream, in fact, of the extreme regionalist, the extreme believer in the fertility of the grass roots. But this demand—that the dramatist be produced locally, in large enough quantities to keep the community-theater projects running all over the country—has expected to turn back, without revision and to the folk level, an artistic form that has reached a great height of artistic creativeness, has expected every village green to produce its Eugene O'Neill. We have kept our standard of individual creativeness, possible only to the genius, at the same time that we have tried for greater participation on the part of the community. Cultivating the grass roots has meant, in effect, scratching in the cornfield for "mute inglorious Miltons." We have tried to bridge the gap between the great dramatic tradition of the capital cities of the world and the capabilities of the small town at the top of the gap instead of at the bottom.

The old minstrel show with its opportunities for local gags and improvised wit gave to local talent a formal outlet that any attempt to write in imitation of a "drama" will never give, and at the same time was free from the tawdriness of the ready-make product. And here again we find a Balinese parallel. In structure the typical Balinese play, which includes acting, singing, dancing, and accompanying music, is rather like a Shakespearian comedy, if we can imagine that each group of performers learns only the parts played by the serious characters, leaving the parts played by servants, clowns, gravediggers, attendants, etc., to be improvised by the local talent. King and queen, prince and princess move through a Balinese play with the same stately gestures whether the part is played by a Brahmană or a person of low caste, by a portly *rajă* or a humble fisherman. The ancient and almost unintelligible language, the fixed poetic measures, the stereotyped gestures, although performed with an almost unbelievable range of skills, are all attempts to approximate one model. They provide the form, rescue the most inept performance from cheapness, maintain a tradition that permeates the whole performance. But the proportion of the play which is theirs is seldom more than a third; the other two thirds of the time belong to the people—to the actors, to the spectators (who sometimes become actors in very truth as the clowns chase one another in and out of the audience). For, to enjoy the complicated improvisations of Balinese comedy, one must attend the rehearsals, and one must also have seen a great many performances of varying degrees of skill. One troupe of players whom we engaged for a special celebration spent two hours in giving us a demonstration —from their point of view bound to delight us—of the way the same cast had performed a different play, working out a double play upon two types of acting and two types of rendering of the roles. The peasant audience, skilled in phantasy participation in every piece of acting they had ever seen, doubled up with laughter.

If we are to have community drama to which the members of the community can make a genuine artistic contribution, there must be a place within the *form* itself for that contribution. I say within the form, for it is too much to ask them to create the form *de novo*, and it is too little to ask them merely to reproduce it in order to perform it once before an audience given too little participation to realize and appreciate their skill. But to allow for such a contribution within the form means a return to faith in the performer, in his wit and resourcefulness, which has practically vanished from contemporary life. It would be, in fact, a real return to the grass roots. To write a play whose main characters will have the dignity and universal significance of great drama but in which there will be room for the agile tongue and graceful wit of the gifted of each small community—that is a feat no one has attempted since the reign of Elizabeth. Everyone recognizes those places in a Shakespearian play in which the actors simply walk through their lines, no matter how well they act, because the lines are greater than they. In genuine grass-roots drama such lines would be needed to provide a framework within which the little gifts of local men could be given free play.

Historically just such a framework has been provided by a great theme, as in the miracle plays, or by a great style, as in the European ballet in which a comparatively poor performance echoed the stylization of the model. So long as the story of Creation was ready to hand, the local tanner and tailor could play their comic roles with dignity; when the second-rate dancer worked hard on a style that had attained completeness, the ineptness of the execution did not make it cheap or tawdry. But an attempt to draw whole masterpieces, with no guidelines of theme or plot or style, out of each local genius is a kind of travesty of the whole history of art. The task of the community theater is to find a form wherein a great tradition can meet and be actively, continuously, creatively used by those whose gifts are small.

Colin McPhee[2] has described how, in the Balinese treatment of music, the contribution of the individual leader or the local club lies in the manner in which the music is played rather than in the composition of new music. So much freedom is left to each orchestra to improvise, to embroider and to alter the emphases of a traditional piece of music that in a sense each composition, beautiful in its basic conformity to an exacting tradition, *is* new after any group has rehearsed it for several months. The peasant, the vendor, the potter who has worked all day with the tireless, dreamy industry of the Balinese, comes to his evening rehearsal, not to learn how to do something that has already been done a thousand times, and much better than he could do it (the position of the little groups that meet to play chamber music in this country), but to change, to add, to recreate a piece of music as familiar as his own breath and as potentially different as the new year. Round about the group that is rehearsing will sit other men, who also play musical instruments. They will be listening, enjoying the nuances and the changes, with hands cupped in readiness for the moment when some player tires or slips away for a rest and some one of the audience can take his place. For every Balinese man is, for part of his life—if that be only once a month when the orchestra of his temple plays for its special temple feast—a professional musician. And herein lies another secret of the Balinese handling of the arts. There is almost no folk art in Bali; none of the clumsy, untutored,

[2]Colin McPhee, "The 'Absolute' Music of Bali," *Modern Music*, XII, No. 4 (1935), 163–69.

traditional performance which has had its quality given it by the
abbreviating and purifying influence of time and often by very little
else. In a few mountain villages, in a few temples, there are religious
ceremonies performed very seldom and carried out by individuals
selected for some reason other than their skill. But these are rare. For
the most part the simplest artistic act in Bali is performed with an
attempt to approximate a professional standard. The special teacher
who, articulately and consciously, teaches for a fee the student who
applies himself to learn, and the group that rehearses and discusses its
performances and strives to improve its work—these are found everywhere. The distinction between amateur activities (our modern version of folk activities) and work done seriously is missing in Bali. One
plants rice, prays to the gods, or plays a musical instrument without
differences of mood, with due attention to established traditional
procedure. For in the arts, to any society that has once known conscious creativeness, the touch of the most highly developed form is
life-giving—if that touch can be made sufficiently gentle. People who
count Shakespeare among their traditions cannot attain dignity by
producing nothing above the level of a college junior show; asked to
produce nothing but Shakespeare, their chance to add something of
their own is too slight, and their interest wilts and dies.

Without, therefore, essaying the impossible task of turning modern
Americans into Balinese, there are various lines along which those
who lead the community arts movement might work. They might
stimulate the production of plays written expressly with the idea that
each group acting them shall add something of its own. They might
propagate the idea that it is the whole act of producing a play that is
interesting, that the lines drawn between the greenroom and the
audience are tiresome—a product of silly overemphasis on stage
realism with its horses prancing on moving tracks, grand-opera boats
coming ashore and other pieces of nonsense. The Balinese theater,
like the Elizabethan stage, is totally innocent of such claptrap, but not
so the primitive theater of the New Guinea head-hunter, whose
primary aim is to impress and mystify the women. For him the greenroom, drums that warn the women to hide their heads while he carries
his contraptions through the village, mysterious ropes and gadgets to
make giant feather snakes lollop enticingly over the heads of admiring
crowds of impressed females, are indispensable properties. On his
primitive stage the whole point is the secret—the secret and the
audience to be impressed by his stage tricks. And if by mistake the
women see through some of their transparent devices, the men go into

childish outbursts of rage, their house of cards collapses about their vain and vulnerable ears.

If it were possible to develop in American life a pattern in which everyone in the community took an interest in rehearsals, and the town gossip centered about how the leading man was getting on with his part; in which everyone turned out for the fun of seeing the coach from the big city criticize and correct the local rendering; in which a play was never given the same way twice and the whole style was altered in the middle because half the cast had just seen a play given by another community in a different style, we might then begin to approximate the community participation that makes the arts in Bali so vital a factor in the life of every member of every community.

A Study of a Balinese Family

JANE BELO

Introductory Note

OF A PEOPLE numbering more than a million, divided into castes, into districts which have felt the varying influences of separate dynasties of rulers, and whose religion and social structure appear in all forms from the ancient Bali-agă to the orthodox order of the Sivaite and Buddhist *pĕdandă*, one would be bold indeed to attempt a study of *the family*. There are no statistics, and generalizations are almost certain to be, in some sense, false. But it is true that more than 90 percent of the Balinese are Sudră, the fourth and lowest Hindu caste, called in Bali *jabă*, or outsiders. This is to distinguish them from the Brahmană, Ksatriyă, and Wĕsyă, who claim descent from the Hindu-Javanese invaders of Majapahit, conquerors of the island in the fourteenth century. These *jabă* are, then, more "insiders" that outsiders, the real Balinese. They are organized into village groups, the *dĕsă*, each with its council to which belong all married men who are house-holders. The *dĕsă* has its individual *adat* (customary law), functioning quite apart from the laws laid down by the *rajă* of the past or the present Dutch administration. The village has a suborganization into two or more *banjar*, spatial divisions, each with its own meeting place for the men. The *banjar* may once have been divisions of family groups, but now they resemble clubs, which rival each other in *gamelan* and theatrical performances, whose young men nourish a feud, and whose children dare not cross the invisible line which limits their own *banjar*, lest they be set upon by "the other gang." Religion to the *jabă* means the regular giving of offerings to the spirit of his

Originally published in *American Anthropologist*, New Ser. XXXVIII, No. 1 (1936), 12–31.

ancestors, in his own *sanggah*, or household temple; offerings to the
gods in the village temples, under the tutelage of the *pĕmangku*, a
priest also of *jabă* caste; propitiation of demons and bad spirits, on the
roadside before the house, at the crossroads, the graveyard; and only
occasionally a pilgrimage to one of the temples of mountain-gods, sea-,
lake-, and sacred spring-gods; proper and suitable celebration, with
offerings and performances according to his means, of births, birthdays, tooth-filings, weddings, deaths, cremations, etc., in the family.
As a rule it is only when some difficulty arises in the carrying out of
the ordinary prescribed rites that the *jabă* turns to the Hindu high
priest, the *pĕdandă*, for advice, and still more rarely, for his offices.

It has occurred to me that a study of one such ordinary Balinese—
one of the 900,000 *jabă*—in his family relations, might be of value,
not to lay down any rules but simply as an illustration of certain
common phenomena in the mores.

I have chosen, therefore, an ordinary family, in an ordinary village,
lying halfway between the modern town, where the old customs are
perforce breaking down, and the region of the old-style Bali-agă
villages which in their isolation have preserved an order which is
today more of a curiosity in Bali, not characteristic of the country as
a whole. And so, although it must not be concluded that what has
happened in this family is what necessarily would happen in any
Balinese family, still the procedures may be taken as fairly typical—
if one remembers that variations are great from village to village, and
that the customs of the high-caste Balinese, as well as those of the
Bali-agă villages are not represented in the general picture.

A Balinese Family

Rendah is the head of his household and therefore a *pengajă*, member
of the village council. He owns his own *pĕkarangan*, a walled courtyard within the village limits, enclosing the shrines of his household
gods, the living quarters of his immediate family, and the place of the
pigs and fowls. He owns also a sufficient portion of the irrigated rice
fields surrounding the village for the maintenance of his family. The
fields are tilled by himself, his brothers, and their sons when they are
old enough. All the old people and the dependent women and children
get enough to eat. If the crop is good and there is rice left over, it may
be sold in the market. The women cook and weave cloth (*kamben*) for
the family and carry up fresh water from the spring, night and morning. The small girls of five or six begin to help their mothers and
aunts at this task, balancing a coconut shell full of water on their erect

heads. The little boys of the same age take charge of the ducks and the
water buffalo, driving them out into the inundated rice fields at
sunrise, driving them back to their shelters near the house-court at
dusk.

Rendah has one wife, Rieh, who has borne him nine children.
Three of these died in infancy. His eldest, a girl, he has just given in
marriage to her paternal parallel second cousin, the eldest son of Gari,
Rendah's own paternal parallel cousin (Fig. 1, I). This girl, Tingglih,
has "followed her husband" and now lives across the street in the
house of her father-in-law Gari. Only five children remain in Rendah's house.

Rendah himself was one of eight children, also borne to his father
by one wife (Fig. 2, II). The children, in the order of their birth,

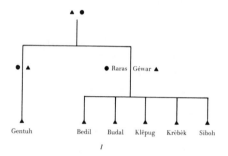

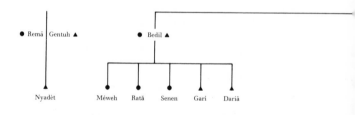

FIG. 2. Genealogies of Balinese families

receive title-names, as follows:

Wayan—First-born; Madé—Second-born;
Nyoman—Third-born; Kĕtut—Fourth-born.

If there are more than four children the series begins over again, and
the fifth child is Wayan, the sixth Madé, and so forth. Every *jabă*
must have one of these title-names, which precedes his given name.
The given name is chosen by a system of divination through fire,
from a group of names suitable to a child born on a certain day of the
astrological calendar. It is rarely used, except when speaking to children and to inferiors in age and in social status. To use the title-name
is always more polite, and compulsory for inferiors in age and in social
status. Thus Rendah, although he is the eldest son, was the fourth-
born of his family. He is called Kĕtut by his equals, or I Kĕtut Rendah
when they are speaking about him, to distinguish him from other

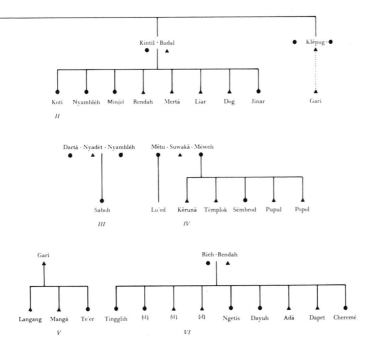

Kĕtuts. After the birth of his first child he is called 'Pan Tingglih,[1] father of Tingglih, and this appellation is still more polite and proper to be used by strangers, equals, and inferiors. All his younger brothers

[1] *Pan* is the abbreviation of *bapan*, from *bapă*, father, with the possessive -n. In certain mountain districts the old word *'nang*, shortened from *nanang*, father, is used. Similarly *bibi* for mother or aunt, is sometimes found instead of the usual *mémé*. On the island of Nusă Pĕnidă, belonging to Bali but with a distinctive dialect, *bibi* and *bébé* are in use for mother and aunt as well as *mémé*, and *maman* for paternal or maternal uncle, reserving *nanang* for the biological father. In Balinese classical literature *paman* is used for uncle and as a familiar form of address to older men (as a

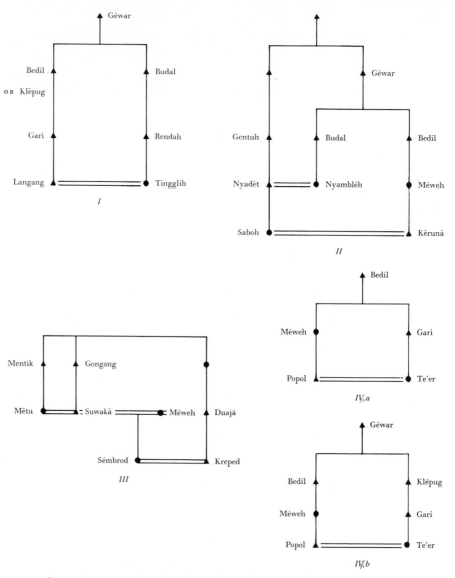

FIG. 1. Genealogies of Balinese families

and cousins call him *bli*, elder brother. His own children, his nephews, and the children of his first and second cousins on both the male and the female sides call him *bapă*, father. In speaking of him, the children of his younger brothers and cousins may call him *uă*, elder uncle (or aunt). His wife generally calls him *bli*, elder brother, or *Kĕtut*, his title-name, and sometimes even *bapă*, as the father of her children. She, as his inferior, may not call him by his given name, Rendah. But he may call her by her given name, although he is more likely to use her title-name, or to call her *mémé*, mother. When Tingglih's first child is born, Rendah and Rieh will be known as Pĕkak——and

young prince speaking to his father's minister). In Malay *paman* may be used in the latter way, though its original meaning is maternal uncle. *Ibu*, mother, and *jajah* or *aji*, father, occur also in the literature. *Ibu* and *aji* are current high Balinese, and *biang*, mother, is found among high-caste people used as a title-name. *Rĕramă* is another old form for mother, found in the texts. *Kaki*, grandfather, appears in the literature more often than the current *pĕkak*. *Nini* and *néné*, old forms for grandmother, are rarely found outside the texts. *Nini* is still in use as the name for the rice-goddess of the harvest ritual, although apparently not universally known.

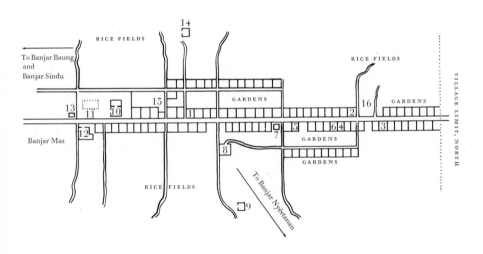

1 house of the great-grandfather, Gentuh-Nyadèt-Kĕrună	9 *pură pĕnataran*, temple
2 house of Géwar-Klĕpug-Gari	10 *pură désă* and *pură pusĕh*, village temple and temple of origin
3 house of Bedil-Dariă	11 *pĕkĕn*, village market place
4 house of Budal-Rendah	12 *puri*, "palace" of the *chokordă*
5 house of Mertă	13 *balè banjar* of Banjar Mas
6 house of Suwakă	14 *pură nagasari*, temple
7 *balé banjar* of Kutuh, meeting house of the men	15 *pură panti*, temple
8 *pură dalĕm*, temple of the dead	16 *semă*, village graveyard and cremation place

FIG. 3. Map of Banjar Kutuh, Village of Sayan

Dadong——, Grandfather of——and Grandmother of——followed by the given name of the child. Thus a man's own name tends to die out even during his own lifetime, as he grows older, and there is no one left to "speak down" to him.

Rendah's eldest sister, Wayan Koti, was married, and later "thrown away." She returned to her father's house. As Rendah has inherited house and household, she now lives within his courts, sharing in the work of the women. The second sister, Madé Njambléh, was given in marriage to the son of her father's male paternal cousin (Fig. 1, II). The third sister died at ten years.

After Rendah came the fifth child, a boy, Wayan Mertă. This boy, on his marriage, moved out of his father's courts and set up a household for himself farther down the road (see map, Fig. 3). Thus he left Rendah, as the eldest son, at the paternal house with his wife and children, to succeed the old man at his death. But this does not always happen, and, as we shall see in other cases, it is more usually the older brothers who move out one by one and set up new households, leaving the youngest boy to succeed and take over the paternal house. (Daughters do not inherit property.) It may be that the desire for independence, when newly married, prompts the elder brother to depart, leaving his right of succession to the youngest. They say also that the youngest son has had, at the time of his father's death, less time to set himself up, and is therefore less able to fend for himself, than the others who have been married several years. Whatever the reasons, the rule is that the eldest or the youngest, not the intermediate son, inherits the paternal house. (See exception, pp. 359–60.)

The sixth child was another boy, who died in childhood. The seventh, Nyoman Dog, another boy, although married for several years, has remained in the paternal house. He and his wife Rawi are now a part of Rendah's household. In Balinese this is called *ngerob*, "to share a kitchen." They say it is because Rendah is not strong, and Dog helps with the cultivation of Rendah's rice fields in return for sharing in the house. Rendah seems to have complete authority over Dog and orders him about as his younger brother, putting most of the heavy work upon him. But it is true that Rendah is not strong and that Dog is not very bright.

Dog and his wife Rawi have no children. This is a tragedy to Balinese. Rendah has recently allowed them to "adopt"[2] one of his little girls, Dayuh. It would not seem to be a very serious change for the child, as they all live together in the same court, and she, with

[2]The term is *anak ngidih*, "asked-for person."

her brothers and sisters, has always called their aunt and uncle by the same names as their mother and father, *mémé* and *bapă*. However, Dayuh senses a difference, and follows Rawi about, always at her heels like a young colt.

The eighth child of Rendah's father was a girl, Kĕtut Jinar, who married and went to live in Nyĕstanan, a different *banjar* of the same village. She is in and out of Rendah's house, helping when there is heavy work with the harvest, rice-pounding, or special preparations for a temple festival. But she neither eats nor sleeps there regularly.

The mother of all these children, whose name, she remembered, was Kintil, is of course also a member of the household. She continues to sleep in the place of honor, the *balé săkănem*, which in her husband's time she shared with him. Although the old man had been for several years in his dotage, unable to fulfill his functions in the village council (where he was represented by Rendah), and rather pushed aside by his grandchildren, Kintil is still a vigorous old woman in full possession of her faculties, respected and esteemed by all the household.

On the plan of Rendah's house (Fig. 4) it will be seen that of the space enclosed by the walls the "highest," that is, the northeast corner, toward the mountains and the abode of the gods, is reserved for the household shrines. The *balé săkănem* is an elevated open pavilion, on a stone foundation, whose thatch roof is supported by six wooden pillars. There is a brick wall at the back, the other three sides are open. The space between four pillars forms a sleeping place, a raised platform built between the pillars. Here the grandmother sleeps, sometimes with one or two of the children.

The *mĕtèn* is a house with mud walls enclosing two sleeping platforms, and outside, on the porch formed by the overhanging roof, are two more sleeping places, with curtains of red print material. Newly married young people, and young unmarried girls sleep in such inner rooms—they have reasons for privacy, or must be protected. Here the two girls Ngetis and Dayuh usually sleep. Rendah sleeps on the porch, in the "higher" bed, toward the east, often with one of his little sons. His wife occupies the other outer bed. The baby sleeps with her or, in fact, any of the younger children, who have no fixed sleeping places but are apt to visit about with their elders.

In the *balé siang-sangă*, which is a sort of family sitting room, also without walls, a place is found for the younger brother Dog and his wife Rawi. There are three platforms, and the children may also sleep here if they please. When guests are spending the night Dog and

Rawi give up to them the largest bed, on a slightly higher level, to do them honor.

Koti, the eldest sister who was married and divorced, sleeps in a little room in the *balé săkăpat*, which is reserved for her.

The kitchen stands opposite to the *mĕtèn*. East of this is the high pointed-roofed *jineng*, the rice-storing place. Behind are the pigs and

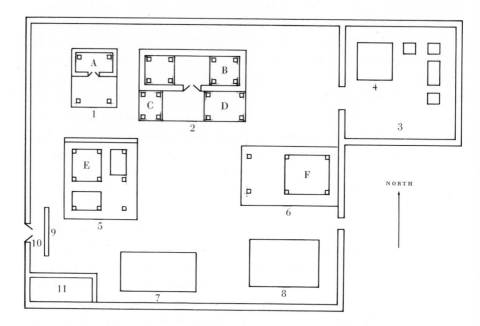

1 *balé săkăpat*, pavilion with four posts	8 *jineng*, rice-storing place
2 *mĕtèn*, house with inner room	9 *aling-aling*, magic wall
3 *sanggah*, household temple	10 *kori*, gateway
4 *balé piasan*, pavilion for offerings	11 pigs
5 *balé siang-sangă*, pavilion with nine posts	A Koti
	B Dayuh, Ngetis
6 *balé săkănem*, pavilion with six posts	C Rieh, Cheremé
	D Rendah, Adă
7 *paon*, kitchen	E Dog, Rawi
	F Kintil, Dapet

FIG. 4. Plan of the house of Rendah

fowls. Immediately opposite the entrance gate, blocking the court from the view of passersby and the attacks of evil spirits, is the *aling-aling*, a single strip of wall. The gate is a sort of stile, covered over by a thatched roof—you go up steps, through a doorway, and down more steps to the roadway without. Cut into the mud wall on either side of the gateway are small niches used for offerings.

The father of Rendah was called Budal. He was one of five sons who were, in order of birth, Bedil, Budal, Klĕpug, Krèbèk, and Siboh (Fig. 2, I). All five served during their adolescence as *parĕkan*, temporary slaves or attendants, to the local *chokordă*, a Ksatriyă prince. In return the prince made them grants of land when they married. He was a prince famous for his generosity. "One was ashamed to ask anything of him, for he gave so much."

The father of these five was called Géwar. No one remembers the name of Géwar's father, nor of his elder brother, who figures in this study (Fig. 2, I). All that we know about the old man, who was Géwar's father and Rendah's great-grandfather, is that he lived in a house next to the old "palace" (now disappeared) of the *chokordă* in Banjar Kutuh, the same *banjar* which Rendah and his cousins still inhabit. Géwar was born in this house, but he did not inherit it. After his marriage, to Raras, also of Banjar Kutuh, he lived in the house marked 2 on the plan (Fig. 3). Possibly this was a grant of the *chokordă*. In those days the region all about the village of Sayan was wilderness, covered with forest. When families grew and the young men wished to set up for themselves, they had to clear the ground for their house-courts and rice fields, level the land into terraces, and extend the canal system to bring water to their fields. This tremendous task must have been carried out by groups. It is known that the parent village of Sayan was Pĕliatan, a village at a distance of five or six miles, and that in the time of Rendah's grandfather and great-grandfather offshoots of many Pĕliatan families, the overflow from a district already fully populated, pushed out to form the new settlement of Sayan.

The five sons of Géwar, then, were born in house 2. The eldest, Bedil, moved out from this house and built house 3 at the time of or shortly after his marriage. He had five children, the three eldest girls, the two youngest boys (Fig. 2, II). They are Rendah's paternal parallel first cousins. It is to the son of one of these cousins, Gari, that Rendah has married his eldest daughter.

The eldest daughter of Bedil, Méweh, became the second wife of a man called Suwakă, who was a *sentană* to his first wife. A *sentană* is a young man, generally a younger son, who marries the daughter of a man without sons. He then becomes the successor of his father-in-law, lives in the house of the bride's parents, makes offerings at the household shrine of her ancestors, and foregoes his own family. He inherits from his father-in-law house and land, and his children continue the line not of his parents but of their maternal grandfather. In this case the man is said to "follow the woman" and becomes a member of her family, just as in the usual marriage the girl gives up her own family and her ancestor gods for those of her husband.

Suwakă was the son of a man whose elder brother had no male child but a daughter. Suwakă married as a *sentană* this daughter, Mĕtu, who was his paternal parallel first cousin. Her father was then to him father-in-law, uncle, and adopted father (Fig. 1, III).[3] Suwakă lived in the house of his father-in-law and later inherited it. Suwakă had only one child by Mĕtu, a daughter. He then took a second wife, who was Méweh (eldest daughter of Bedil and paternal parallel cousin of Rendah), and had by her five children, two of whom have married back into the family which concerns us here (Fig. 2, IV).

It is customary, and considered more suitable, for a man who takes a second wife to provide her with a house of her own, so that the two wives, at least during the early years, will not have to live in too close proximity.[4] Suwakă built for Méweh what is called a *kubu*, an informal sort of house, set out in the rice fields, not within the circumscribed

[3] A Balinese states the custom for choosing a *sentană*: "Take the family nearest on the male side, and, if there is none (no son), only then can he be taken from the female side" (Idă Bagus Adiptă, in article on ancient *adat*, "Menjelidiki adat-adat koena didésa-désa dalem bilangan negara Bangli," in *Bhāwanāgara*, III, Nos. 4–5 (1933), 73).

[4] Household and dependents of Suwakă:

"Town House"
Suwakă	
Mĕtu	his first wife
Popol	youngest son of Suwakă by his second wife
Te'er	wife of Popol
child of	
Popol and Te'er	
Sampring	mother of Mĕtu

Kubu No. 1
Méweh	second wife of Suwakă
Tĕmplok	son of Suwakă and Méweh
Kébek	wife of Tĕmplok
2 children	
of Tĕmplok and Kébek	
Pupul	son of Suwakă and Méweh

Kubu No. 2
Lu'ed	daughter of Suwakă by Mĕtu (first wife)
Gemuh	husband of Lu'ed
6 children	
of Gemuh and Lu'ed	

The total is twenty people, eleven adults and nine children, living in the three houses, but receiving their share of the common rice supply, kept in the "town house." Suwakă and all the young men of three households work the rice fields which he inherited from Mĕtu's father.

limits of the village. Here Méweh still lives, although her children
are grown up and married. With her are her second son, Tèmplok,
with his wife and two children, and her third son, Pupul, who is
unmarried. Her youngest son, Popol, lives with his wife and child in
the "town house" with his father and Mĕtu. Mĕtu's daughter Lu'ed
lives with her husband and six children in another *kubu* also on her
father-in-law's land, for the husband is poor and landless, and glad
to work his father-in-law's fields in return for his share of the crop.
(He is not a *sentană*, as Méweh has sons enough to carry on the line.
Such a working relationship is called *silih*, which has the meaning of
borrowing or repaying a debt, in friendly exchange.) Suwakă says that
all these people—that is, the two wives with all their children, sons
and daughters-in-law, and grandchildren (with the exception of the
daughter Sémbrod and the son Kĕrună), and including also the old
mother of Mĕtu—"get rice at his house." But those who live in the
two *kubu* cook it in their own houses. Here the term which was used
for the dependence of Dog in Rendah's house, *ngerob*, does not apply,
for, although they share the crop, they do not share a kitchen. Nevertheless Mĕtu's portion, which came to Suwakă as *sentană*, has sufficed
to maintain his entire second family, as well as Mĕtu's daughter, with
her husband and six children.

Kĕruna, the eldest son of Suwakă and Méweh, also became a
sentană. He married Saboh, the only daughter of Nyadèt and Nyambléh. Nyambléh is his mother's paternal parallel cousin, and Nyadèt
the son of his mother's father's paternal parallel cousin (Fig. 1, II). It
will be remembered that Nyadèt and Nyambléh were the children of
paternal parallel cousins (see p. 356).

The youngest son of Méweh, Popol, has married his maternal cross-
cousin, Te'er, the daughter of Gari (Fig. 1, IV, a). But this description,
though biologically true, does not fit the case. Gari, born the brother
of Méweh, was adopted at the age of three months by a childless
uncle, Klĕpug. He became, then, by adoption, Méweh's paternal
parallel cousin, instead of her brother. The marriage of Popol and
Te'er is to be considered socially as another marriage of the children
of paternal parallel cousins (Fig. 1, IV, b).

There is one more child of Méweh who concerns us here, the
daughter Sémbrod, who married the son of her father's male paternal
cross-cousin (Fig. 1, III). Her case differs from that of her brother
Popol, in that her relation to her husband sprang from an original
cross-cousinship, carried through a parallel phase in the second generation; and Popol's relation to his wife (considered socially) sprang from

an original parallel cousinship, carried through a cross phase in the
second generation. Note that the description of Sémbrod's case holds
true whether she is considered as the child of the line of Gongang,
Suwakă's own father, or of the line of Mentik, father of Mĕtu, who
became Suwakă's social and religious father when Suwakă married
Mĕtu as a *sentană*. It is impossible for a Balinese to state definitely to
which line Sémbrod belongs, as she calls both Mentik and Gongang
pĕkak, grandfather, just as she calls all her uncles *bapă*, father. Even
Rendah, who is her mother's cousin, she calls *bapă*. That is why the
matter of inheritance is significant in tracing the emphasis of kinship,
for it is only after the fact of succession to property that one can be
sure where the emphasis lies. In this particular family, of Mĕtu-
Suwakă-Mĕweh, complicated by the *sentană* marriage on one side and
the ordinary marriage on the other, we shall have to await Suwakă's
death to see what transpires. One can only note probabilities from the
present distribution of the family in the three houses, the "town
house," and the two *kubu* in the fields (see footnote 5 and Fig. 2, IV).
Mĕtu's only daughter Lu'ed did not marry a *sentană*, as might have
been expected, although her husband is a poor man. They do not live
in the town house, but in a *kubu* of their own on Suwakă's land. There
is no chance of their inheriting the town house, since succession does
not go through daughters. Probably they will inherit a tenantry right
to a portion of the rice fields. Mĕweh's eldest son, Kĕrună, married as
a *sentană* into the family of Nyadèt, and therefore has no further
claim on his own family, but will inherit from Nyadèt. He is already
pengajă, member of the village council, for that household, because
Nyadèt has become too deaf to fulfill his functions. Mĕweh's second
son, Tèmplok, lives with his mother in her *kubu*, and he is *pengajă* for
that household. Pupul, the third son, also lives there. Probably either
Tèmplok or Pupul will inherit that house, perhaps share it. In any
case they have no chance for the town house, as they are intermediate
sons. The daughter Sémbrod is now a member of her husband's
family and can expect nothing from her father's estate. This leaves
Popol, Mĕweh's youngest son, who would seem to be the logical heir
to the town house. As we should expect, we find him living there with
his father and his co-mother Mĕtu, ready to take over the rights on
the death of his father.

Let us go back now two generations to the family of Géwar, where
we find another curious case of inheritance, not conjecture this time
but accomplished fact (Fig. 2, I). It will be remembered that Géwar
had five sons who served as *parĕkan* of the local prince. He lived in

the house marked 2 on the map. His eldest son, Bedil, after his marriage, lived in house 3, and the second son Budal, in house 4 (which is now Rendah's). It was the third son, Klĕpug, who inherited the paternal house, house 2.

It came about in this way: The *chokordă*, prince of the district, was waging war on the region to the south of Sayan. He was victorious, and the inhabitants fled, leaving the country deserted. Krèbèk, the fourth son of Géwar, was sent away by the *chokordă* to Banjar Tunon, in the conquered district, as a settler. He was given a grant of land and therefore did not succeed to any of his father's lands in Sayan.

The fifth son, Siboh, who might have been expected to inherit the paternal house, was married as a *sentană* and moved away to the house of his father-in-law in Banjar Mas, thereby forfeiting his claim. And so it was that the third son, Klĕpug, was the only one left to inherit the house of Géwar. His two elder brothers already had houses of their own, and his two younger brothers had departed from the *banjar* before their father's death.

Now Klĕpug had the house, and he took two wives, but he had no children. This was an important matter not only to him but to the entire family. For although each *pĕkarangan* must contain its individual household temple, the *sanggah* of the paternal house is larger, and all the children and grandchildren feel a responsibility for keeping up this parent temple, whence their own house temples spring. Surely the spirit of the forefathers is more powerful there! And so an heir must be found for Klĕpug, who has inherited the house of Géwar and become guardian of his *sanggah*. The eldest brother, Bedil, who has already three daughters, hands over to Klĕpug his first-born son, at the age of three months. This child, who is Gari, still lives in the house of Géwar. He has inherited his grandfather's house, not as the child of the eldest son but as the adopted child of the youngest son who remained at home.

The house in which Bedil lived has passed on to his younger son Dariă, who lives there now with his wife and four children (house 3).

It is difficult to trace the inheritance of property other than the dwelling house. For the rice fields are loaned, mortgaged, paid for in labor, or held by a system of tenantry with a sharing of the crops, all arrangements made between individuals, rarely with a written agreement. Within the family land is loosely held, and a man will speak of as his all property belonging to himself and his brothers, even of his cousins. Princes claim as theirs land which may have been given as a grant by their father or grandfather in return for services already rendered, or else let out on a crop-sharing basis, or even land originally owned by the commoner, but which the prince has planted with lines of his own coconut trees between the fields. The Balinese have an extraordinary memory for their relative indebtedness to every individual of their acquaintance, and the balance of favors given and received swings back and forth through the generations. But all the same when quarrels arise, the present government has difficulty in settling the ownership of property to which one man may hold the deed,[5] whereas another has been farming it and paying the taxes on it for ten or fifteen years.

In the case of Rendah and his two surviving brothers, the rice fields of their father are supposed to have been divided between them. Rendah, as the eldest, claims to have got a larger share than Mertă and Dog. Now Mertă maintains a separate household, whereas Dog lives in the house of Rendah and has no child (except the daughter of Rendah whom he has adopted). Rendah says that two thirds of the land belong to him but that, as the land is all lumped together and worked chiefly by Mertă and Dog, they divide the crops between the two households, that of Mertă and that of Rendah, which includes Dog. Rendah's household consists of six adults and five children, Mertă's of two adults and seven children. "If he has not got enough rice, I give it to him, whereas, if I am lacking, he gives to me," says Rendah. Hence we assume that the division of the crop is done on a friendly basis according to necessity, and, if Rendah's household should diminish through the death of the old mother and sister, or the marriage of his daughters, and Mertă's increase with the birth of more children, the ratio could be proportionately altered. But it is hard to tell, when Rendah says he owns two thirds of the land, whether this is really all his, or whether he is counting with his own Dog's share, since Dog is in the position of a dependent in his household. In this case it is of no particular importance, as Dog has no son to inherit from him.

It will be noted that of the eleven marriages recorded in Rendah's generation, only two were polygynous. Nyadèt married Dartă and, having no children by her, took his paternal parallel second cousin Nyambléh, who gave him one daughter. When she grew up, a *sentană* marriage was arranged with her cousin Kĕrună, who is

---

[5] The deed, called *pipil*, is in writing, engraved upon a leaf of the tal palm. It is tucked away in a safe place, and forgotten. In the case of land which I rented, the search for the *pipil* lasted six weeks. It was finally discovered in a roof-bamboo of the house of the paternal second cousin of the "owner."

related to her both on her mother's and on her father's side (Fig. 1, II). In the son of this marriage, Nyadèt has at last got his heir to carry on the line. The other marriage of two wives was when Suwakǎ, who, as *sentanǎ* husband to Mětu, had only a daughter, wedded his second cousin Méweh as a second wife and by her got four sons.

In the preceding generation Klěpug and Krèbèk each had two wives. Klěpug's first wife seems to have been unsatisfactory and was divorced. She had no children. Neither did her successor, Giyur. Klěpug obtained an heir by adopting the son of his brother. On Krèbèk, who moved away to another district, we have no information beyond the fact of his marrying twice.

It is of course impossible to draw any conclusions on polygyny from such a limited study. The cases mentioned only illustrate how the taking of a second wife is more strongly motivated by the need for sons than by an affectional urge toward the woman. It would be expected that the young men for whom initial marriages have been arranged would later wish to exercise an independent choice. But, as we have seen, even the second marriage may be an arranged one, between cousins. The Balinese say that a poor man who has one good wife can ill afford to take another. As a rule any wife who is not unfaithful and who has borne a son, is considered "good." It is the son, in Balinese culture, who is of most importance—a social and religious necessity.

Additional Remarks

It is generally said of Bali that marriage is by abduction, the husband subsequently making a payment to the bride's father, varying from 10,000 to 50,000 *kèpèng* (value approximately 12 to 65 Dutch guilders). It is true that this custom is widespread, and prevalent in the districts around Den Pasar and Bulèlèng, the big townships. It may be found surprising that no such marriage is mentioned in the study of Rendah's family. There is much evidence to show that the form of arranged marriage practiced in Rendah's family, planned to link the households of relatives and friends, and without monetary compensation, is the older and more characteristic procedure. In fact, the old men of Sayan say that in their generation (before the Dutch occupation) girls were often stolen from one village by the young men of an enemy village, but that, instead of the husband's making a payment to the bride's father, the father would make a payment to the young man so that the girl should be returned to her village and the marriage dissolved. To have one's daughter marry in a hostile village was to lose sight of her completely. They say that if the match is suitable the father asks no payment, and only if he were angry would he require compensation of the bridegroom. Cynical and commercial-minded young men of the towns say, "The father always manages to be angry, so that he will get the money."[6] But for the old-fashioned people of Sayan this is not true. Rendah said to me, on the occasion of his daughter's marriage to her cousin, whose house is across the street, "I would rather *rugi* [take a financial loss] than to have my child marry away from home. If she married in another village, I should have the money, but my heart would be sick."

Such a remark, reflecting a sentiment of paternal devotion, must not be taken only at its face value. The Balinese, like other races, often say things which "sound well" but do not render their complete thought process, and are therefore misleading. It is not to be assumed that a man like Rendah, in giving away his daughter to her cousin, is actually casting to the winds a profit of 10,000 or 20,000 *kèpèng*, having weighed them as nothing beside the possibility of losing sight of his child. Certainly he would prefer to have her near home. But to have her marry into a family with which he already has an established relation of favors given and received is more satisfactory than to set up a new link with a family of comparative strangers. And if he should accept compensation, he would be sanctioning a system which would not profit him in the end, for might not his own sons then have to pay for their brides? It would seem that these indebtedness relations are best carried on within the family group.

In connection with this it must be mentioned that sister exchange between parallel cousins, maternal or paternal, is not permitted. This statement was made to me by various informants. None mentioned the prohibition of sister exchange between cross-cousins, nor between unrelated families. I did not find any reference to sister exchange in Balinese texts. The term used for the forbidden sister exchange of parallel cousins is *malik-terbalik*, meaning a reversal, a going-and-coming. *Malik* may be a Balinese form of the root *balik*, although *balik* or *walik* are those commonly used in other connections; *terbalik* is definitely a Malay form, foreign to the Balinese language. But as many informants speak Malay fluently, and consider it a more polite

---

[6]Certainly it is considered decorous for the father to at least pretend anger at the ravishing of his daughter, just as the girl herself must weep and struggle to escape at the time of her capture, even though she has previously agreed and helped to plot that capture.

usage to foreigners, the form of the term is not a proof of the late introduction of the taboo.

The difference in the two marriage schemes, that of the arranged marriage as against the marriage by abduction, reflects on the divorce. A woman may be "thrown away" by her husband for various reasons: she is barren, quarrelsome, or unfaithful. She may either return to her father's house, or, if she has a lover, marry him. Whether or not a payment has been made to the father, the father does not have to make any restitution to the husband in case the marriage fails. But the lover or second husband must in either case pay compensation money to the wronged husband. This is rather more expensive than the cost of an unmarried girl, for, besides the cost of the woman, a fine must be paid to the community. This is part of the old village law, now taken over by the courts—a sort of punishment and compensation for disturbing the "balance" of the social group. I have known a case of an unusually fickle woman, who passed from one husband to another in such rapid succession that none had had time to pay for her before being deserted. Husband Number 4 found himself sued for a sum in which each of her previous husbands had a share: Number 4 was to pay Number 3, who owed Number 2, who still had not paid Number 1. The father also had a claim, but with faint hopes of recovery.

A wife who is maltreated by her husband has the option of returning to her family, where she will be graciously received if they do not consider her in the wrong. At the present time, if she can prove her husband's delinquency in the courts, she may obtain some right over the children. However, even under the old regime, a husband has been known to allow the wife to bring up the children in a separate establishment, although they are considered chiefly his and the descendants of his ancestral line.

There was the case of a girl for whom a marriage was arranged with her cousin, the son of her father's elder brother. Her father had died, leaving his wife with four girls and a baby boy, and no one to provide for them. The cousin's branch owned house and land, whereas the girl's family had nothing, not even the space on which their house stood. Her father had occupied the land as tenant farmer to the *chokordă*, and after his death, as there was no man left to till it, the land was forfeit. Obviously the marriage of the eldest daughter to her cousin would have been advantageous, and all her relations urged her to agree to it. The wealthy branch could have advanced the money needed to buy the land on which her house stood, and thus saved the house for her mother and sisters and eventually as a heritage for the small brother. But the girl resisted all persuasion to the match. Finally the grandmother resorted to a ruse. She came to the girl, asking her to prepare medicine for her cousin lying ill with a fever. The girl collected the necessary herbs and spices, pounded them together, and brought them to her cousin's house. Although she hated him, she could not refuse to help a relative in illness.

"He lies within," said the grandmother, indicating the *mětèn*, the room enclosed with walls. "Take it in to him."

The girl entered the room. At once the old woman pulled the door to and bolted it on the outside. The young man leapt up from the couch to embrace his unwilling bride.

For several days the girl was kept a prisoner. When they began to relax their vigilance, she ran away, but her cousins always pursued her and brought her back. They believed that once used to the young man, she would give in. After a time she did relent and, when a month had passed, agreed to the purification ceremony, *mĕsakapan*, which solemnizes a marriage. But within three days of the ceremony she could stand no more and again escaped. It was too late to return to her home, especially as her mother and sisters had been in favor of the marriage from the beginning. She ran away to the town, where she lives at the present time, kept by an Arab merchant.

This case suggests that the women can, and sometimes do, rebel against marriages arranged with their cousins. Certainly with the peaceful times under the Dutch administration, when it is safe to visit other villages without fearing assault, and the increased freedom of communication by motorbus and bicycle, the young people are more apt to resist an unwelcome marriage. There is infinitely more opportunity for a free choice, based on mutual attraction, than there was. In the old days, living in the enforced isolation of the village surrounded by hostile camps, if a girl refused her cousin or neighbor she might get no husband at all. Also, she was the more likely to be pleased with him, so few were the youths of her acquaintance with whom she might compare him.

We have seen that marriages of first and second cousins, both maternal and paternal, are frequent, and that no special distinction is made between parallel and cross-cousins. In Balinese the name for them is the same: *misan*, first cousin, *mindon*, second cousin, whether paternal or maternal, whether cross or parallel. Marriages of third cousins are more difficult to trace, as there is no term for them other than the general term for brother, relative, *nyamă* (low Balinese), *sĕmotonan* (high Balinese).

The ordinary incest taboos are as follows: A man may not have sexual connection with his mother, his sister, his half-sister, or the mother of his half-sister or half-brother (that is, his mother's co-wife). The penalty for this first degree incest, according to records of ancient *adat*, includes immediate banishment from the formal limits of the village, a great purification ceremony with animal offering to the bad spirits, and sometimes a rite whereby the offending pair are dressed in the yokes worn by pigs and made to approach on all four and drink out of a pig's drinking trough.[7] Subsequently the two are to be banished from the village for life and their lands confiscated. As such banishment in the old days left them no recourse but to wander off in the jungle, there to be hunted by wild beasts or to face death from starvation, the punishment amounted in fact to a death sentence. No other village would take in people banished from their own village, lest they bring ill luck and disaster. It can be imagined that the infringement of this incest law has not been frequent.

Less serious punishment falls upon the offenders in second degree incest, which is (1) sexual connection of a man with his aunt, either his father's or his mother's sister; or (2) connections with his first cousin once removed, that is, his father's or his mother's first cousin. The first is called *rĕramă dimisan*, "mother at (or of) the first cousin," the second *rĕramă dimindon*, "mother at (or of) the second cousin." Offenders in these cases are banished from the village for a period of a year (420 days) but are allowed to return to the village after the completion of the necessary purification rites. They spend the intervening year in a hut put up for them on some unholy ground, the graveyard or the crossroads, and are not allowed during that time even to enter the village limits. It will be noted that both relations have the mother element reflected in the terminology, and that the man belongs to the generation younger than the woman, and therefore stands with her as a child to its mother. Similar relations but reversed, as of a man to his niece, or to his first cousin's daughter, are not forbidden and entail no banishment, according to the old *adat*. There is here a feeling that the male should be older than the female, as he is her superior, and that he should not marry, or have connection with, a woman belonging to an older generation, even though he might be her senior in actual age. The law also may be based on a desire of the older males to maintain their authority within the household, and to

[7] Recorded as part of the *adat* of the village Bu'ungan, district of Bangli; Idă Bagus Adiptă, "Menjelidiki adat-adat koena didésa-désa bilangan negara Bangli," *Bhāwanāgara*, III, Nos. 4–5 (1933), 71.

prevent younger males from threatening their authority by marrying into a generation equal to their own. And perhaps it may have originated as a safeguard to the morality of the household during the absence, at work or at war, of the father, the head of the family.

In connection with the incest laws an exception may be mentioned, that of boy and girl twins, who may marry each other.[8] Among the *jabă* the birth of such twins is considered a great wrong (*manak salah*), for the brother and sister are thought to have had a too intimate contact in the womb of their mother. The event will bring famine and disaster upon the entire village, unless averted by the temporary banishment of the children and their parents, followed by great offerings for purification and the propitiation of evil spirits. When these rites are completed, and the twins have grown up, they may marry, for their incestuous connection is considered to be already atoned for. Since Balinese legendary history contains many examples of boy and girl twins who married and brought forth a tribe, or a line of kings, there is a certain feeling that boy and girl twins are intended to be man and wife, even though it is wrong for them to be so connected. At the present time it is rare for such twins to marry, although the banishment and propitiatory ceremonies are still widely practiced.

Curiously enough, it is not considered a wrong for very high-caste people to have such twins. But there are many divergences in the customs of the high-caste Balinese from those of the *jabă*. In passing, it may be mentioned that men of the three higher castes may marry women who are *jabă*, whereas it is a crime for high-caste women to marry or to have relations with a man of lower caste than their own. Offenders used to be either drowned in the sea or banished to another island. Within the past five years the government was forced to deport a Brahmană woman and a *jabă* man, who, banished from their own village, were refused admittance to all other villages and towns.

The Balinese *lontar*, sacred texts written on leaves of the tal palm, describe in full the penalties and atonements for the unusual case in family matters: incestuous unions, birth of twins, seductions, suicides, and so forth. These are the things that are "not done." But for the things that are done, the customary, everyday occurrences, there are no written rules. That is why I have presented this study of a single family in its intimate relations, with the hope that it will give some picture of the family life running its ordinary course.

[8] See Belo, "A Study of Customs Pertaining to Twins in Bali," in this volume, pp. 25–29.

Free Designs of Limited Scope as a Personality Index

A Comparison of Schizophrenics with Normal, Subnormal, and Primitive Culture Groups

THEODORA M. ABEL

THE PURPOSE of this investigation was to study the performance of
schizophrenics on a drawing test that allowed for freedom of expression and interpretation but at the same time definitely limited the
scope of the task.

The more spontaneous drawings of psychotics and neurotics have
become valuable material in the study of personality, for they so often
reflect either directly or indirectly expressions or symptoms of behavior, that is, meticulousness, stereotypes, indifference, or hyperactivity,
as well as the more symbolic representations of deep-seated and unconscious trends. Even in fairly rigid, limited, and less spontaneous
drawing tasks included among test items of intelligence examinations
(copying a diamond or designs, tracing pathway in ball and field,
drawing a man), personality differences are indicated, particularly
among psychopathic subjects. In fact, the qualitative differences in
drawing are often more significant as keys to personality traits than
the quantitative ratings of mental age and IQ. As such they can be
and are being used considerably in psychiatric work.

We decided to study the modes of performance on a drawing task
that allowed for some freedom of expression and interpretation, as in a
spontaneous drawing, but which at the same time restricted the

Originally published in *Character and Personality*, VII, No. 1 (September, 1938),
50–62. Reprinted with permission of the author.

activity of the subject to a limited and fixed goal. In other words, we wanted to control the situation, as in a test, but still give the individual a chance to do some imagining rather than merely perceive or recall spatial relationships.

The Task

The subject was presented with a sheet of paper on which a rectangle was traced longitudinally (4 inches by 6 inches). He was told to make any kind of a balanced or even design he desired in the rectangle, but he must use only a certain number of lines. This number was to be nineteen straight and six curved lines. The lines could be of any length, and any kind of line that was not straight was considered as curved. He was given as much time as he wanted to make the design. Any questions the subject raised were answered before he began to draw. Often a question concerning the meaning of *balanced* or *even* was brought up. The subject was told that this meant making the design sort of balanced or even, either left and right or top and bottom but he need not be too particular about the balance. The experimenter always noted the manner in which the subject proceeded with the task, whether he worked slowly and cautiously or fast and impetuously, which type of lines he drew first, or any spontaneous comments he made that threw light on his attitudes in making the design.

The Subjects

Group I. The test was given individually to 58 schizophrenic patients, 53 males and 5 females, who were sufficiently cooperative to have some rapport with the experimenter and were willing to do the task. They were classified in the hospitals as follows:

Paranoid or paranoid condition	36
Catatonic	5
Hebephrenic	13
Simple	1
Recovered paranoid (still hospitalized but ready to go on parole)	3

We attempted to test about 20 more subjects, but they refused to do the task either because of negativism and hostility (catatonics) or distractability (hebephrenics). It is for this reason that we have the largest number of paranoid patients, as they were more willing to cooperate. Also, the classification is naturally quite arbitrary, and there were overlapping behavior trends in the different groups. All the catatonics we tested had predominantly paranoid trends, while two of the paranoids were silly and distractable in their attitudes during the testing. Several of the hebephrenics behaved seriously and conscientiously during the testing, and their protocols revealed that they had either marked or fleeting persecutory paranoid trends. No cases of obvious deterioration or of known accompanying organic disorder were included.[1]

The subjects were patients in New York State hospitals (Psychiatric Institute and Hospital—12 cases, Rockland—38 cases, Harlem Valley —8 cases).[2] Their chronological ages ranged from 18 to 53 (only 3 cases over 40). They had been of normal or superior intelligence prior to their illness, judging from the amount of schooling, type of employment, and level and mode of conversation during a psychiatric interview. The majority had had two or more years of high school; several were college and university graduates and had held professional positions.

We have given this designs test to a large number of nonpsychotic individuals and are planning in a subsequent paper to report the use of the test as a personality index among normal subjects. For purposes of comparison with the schizophrenics, however, we shall here indicate roughly the types of designs made by some of our groups of normal subjects. The following groups were tested:

Group II. Seventy-five boys and girls (33 boys, 42 girls) in a high school in Holland, Michigan. C.A. 14 to 20. Tested in groups.[3]

Group III. Eighty-two girls in an industrial high school in New York City. C.A. 15 to 16, IQ 80 to 115. Tested in groups.

Group IV. Fifty adults, male and female, with C.A. 20 to 60, of normal intelligence, or superior, largely employed in the professions. Tested individually.[4]

In addition to comparing the behavior of the schizophrenic patients with the normal subjects indicated, we have made three comparisons with quite specialized groups in order to see what further possibilities there were for understanding the personality of the psychotics. Our

[1] Two alcoholics and one general paretic were given the test before a definite diagnosis had been made of their psychosis. All three drew designs, as did the majority of schizophrenics. We have not included these results, however.

[2] Thanks are due Dr. H. Starks of Rockland State Hospital, Dr. Z. Piotrowski of the Psychiatric Institute, New York, and Dr. E. J. Weiss, formerly of Harlem Valley Hospital, for their cooperation in either administering the test or making arrangements for the author to do so.

[3] Thanks are due Dr. Morris Steggerda, Department of Genetics, Carnegie Institution of Washington, for having these tests given at Holland, Mich.

[4] Groups III and IV were tested by the author.

first comparisons are with drawings of individuals in more primitive cultures.

Group V. Twenty-three Navajo Indians (20 females, 3 males) who had been at the government school at Fort Wingate, New Mexico. C.A. 13 to 27. Tested individually.[5]

Group VI. Thirty Balinese of Bayung, in Bali, Netherland East Indies (29 males, 1 female). Tested individually. Twenty-seven were a group of artists, selected for study by Dr. Mead, who is at present on a field expedition in Bali. Three were informants with special abilities; three were about 11 years old; two were 14; the others, older.[6]

Our final comparison is with a group of subnormal subjects. Group VII consisted of 24 subnormals, 14 at Letchworth (9 boys, 5 girls), with C.A. 13 to 21 and IQ 60 to 79 (Stanford-Binet), and 10 girls in the Trade Extension Classes in New York City, with C.A. 15 to 16 and IQ 60 to 79 (Otis Self-Administering).[7] Tested individually. The number of straight lines to be drawn was reduced to 13, as 19 was found to be too large a number concept for these subjects to handle (a difference in itself between the subnormals and the abnormals).

Results

Schizophrenic Patients. The performance of the patients in Group I could be divided into the following categories on the basis of the kind of design made. A. No design at all, but the instruction as to the number of straight and curved lines was explicitly carried out. Fig. 1a shows a reproduction typical of this group. B. Very crude and rudimentary design. The number of lines is correct. The only attempt at design is either to cross the straight and curved lines in a very simple manner or to make the rudimentary spatial arrangement of lines. Fig. 1b gives a sample of a typical drawing of this kind.

Most of the drawings in both A and B fill the greater part of the space of the rectangle. A very few are small and placed in or near the center of the space allowed.[8]

C. Definite attempt to make a design or pattern with interplay and

---

[5] Thanks are again due Dr. Steggerda for giving these tests to the Navajo subjects.

[6] Thanks are due Dr. Margaret Mead of the American Museum of Natural History for giving these tests.

[7] Thanks are due Dr. Elaine F. Kinder for giving these tests at Letchworth Village. The other subjects were tested by the author.

[8] Occasionally a design was made where the lines "clung" to the boundary of the rectangle. This characteristic as well as that of "smallness" are of psychiatric interest, but we cannot deal with these problems in the present paper. Cf. E. Liss, "The Graphic Arts," *American Journal of Orthopsychiatry,* VIII (1938), 95–99.

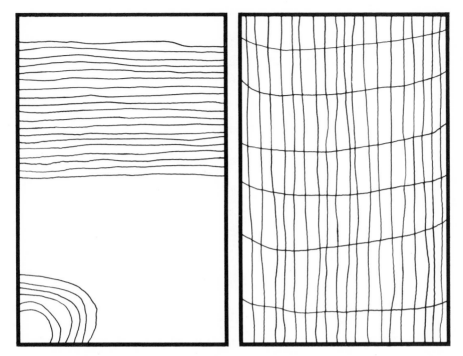

FIG. 1a. Male. D.P. Paranoid. C.A. 42. Suspicious of being followed. Carried bread knife for self-protection.

FIG. 1b. Male. D.P. Catatonic. C.A. 30. Intense. Had been assaultive. Feelings of influence and power.

FIG. 2a. Female. Normal 2d yr. High-School student. Italian descent. C.A. 15.6. IQ 102.

FIG. 2b. Female. Superior adult. C.A. 26. Neurotic and paranoid trends.

spatial arrangement of straight and curved lines (Fig. 2a). D. Design drawn in form of concrete object (garage, flower garden).

We have placed in Table 1 the number of cases falling into the four categories just described.

TABLE 1

Classified Psychosis	No. Cases	A No Design	B Crude Design	Total A and B	C Definite Pattern	D Object Drawn
Paranoid	36	15	17	32	4	0
Catatonic	5	3	1	4	0	1
Hebephrenic	13	2	6	8	0	5
Simple D.P.	1	0	0	0	1	0
Total	55	20	24	44	5	6
Recovered paranoid	3				3	

The outstanding characteristic of the performance of the schizophrenics is that a considerable majority (44, i.e., 80 percent) made either no design or only a simple and rudimentary one. This group (A and B) followed the instructions meticulously and conscientiously in drawing the required number of lines. The usual procedure was to draw the 19 straight lines first, to verify the number as they went along or to inquire if 19 was the current number, and then to draw the 6 curved lines. Some of the patients asked for rulers or compasses to make the lines more even. (They were told that this was not necessary.) Several, if they commented at all, said that they were not artists but would do their best. Their attitude was one of extreme seriousness, obsessiveness about getting in the correct number of lines, and rigidity and inflexibility toward making a definite pattern. Either the effort was too great or they did not feel free to work out a constructive idea about a design. Their obsessiveness and punctiliousness overshadowed any possible play of the imagination. It was as if they were on their guard and could not or would not give themselves away. One patient, a catatonic, showed this characteristic in an exaggerated manner. He drew the 19 straight lines in the rectangle diagonally filling up all the space. Then, in order to complete the task, he drew the 6 curved lines as thumbnails at the bottom of the paper outside of the rectangle.

The reasons for this inflexibility on the part of 80 percent of the patients we may only surmise. Probably they were unable to enter into a situation as demanding as drawing a design of limited scope, but yet felt under compulsion to complete the task in order to get out of the situation as soon as possible. It is a well-known fact that psychotics do less well in performance tests than in verbal ones.[9] Verbal contacts with the world around them are less exacting than definite manipulative tasks requiring planning and organization of overt activity.

Among the 11 patients (20 percent) who made a definite design or drew an object, we know, in the case of a few of them, something about why their performance was different from the majority. One was a case of simple schizophrenia who had never had paranoid trends. Six patients who drew concrete objects volunteered at first quite seriously to do the task, but as they got started, their attitude became silly and distracted. Not one of them employed the correct number of lines. One of them drew a profile, employing the curved lines as features and the straight ones for the hair. His comment was "Ha! Ha! There's something for you!" The drawings, then, reflected the attitudes of the patients at the time. We have noted this same type of performance in making the designs in the case of two hypomaniacs and of normals with highly extroverted and distractible trends of behavior.

Two paranoid patients who made rather elaborate and intricate designs were particularly pleasant and cooperative and seemed only mildly obsessive about the task. Probably they were more nearly recovered than were the other patients. Certainly the three definitely recovered paranoid cases who made fairly elaborate designs, as do intelligent normals, were obviously in good contact with the external world, in their rapport with the experimenter and in carrying out the task.

Normal Subjects. If the performance of the schizophrenics is compared with that of normal subjects, we find a marked difference. Table 2 shows the number of subjects in our three normal control groups, classified according to whether they made no design or a very crude one, a definite design with interplay of curved and straight lines, or drew a concrete object.

As can be seen, nearly all of the normal subjects drew definitely thought-out patterns where there were at least some arrangement and interplay between the straight and curved lines. Fig. 2a represents a

[9] Z. A. Piotrowski, "A Comparison of Congenitally Defective Children with Schizophrenic Children in Regard to Personality Structure and Intelligence Type," *Proceedings of American Association on Mental Deficiency*, XLII (1937), 78–90; M. Davidson, "A Study of Schizophrenic Performance on the Stanford-Binet Scale," *British Journal of Medical Psychology*, VII (1937), 93–97.

TABLE 2

Group	No. Cases	A and B No Design or Crude One	C Definite Pattern	D Object Drawn
II.				
Dutch-American				
High-School Boys and Girls	75	5	69	1
III.				
Industrial High-School Girls	98	9	83	6
IV.				
Adults (mostly superior intell.)	50	2	40	8
Total	223	16	192	15

very frequent type of design. Only 16, or 7 percent, of the total number of subjects made no design or only a very crude one, in which the correct number of lines was drawn but little or no account was taken of a possible pattern. This percentage is decidedly smaller than that of the schizophrenic patients who performed in the same manner.

Unfortunately we were not able to obtain reliable accounts of the personality make-up of the 14 subjects in the high school who made no, or only crude, designs. We have considerable information, however, about the two superior adults (in Group IV) who made crude but meticulous drawings. Fig. 2b shows one of these designs. The other is fairly similar. Interestingly enough, both of these subjects show marked paranoid trends of behavior, although they were able to adjust in the social world. One of them (whose design is represented in Fig. 2b), feels that her family has always discriminated against her and in favor of her sister, and that her husband abuses her sadistically. She also has a "breast" phobia, is afraid of touching a bare breast, of exposing her own breasts, or of seeing anyone nursing. (Her design seems also to be of interest symbolically in view of this phobia.) The other subject is extremely critical of others and feels that only she is correct in her judgments.

Primitive Groups. NAVAJO INDIANS. The performance of the Navajo Indians was more like that of the normal whites than that of the schizophrenics in that they were able to enter into the constructive requirements of the task. Twenty-one of the twenty-three subjects made definite designs. Of this number, sixteen, or 70 percent, made patterns characteristic of an Indian culture, that is, the designs looked like those seen on Navajo rugs. Two drew definite objects (Indian head and horse). Three made designs that resembled designs of our normal subjects (Fig. 2a). None of these 21 designs were at all crude; rather they showed flexibility and ability in the making of a pattern.

The other two subjects, yet unaccounted for, made designs like those of the majority of psychotics (categories A and B in Group I), putting in the correct number of lines but making little attempt to arrange the lines in a pattern. These two Navajos were both high-school graduates and the two oldest members of the group (C.A. 23 and 27). Consequently, lack of understanding and immaturity were

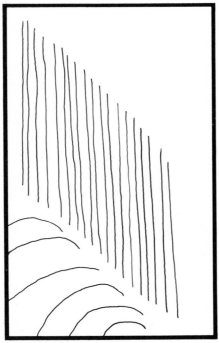

FIG. 3. Male. Navajo Indian. High-School graduate. C.A. 23. Gifted artist. Unstable, psychotic trends.

not the reasons for their performance. We could obtain no further information about the personality characteristics of one of these subjects. The other one, however, was well known at the school. He was described as having been a gifted artist but had become very temperamental, obstinate, and impossible to handle. Consequently, he was dismissed from the school. When he was given the test, he was quiet and cooperative. It is apparent from this description that he had developed at least some psychotic trends of behavior. Fig. 3 shows the design he made, which is very much like the predominant one among the schizophrenics (compare with Fig. 1a and b).

BALINESE. The other primitive group, the Balinese (Group VI), has had much less cultural contact with white people. Giving the Balinese a paper and pencil performance test devised by individuals in an alien culture puts them at quite a disadvantage. But the task was given mostly to subjects who were artists and had had plenty of experience in painting the elaborate and stylized patterns characteristic of the Balinese culture.[10] The other three subjects, as informants, had had contacts with white people and could be considered as willing to cooperate. As yet we have not received the designs from Bali, but Dr. Mead has written us at length what the results are like. In the first place, she had considerable difficulty getting in rapport with the subjects. They hate tests and are suspicious of their purpose. An informant, a highly intelligent and cooperative individual, who had received a good education in Java, was finally able to obtain designs from 30 subjects, as we have indicated. He gave the instructions, while Dr. Mead observed behavior and method of proceeding with the task.

The Balinese fussed a good deal, asked over and over again for reassurance which the informant gave by repeating bits of the directions. Unless this was done, they simply balked. The majority attacked the problem linearly, drawing first 19 straight lines and then 6 curved lines. The results are all very similar in appearance and similar to the majority of drawings of our schizophrenic group. Dr. Mead sent three samples which she said were the commonest types of response. These three drawings are all slight modifications of the sample given in Fig. 1a. The 19 straight lines are above the curved lines, either longer lines drawn across the whole width of the rectangle or shorter parallel and horizontal lines in the center of the space. The curved lines are also drawn in sequence, either concavely up or down or to the left or right as was the case with the mental patients.

In order to reveal their individuality in drawing, the Balinese have to be left alone to do their work more spontaneously or at least under conditions where there is less censorship or weight of an authoritative culture directed against them. These subjects had been voluntarily making sketches and paintings for Dr. Mead over a period of several months. The same difficulty, most likely, holds true for schizophrenics with persecutory paranoid trends, who feel they are under scrutiny in any social situation, particularly in a test situation. Herein lies the advantage of allowing for spontaneity of response as in voluntary

[10] M. Covarrubias, *Island of Bali* (New York, Knopf, 1937), pp. 160–204.

drawing, where the individual is less formally and consciously aware of carrying out a manipulative organized task.

Dr. Mead further described the personality structure of the Balinese as follows: "The whole emphasis of the education is to scatter, disintegrate, separate one response from another, and to make only very superficial, verbalistic associations. It's not so much that the Balinese can't take in a new idea, as that they can't take in anything *whole*; their own receptivity is a honeycomb. Every new idea has to be chopped into little bits."[11] This factor probably accounts for the making of the discrete ununified lines in the designs. This same factor may be the one dominant in the behavior of the schizophrenics. Certainly, one of their marked characteristics is disorganization of the total personality, and inability to integrate different aspects of their world of new experiences. They failed to build up a constructive plan for a design, but were successful in drawing the correct number of lines. We may suggest, then, that they were unable to integrate the new idea as a whole; the task that allowed for freedom of expression in making a design but one to be constructed on the basis of a limited goal.

Also, the psychotics showed another characteristic in their drawings, that of being obsessive about getting in the correct number of lines in rigid formation. The behavior of the Balinese seemed obsessive also. They carefully put in the correct number of lines, likewise in an inflexible manner. In commenting on the characteristics of painters and sculptors in Bali, Covarrubias indicated this obsessive trait: "They admire technique and good craftsmanship above other points and when I showed a Balinese friend a beautiful sculpture I had just acquired, he found fault with the minute parallel grooves that marked the strands of hair because in places they ran together."[12] Except on festival occasions, the Balinese are quite restrained in their daily lives, a great deal of their behavior is formal and ritualistic, dictated by long established customs and traditions. They show an "habitual avoidance of any impulsive movement." Consequently, their attitude toward a novel situation, as making a design of limited scope, was in keeping with their predominant mode of self-conscious behavior.[13]

Subnormal Subjects. Our final comparison takes us into a different problem entirely, that of limited intelligence. We wanted to see

[11] Excerpt from a letter sent to the author, February 12, 1938.
[12] Covarrubias, *Island of Bali*, p. 165.
[13] Jane Belo, "The Balinese Temper," in this volume, p. 87.

whether the performance of subnormals in making designs would be more like the normals or more like the schizophrenics. As previously mentioned, only 13 straight lines were required. The performance of the 24 mental defectives in Group VII was as follows: Twelve made definite patterns (none very intricate) where they made use of spatial relationships. Four made a design by drawing a concrete object (flowers, airplane). One drew a concrete object but forgot about the correct number of lines. One did not understand the complete instructions and only made a few lines. Six made no or hardly any design, merely followed instructions, as had the psychotics, about drawing the correct number of straight and curved lines.

We can see then that relatively more of the subjects in Group VII performed as did the schizophrenics than did the normal groups (II, III, IV). But still this number was in the minority (6, or 25 percent). The majority (71 percent) made some kind of definite design, whereas, as can be recalled, only 20 percent of the psychotics did so. Obviously the factor of retarded intelligence was not the main cause of the performance of the schizophrenics. The latter were potentially, if not functionally, a good deal more intelligent than the subnormals. The difference then seems to be more one of attitude and quality of mental functioning. The subnormals were flexible enough to allow for some freedom of imagination and of expression in a constructive manner. They did draw a design, making use of spatial relationships in the rectangle rather than merely putting in the correct number of lines.

Conclusions

Schizophrenics whose predominant and prevailing attitude is a persecutory paranoid trend perform in a characteristic manner when asked to make a design of limited scope. They are unable and unwilling to build up a constructive idea about arranging straight and curved lines in a pattern as do normal subjects, and are obsessive about following explicitly the instructions concerning the limitations of the task, namely, employing a certain number of lines. They do what they are told as long as the task is one of simple understanding and recall (drawing 19 straight and 6 curved lines), but do not carry out the other part of the task which requires some use of thinking and imagination.

The task, then, is a failure as far as revealing individual differences among paranoids in the making of designs is concerned. For them a freer situation needs to be provided. They must be left alone with paper and pencil, or better yet, with finger paints and clay, in order that any emotional imaginative trends may be expressed in a manipulative rather than verbal manner. As a personality index or classificatory device for schizophrenics with persecutory paranoid attitudes, the designs test may be of some use: the patients behaved so consistently alike.

We have indicated that more normal individuals, but those who have some characteristic paranoid trends, perform more like the patients than like normal people in making the design. We have pointed out also that a maladjusted Navajo Indian, who was a gifted artist, made no attempt at making a pattern but drew the straight and curved lines linearly and rigidly as did the schizophrenics, whereas the other Navajos tested showed flexibility in working out definite patterns in their designs.

In addition, a group of Balinese artists, who had been making sketches and paintings in a freer and more voluntary situation, in a test situation which they were prevailed upon to try out, drew rigid and stereotyped lines with no attempt at spatial arrangement and interplay of straight and curved lines. Their behavior was due to the facts that they did not only dislike the test situation, but that they were unable to grasp a new idea as a whole, to use a certain number of lines and to build up a design. It was easier to get out of the situation by conscientiously putting in the correct number of lines and letting it go at that. Their performance was like that of the paranoid schizophrenics, and we have suggested that their attitude and modes of thinking were the same.

We have shown finally that the performances of schizophrenics and of subnormals was not similar in making the designs. Although the subnormals are limited in their range of understanding and imagination, their designs were more flexible in pattern arrangement than that of the patients. They were not obsessive about getting in the correct number of lines at the expense of developing a constructive idea. Qualitative rather than quantitative differences in modes of function, then, accounted for the difference in performance of the abnormals and normals.

Bali: The Value System
of a Steady State[1]

GREGORY BATESON

"Ethos" and "Schismogenesis"

IT WOULD BE an oversimplification—it would even be false—to say that science necessarily advances by the construction and empirical testing of successive working hypotheses. Among the physicists and chemists there may be some who really proceed in this orthodox manner, but among the social scientists there is perhaps not one. Our concepts are loosely defined—a haze of chiaroscuro prefiguring sharper lines still undrawn—and our hypotheses are still so vague that rarely can we imagine any crucial instance whose investigation will test them.

The present paper is an attempt to make more precise an idea which I published in 1936[2] and which has lain fallow since that time. The notion of ethos had proved a useful conceptual tool for me, and with it I had been able to get a sharper understanding of Iatmul culture. But this experience by no means proved that this tool would necessarily be useful in other hands or for the analysis of other cultures. The most general conclusion I could draw was of this order: that my own mental processes had certain characteristics; that the sayings, actions, and organization of the Iatmul had certain characteristics; and that the abstraction "ethos" performed some role—catalytic, perhaps —in easing the relation between these two specificities, my mind and the data which I myself had collected.

Originally published in Meyer Fortes, ed., *Social Structure* (Oxford, Clarendon Press, 1949), pp. 35–53. Reprinted with permission of the author.

[1] A term borrowed from communications engineering: that ongoing state of a system of interdependent variables which shows no progressive or irreversible change. The homeostasis of the internal environment of an organism is an example of "steady state."

[2] Gregory Bateson, *Naven* (Cambridge, Cambridge University Press, 1936).

Immediately after completing the manuscript of *Naven* I went to Bali with the intention of trying upon Balinese data this tool which had been evolved for the analysis of Iatmul. For one reason or another, however, I did not do this, partly because in Bali Margaret Mead and I were engaged in devising other tools—photographic methods of record and description—and partly because I was learning the techniques of applying genetic psychology to cultural data, but more especially because at some inarticulate level I felt that the tool was unsuitable for this new task.

It was not that ethos was in any sense disproved—indeed, a tool or a method can scarcely be proved false. It can only be shown to be not useful, and in this case there was not even a clear demonstration of uselessness. The method remained almost untried, and the most I could say was that, after that surrender to the data which is the first step in all anthropological study, ethological analysis did not seem to be the next thing to do.

It is now possible to show with Balinese data what peculiarities of that culture may have influenced me away from ethological analysis, and this demonstration will lead to a greater generalization of the abstraction ethos. We shall in the process make certain heuristic advances which may guide us to more rigorous descriptive procedures in dealing with other cultures.

1. The analysis of Iatmul data led to the definition of ethos as: "The expression of a culturally standardized system of organization of the instincts and emotions of the individuals."[3]

2. Analysis of Iatmul ethos—consisting in the ordering of data so as to make evident certain recurrent "emphases" or "themes"—led to recognition of schismogenesis. It appeared that the working of Iatmul society involved *inter alia* two classes of regenerative[4] or "vicious" circles. Both of these were sequences of social interaction

---

[3] *Ibid.*, p. 118.

[4] The terms "regenerative" and "degenerative" are borrowed from communications engineering. A regenerative or "vicious" circle is a chain of variables of the general type: increase in A causes increase in B; increase in B causes increase in C; . . . increase in N causes increase in A. Such a system, if provided with the necessary energy sources and if external factors permit, will clearly operate at a greater and greater rate of intensity. A "degenerative" or "self-corrective" circle differs from a regenerative circle in containing at least one link of the type: "increase in N causes decrease in M." The house thermostat or the steam engine with a governor are examples of such self-correcting systems. It will be noted that in many instances the same material circuit may be either regenerative or degenerative according to the amount of loading, frequency of impulses transmitted around the path, and time characteristics of the total path.

such that A's acts were stimuli for B's acts, which in turn became stimuli for more intense action on the part of A, and so on, A and B being persons acting either as individuals or as group members.

3. These schismogenic sequences could be classified into two classes: (*a*) symmetrical schismogenesis, where the mutually promoting actions of A and B were essentially similar, for example, in cases of competition, rivalry, and the like; and (*b*) complementary schismogenesis, where the mutually promoting actions are essentially dissimilar but mutually appropriate, for example, in cases of dominance-submission, succouring-dependence, exhibitionism-spectatorship, and the like.

4. In 1939 a considerable advance was made in defining the formal relations between the concepts of symmetrical and complementary schismogenesis. This came from an attempt to state schismogenenic theory in terms of Richardson's equations for international armaments races.[5] The equations for rivalry evidently gave a first approximation to what I had called "symmetrical schismogenesis." These equations assume that the intensity of A's actions (the rate of his arming, in Richardson's case) is simply proportional to the amount by which B is ahead of A. The stimulus term in fact is $(B - A)$, and when this term is positive it is expected that A will engage in efforts to arm. Richardson's second equation makes the same assumption *mutatis mutandis* about B's actions. These equations suggested that other simply rivalrous or competitive phenomena—for example, boasting— though not subject to such simple measurement as expenditure on armament, might yet when ultimately measured be reducible to a simply analogous set of relations.

The matter was, however, not so clear in the case of complementary schismogenesis. Richardson's equations for "submission" evidently define a phenomenon somewhat different from a progressive complementary relationship, and the form of his equations describes the action of a factor "submissiveness" which slows down and ultimately reverses the sign of warlike effort. What was, however, required to describe complementary schismogenesis was an equational form giving a sharp and discontinuous reversal of sign. Such an equational form is achieved by supposing A's actions in a complementary relationship to be proportional to a stimulus term of the type $(A - B)$. Such a form has also the advantage of automatically defining the actions of one of the participants as negative, and thus gives some mathematical

[5] L. F. Richardson, "Generalized Foreign Politics," *British Journal of Psychology*, Monograph Supplement XXIII (1939).

analogue for the apparent psychological relatedness of domination to submission, exhibitionism to spectatorship, succouring to dependence, and so forth.

Notably this formulation is itself a negative of the formulation for rivalry, the stimulus term being the opposite. It had been observed that symmetrical sequences of actions tend sharply to reduce the strain of excessively complementary relationships between persons or groups.[6] It is tempting to ascribe this effect to some hypothesis which would make the two types of schismogenesis in some degree psychologically incompatible, as is done by the above formulation.

5. It is of interest to note that all the modes associated with the erogenous zones,[7] though not clearly quantifiable, define themes for *complementary* relationship.

6. The link with erogenous zones suggested in 5, above, indicates that we ought, perhaps, not to think of simple rising exponential curves of intensity limited only by factors analogous to fatigue, such as Richardson's equations would imply; but rather that we should expect our curves to be bounded by phenomena comparable to orgasm—that the achievement of a certain degree of bodily or neural involvement or intensity may be followed by a release of schismogenic tension. Indeed, all that we know about human beings in various sorts of simple contests would seem to indicate that this is the case, and that the conscious or unconscious wish for release of this kind is an important factor which draws the participants on and prevents them from simply withdrawing from contests which would otherwise not commend themselves to "common sense." If there be any basic human characteristic which makes man prone to struggle, it would seem to be this hope of release from tension through total involvement. In the case of war this factor is undoubtedly often potent. (The real truth—that in modern warfare only a very few of the participants achieve this climactic release—seems hardly to stand against the insidious myth of "total" war.)

[6] Bateson, *Naven*, p. 173.

[7] E. H. Homburger, "Configurations in Play: Psychological Notes," *Psychoanalytic Quarterly*, VI (1937), 138–214. This paper, one of the most important in the literature seeking to state psychoanalytic hypotheses in more rigorous terms, deals with the "modes" appropriate to the various erogenous zones—intrusion, incorporation, retention, and the like—and shows how these modes may be transferred from one zone to another. This leads the writer to a chart of the possible permutations and combinations of such transferred modalities. This chart provides precise means of describing the course of the development of a large variety of different types of character structure (for example, as met with in a different culture).

7. In 1936 it was suggested that the phenomenon of "falling in love" might be comparable to a schismogenesis with the signs reversed, and even that "if the course of true love ever ran smooth it would follow an exponential curve."[8] Richardson[9] has since, independently, made the same point in more formal terms. Paragraph 6, above, clearly indicates that the "exponential curves" must give place to some type of curve which will not rise indefinitely but will reach a climax and then fall. For the rest, however, the obvious relationship of these interactive phenomena to climax and orgasm very much strengthens the case for regarding schismogenesis and those cumulative sequences of interaction which lead to love as often psychologically equivalent. (Witness the curious confusions between fighting and love-making, the symbolic identifications of orgasm with death, the recurrent use by mammals of organs of offense as ornaments of sexual attraction, and so forth.)

8. Schismogenic sequences were not found in Bali. This negative statement is of such importance and conflicts with so many theories of social opposition and Marxian determinism that, in order to achieve credibility, I must here describe schematically the process of character formation, the resulting Balinese character structure, the exceptional instances in which some sort of cumulative interaction can be recognized, and the methods by which quarrels and status differentiation are handled. (Detailed analysis of the various points and the supporting data cannot here be reproduced, but references will be given to published sources where the data can be examined.)[10]

Balinese Character

(*a*) The most important exception to the above generalization occurs in the relationship between adults (especially parents) and children. Typically, the mother will start a small flirtation with the child, pulling its penis or otherwise stimulating it to interpersonal activity. This will excite the child, and for a few moments cumulative interaction will occur. Then just as the child, approaching some small climax, flings its arms round the mother's neck, her attention wanders. At this point the child will typically start an alternative cumulative interaction, building up toward temper tantrum. The mother will

---

[8] Bateson, *Naven*, p. 197.

[9] Richardson, "Generalized Foreign Politics."

[10] See especially Gregory Bateson and Margaret Mead, *Balinese Character* (New York, New York Academy of Sciences, 1942). Since this photographic record is available, no photographs are included in the present paper.

either play a spectator's role, enjoying the child's tantrum, or, if the child actually attacks her, will brush off his attack with no show of anger on her part. These sequences can be seen either as an expression of the mother's distaste for this type of personal involvement or as contexts in which the child acquires a deep distrust of such involvement. The perhaps basically human tendency toward cumulative personal interaction is thus muted.[11] It is possible that some sort of continuing plateau of intensity is substituted for climax as the child becomes more fully adjusted to Balinese life. This cannot at present be clearly documented for sexual relations, but there are indications that a plateau type of sequence is characteristic for trance and for quarrels (see *d* below).

(*b*) Similar sequences have the effect of diminishing the child's tendencies toward competitive and rivalrous behavior. The mother will, for example, tease the child by suckling the baby of some other woman and will enjoy her own child's efforts to push the intruder from the breast.[12]

(*c*) In general the lack of climax is characteristic for Balinese music, drama, and other art forms. The music typically has a progression, derived from the logic of its formal structure, and modifications of intensity determined by the duration and progress of the working out of these formal relations. It does not have the sort of rising intensity and climax structure characteristic of modern occidental music, but rather a formal progression.[13]

(*d*) Balinese culture includes definite techniques for dealing with quarrels. Two men who have quarreled will go formally to the office of the local representative of the *rajă* and will there register their quarrel, agreeing that whichever speaks to the other shall pay a fine or make an offering to the gods. Later, if the quarrel terminates, this contract may be formally nullified. Smaller—but similar—avoidances (*pwik*) are practiced, even by small children in their quarrels. It is significant, perhaps, that this procedure is not an attempt to influence the protagonists away from hostility and toward friendship. Rather, it is a formal recognition of the state of their mutual relationship, and possibly, in some sort, of a pegging of the relationship at that state. If this interpretation is correct, this method of dealing with quarrels would correspond to the substitution of a plateau for a climax.

---

[11] Bateson and Mead, *Balinese Character*, Pl. 47 and pp. 32–36.

[12] *Ibid.*, Pls. 49, 52, 53, and 69–72.

[13] See Colin McPhee, "The 'Absolute' Music of Bali," *Modern Music*, XII, No. 4 (1935), 163–69, and his *A House in Bali* (New York, John Day, 1946).

(*e*) In regard to warfare, contemporary comment on the old wars between the *rajă* indicates that in the period when the comments were collected (1936–39) war was thought of as containing large elements of mutual avoidance. The village of Bayung Gĕdè was surrounded by an old vallum and foss, and the people explained the functions of these fortifications in the following terms: "If you and I had a quarrel, then you would go and dig a ditch around your house. Later I would come to fight with you, but I would find the ditch and then there would be no fight"—a sort of mutual Maginot Line psychology. Similarly the boundaries between neighboring kingdoms were, in general, a deserted no-man's land inhabited only by vagrants and exiles. (A very different psychology of warfare was no doubt developed when the kingdom of Karangasĕm embarked on the conquest of the neighboring island of Lombok in the beginning of the eighteenth century. The psychology of this militarism has not been investigated, but there is reason to believe that the time perspective of the Balinese colonists in Lombok is today significantly different from that of Balinese in Bali.)[14]

(*f*) The formal techniques of social influence—oratory and the like—are almost totally lacking in Balinese culture. To demand the continued attention of an individual or to exert emotional influence upon a group are alike distasteful and virtually impossible; because in such circumstances the attention of the victim rapidly wanders. Even such continued speech as would, in most cultures, be used for the telling of stories does not occur in Bali. The narrator will, typically, pause after a sentence or two and wait for some member of the audience to ask him a concrete question about some detail of the plot. He will then answer the question and so resume his narration. This procedure apparently breaks the cumulative tension by irrelevant interaction.

(*g*) The principal hierarchical structures in the society—the caste system and the hierarchy of full citizens who are the village council—are rigid. There are no contexts in which one individual could conceivably compete with another for position in either of these systems. An individual may lose his membership in the hierarchy for various acts, but his place in it cannot be altered. Should he later return to orthodoxy and be accepted back, he will return to his original position in relation to the other members.[15]

---

[14] See Bateson, "An Old Temple and a New Myth," in this volume, p. 111.

[15] See Margaret Mead, "Public Opinion Mechanisms among Primitive Peoples," *Public Opinion Quarterly*, I, No. 3 (1937), 5–16.

The foregoing descriptive generalizations are all partial answers to a negative question—"Why is Balinese society nonschismogenic?"—and from the combination of these generalizations we arrive at a picture of a society differing very markedly from our own, from that of the Iatmul, from those systems of social opposition which Radcliffe-Brown has analyzed, and from any social structure postulated by Marxian analysis.

We started with the hypothesis that human beings have a tendency to involve themselves in sequences of cumulative interaction, and this hypothesis is still left virtually intact. Among the Balinese the babies, at least, evidently have such tendencies. But for sociological validity this hypothesis must now be guarded with a parenthetical clause stipulating that these tendencies are operative in the dynamics of society only if the childhood training is not such as to prevent their expression in adult life.

We have made an advance in our knowledge of the scope of human character formation in demonstrating that these tendencies toward cumulative interaction are subject to some sort of modification, deconditioning, or inhibition.[16] And this is an important advance. We know how it is that the Balinese are nonschismogenic, and we know how their distaste for schismogenic patterns is expressed in various details of the social organization—the rigid hierarchies, the institutions for the handling of quarrels, and so forth—but we still know nothing of the positive dynamics of the society. We have answered only the negative question.

Balinese Ethos

The next step, therefore, is to ask about Balinese ethos. What actually are the motives and the values which accompany the complex and rich cultural activities of the Balinese? What, if not competitive and other types of cumulative interrelationship, causes the Balinese to carry out the elaborate patterns of their lives?

1. It is immediately clear to any visitor to Bali that the driving force for cultural activity is *not* either acquisitiveness or crude physiological need. The Balinese, especially in the plains, are not hungry or poverty-stricken. They are wasteful of food, and a very considerable part of their activity goes into entirely nonproductive activities of an

---

[16] As is usual in anthropology, the data are not sufficiently precise to give us any clue as to the nature of the learning processes involved. Anthropology, at best, is only able to *raise* problems of this order. The next step must be left for laboratory experimentation.

artistic or ritual nature in which food and wealth are lavishly expended. Essentially, we are dealing with an economy of plenty rather than an economy of scarcity. Some, indeed, are rated "poor" by their fellows, but none of these poor are threatened by starvation, and the suggestion that human beings may actually starve in great occidental cities, was, to the Balinese, unutterably shocking.

2. In their economic transactions the Balinese show a great deal of carefulness in their small dealings. They are "penny wise." On the other hand this carefulness is counteracted by occasional "pound foolishness" when they will expend large sums of money upon ceremonials and other forms of lavish consumption. There are very few Balinese who have the idea of steadily maximizing their wealth or property; these few are partly disliked and partly regarded as oddities. For the vast majority the "saving of pennies" is done with a limited time perspective and a limited level of aspiration. They are saving until they have enough to spend largely on some ceremonial. We should not describe Balinese economics in terms of the individual's attempt to maximize value but rather compare it with the relaxation oscillations of physiology and engineering, realizing that not only is this analogy descriptive of their sequences of transactions but that they themselves see these sequences as naturally having some such form.

3. The Balinese are markedly dependent upon spatial orientation. In order to be able to behave they must know their cardinal points, and, if a Balinese is taken by motorcar over twisting roads so that he loses his sense of direction, he may become severely disorientated and unable to act (for example, a dancer may become unable to dance) until he has got back his orientation by seeing some important landmark, such as the central mountain of the island around which the cardinal points are structured. There is a comparable dependence upon social orientation, but with this difference: that where the spatial orientation is in a horizontal plane, social orientation is felt to be, in the main, vertical. When two strangers are brought together, it is necessary, before they can converse with any freedom, that their relative caste positions be stated. One will ask the other, "Where do you sit?" and this is a metaphor for caste. It is asking, essentially, "Do you sit high or low?" When each knows the caste of the other, each will then know what etiquette and what linguistic forms he should adopt, and conversation can then proceed. Lacking such orientation, a Balinese is tongue-tied.

4. It is common to find that activity (other than the "penny-wisdom" mentioned above) rather than being purposive, that is,

aimed at some deferred goal, is valued for itself. The artist, the dancer, the musician, and the priest may receive a pecuniary reward for their professional activity, but only in rare cases is this reward adequate to recompense the artist even for his time and materials. The reward is a token of appreciation, it is a definition of the context in which the theatrical company performs, but it is not the economic mainstay of the troupe. The earnings of the troupe may be saved up to enable them to buy new costumes, but when finally the costumes are bought it is usually necessary for every member to make a considerable contribution to the common fund in order to pay for them. Similarly, in regard to the offerings which are taken to every temple feast, there is no purpose in this enormous expenditure of artistic work and real wealth. The god will not bring any benefit because you made a beautiful structure of flowers and fruit for the calendric feast in his temple, nor will he avenge your abstention. Instead of deferred purpose there is an immediate and imminent satisfaction in performing beautifully, with everybody else, that which it is correct to perform in each particular context.

5. In general there is evident enjoyment to be had from doing things busily with large crowds of other people.[17] Conversely there is such misfortune inherent in the loss of group membership that the threat of this loss in one of the most serious sanctions in the culture.

6. It is of great interest to note that many Balinese actions are articulately accounted for in sociological terms rather than in terms of individual goals or values.[18]

This is the most conspicuous in regard to all actions related to the village council, the hierarchy which includes all full citizens. This body, in its secular aspects, is referred to as *I Désa* (literally, "Mr. Village"), and numerous rules and procedures are rationalized by reference to this abstract personage. Similarly, in its sacred aspects, the village is deified as *Batară Désă* (God Village), to whom shrines are erected and offerings brought. (We may guess that a Durkheimian analysis would seem to the Balinese to be an obvious and appropriate approach to the understanding of much of their public culture.)

In particular all money transactions which involve the village treasury are governed by the generalization, "The village does not

---

[17] Bateson and Mead, *Balinese Character*, Pl. 5.

[18] Cf. Bateson, *Naven*, pp. 250 ff., where it was suggested that we must expect to find that some peoples of the world would relate their actions to the sociological frame.

lose" (*Désanne sing dadi pochol*). This generalization applies, for example, in all cases in which a beast is sold from the village herd. Under no circumstances can the village accept a price less than that which it actually or nominally paid. (It is important to note that the rule takes the form of fixing a lower limit and is not an injunction to maximize the village treasury.)

A peculiar awareness of the nature of social processes is evident in such incidents as the following: A poor man was about to undergo one of the important and expensive *rites de passage* which are necessary for persons as they approach the top of the council hierarchy. We asked what would happen if he refused to undertake this expenditure. The first answer was that, if he were too poor, *I Désă* would *lend* him the money. In response to further pressing as to what would happen if he really refused, we were told that nobody ever had refused but that if somebody did nobody would go through the ceremony again. Implicit in this answer and in the fact that nobody ever does refuse is the assumption that the ongoing cultural process is itself to be valued.

7. Actions which are culturally correct (*patut*) are acceptable and aesthetically valued. Actions which are permissible (*dadi*) are of more or less neutral value; while actions which are not permissible (*sing dadi*) are to be deprecated and avoided. These generalizations, in their translated form, are no doubt true in many cultures, but it is important to get a clear understanding of what the Balinese mean by *dadi*. The notion is not to be equated with our "etiquette" or "law," since each of these invokes the value judgment of some other person or sociological entity. In Bali there is no feeling that actions have been or are categorized as *dadi* or *sing dadi* by some human or supernatural authority. Rather, the statement that such-and-such an action is *dadi* is an absolute generalization to the effect that under the given circumstances this action is regular.[19] It is wrong for a casteless person to address a prince in other than the "polished language," and it is wrong for a menstruating woman to enter a temple. The prince or the deity may express annoyance, but there is no feeling that either the prince, the deity, or the casteless person made the rules. The offense is felt to be against the order and natural structure of the universe rather than against the actual person offended. The offender, even in such serious matters as incest (for which he may be extruded

[19] The word *dadi* is also used as a copula referring to changes in social status. *I Anu dadi Kubayan* means "So and so has become a village official."

from the society)[20] is not blamed for anything worse than stupidity and clumsiness. Rather, he is "an unfortunate person" (*anak lachur*), and misfortune may come to any of us "when it is our turn." Further, it must be stressed that these patterns which define correct and permissive behavior are exceedingly complex (especially the rules of language) and that the individual Balinese (even to some degree inside his own family) has continual anxiety lest he make an error. Moreover, the rules are not of such a kind that they can be summarized either in a simple recipe or an emotional attitude. Etiquette cannot be deduced from some comprehensive statement about the other person's feelings or from respect for superiors. The details are too complex and too various for this, and so the individual Balinese is forever picking his way, like a tightrope walker, afraid at any moment lest he make some misstep.

8. The metaphor from postural balance used in the last paragraph is demonstrably applicable in many contexts of Balinese culture:

(*a*) The fear of loss of support is an important theme in Balinese childhood.[21]

(*b*) Elevation (with its attendant problems of physical and metaphorical balance) is the passive complement of respect.[22]

(*c*) The Balinese child is elevated like a superior person or a god.[23]

(*d*) In cases of actual physical elevation[24] the duty of balancing the system falls on the supporting lower person, but control of the direction in which the system will move is in the hands of the elevated. The little girl standing in trance on a man's shoulders can cause her bearer to go wherever she desires by merely leaning in that direction. He must then move in that direction in order to maintain the balance of the system.

(*e*) A large proportion of our collection of 1200 Balinese carvings shows preoccupation on the part of the artist with problems of balance.[25]

(*f*) The witch, the personification of fear, frequently uses a gesture called *kapar*, which is described as that of a man falling from a coconut palm on suddenly seeing a snake. In this gesture the arms are raised sideways to a position somewhat above the head.

(*g*) The ordinary Balinese term for the period before the coming of the white man is "when the world was steady" (*dugas gumine entég*).

[20] Mead, "Public Opinion Mechanisms among Primitive People."

[21] Bateson and Mead, *Balinese Character*, Pls. 17, 67, and 79.

[22] *Ibid.*, Pls. 10–14.   [23] *Ibid.*, Pl. 45.   [24] *Ibid.*, Pl. 10, Fig. 3.

[25] At present it is not possible to make such a statement in sharply defined quantitative terms, the available judgments being subjective and occidental.

Applications of the Von Neumannian Game

Even this very brief listing of some of the elements in Balinese ethos suffices to indicate theoretical problems of prime importance. Let us consider the matter in abstract terms. One of the hypotheses underlying most sociology is that the dynamics of the social mechanism can be described by assuming that the individuals constituting that mechanism are motivated to maximize certain variables. In conventional economic theory it is assumed that the individuals will maximize value, while in schismogenic theory it was tacitly assumed that the individuals would maximize intangible but still simple variables such as prestige, self-esteem, or even submissiveness. The Balinese, however, do not maximize any such simple variables.

In order to define the sort of contrast which exists between the Balinese system and any competitive system, let us start by considering the premises of a strictly competitive Von Neumannian game and proceed by considering what changes we must make in these premises in order to approximate more closely to the Balinese system.

1. The players in a Von Neumannian game are, by hypothesis, motivated only in terms of a single linear (sc. monetary) scale of value. Their strategies are determined: (*a*) by the rules of the hypothetical game; and (*b*) by their intelligence, which is, by hypothesis, sufficient to solve all problems presented by the game. Von Neumann shows that, under certain definable circumstances depending upon the number of players and upon the rules, coalitions of various sorts will be formed by the players, and in fact Von Neumann's analysis concentrates mainly upon the structure of these coalitions and the distribution of value among the members. In comparing these games with human societies we shall regard social organizations as analogous to coalition systems.[26]

---

[26] Alternatively, we might handle the analogy in another way. A social system is, as Von Neumann and Morgenstern point out, comparable to a nonzero sum game in which one or more coalitions of people play against each other and against nature. The nonzero sum characteristic is based on the fact that value is continually extracted from the natural environment. Inasmuch as Balinese society exploits nature, the total entity, including both environment and people, is clearly comparable to a game requiring coalition between people. It is possible, however, that the subdivision of the total game comprising the *people only* might be such that the formation of coalitions within it would not be essential—that is, Balinese society may differ from most other societies in that the "rules" of the relationship between people define a "game" of the type Von Neumann would call "nonessential." This possibility is not here examined. (See John Von Neumann and Oskar Morgenstern, *Theory of Games and Economic Behavior* [Princeton, Princeton University Press, 1944].)

2. Von Neumannian systems differ from human societies in the following respects:

(*a*) His "players" are from the start completely intelligent, whereas human beings learn. For human beings we must expect that the rules of the game and the conventions associated with any particular set of coalitions will become incorporated into the character structures of the individual players.

(*b*) The mammalian value scale is not simple and monotone but may be exceedingly complex. We know, even at a physiological level, that calcium will not replace vitamins, nor will an amino acid replace oxygen. Further, we know that the animal does not strive to maximize its supply of any of these discrepant commodities, but rather is required to maintain the supply of each within tolerable limits. Too much may be as harmful as too little. It is also doubtful whether mammalian preference is always transient.

(*c*) In the Von Neumannian system the number of moves in a given "play" of a game is assumed to be finite. The strategic problems of the individuals are soluble because the individual can operate within a limited time perspective. He need only look forward a finite distance to the end of the play when the gains and losses will be paid up and everything will start again from a *tabula rasa*. In human society life is not punctuated in this way, and each individual faces a vista of unknowable factors whose number increases (probably exponentially) into the future.

(*d*) The Von Neumannian players are, by hypothesis, not susceptible either to economic death or to boredom. The losers can go on losing forever, and no player can withdraw from the game, even though the outcome of every play is definitely predictable in probability terms.

3. Of these differences between Von Neumannian and human systems, only the differences in value scales and the possibility of "death" concern us here. For the sake of simplicity we shall assume that the other differences, though very profound, can for the moment be ignored.

4. Curiously, we may note that, although men are mammals and therefore have a primary value system which is multidimensional and nonmaximizing, it is yet possible for these creatures to be put into contexts in which they will strive to maximize one or a few simple variables (money, prestige, power, and so forth).

5. Since the multidimensional value system is apparently primary, the problem presented by, for example, Iatmul social organization is not so much to account for the behavior of Iatmul individuals by

invoking (or abstracting) their value system; we should ask also how that value system is imposed on the mammalian individuals by the social organization in which they find themselves. Conventionally in anthropology this question is attacked through genetic psychology. We endeavor to collect data to show how the value system implicit in the social organization is built into the character structure of the individuals in their childhood. There is, however, an alternative approach which would momentarily ignore, as Von Neumann does, the phenomena of learning and consider merely the strategic implications of those contexts which must occur in accordance with the given "rules" and the coalition system. In this connection it is important to note that competitive contexts—provided the individuals can be made to recognize the contexts as competitive—inevitably reduce the complex gamut of values to a very simple and even linear and monotone term.[27] Considerations of this sort, *plus* descriptions of the regularities in the process of character formation, probably suffice to describe how simple value scales are imposed upon mammalian individuals in competitive societies such as that of Iatmul or twentieth-century America.

6. In Balinese society, on the other hand, we find an entirely different state of affairs. Neither the individual nor the village is concerned to maximize any simple variable. Rather, they would seem to be concerned to maximize something which we may call stability, using this term perhaps in a highly metaphorical way. (There is, in fact, one simple quantitative variable which does appear to be maximized. This variable is the amount of any fine imposed by the village. When first imposed the fines are mostly very small, but if payment is delayed the amount of the fine is increased very steeply, and if there be any sign that the offender is *refusing* to pay—"opposing the village"—the fine is at once raised to an enormous sum and the offender is deprived of membership in the community until he is willing to give up his opposition. Then a part of the fine may be excused.)

7. Let us now consider a hypothetical system consisting of a number of identical players, plus an umpire who is concerned with the maintenance of stability among the players. Let us further suppose that the players are liable to economic death, that our umpire is concerned to see that this shall not occur, and that the umpire has power to make certain alterations in the rules of the game or in the probabilities associated with chance moves. Clearly this umpire will be in

[27] L. K. Frank, "The Cost of Competition," *Plan Age*, VI (1940), 314–24.

more or less continual conflict with the players. He is striving to maintain a dynamic equilibrium or steady state, and this we may rephrase as the attempt to maximize the chances *against* the maximization of any single simple variable.

8. Ashby has pointed out in rigorous terms that the steady state and continued existence of complex interactive systems depend upon preventing the maximization of any variable, and that any continued increase in any variable will inevitably result in, and be limited by, irreversible changes in the system. He has also pointed out that in such systems it is very important to permit certain variables to alter.[28] The steady state of an engine with a governor is unlikely to be maintained if the position of the balls of the governor is clamped. Similarly a tightrope walker with a balancing pole will not be able to maintain his balance except by *varying* the forces which he exerts upon the pole.

9. Returning now to the conceptual model suggested in paragraph 7, let us take one further step toward making this model comparable with Balinese society. Let us substitute for the umpire a village council composed of all the players. We now have a system which presents a number of analogies to our balancing acrobat. When they speak as members of the village council, the players by hypothesis are interested in maintaining the steady state of the system—that is, in preventing the maximization of any simple variable the excessive increase of which would produce irreversible change. In their daily life, however, they are still engaged in simple competitive strategies.

10. The next step toward making our model resemble Balinese society more closely is clearly to postulate in the character structure of the individuals and/or in the contexts of their daily life those factors which will motivate them toward maintenance of the steady state not only when they speak in council but also in their other interpersonal relations. These factors are in fact recognizable in Bali and have been enumerated above. In our analysis of why Balinese society is nonschismogenic, we noted that the Balinese child learns to avoid cumulative interaction, that is, the maximization of certain simple variables, and that the social organization and contexts of daily life are so constructed as to preclude competitive interaction. Further, in our analysis of the Balinese ethos, we noted recurrent valuation: (*a*) of the clear and static definition of status and spatial orientation, and (*b*) of balance and such movement as will conduce to balance.

---

[28] W. R. Ashby, "Effect of Controls on Stability," *Nature*, CLV, No. 3930 (February 24, 1945), 242–43.

In sum it seems that the Balinese extend to human relationships attitudes based upon bodily balance and that they generalize the idea that motion is essential to balance. This last point gives us, I believe, a partial answer to the question of why society not only continues to function but functions rapidly and busily, continually undertaking ceremonial and artistic tasks which are not economically or competitively determined. This steady state is maintained by continual nonprogressive change.

Schismogenic System versus the Steady State

I have discussed two types of social system in such schematic outline that it is possible to state clearly a contrast between them. Both types of system, so far as they are capable of maintaining themselves without progressive or irreversible change, achieve the steady state. There are, however, profound differences between them in the manner in which the steady state is regulated.

The Iatmul system, which is here used as a prototype of schismogenic systems, includes a number of regenerative causal circuits or vicious circles. Each such circuit consists of two or more individuals (or groups of individuals) who participate in potentially cumulative interaction. Each human individual is an energy source or "relay," such that the energy used in his responses is not derived from the stimuli but from his own metabolic processes. It therefore follows that such a schismogenic system is—unless controlled—liable to excessive increase of those acts which characterize the schismogeneses. The anthropologist who attempts even a qualitative description of such a system must therefore identify: (1) the individuals and groups involved in schismogenesis and the routes of communication between them; (2) the categories of acts and contexts characteristic of the schismogeneses; (3) the processes whereby the individuals become psychologically apt to perform these acts and/or the nature of the contexts which force these acts upon them; and lastly, (4) he must identify the mechanisms of factors which control the schismogeneses. These controling factors may be of at least three distinct types: (a) degenerative causal loops may be superposed upon the schismogeneses so that when the latter reach a certain intensity some form of restraint is applied—as occurs in occidental systems when a government intervenes to limit economic competition; (b) there may be, in addition to the schismogeneses already considered, other cumulative interactions acting in an opposite sense and so promoting social integration rather than fission; (c) the increase in schismogenesis may be limited by factors which are internally or externally environmental to the parts of the schismogenic circuit. Such factors which have only small restraining effect at low intensities of schismogenesis may increase with increase of intensity. Friction, fatigue, and limitation of energy supply would be examples of such factors.

In contrast with these schismogenic systems, Balinese society is an entirely different type of mechanism, and in describing it the anthropologist must follow entirely different procedures, for which rules cannot as yet be laid down. Since the class of "nonschismogenic" social systems is defined only in negative terms, we cannot assume that members of the class will have common characteristics. In the analysis of the Balinese system, however, the following steps occurred, and it is possible that some at least of these may be applicable in the analysis of other cultures of this class: (1) it was observed that schismogenic sequences are rare in Bali; (2) the exceptional cases in which such sequences occur were investigated; (3) from this investigation it appeared, (a) that in general the contexts which recur in Balinese social life preclude cumulative interaction and (b) that childhood experience trains the child away from seeking climax in personal interaction; (4) it was shown that certain positive values—related to balance—recur in the culture and are incorporated into the character structure during childhood, and, further, that these values may be specifically related to the steady state; (5) a more detailed study is now required to arrive at a systematic statement about the self-correcting characteristics of the system. It is evident that the ethos alone is insufficient to maintain the steady state. From time to time the village or some other entity does step in to correct infractions. The nature of these instances of the working of the corrective mechanism must be studied; but it is clear that this intermittent mechanism is very different from the continually acting restraints which must be present in all schismogenic systems.

Bibliography

PUBLICATIONS

Abel, Theodora M. "Free Designs of Limited Scope as a Personality Index," *Character and Personality*, VII, No. 1 (September, 1938), 50–62. Reprinted in this volume, pp. 371–83.

Bateson, Gregory. *Bali: The Human Problem of Reoccupation.* New York, The Museum of Modern Art, 1942. Mimeographed.

—— "Bali: The Value System of a Steady State," in Meyer Fortes, ed., *Social Structure: Studies Presented to A. R. Radcliffe-Brown.* Oxford, Clarendon Press, 1949, pp. 35–53. Reprinted in this volume, pp. 384–401.

—— "Comment on 'The Comparative Study of Culture and the Purposive Cultivation of Democratic Values,' by Margaret Mead," in Conference on Science, Philosophy, and Religion in Their Relation to the Democratic Way of Life, *Science, Philosophy, and Religion: 2d Symposium.* New York, The Conference, 1942, pp. 81–97.

—— "Cultural Determinants of Personality," in J. McV. Hunt, ed., *Personality and the Behavior Disorders.* New York, Ronald Press Co., 1944, Vol. II, pp. 714–36.

—— Equilibrium and Climax in Interpersonal Relations. Paper read at the Conference of Topological Psychologists, held at Smith College, Northampton, Mass., December 31, 1940–January 2, 1941.

—— "Experiments in Thinking about Observed Ethnological Material," *Philosophy of Science*, VIII, No. 1 (1941), 53–68.

—— "The Frustration-Agression Hypothesis," *Psychological Review*, XLVIII, No. 4 (1941), 350–55. Reprinted in Society for the Psychological Study of Social Issues, *Readings in Social Psychology*, ed. by Theodore M. Newcomb, Eugene L. Hartley, *et al.* New York, Holt, 1947, pp. 267–68.

——"Morale and National Character," in Goodwin Watson, ed., *Civilian Morale; Second Yearbook of the Society for the Psychological Study of Social Issues.* Boston, Houghton Mifflin, 1942, pp. 71–91.

This bibliography lists studies based primarily on research done prior to World War II. Most of the items listed herein are from "Balinese Bibliography," in Margaret Mead and Martha Wolfenstein, eds., *Childhood in Contemporary Cultures* (Chicago, University of Chicago Press, 1955), pp. 95–98. A few later works by the authors of the essays in this volume have been added.

—— "An Old Temple and a New Myth," *Djawa*, XVII, Nos. 5–6 (1937), 291–307. Reprinted in this volume, pp. 111–36.

Bateson, Gregory, and Margaret Mead. *Balinese Character: A Photographic Analysis*. Special Publications of the New York Academy of Sciences, Vol. II. New York, the Académy, 1942; reissued 1962.

Belo, Jane. *Bali: Rangda and Barong*. American Ethnological Society Monographs, 16. New York, J. J. Augustin, 1949.

—— *Bali: Temple Festival*. American Ethnological Society Monographs, 22. Locust Valley, N.Y., J. J. Augustin, 1953.

—— "Balinese Children's Drawing," *Djawa*, XVII, Nos. 5–6 (1937), 248–59. Reedited version in Margaret Mead and Martha Wolfenstein, eds., *Childhood in Contemporary Cultures*. Chicago, University of Chicago Press, 1955, pp. 52–69. Reprinted in this volume, pp. 240–59.

—— "The Balinese Temper," *Character and Personality*, IV (December, 1935), 120–46. Reprinted in this volume, pp. 85–110.

—— "A Study of a Balinese Family," *American Anthropologist*, New Ser., XXXVIII, No. 1 (1936), 12–31. Reprinted in this volume, pp. 350–70.

—— "A Study of Customs Pertaining to Twins in Bali," *Tijdschrift voor Indische Taal-, Land-, en Volkenkunde*, LXXV, No. 4 (1935), 483–549. Reprinted in this volume, pp. 3–56.

Covarrubias, Miguel. *Island of Bali*. New York, Knopf, 1937.

Eissler, Kurt, R. "Balinese Character," *Psychiatry*, VII, No. 2 (1944), 139–44.

Gorer, Geoffrey. *Bali and Angkor; or, Looking at Life and Death*. London, Michael Joseph, 1936.

Goris, R. "Overzicht over de belangrijste Litteratuur betreffende de Cultur van Bali over het Tijdvak 1920–1935," *Medeelingen Kirtya Liefrinck van der Tuuk*, Aflevering 5, 1936 (?).

Holt, Claire. Analytical Catalogue of Collection of Balinese Carvings. MS, American Museum of Natural History, New York.

—— *Art in Indonesia; Continuities and Change*. Ithaca, N.Y., Cornell University Press, 1967.

—— " 'Bandit Island,' " a Short Exploratory Trip to Nusă Pĕnida," *Djawa*, *XVI*, Nos. 1–3 (1936). Reprinted in this volume, pp. 67–84.

—— "Les Danses de Bali," *Archives internationales de la danse*, 1935, Pt. I, pp. 51–53; Pt. II, pp. 84–86.

—— "Théâtre et danses aux Indes néerlandaises," in Exposition des archives internationales de la danse, XIIIe, *Catalogue et commentaires*. Paris, Masson, 1939, p. 86.

Holt, Claire, and Gregory Bateson. "Form and Function of the Dance in Bali," in *The Function of the Dance in Human Society, a Seminar Directed by Franziska Boas*. New York, The Boas School, 1944, pp. 46–52. Reprinted in this volume, pp. 322–30.

Kat Angelino, A. D. A. de, and Tyra de Kleen. *Mudras auf Bali*. Hagen i. W., Folkwang-Verlag, 1923.

Lekkerkerker, Cornelis. *Bali en Lombok: Overzicht der Litteratuur omtrent deze Eilanden tot einde 1919*. Uitgave van het Bali-Instituut. Rijswijk, Blankwaardt & Schoonhoven, 1920.

McPhee, Colin. "The 'Absolute' Music of Bali," *Modern Music*, XII, No. 4 (1935), 163–69.

—— "*Angkloeng* Music in Bali," *Djawa*, XVII (1937), 322–66.

—— "The Balinese *Wajang Koelit* and Its Music," *Djawa*, XVI, No. 1 (1936), 1–34. Reprinted in this volume, pp. 146–97.

—— "Children and Music in Bali," *Djawa*, XVIII, No. 6 (1938), 1–15. Reprinted in Margaret Mead and Martha Wolfenstein, eds., *Childhood in Contemporary Cultures*. Chicago, University of Chicago Press, 1955, pp. 70–94. Reprinted in this volume, pp. 212–39.

—— *A Club of Small Men*. New York, John Day, 1947.

—— "Dance in Bali," *Dance Index*, VII, Nos. 7–8 (1948), 156–207. Reprinted in this volume, pp. 290–321.

—— "Figuration in Balinese Music," *Peabody Bulletin*, Ser. XXXVI, No. 2 (1940), pp. 23–26.

—— "Five-Tone *Gamelan* Music of Bali," *Musical Quarterly*, XXXV, No. 2 (1949), 250–81.

—— "*Gamelan*-Muziek van Bali, Ondergangschemering van een Kunst,"*Djawa* XIX (1939), 183–85.

—— *A House in Bali*. New York, John Day, 1946.

—— "In This Far Island," *Asia Magazine*, XLIV (1944), 532–37; XLV (1945), 38–43, 109–14, 157–62, 206–10, 257–61, 305–9, 350–54.

—— *Music in Bali: A Study in Form and Instrumental Organization in Balinese Orchestral Music*. New Haven, Conn., Yale University Press, 1966.

Mead, Margaret. "Administrative Contributions to Democratic Character Formation at the Adolescent Level," *Journal of the National Association of Deans of Women*, IV, No. 2 (1941), 51–57. Reprinted in Clyde Kluckhohn and Henry A. Murray, eds., *Personality in Nature, Society, and Culture*, New York, Knopf, 1948, pp. 523–30.

—— "Age Patterning in Personality Development," *American Journal of Orthopsychiatry*, XVII, No. 2 (1947), 231–40.

—— "The Arts in Bali," *Yale Review*, XXX, No. 2 (1940), 335–47. Reprinted in this volume, pp. 331–40.

—— "Back of Adolescence Lies Early Childhood," *Childhood Education*, XVIII, No. 5 (1941), 58–61.

—— "Bali in the Market Place of the World," *Proceedings of the American Academy of Arts and Letters and the National Institute of Arts and Letters*, Series II, No. 1 (1959), 286–93.

—— "Character Formation in Two South Seas Societies," American Neurological Association, *Transactions*, 66th Annual Meeting (June, 1940), pp. 99–103.

—— "Children and Ritual in Bali," in Margaret Mead and Martha Wolfenstein, eds., *Childhood in Contemporary Cultures* (Chicago, University of Chicago Press, 1955), pp. 40–51. Reprinted in this volume, pp. 198–211.

—— "Community Drama, Bali and America," *American Scholar*, XI, No. 1 (January, 1942), 79–88. Reprinted in this volume, pp. 341–49.

—— "Conflict of Cultures in America," in Middle States Association of Colleges and Secondary Schools, *Proceedings*, 54th Annual Convention (November 23–24, 1940), pp. 30–44.

—— "Cultural Determinants of Sexual Behavior," in William C. Young, ed., *Sex and Internal Secretions*. 3d ed. Baltimore, Williams & Wilkins, 1961, pp. 1433–97.

—— "Educative Effects of Social Environment as Disclosed by Studies of Primitive Societies," in E. W. Burgess, *et al.*, eds., *Symposium of Environment and Education*. University of Chicago, Supplementary Educational Monographs, No. 54, Human Development Series, Vol. I. Chicago, University of Chicago Press, 1942, pp. 48–61.

—— "The Family in the Future." in Ruth Nanda Anshen, ed., *Beyond Victory*. New York, Harcourt, Brace, 1943, pp. 66–87.

—— "Family Organization and the Super-ego." Paper presented at the Conference of Topological Psychologists, Smith College, Northampton, Mass., December 31, 1940–January 2, 1941. Mimeographed.

—— *Male and Female*. New York, Morrow, 1949. Reprinted, Mentor MP369, New York, New American Library, 1955.

—— "Men and Gods in a Bali Village," *New York Times Magazine*, July 16, 1939, pp. 12–13, 23.

—— "Public Opinion Mechanisms among Primitive Peoples," *Public Opinion Quarterly*, I, No. 3 (1937), 5–16.

—— "Research on Primitive Children," in Leonard Carmichael, ed., *Manual of Child Psychology*. New York, Wiley, 1954, pp. 735–80.

—— "Researches in Bali, 1936–1939: on the Concept of Plot in Culture," *Transactions of the New York Academy of Sciences*, Ser. II, Vol. II, No. 1 (November, 1939), pp. 1–4.

—— "Social Change and Cultural Surrogates," *Journal of Educational Sociology*, XIV, No. 2 (1940), 92–109. Reprinted in Clyde Kluckhohn and Henry A. Murray, eds., *Personality in Nature, Society, and Culture*. New York, Knopf, 1948, pp. 511–22.

—— "The Strolling Players in the Mountains of Bali," *Natural History*, XLIII, No. 1 (January, 1939), 17–26. Reprinted in this volume, pp. 137–45.

Mead, Margaret, and Frances Cooke Macgregor. *Growth and Culture: A Photographic Study of Balinese Childhood*. New York, Putnam, 1951.

Murphy, Gardner, and Lois Murphy. "Review of 'Balinese Character: A Photographic Analysis,'" *American Anthropologist*, XLV, No. 4, Pt. I (October–December, 1943), 615–19.

Zoete, Beryl de, and Walter Spies. *Dance and Drama in Bali*. Preface by Arthur Waley. London, Faber & Faber, 1938. Extracts reprinted in this volume, pp. 260–89.

FILMS

Bateson, Gregory, and Margaret Mead. Films on character formation in different cultures. Institute for Intercultural Studies. Distributed by New York University Film Library, New York, N.Y. 10003.
A Balinese Family. 2 reels, sound.
Bathing Babies in Three Cultures. 1 reel, sound.
Childhood Rivalry in Bali and New Guinea. 2 reels, sound.
Karba's First Years. 2 reels, sound.
Trance and Dance in Bali. 2 reels, sound.

MUSIC

Recorded Music

From album of *Music of Indonesia*
  Bali:
    1. *Ganda Pura* (instrumental with *gamelan* and *rebab*)
    2. *Peperangan Sira Pandji Perabangsa* (classic opera); with notes by
       Raden Suwanto. Information Services, Indonesian Government, No.
       P-406. New York, Folkways Records, 1950.
Dancers of Bali: Gamelan Orchestra of the Village of Pliatan, Bali, Indonesia,
  directed by AnakAgung Gde Mandera. ML-4618. New York, Columbia Records,
  1952.
McPhee, Colin. *Music of Bali*. Album of Balinese flute melodies and *gamelan*
  compositions, arranged for flute and piano, and for two pianos. Performers,
  George Barrère, Benjamin Britten, and Colin McPhee. New York, G. Schirmer,
  1940.

Published Music

McPhee, Colin. *Balinese Ceremonial Music: Gambangan, Pemungkah, Taboeh
  Teloe*. Transcribed for two pianos. New York, G. Schirmer, 1940.
—— Orchestra score of *Tabuh-Tabuhan*, symphonic work for two pianos and
  orchestra based on Balinese *gamelan* technique. New York, Associated Music
  Publishers, 1960.

Glossary

adat recognized rules for conduct; prescribed manner of behavior

agung great

anak man; person

Anak Agung title applied to man of princely caste, Ksatriyă

anak chenik "small man," i.e., child (polite form)

anak cherik "small man," i.e., child (familiar form)

anak luh woman

ari-ari afterbirth; placenta

arjă modern operetta based on traditional theater, with songs in old Javanese meters

Bagus splendid, magnificent; used in title for Brahmană men

balé house, pavilion, small building; raised platform for sleeping

balé agung large pavilion; council house

balé banjar pavilion used for headquarters of the ward (*banjar*)

Bali-agă aboriginal religion practiced in the northern mountain areas of Bali

balian ritual specialist

banjar ward of a village

bantèn offerings to the gods

bapă father

baris ancient warrior's drill dance

barong fanciful beast mask worn by two men; Balinese version of dragon mask

bau priest or ruler of a village

bibi mother; aunt

Brahmană member of the highest caste in Bali

bută elemental; demon

Chalonarang the witch drama

charu ground offering for an elemental (*bută*)

chèng-chèng cymbals

Chokordă title applied to man of princely caste, Ksatriyă

chondong lady-in-waiting in a dance or play

dalang puppet operator in the shadow play (*wayang kulit*)

dalěm deep, majestic; see *pură dalém*

dĕdari "heavenly nymphs"; see *sanghyang dĕdari*

désă village

dèwă a sort of priestess

engotan rhythmic shifting of the head from side to side in a dance

gabor women's ceremonial dance with offerings

The glossary contains only those words that are used in more than one essay in this volume. Thanks are due to Katharane Mershon for her generous assistance in the preparation of the definitions.

Galungan a yearly festival celebrating the New Year

gambuh ancient court theater

gamelan orchestra of gongs, keyed instruments, drums, and cymbals

gamelan gong a type of *gamelan*, using a special scale

gandrung popular street dance performed by a boy

gangsă keyed instrument which plays ornamental parts or basic melody

gĕdé large, great

gĕndèr keyed instrument which plays the melody

gună general term for magic

gunung mountain

guru teacher; holy man

Gusti title applied to Wesyă caste

jabă low-caste

jagung corn

jangèr modern secular dance for young people

jauk male dancer, wearing a round-eyed mask and long-nailed gloves, who performs in the *barong* drama

jogèd popular street dance performed by a girl who engages male partners from the audience

kain unsewn material forming lower portion of a man's dress

kajă in the direction of the mountains, the abode of the gods; north or south (see note on pp. 86–87)

kangin east

kauh west

kawi archaic religious language containing Javanese and Sanskrit terms

kĕbo water buffalo

kĕbyar modern exhibition dance performed by a young boy

kechak lively rhythmic male chorus performed with rhythmic movements

kĕlod in the direction of the sea; north or south (see note on pp. 86–87)

kèpèng Chinese coin with a hole in the center

kĕtipat small woven basket for cooked rice used in offerings

klian head of a village ward

kras strong; coarse; loud

Ksatriyă member of the second of the three high-caste divisions

kubu a pavilion or hut

kulit skin; see *wayang kulit*

kul-kul ceremonial drums

légong dance performed by little girls

léyak evil spirit; elemental; witch

lontar technical book made on palm leaf

luh female

main-main play; entertainment

manak salah to have children the wrong way; i.e., to have twins

manis sweet

mantră prayers

mémé mother; aunt

mĕcharu ground offerings for a purification ceremony

mendét variation of *gabor* dance, generally performed by women or girls

mèru mountain symbol for mountain of the gods

mĕtèn conjugal house where children are born

mindon second cousin

misan first cousin

mudras sign language of the hands; hand gestures which accompany prayers (*mantră*)

nagă serpent; dragon

ngurek self-stabbing in trance

nyamă low language for brothers, sisters, all relatives; placenta of new-born child

odalan temple feast

paling disoriented; drunk; confused; lost

paon   hearth

paras   a kind of stone

parĕkan   slave; attendant

pĕdandă   a priest, generally a Brahmană

pĕkarangan   walled courtyard within the village limits

pĕkĕn   village market place

pĕmangku   temple official

pĕnasar   followers

pĕngipuk   introductory theme for love music

pĕras   a kind of offering

pĕrbĕkĕl   a village official

punggawă   appointed head of a district

pură   temple

pură balé agung   temple connected with the council house (*balé agung*)

pură dalĕm   temple outside of a village, sometimes called a "death" temple

pură dĕsă   village temple (temple of the *dĕsă*)

pură pĕnataran   a temple

pură puseh   "navel" temple; temple of origin

puri   palace of a *rajă*

pusĕh   see *pura puseh*

putih   white

rajă   prince or ruler; member of Ksatriyă caste

raksasă   a demon

rangdă   literally, widow; the witch in the Chalonarang drama

rejang   ritual dance performed by young, unmarried girls

rĕramă di mindon   marry the mother of his second cousin

rĕramă di misan   marry the mother of his first cousin

sakti   supernaturally powerful through holiness

sanggah   shrine or household temple to one's ancestors

sanggar   a shrine where meditation is practiced

sanghyang   a protective divinity

sanghyang dĕdari   small girls, entranced, dancing as "heavenly nymphs"

sawah   rice fields

sĕbĕl   ritually unclean

sĕkă; sĕkĕhă   club (association)

semă   village graveyard and cremation place

sĕmbah   bow with clasped hands

sĕpi   dead silent

sirih   a form of pepper vine used to chew with the betel nut

suară   sound

sudamala   a special form of holy water given to a child unfortunate enough to have been born on the day *tumpak wayang*

Sudră   low-caste person

tapakan   basket containing a coconut, rice, money, etc., used in offerings

tĕrună   youths

tonyă   an animistic spirit

topéng   ancient play with masked actors

Triwangsă   the three high-caste divi-divisions: Brahmană, Ksatriyă, and Wĕsyă

tuak   palm beer

wadah   cremation tower

wayang   shadow

wayang kulit   shadow play using puppets made from hide (*kulit*)

wayang wong   play in which men are the actors

Wĕsyă   the third high-caste division

wong   people

Index

Unless otherwise noted, the categories indexed
pertain only to Bali and the Balinese.